374

D0277974

Boundaries of Adult Learning

Adult Learners, Education and Training 1

THE OPEN UNIVERSITY MA IN EDUCATION

This Reader, *Boundaries of Adult Learning*, and its companion volume, *The Learning Society: Challenges and Trends*, are both part of a course, *Adult Learners, Education and Training*, that is itself part of the Open University MA in Education programme.

The Open University MA in Education is now firmly established as the most popular postgraduate degree for education professionals in Europe, with over 3,500 students registering each year. The MA in Education is designed particularly for those with experience of teaching, the advisory service, educational administration or allied fields.

Structure of the MA

The MA is a modular degree, and students are therefore free to select from a range of options the programme which best fits in with their interests and professional goals. Specialist lines in management and primary education are also available. Study in the Open University's Advanced Diploma and Certificate Programmes can also be counted towards the MA, and successful study in the MA programme entitles students to apply for entry into the Open University Doctorate in Education programme.

COURSES CURRENTLY AVAILABLE:

- Management • Child Development • Primary Education
- Curriculum, Learning and Assessment • Special Needs
- Language and Literacy • Mentoring • Classroom Studies
  - Education Training and Employment • Gender
  - Educational Research • Science Education
  - Adult Learners • Maths Education

OU supported open learning

The MA in Education programme provides great flexibility. Students study at their own pace, in their own time, anywhere in the European Union. They receive specially prepared study materials, supported by tutorials, thus offering the chance to work with other students.

How to apply

If you would like to register for this programme, or simply to find out more information, please write for the *Professional Development in Education* prospectus to the Central Enquiry Service, PO Box 200, The Open University, Walton Hall, Milton Keynes, MK7 6YZ, UK (Telephone 01908 653231).

Adult Learners, Education and Training 1

Boundaries of Adult Learning

Edited by Richard Edwards, Ann Hanson and
Peter Raggatt at The Open University

London and New York in association with
The Open University

First published 1996
by Routledge
11 New Fetter Lane, London EC4P 4EE

Simultaneously published in the USA and Canada
by Routledge
29 West 35th Street, New York, NY 10001

Reprinted 2000

Routledge is an imprint of the Taylor & Francis Group

© 1996 Selection and editorial matter, The Open University, individual
chapters, the contributors

Typeset in Garamond by Datix International Limited, Bungay, Suffolk
Printed and bound in Great Britain by Biddles Ltd, www.Biddles.co.uk

British Library Cataloguing in Publication Data
A catalogue record for this book is available from the British Library

Library of Congress Cataloguing in Publication Data
A catalogue record for this book has been requested

ISBN 0–415–13614–8

Contents

List of illustrations   vii
Acknowledgements   ix

Introduction: beyond the bounds   1
Richard Edwards, Ann Hanson and Peter Raggatt

1 **From technical rationality to reflection-in-action**   8
Donald Schön

2 **Promoting reflection in learning: a model**   32
David Boud, Rosemary Keogh and David Walker

3 **Breaking the code: engaging practitioners in critical analysis of adult educational literature**   57
Stephen Brookfield

4 **Andragogy: an emerging technology for adult learning**   82
Malcolm Knowles

5 **The search for a separate theory of adult learning: does anyone really need andragogy?**   99
Ann Hanson

6 **On contemporary practice and research: self-directed learning to critical theory**   109
Michael Collins

7 **Freire and a feminist pedagogy of difference**   128
Kathleen Weiler

8 **The British adult education tradition: a re-examination**   152
Bob Bell

9 **Concepts, organization and current trends of lifelong education in Sweden**   169
Kenneth Abrahamsson

10 **The second chance: the vital myth of equal opportunities in adult education**   183
Risto Rinne and Osmo Kivinen

11 **Learning and 'leisure'**   196
Naomi Sargant

12 **Part-time: whose time? Women's lives and adult learning**   211
Marlene Morrison

13 **Learner autonomy in a changing world**   232
Stephen McNair

14 **Professions and competencies**   246
Paul Hager and Andrew Gonczi

15 **Personal skills and transfer: meanings, agendas and possibilities**   261
Roger Harrison

16 **Policy continuity and progress in the reform of post-compulsory and higher education**   276
David Robertson

Index   295

Illustrations

FIGURES

2.1 A model of reflection in the learning process   34
2.2 Components of reflection   42
2.3 The reflection process in context   52
4.1 The relationship of the time-span of social change to individual life-span   83
10.1 Distribution of adult education courses, by mode of education and major objectives (%)   187
10.2 Participation in adult education, by socio-economic status (%)   189
10.3 Annual and lifetime participation rates in adult education, by previous level of education (%)   191
10.4 Characterization of the labour force in relation to participation rates in adult education   194
15.1 Changing structure of curriculum objectives: a schema   268

TABLES

4.1 Superior conditions of learning   97
10.1 Number of adults participating in different forms of adult education in Finland, 1990   186
10.2 Participation in adult education, by sex (%)   187
10.3 High participants and non-participants in adult education, by previous levels of education (%)   193
10.4 High participants and non-participants in adult education, by socio-economic status   193
11.1 Main leisure interests and activities, by age   199
11.2 Main subjects studied – the surveys compared   205
11.3 Comparison between main subjects both being studied and learned informally   206
11.4 Main groupings of 'new' subjects people would like to learn about, by age-group   207

12.1 Time spent in study   222
14.1 Ways in which Australian professions employ competency
       standards (%)   252
16.1 Existing credit frameworks: a comparison and evaluation   286
16.2 Credit frameworks: towards a synthesis   290

Acknowledgements

Acknowledgement is gratefully expressed for material from the following publications:

1 Schön, D. (1983) 'From technical rationality to reflection-in-action', *The Reflective Practitioner: How Professionals Think in Action*, London: Basic Books. (Edited version.)

2 Boud, D. Keogh, R. and Walker, D. (1985) 'Promoting reflection in learning: a model', in *Reflection: Turning Experience into Learning*, London: Croom Helm. (Edited version.)

3 Brookfield, S. (1993) 'Breaking the code: engaging practitioners in critical analysis of adult educational literature', in *Studies in the Education of Adults*, vol. 25 (2) pp. 64–91 April, National Institute for Adult and Continuing Education: Leicester. (Edited version.)

4 Knowles, M. (1983)'Andragogy: an emerging technology for adult learning', in M. Tight (ed.) *Adult Learning and Education*, London: Croom Helm. Reprinted by permission of Routledge.

6 Collins, M. (1991) 'On contemporary practice and research: self-directed learning to critical theory', in *Adult Education as Vocation*, London: Routledge. (Edited version.) Reproduced by permission of Routledge.

7 Weiler, K. (1991)'Freire and a feminist pedagogy of difference', in *Harvard Educational Review*, vol. 61 (4), Harvard University: Cambridge, Massachussets, pp. 449–73.

9 Abrahamsson, K. (1993) 'Concepts, organisation and current trends of lifelong education in Sweden', in *International Journal of University Adult Education*, vol. xxxii (3), International Congress of University Adult Education: Canada, pp. 47–69.

10 Rinne, R. and Kivinen, O. (1993) 'Adult education, the second chance: fact and fiction', in *Scandinavian Journal of Educational Research*, vol. 37 (2), Carfax

Publishing Company, P.O. Box 25, Abingdon, Oxfordshire, OX14 3UE, pp. 115–28.

12 Morrison, M. (1992) 'Part-time: whose time? Women's lives and adult learning', in *Managing Time for Education*, CEDAR Paper 3, Centre for Educational Development, Appraisal and Research, University of Warwick.

16 Robertson, D. 'Policy continuity and progress in the reform of post-compulsory and higher education', revised from 'Flexibility and mobility in Further and Higher Education: policy continuity and progress and choosing to change', in *Journal of Further and Higher Education*, vol. 17 (1), NATFE: London, pp. 68–79.

While the publishers have made every effort to contact copyright holders of material used in this volume, they would be grateful to hear from any they were unable to contact.

Introduction

Beyond the bounds

Richard Edwards, Ann Hanson and Peter Raggatt

The theme of this book is the varying and contested attempts to provide some boundaries for the range and variety of lifelong learning. The significance of boundaries is that in providing a border around a specific set of activities – adult education, training, human resource development, adult learning – they provide the grounds for delineating what constitutes the legitimate object of study and the locus of practice. Boundaries therefore provide the grounds for bringing a certain order to the apparently chaotic, unpredictable and changing activities in which adult learners engage. They provide the basis for deciding what is to be included and what is to be excluded. In this way boundaries are powerful in deciding what constitutes a field of practice and a field of study in what could otherwise be considered an expansive moorland of adult learning. Who has the power to set boundaries and what boundaries are set have powerful effects on the opportunities available for adults to learn. This makes boundaries controversial and subject to debate and struggle linking the world of ideas and practice to the world of politics and policy-making. For instance, if certain forms of learning can be demonstrated to enhance economic development – a position of great significance in the 1990s – governments concerned about the competitiveness of their economies may be more inclined to include them within the boundaries of public policy-making.

This book therefore brings together a variety of chapters drawn from Europe, North America and Australia to explore, illustrate and challenge the notion of boundaries in lifelong learning. As will be immediately clear, this has involved setting certain boundaries ourselves. For instance, we could have included chapters from Africa or Asia and the chapters from Europe we have chosen are largely from northern Europe and primarily the UK. It may also be that certain boundaries of gender and ethnocentricity are reproduced by the selection for this text and may even be inscribed in the content of some of the chapters. For instance, Schön (Chapter 1) uses the masculine pronoun to refer to all professionals, which can be interpreted as excluding women from his discourse. A book on boundaries cannot but be aware of its own boundaries and we invite you as readers to challenge the chapters in this book and the boundaries within which they are framed and set in the same way as we hope they are challenging to you.

In recent years the boundaries for adults' learning have become both more important and more difficult to draw. For much of the post-war period boundaries were established around certain forms of provision which were solely concerned with adults. As Bell (Chapter 8) argues, unlike in other parts of northern Europe, in the UK this was largely focused on non-vocational adult education provided through local authorities, university extra-mural departments and the Workers Education Association (WEA). The field of adult education was established and policy was largely formed and framed by assumptions that this was the arena in which adults learned. Within this boundary there were debates and discussions about the curriculum and the nature of participation, but adult education was a clearly bounded form of practice. In the process other settings for and forms of adult learning were excluded and placed outside the boundaries of practitioner, policy and academic concern.

The question of boundaries is played out in different countries and cultures in different ways. Abrahamsson (Chapter 9) and Rinne and Kivinen (Chapter 10) provide us with examples from Sweden and Finland respectively. In each there has been and remains the struggle to delineate a certain field as the primary focus of those concerned with adult learning. This might embrace a wider range of organizations than that in the UK, such as the folk high schools and study circles of Scandanavia. However, boundaries remain which privilege certain forms of provision over others. Abrahamsson charts the increased significance of economically relevant learning to the Swedish government during the early 1990s. This creates the grounds for a shared concern by some at the cutbacks in expenditure of non-vocational adult education in the UK and the funding of study circles in Sweden. By contrast, Rinne and Kivinen examine the attempts to make the boundaries around Finnish adult education more permeable in order to increase accessibility and extend participation. This is key to certain notions of lifelong learning and the learning society. However, they clearly demonstrate the difficulty of extending participation if measures are solely taken by practitioners and institutions. This is not to deny the importance of such measures for, as Morrison (Chapter 12) suggests, important steps can be taken to enhance participation by examining how adults – and in her study women – make time to study.

A set of arguments were and continue to be deployed to maintain boundaries around certain institutional arrangements. Part of this involves for some distinguishing adult education from training or leisure, distinguishing the non-vocational uncertificated learning of adults from certificated and vocational learning, distinguishing adult learning from that of children. Bell (Chapter 8) and Sargant (Chapter 11) both point to the increasingly problematic nature of such boundaries. They suggest that for many adults, particularly those who do not normally participate in formal education and training, learning may indeed be a leisure activity. Bell goes further and argues that most adults participate in learning as a leisure and consumer activity and that adult educators, particularly university based adult educators, have tended to marginalize this which has resulted in a misleading picture of what constitutes 'adult education'.

Some theories have developed which attempt to delineate what is particular to adults as learners. Knowles' (Chapter 4) theory of andragogy – the practice of helping adults to learn – has been influential in North America and the UK, but less so in the rest of Europe where different intellectual and cultural traditions developed andragogy as an academic discipline rather than as a description of how adults differ from children. Boud, Keogh and Walker (Chapter 2) argue that reflection is central to adult learning. Particularly important is reflection on experience, including the affective dimensions of experience. It is through reflection that adults are enabled to learn more effectively. Others have argued that the boundaries between adults and children are not as clear-cut as they are often presented and that practitioners need to draw on such theories, to be aware of concepts such as reflection, experiential learning and perspective transformation, and their implications for practice, but not adopt them into all-embracing ideologies of adult learning. Attention needs to be given to particular adults and their contexts and the settings and circumstances with which one works. Drawing on her own research with adult learners, Hanson (Chapter 5) offers one such contribution.

As well as distinguishing adult learning from that of children, attempts have also been made to distinguish adult education as a distinctly emancipatory practice, aimed at supporting progressive social change. From different perspectives, Collins (Chapter 6) and Weiler (Chapter 7) examine certain dimensions of such claims. Writing from Canada, Collins argues that attention given to facilitating self-directed adult learning keeps adult education practice within the existing boundaries of economic and social inequality. It induces an obsession with technique or technical rationality which results in an avoidance of adult education's role as part of a social movement for equality and a form of emancipatory practice. For Collins, unlike Bell, this goal has been central rather than marginal to the adult education tradition, but is not built around a distinct form or theory of adult learning. However, drawing on feminist theory and practice, Weiler argues that emancipatory adult education, often associated with figures such as the Brazilian Freire, tends to produce fresh forms of oppression unless it takes account of the differences that exist between groups of adults, even where they seem to share similar situations and have similar interests. Weiler suggests that, even as certain boundaries are challenged, new boundaries and fresh inequalities can be produced unless people's differences are acknowledged. It is on this basis that she agues for a feminist pedagogy of difference.

A set of institutions and/or practices are often suggested to be the basis for establishing a boundary around a specific field of adult education. However, the very concern with adult *learning* rather than adult *education* challenges the boundaries established on the basis of certain forms of provision. Recognition is given to the fact that adults learn in a whole variety of settings – in the home, workplace, community – which cannot be contained within a boundary of education or training focused on the formal provision of learning opportunities. So, a shift from a concern with provision to a concern with learning threatens boundaries built up around certain institutional arrangements in the provision of learning opportunities for adults. Sargant's study of participation demonstrates that as the wider settings for adult learning are examined so profiles of participation are altered, with a greater diversity of adults learning than participating in formal institutional provision. In this way a more diverse range of activities can be said to come inside the boundaries, to be part of a larger field of adult or lifelong learning. Alternatively, it can be argued that the diversity is so great it cannot be embraced by the notion of a bounded field, but rather is closer to an unbounded moorland.

This needs to be set alongside the recent, growing interest in adults as learners among policy-makers, academics, employers and individuals themselves. In the UK and elsewhere, this has stemmed from and resulted in a huge growth in the numbers and percentage of adults participating in the various sectors of post-compulsory education and training. In the UK, as adults over 21 have come to be the majority in further education and over 25-year-olds are the majority in higher education institutions, the possibility of maintaining adult education as a bounded and distinct area of policy, practice and concern has been brought into question. In addition, there has been a growth in the non-formal sector of provision, of private providers and employers concerned to develop and train their workforces. In addition, social trends surveys demonstrate increased participation in home based forms of learning through the various media. Learning here is initiated and undertaken by learners beyond the boundaries of organized provision. Learning activities are therefore far more extensive than can be contained within a tidy institutional boundary.

The challenges to boundaries extends, therefore, to the settings in which adults learn, the nature of that learning and the content of the learning. In the process a set of boundaries established to differentiate a specific field of practice and study, based on the provision of learning opportunities, has begun to break down. Yet even as learning is recognized as far more extensive than encompassed by formal providers of learning opportunities, new structures and approaches have been developed to try and embrace that wider moorland of experiential, informal, incidental and uncertificated learning. It is this which has provided in part the basis for the interest in, and development of, the assessment and accreditation of learning outcomes and credit frameworks. Here boundaries can be said to have shifted from being constituted by inputs – certain institutional arrangements – to outputs – arrangements for the assessment and accreditation of learning wherever it takes place. This has provided the basis for new and more fluid sets of institutional relationships between the different sectors of education and training – formal, non-formal and informal – and attempts to provide permeability and mobility for adult learners. Robertson (Chapter 16) charts the moves to provide a coherent framework for the accumulation and transfer of credit across post-secondary education and training in England in the mid-1990s. For McNair (Chapter 13) such moves, particularly where based on the explicit expression of learning outcomes, enhance the autonomy of adults. He argues that, despite problems, this has become important for a variety of social, economic and cultural reasons and is desirable for supporting lifelong learning.

However, even in this process of extending and breaking down boundaries, fresh exclusions are introduced. First, over what is valued as learning and the relative values of different types of learning. Establishing the skills, knowledge and understanding for which credit can be awarded is a powerful position, as the chapters by Hager and Gonczi (Chapter 14) and Harrison (Chapter 15) illustrate. Writing from Australia, Hager and Gonczi argue that very different notions of competence have been built into the reforms of vocational qualifications in that country by contrast with the UK, excluding Scotland, with consequences for what is assessed and accredited and how that process occurs. They suggest that a more holistic notion of competence has been developed in Australia and that this is partly due to the professions rather than employers providing the lead in developing standards of competence. Harrison explores the varying support for clarifying and assessing core and personal skills in the UK since the mid-1980s. He demonstrates the differing meanings and significance given to these notions by different groups – practitioners, employers, trades unions – and how that is manifested in what is assessed and valued. Learning which is not valued and certificated can therefore become excluded from and by the credit framework ostensibly set up to embrace the various settings in which adults learn.

A second boundary which can develop is over who awards credit, as new settings and organizations, such as employers, come to play a role in what has previously been the concern of formal education and training institutions. Which institutions are given the right to be awarding bodies and the impact on what is assessed and the quality of the assessment processes become a central concern. A third set of boundaries is that between different credit systems. This is most notable where there are demarcations between traditional academic awards, based on input ideas of notional study time, and occupational awards, based on outcomes or standards of competence. Creating the conditions for the recognition and valuing of different types of learning and credit, as Robertson suggests, may be a necessary feature of a learning society but is not straightforward. Powerful interests invest different value and significance to different forms of learning and that is a wider cultural and political issue, as well as one for practitioners working with adults. It is also an issue which affects the ability of adults to cross the boundaries between life and learning, to be mobile within and between learning settings wherever they may be.

For those working with adults, practitioners in the diverse settings within which adults learn, the changing boundaries in the moorland of lifelong learning presents an ongoing set of challenges. Shifting boundaries, the engendering of different boundaries and different forms of permeability offer circumstances, which are uncertain in their consequences. It is for this reason that Schön, like Collins, rejects the adequacy of technical rationality, the learning of a certain set of rules to be applied in all circumstances, as an adequate basis for professionals to work within. Unlike Collins, with his emphasis on emancipatory adult education, Schön argues that all professionals are faced with varying and different circumstances, wherein they have to interpret and form judgements about what constitutes an effective response. He argues for the centrality of reflection-in-action to professional judgements which, with the uncertainty and unpredictability within and beyond the shifting boundaries of lifelong learning, mean that practitioners with adults would appear to require and need to develop this form of professional knowledge and understanding. It is for similar reasons that Brookfield (Chapter 3) suggests a range of strategies for practitioners to be able to interrogate texts in order to develop their critical understanding on and about lifelong learning and thereby the influences to which they, their workplaces and their practices with adults are subject.

If change and uncertainty have become part of the practices of lifelong learning, in which the varying boundaries around and within the field are challenged and shift, then developing strategies to identify, interpret and make judgements about the significance of such changes becomes critical. The concern with boundaries suggests that practitioners are constantly needing to negotiate borders of varying forms in developing practices for working effectively with diverse adults in varying settings. This can be unsettling and challenging, for in the borderlands we can be bound for glory or bound and gagged!

Chapter 1

From technical rationality to reflection-in-action†

Donald Schön

THE DOMINANT EPISTEMOLOGY OF PRACTICE

According to the model of Technical Rationality – the view of professional knowledge which has most powerfully shaped both our thinking about the professions and the institutional relations of research, education, and practice – professional activity consists of instrumental problem solving made rigorous by the application of scientific theory and technique. Although all occupations are concerned, in this view, with the instrumental adjustment of means to ends, only the professions practice rigorously technical problem solving based on specialized scientific knowledge. [. . .]

The prototypes of professional expertise are the 'learned professions' of medicine and law and, close behind these, business and engineering. These are, in Nathan Glazer's terms, the 'major' or 'near-major' professions (Glazer 1974: 345). They are distinct from 'minor' professions such as social work, librarianship, education, divinity, and town planning. In the essay from which these terms are drawn, Glazer (1974) argues that the schools of the minor professions are hopelessly non-rigorous, dependent on representatives of academic disciplines, such as economics or political science, who are superior in status to the professions themselves. But what is of greatest interest from our point of view, Glazer's distinction between major and minor professions rests on a particularly well-articulated version of the model of Technical Rationality. The major professions are 'disciplined by an unambiguous end – health, success in litigation, profit – which settles men's minds' (Glazer 1974: 363) and they operate in stable institutional contexts. Hence they are grounded in systematic, fundamental knowledge, of which scientific knowledge is the prototype, or else they have 'a high component of strictly technological knowledge based on science in the education

† This is an edited version of a chapter that appeared in *The Reflective Practitioner: How Professionals Think in Action*, London: Basic Books 1983.

which they provide' (Glazer 1974: 349). In contrast, the minor professions suffer from shifting, ambiguous ends and from unstable institutional contexts of practice, and are *therefore* unable to develop a base of systematic, scientific professional knowledge. For Glazer, the development of a scientific knowledge base depends on fixed, unambiguous ends because professional practice is an instrumental activity. If applied science consists of cumulative, empirical knowledge about the means best suited to chosen ends, how can a profession ground itself in science when its ends are confused or unstable?

The systematic knowledge base of a profession is thought to have four essential properties. It is specialized, firmly bounded, scientific, and standardized. This last point is particularly important, because it bears on the paradigmatic relationship which holds, according to Technical Rationality, between a profession's knowledge base and its practice. In Wilbert Moore's words:

> If every professional problem were in all respects unique, solutions would be at best accidental, and therefore have nothing to do with expert knowledge. What we are suggesting, on the contrary, is that there are sufficient uniformities in problems and in devices for solving them to qualify the solvers as professionals ... professionals apply very general principles, *standardized* knowledge, to concrete problems ...
>
> (Moore 1970: 56)

This concept of 'application' leads to a view of professional knowledge as a hierarchy in which 'general principles' occupy the highest level and 'concrete problem solving' the lowest. As Edgar Schein has put it, there are three components to professional knowledge:

> 1 An *underlying discipline* or *basic science* component upon which the practice rests or from which it is developed.
> 2 An *applied science* or *'engineering'* component from which many of the day-to-day diagnostic procedures and problem-solutions are derived.
> 3 A *skills and attitudinal* component that concerns the actual performance of services to the client, using the underlying basic and applied knowledge.
>
> (Schein 1973: 39)

The application of basic science yields applied science. Applied science yields diagnostic and problem solving techniques which are applied in turn to the actual delivery of services. Applied science is said to 'rest on' the foundation of basic science. And the more basic and general the knowledge, the higher the status of its producer.

When the representatives of aspiring professions consider the problem of rising to full professional status, they often ask whether their knowledge base has the requisite properties and whether it is regularly applied to the everyday problems of practice. Thus, in an article entitled 'The Librarian: from occupation to profession' the author states that:

> the central gap is of course the failure to develop a general body of scientific knowledge bearing precisely on this problem, in the way that the medical profession with its auxiliary scientific fields has developed an immense body of knowledge with which to cure human diseases.
>
> (Goode 1966: 39)

The sciences in which he proposes to ground his profession are 'communications theory, the sociology or psychology of mass communications, or the psychology of learning as it applies to reading' (Goode 1966: 39). Unfortunately, however, he finds that:

> most day-to-day professional work utilizes rather concrete rule-of-thumb local regulations and rules and major catalog systems . . . The problems of selection and organization are dealt with on a highly empiricist basis, concretely, with little reference to general scientific principles.
>
> (Goode 1966: 39)

And a social worker, considering the same sort of question, concludes that 'social work is already a profession' because it has a basis in:

> theory construction via systematic research. To generate valid theory that will provide a solid base for professional techniques requires the application of the scientific method to the service-related problems of the profession. Continued employment of the scientific method is nurtured by and in turn reinforces the element of *rationality*.
>
> (Greenwood 1966: 11)

It is by progressing along this route that social work seeks to 'rise within the professional hierarchy so that it, too, might enjoy maximum prestige, authority, and monopoly which presently belong to a few top professions' (Greenwood 1966: 19).

If the model of Technical Rationality appeared only in such statements of intent, or in programmatic descriptions of professional knowledge, we might have some doubts about its dominance. But the model is also embedded in the institutional context of professional life. It is implicit in the institutionalized relations of research and practice, and in the normative curricula of professional education. Even when practitioners, educators, and researchers question the model of technical rationality, they are party to institutions that perpetuate it.

As one would expect from the hierarchical model of professional knowledge, research is institutionally separate from practice, connected to it by carefully defined relationships of exchange. Researchers are supposed to provide the basic and applied science from which to derive techniques for diagnosing and solving the problems of practice. Practitioners are supposed to furnish researchers with problems for study and with tests of the utility of research results. The researcher's role is distinct from, and usually considered superior to, the role of the practitioner. [. . .]

The hierarchical separation of research and practice is also reflected in the normative curriculum of the professional school. Here the order of the curriculum parallels the order in which the components of professional knowledge are 'applied'. The rule is: first, the relevant basic and applied science; then, the skills of application to real-world problems of practice. Edgar Schein's study of professional education led him to describe the dominant curricular pattern as follows:

> Most professional school curricula can be analyzed in terms of the form and timing of these three elements [of professional knowledge]. Usually the professional curriculum starts with a common science core followed by the applied science elements. The attitudinal and skill components are usually labelled 'practicum' or 'clinical work' and may be provided simultaneously with the applied science components or they may occur even later in the professional education, depending upon the availability of clients or the ease of simulating the realities that the professional will have to face.
>
> (Schein 1973: 44)

Schein's use of the term 'skill' is of more than passing interest. From the point of view of the model of Technical Rationality institutionalized in the professional curriculum, real knowledge lies in the theories and techniques of basic and applied science. Hence, these disciplines should come first. 'Skills' in the use of theory and technique to solve concrete problems should come later on, when the student has learned the relevant science – first, because he cannot learn skills of application until he has learned applicable knowledge; and second, because skills are an ambiguous, secondary kind of knowledge. There is something disturbing about calling them 'knowledge' at all.

Again, medicine is the prototypical example. Ever since the Flexner Report, which revolutionized medical education in the early decades of this century, medical schools have devoted the first two years of study to the basic science – chemistry, physiology, pathology – as 'the appropriate foundation for later clinical training' (Thorne 1973: 30). Even the physical arrangement of the curriculum reflects the basic division among the elements of professional knowledge:

The separation of the medical school curriculum into two disjunctive stages, the preclinical and the clinical, reflects the division between theory and practice. The division also appears in the location of training and in medical school facilities. The sciences of biochemistry, physiology, pathology and pharmacology are learned from classrooms and laboratories, that is, in formal academic settings. More practical training, in clinical arts such as internal medicine, obstetrics and pediatrics, takes place in hospital clinics, within actual institutions of delivery.

(Thorne 1973: 31)

[. . .]

THE ORIGINS OF TECHNICAL RATIONALITY

It is striking that the dominant model of professional knowledge seems to its proponents to require very little justification. How comes it that in the second half of the twentieth century we find in our universities, a dominant view of professional knowledge as the application of scientific theory and technique to the instrumental problems of practice?

The answer to this question lies in the last three hundred years of the history of Western ideas and institutions. Technical Rationality is the heritage of Positivism, the powerful philosophical doctrine that grew up in the nineteenth century as an account of the rise of science and technology and as a social movement aimed at applying the achievements of science and technology to the well-being of mankind. It became institutionalized in the modern university, founded in the late nineteenth century when Positivism was at its height, and in the professional schools which secured their place in the university in the early decades of the twentieth century.

Since the Reformation, the history of the West has been shaped by the rise of science and technology and by the industrial movement which was both cause and consequence of the increasingly powerful scientific world-view. As the scientific world-view gained dominance, so did the idea that human progress would be achieved by harnessing science to create technology for the achievement of human ends. This Technological Programme[1] became a major theme for the philosophers of the Enlightenment in the eighteenth century, and by the late nineteenth century had been firmly established as a pillar of conventional wisdom. By this time, too, the professions had come to be seen as vehicles for the application of the new sciences to the achievement of human progress. The engineers, closely tied to the development of industrial technology, became a model of technical practice for the other professions. Medicine, a learned profession with origins in the medieval universities, was refashioned in the new image of a science-based technique for the preservation of health. And statecraft came to be seen as a kind of social engineering. As the professions evolved and proliferated, they became, increasingly, the principal agents of the Technological Programme.

As the scientific movement, industrialism, and the Technological Programme became dominant in Western society, a philosophy emerged which sought both to give an account of the triumphs of science and technology and to purge mankind of the residues of religion, mysticism, and metaphysics which still prevented scientific thought and technological practice from wholly ruling over the affairs of men. It was in this spirit that, in the first half of the nineteenth century, Auguste Comte first expressed the three principal doctrines of Positivism. First, there was the conviction that empirical science was not just a form of knowledge but the only source of positive knowledge of the world. Second, there was the intention to cleanse men's minds of mysticism, superstition, and other forms of pseudoknowledge. And finally, there was the programme of extending scientific knowledge and technical control to human society. [. . .]

As Positivists became increasingly sophisticated in their efforts to explain and justify the exclusivity of scientific knowledge, they recognized to what extent observational statements were theory-laden, and found it necessary to ground empirical knowledge in irreducible elements of sensory experience. They began to see laws of nature not as facts inherent in nature but as constructs created to explain observed phenomena, and science became for them a hypothetico–deductive system. In order to account for his observations, the scientist constructed hypotheses, abstract models of an unseen world which could be tested only indirectly through deductions susceptible to confirmation or disconfirmation by experiment. The heart of scientific inquiry consisted of the use of crucial experiments to choose among competing theories of explanation.

In the light of Positivist doctrines such as these, practice appeared as a puzzling anomaly. Practical knowledge exists, but it does not fit neatly into Positivist categories. We cannot readily treat it as a form of descriptive knowledge of the world, nor can we reduce it to the analytic schemas of logic and mathematics. Positivism solved the puzzle of practical knowledge in a way that had been foreshadowed by the Technological Programme and by Comte's programme for applying science to morality and politics. Practical knowledge was to be construed as knowledge of the relationship of means to ends. Given agreement about ends,[2] the question, 'How ought I to act?' could be reduced to a merely instrumental question about the means best suited to achieve one's ends. Disagreement about means could be resolved by reference to facts concerning the possible means, their relevant consequences, and the methods for comparing them with respect to the chosen ends of action. Ultimately, the instrumental question could be resolved by recourse to experiment. And as men built up scientific understandings of cause and effect, causal relationships could be mapped on to instrumental ones. It would be possible to select the means appropriate to one's ends by applying the relevant scientific theory. The question, 'How ought I to act?' could become a scientific one, and the best means could be selected by the use of science-based technique.

In the late nineteenth and early twentieth centuries, the professions of engineering and medicine achieved dramatic successes in reliably adjusting means to ends and became models of instrumental practice. The engineer's design and analysis of materials and artifacts, the physician's diagnosis and treatment of disease, became prototypes of the science-based, technical practice which was destined to supplant craft and artistry. For according to the Positivist epistemology of practice, craft and artistry had no lasting place in rigorous practical knowledge.

Universities came of age in the United States, assumed their now familiar structure and styles of operation, in the late nineteenth and early twentieth centuries when science and technology were on the rise and the intellectual hegemony of Positivism was beginning to be established. Although other traditions of thought were never wholly extinguished in American universities – indeed, in some places managed to preserve a kind of local dominance – nevertheless in the United States more than in any other nation except Germany the very heart of the university was given over to the scientific enterprise, to the ethos of the Technological Programme, and to Positivism. [. . .]

But for this, the professionalizing occupations paid a price. They had to accept the Positivist epistemology of practice which was now built into the very tissue of the universities. And they had also to accept the fundamental division of labour on which Veblen (1962) had placed so great an emphasis. It was to be the business of university-based scientists and scholars to create the fundamental theory which professionals and technicians would apply to practice. The function of the professional school would be:

> the transmission to its students of the generalized and systematic knowledge that is the basis of professional performance.
>
> (Hughes 1973: 660)

But this division of labour reflected a hierarchy of kinds of knowledge which was also a ladder of status. Those who create new theory were thought to be higher in status than those who apply it, and the schools of 'higher learning' were thought to be superior to the 'lower'. [. . .]

EMERGING AWARENESS OF THE LIMITS OF TECHNICAL RATIONALITY

[. . .]

Following World War II, the United States Government began an unparalleled increase in the rate of spending for research. As government spending for research increased, research institutions proliferated. Some were associated with the universities, others stood outside them. All were organized around the production of new scientific knowledge and were largely promoted on the basis of the proposition that the production of new scientific knowledge could be used to create wealth, achieve national goals, improve human life, and solve social problems. Nowhere was the rate of increase in research spending more dramatic, and nowhere were the results of that spending more visible, than in the field of medicine. The great centres of medical research and teaching were expanded, and new ones were created. The medical research centre, with its medical school and its teaching hospital, became the institutional model to which other professions aspired. Other professions, hoping to achieve some of medicine's effectiveness and prestige, sought to emulate its linkage of research and teaching institutions, its hierarchy of research and clinical roles, and its system for connecting basic and applied research to practice.

The prestige and apparent success of the medical and engineering models exerted a great attraction for the social sciences. In fields such as education, social work, planning, and policy making, social scientists attempted to do research, to apply it, and to educate practitioners, all according to their perceptions of the models of medicine and engineering. Indeed, the very language of social scientists, rich in references to measurement, controlled experiment, applied science, laboratories, and clinics, was striking in its reverence for these models. [. . .]

However, both the general public and the professionals have become increasingly aware of the flaws and limitations of the professions. The professions have suffered a crisis of legitimacy rooted both in their perceived failure to live up to their own norms and in their perceived incapacity to help society achieve its objectives and solve its problems. Increasingly, we have become aware of the importance to actual practice of phenomena – complexity, uncertainty, instability, uniqueness, and value-conflict – which do not fit the model of Technical Rationality. Now, in the light of the Positivist origins of Technical Rationality, we can more readily see why these phenomena are so troublesome.

From the perspective of Technical Rationality, professional practice is a process of problem *solving*. Problems of choice or decision are solved through the selection, from available means, of the one best suited to established ends. But with this emphasis on problem solving, we ignore problem *setting*, the process by which we define the decision to be made, the ends to be achieved, the means which may be chosen. In real-world practice, problems do not present themselves to the practitioner as givens. They must be constructed from the materials of problematic situations which are puzzling, troubling, and uncertain. In order to convert a problematic situation to a problem, a practitioner must do a certain kind of work. He must make sense of an uncertain situation that initially makes no sense. When professionals consider what road to build, for example, they deal usually with a complex and ill-defined situation in which geographic, topological, financial, economic, and political issues are are mixed up together. Once they have somehow decided what road to build and go on to consider how best to build it, they may have a problem they can solve by the application of available techniques; but when the road they have built leads unexpectedly to the destruction of a neighbourhood, they may find themselves again in a situation of uncertainty.

It is this sort of situation that professionals are coming increasingly to see as central to their practice. They are coming to recognize that although problem setting is a necessary condition for technical problem solving, it is not itself a technical problem. When we set the problem, we select what we will treat as the 'things' of the situation, we set the boundaries of our attention to it, and we impose upon it a coherence which allows us to say what is wrong and in what directions the situation needs to be changed. Problem setting is a process in which, interactively, we *name* the things to which we will attend and *frame* the context in which we will attend to them.

Even when a problem has been constructed, it may escape the categories of applied science because it presents itself as unique or unstable. In order to solve a problem by the application of existing theory or technique, a practitioner must be able to map those categories on to features of the practice situation. When a nutritionist finds a diet deficient in lysine, for example, dietary supplements known to contain lysine can be recommended. But a unique case falls outside the categories of applied theory; an unstable situation slips out from under them. A nutritionist attempting a planned nutritional intervention in a rural Central American community may discover that the intervention fails because the situation has become something other than the one planned for.

Technical Rationality depends on agreement about ends. When ends are fixed and clear, then the decision to act can present itself as an instrumental problem. But when ends are confused and conflicting, there is as yet no 'problem' to solve. A conflict of ends cannot be resolved by the use of techniques derived from applied research. It is rather through the non-technical process of framing the problematic situation that we may organize and clarify both the ends to be achieved and the possible means of achieving them.

Similarly, when there are conflicting paradigms of professional practice, such as we find in the pluralism of psychiatry, social work, or town planning, there is no clearly established context for the use of technique. There is contention over multiple ways of framing the practice role, each of which entrains a distinctive approach to problem setting and solving. And when practitioners do resolve conflicting role frames, it is through a kind of inquiry which falls outside the model of Technical Rationality. Again, it is the work of naming and framing that creates the conditions necessary to the exercise of technical expertise.

We can readily understand, therefore, not only why uncertainty, uniqueness, instability, and value conflict are so troublesome to the Positivist epistemology of practice but also why practitioners bound by this epistemology find themselves caught in a dilemma. Their definition of rigorous professional knowledge excludes phenomena they have learned to see as central to their practice. And artistic ways of coping with these phenomena do not qualify, for them, as rigorous professional knowledge.

This dilemma of 'rigour or relevance' arises more acutely in some areas of practice than in others. In the varied topography of professional practice, there is a high, hard ground where practitioners can make effective use of research-based theory and technique, and there is a swampy lowland where situations are confusing 'messes' incapable of technical solution. The difficulty is that the problems of the high ground, however great their technical interest, are often relatively unimportant to clients or to the larger society, whereas in the swamp are the problems of greatest human concern. Shall the practitioner stay on the high, hard ground where he can practise rigorously, as he understands rigour, but where he is constrained to deal with problems of relatively little social importance? Or shall he descend to the swamp where he can engage the most important and challenging problems if he is willing to forsake technical rigour?

In 'major' professions such as medicine, engineering, or agronomy there are zones where practitioners can function as technical experts. But there are also zones where the major professions resemble the minor ones. Medical technologies, such as kidney dialysis, generate demands in excess of the willingness of the nation to invest in medical care. Engineering that seems powerful and elegant when judged from a narrowly technical perspective may also carry unacceptable risks to environmental quality or human safety. Large-scale, industrialized agriculture destroys the peasant economies of the developing worlds. How should professionals take account of such issues as these?

There are those who choose the swampy lowlands. They deliberately involve themselves in messy but crucially important problems and, when asked to describe their methods of inquiry, they speak of experience, trial and error, intuition, and muddling through.

Other professionals opt for the high ground. Hungry for technical rigour, devoted to an image of solid professional competence, or fearful of entering a world in which they feel they do not know what they are doing, they choose to confine themselves to a narrowly technical practice. [. . .]

Many practitioners have [responded] to the dilemma of rigour or relevance [by] cutting the practice situation to fit professional knowledge. This they do in several ways. They may become selectively inattentive to data that fall outside their categories. Designers of management information systems may simply avoid noticing, for example, how their systems trigger games of control and evasion. They may use 'junk categories' to explain away discrepant data, as technical analysts sometimes attribute the failure of their recommendations to 'personality' or to 'politics'.[3] Or they may try to force the situation into a mould which lends itself to the use of available techniques. Thus, an industrial engineer may simplify the actual arrangement of a manufacturing system in order to make it easier to analyse; or, more ominously, members of the helping professions may get rid of clients who resist professional help, relegating the categories such as 'problem tenant' or 'rebellious child'. All such strategies carry a danger of misreading situations, or manipulating them, to serve the practitioner's interest in maintaining his confidence in his standard models and techniques. When people are involved in the situation, the practitioner may preserve his sense of expertise at his clients' expense.

Some students of the professions have tried to take account of the limitations of technical expertise and have proposed new approaches to the predicament of professional knowledge. Among these are Edgar Schein and Nathan Glaze and Herbert Simon. Each of these writers has identified a gap between professional knowledge and the demands of real-world practice. [. . .]

Schein (1973), Glazer (1974) and Simon (1972) propose three different approaches to the limitations of Technical Rationality and the related dilemma of rigour or relevance. All three employ a common strategy, however. They try to fill the gap between the scientific basis of professional knowledge and the demands of real-world practice in such a way as to preserve the model of Technical Rationality. Schein does it by segregating convergent science from divergent practice, relegating divergence to a residual category called 'divergent skill'. Glazer does it by attributing convergence to the major professions, which he applauds, and divergence to the minor professions, which he dismisses. Simon does it by proposing a science of design which depends on having well-formed instrumental problems to begin with.

Yet the Positivist epistemology of practice, the model of professional knowledge to which these writers cling, has fallen into disrepute in its original home, the philosophy of science. [. . .]

Among philosophers of science no one wants any longer to be called a Positivist, and there is a rebirth of interest in the ancient topics of craft, artistry, and myth – topics whose fate Positivism once claimed to have sealed. It seems clear, however, that the dilemma which afflicts the professions hinges not on science *per se* but on the Positivist view of science. From this perspective, we tend to see science, after the fact, as a body of established propositions derived from research. When we recognize their limited utility in practice, we experience the dilemma of rigour or relevance. But we may also consider science before the fact as a process in which scientists grapple with uncertainties and display arts of inquiry akin to the uncertainties and arts of practice.

Let us then reconsider the question of professional knowledge; let us stand the question on its head. If the model of Technical Rationality is incomplete, in that it fails to account for practical competence in 'divergent' situations, so much the worse for the model. Let us search, instead, for an epistemology of practice implicit in the artistic, intuitive processes which some practitioners do bring to situations of uncertainty, instability, uniqueness, and value conflict.

REFLECTION-IN-ACTION

When we go about the spontaneous, intuitive performance of the actions of everyday life, we show ourselves to be knowledgeable in a special way. Often we cannot say what it is that we know. When we try to describe it we find ourselves at a loss, or we produce descriptions that are obviously inappropriate. Our knowing is ordinarily tacit, implicit in our patterns of action and in our feel for the stuff with which we are dealing. It seems right to say that our knowing is *in* our action.

Similarly, the workaday life of the professional depends on tacit knowing-in-action. Every competent practitioner can recognize phenomena – families of symptoms associated with a particular disease, peculiarities of a certain kind of building site, irregularities of materials or structures – for which he cannot give a reasonably accurate or complete description. In his day-to-day practice he makes innumerable judgments of quality for which he cannot state adequate criteria, and he displays skills for which he cannot state the rules and procedures. Even when he makes conscious use of research-based theories and techniques, he is dependent on tacit recognitions, judgments, and skilful performances.

On the other hand, both ordinary people and professional practitioners often think about what they are doing, sometimes even while doing it. Stimulated by surprise, they turn thought back on action and on the knowing which is implicit in action. They may ask themselves, for example, 'What features do I notice when I recognize this thing? What are the criteria by which I make this judgment? What procedures am I enacting when I perform this skill? How am I framing the problem that I am trying to solve?' Usually, reflection on knowing-in-action goes together with reflection on the stuff at hand. There is some puzzling, or troubling, or interesting phenomenon with which the individual is trying to deal. As he tries to make sense of it, he also reflects on the understandings which have been implicit in his action, understandings which he surfaces, criticizes, restructures, and embodies in further action.

It is this entire process of reflection-in-action which is central to the 'art' by which practitioners sometimes deal well with situations of uncertainty, instability, uniqueness, and value conflict.

Knowing-in-action. Once we put aside the model of Technical Rationality, which leads us to think of intelligent practice as an *application* of knowledge to instrumental decisions, there is nothing strange about the idea that a kind of knowing is inherent in intelligent action. Common sense admits the category of know-how, and it does not stretch common sense very much to say that the know-how is *in* the action – that a tightrope walker's know-how, for example, lies in, and is revealed by, the way he takes his trip across the wire, or that a big-league pitcher's know-how is in his way of pitching to a batter's weakness, changing his pace, or distributing his energies over the course of a game. There is nothing in common sense to make us say that know-how consists of rules or plans which we entertain in the mind prior to action. Although we sometimes think before acting, it is also true that in much of the spontaneous behaviour of skilful practice we reveal a kind of knowing which does not stem from a prior intellectual operation.

As Gilbert Ryle has put it:

> What distinguishes sensible from silly operations is not their parentage but their procedure, and this holds no less for intellectual than for practical performances. 'Intelligent' cannot be defined in terms of 'intellectual' or 'knowing *how*' in terms of 'knowing *that*'; 'thinking what I am doing' does not connote 'both thinking what to do and doing it.' When I do something intelligently . . . I am doing one thing and not two. My performance has a special procedure or manner, not special antecedents.
>
> (Ryle 1949: 32)

[. . .]

Over the years, several writers on the epistemology of practice have been struck by the fact that skilful action often reveals a 'knowing more than we can say'. [. . .]

Psycholinguists have noted that we speak in conformity with rules of phonology and syntax which most of us cannot describe.[4] Alfred Schultz (1962) and his intellectual descendants have analysed the tacit, everyday know-how that we bring to social interactions such as the rituals of greeting, ending a meeting, or standing in a crowded elevator. Bird-whistell (1970) has made comparable contributions to a description of the tacit knowledge embodied in our use and recognition of movement and gesture. In these domains, too, we behave according to rules and proced-ures that we cannot usually describe and of which we are often unaware.

In examples like these, knowing has the following properties:

- There are actions, recognitions, and judgments which we know how to carry out spontaneously; we do not have to think about them prior to or during their performance.
- We are often unaware of having learned to do these things; we simply find ourselves doing them.
- In some cases, we were once aware of the understandings which were subsequently internalized in our feeling for the stuff of action. In other cases, we may never have been aware of them. In both cases, however, we are usually unable to describe the knowing which our action reveals.

It is in this sense that I speak of knowing-*in*-action, the characteristic mode of ordinary practical knowledge.

Reflecting-in-action. If common sense recognizes knowing-in-action, it also recognizes that we sometimes think about what we are doing. Phrases such as 'thinking on your feet', 'keeping your wits about you', and 'learning by doing' suggest not only that we can think about doing but that we can think about doing something while doing it. Some of the most interesting examples of this process occur in the midst of a performance.

Big-league baseball pitchers speak, for example, of the experience of 'finding the groove':

> Only a few pitchers can control the whole game with pure physical ability. The rest have to learn to adjust once they're out there. If they can't, they're dead ducks.

> [You get] a special feel for the ball, a kind of command that lets you repeat the exact same thing you did before that proved successful.

> Finding your groove has to do with studying those winning habits and trying to repeat them every time you perform.

> (Maslow 1981: 34)

I do not wholly understand what it means to 'find the groove'. It is clear, however, that the pitchers are talking about a particular kind of reflection. What is 'learning to adjust once you're out there'? Presumably it involves noticing how you have been pitching to the batters and how well it has been working, and on the basis of these thoughts and observations, changing the way you have been doing it. When you get a 'feel for the ball' that lets you 'repeat the exact same thing you did before that proved successful', you are noticing, at the very least, that you have been doing something right, and your 'feeling' allows you to do that something again. When you 'study those winning habits', you are thinking about the know-how that has enabled you to win. The pitchers seem to be talking about a kind of reflection on their patterns of action, on the situations in which they are performing, and on the know-how implicit in their performance. They are reflecting *on* action and, in some cases, reflecting *in* action.

When good jazz musicians improvise together, they also manifest a 'feel for' their material and they make on-the-spot adjustments to the sounds they hear. Listening to one another and to themselves, they feel where the music is going and adjust their playing accordingly. They can do this, first of all, because their collective effort at musical invention makes use of a schema – a metric, melodic, and harmonic schema familiar to all the participants – which gives a predictable order to the piece. In addition, each of the musicians has at the ready a repertoire of musical figures which he can deliver at appropriate moments. Improvisation consists of varying, combining, and recombining a set of figures within the schema which bounds and gives coherence to the performance. As the musicians feel the direction of the music that is developing out of their interwoven contributions, they make new sense of it and adjust their performance to the new sense they have made. They are reflecting-in-action on the music they are collectively making and on their individual contributions to it, thinking what they are doing and, in the process, evolving their way of doing it. Of course, we need not suppose that they reflect-in-action in the medium of words. More likely, they reflect through a 'feel for the music' which is not unlike the pitcher's 'feel for the ball'.

Much reflection-in-action hinges on the experience of surprise. When intuitive, spontaneous performance yields nothing more than the results expected for it, then we tend not to think about it. But when intuitive performance leads to surprises, pleasing and promising or unwanted, we may respond by reflecting-in-action. Like the baseball pitcher, we may reflect on our 'winning habits'; or like the jazz musician, on our sense of the music we have been making; or like the designer, on the misfit we have unintentionally created. In such processes, reflection tends to focus interactively on the outcomes of action, the action itself, and the intuitive knowing implicit in the action.

Let us consider an example which reveals these processes in some detail.

In an article entitled 'If you want to get ahead, get a theory', Inhelder and Karmiloff-Smith describe a rather unusual experiment concerning 'children's processes of discovery in action' (Inhelder and Karmiloff-Smith 1975:195). They asked their subjects to balance wooden blocks on a metal bar. Some of the blocks were plain wooden blocks, but others were conspicuously or inconspicuously weighted at one end. The authors attended to the spontaneous processes by which the children tried to learn about the properties of the blocks, balance them on the bar, and regulate their actions after success or failure.

They found that virtually all children aged six to seven began the task in the same way:

> *all* blocks were systematically first tried at their geometric centre.
>
> (Inhelder and Karmiloff-Smith 1975: 202)

And they found that slightly older children would not only place all blocks at their geometric centre but that:

> when asked to add small blocks of varying shapes and sizes to blocks already in balance, they added up to ten blocks precariously one on top of the other at the geometric centre rather than distributing them at the extremities.
>
> (Inhelder and Karmiloff-Smith 1975: 203)

They explain this persistent and virtually universal behaviour by attributing to the children what they call a 'theory-in-action': a 'geometric centre theory' of balancing, or, as one child put it, a theory that 'things always balance in the middle'.

Of course, when the children tried to balance the counterweighted blocks at their geometric centres, they failed. How did they respond to failure? Some children made what the authors called an 'action-response':

> They now placed the very same blocks more and more systematically at the geometric centre, with only very slight corrections around this point. They showed considerable surprise at not being able to balance the blocks a second time ('Heh, what's gone wrong with this one, it worked before') ... Action sequences then became reduced to: Place carefully at geometric centre, correct very slightly around this centre, abandon all attempts, declaring the object 'impossible' to balance.
>
> (Inhelder and Karmiloff-Smith 1975: 203)

Other children, generally between the ages of seven and eight, responded in a very different way. When the counterweighted blocks failed to balance at their geometric centres, these children began to de-centre them. They did this first with conspicuously counterweighted blocks. Then:

> gradually, and often almost reluctantly, the 7 to 8 year olds began to make corrections also on the inconspicuous weight blocks ... At this

point, we observed many pauses during action sequences on the
inconspicuous weight items.

(Inhelder and Karmiloff-Smith 1975: 205)

Later still:

> As the children were now really beginning to question the generality
> of their geometric centre theory, a negative response at the geometric
> centre sufficed to have the child rapidly make corrections toward the
> point of balance.

(Inhelder and Karmiloff-Smith 1975: 205)

And finally:

> children paused *before* each item, roughly assessed the weight distribu-
> tion of the block by lifting it ('you have to be careful, sometimes it's
> just as heavy on each side, sometimes it's heavier on one side'),
> inferred the probable point of balance and then placed the object
> immediately very close to it, without making any attempts at first
> balancing at the geometric centre.

(Inhelder and Karmiloff-Smith 1975: 205)

The children now behaved as though they had come to hold a theory-in-
action that blocks balance, not at their geometric centres, but at their
centres of gravity.

This second pattern of response to error, the authors call 'theory-
response'. Children work their way toward it through a series of stages.
When they are first confronted with a number of events which refute
their geometric centre theories-in-action, they stop and think. Then,
starting with the conspicuous-weight blocks, they begin to make correc-
tions away from the geometric centre. Finally, when they have really
abandoned their earlier theories-in-action, they weigh all the blocks in
their hands so as to infer the probable point of balance. As they shift
their theories of balancing from geometric centre to centre of gravity,
they also shift from a 'success orientation' to a 'theory orientation'.
Positive and negative results come to be taken not as signs of success or
failure in action but as information relevant to a theory of balancing.

It is interesting to note that as the authors observe and describe this
process, they are compelled to invent a language. They describe
theories-in-action which the children themselves cannot describe:

> Indeed, although the (younger) child's action sequences bear eloquent
> witness to a theory-in-action implicit in his behavior, this should not
> be taken as a capacity to conceptualize explicitly on what he is doing
> and why.

(Inhelder and Karmiloff-Smith 1975: 203)

Knowing-in-action which the child may represent to himself in terms of a 'feel for the blocks', the observers redescribe in terms of 'theories'. I shall say that they convert the child's know*ing*-in-action to know*ledge*-in-action.

A conversion of this kind seems to be inevitable in any attempt to talk about reflection-in-action. One must use words to describe a kind of knowing, and a change of knowing, which are probably not originally represented in words at all. Thus, from their observations of the children's behaviour, the authors make verbal descriptions of the children's intuitive understandings. These are the authors' theories about the children's knowing-in-action. Like all such theories, they are deliberate, idiosyncratic constructions, and they can be put to experimental test:

> just as the child was constructing a theory-in-action in his endeavour to balance the blocks, so we, too, were making on-the-spot hypotheses about the child's theories and providing opportunities for negative and positive responses in order to verify our own theories!
>
> (Inhelder and Karmiloff-Smith 1975: 199)

Reflecting-in-practice The block-balancing experiment is a beautiful example of reflection-in-action, but it is very far removed from our usual images of professional practice. If we are to relate the idea of reflection-in-action to professional practice, we must consider what a practice is and how it is like and unlike the kinds of action we have been discussing.

The word 'practice' is ambiguous. When we speak of a lawyer's practice, we mean the kinds of things he does, the kinds of clients he has, the range of cases he is called upon to handle. When we speak of someone practising the piano, however, we mean the repetitive or experimental activity by which he tries to increase his proficiency on the instrument. In the first sense, 'practice' refers to performance in a range of professional situations. In the second, it refers to preparation for performance. But professional practice also includes an element of repetition. A professional practitioner is a specialist who encounters certain types of situations again and again. This is suggested by the way in which professionals use the word 'case' – or project, account, commission, or deal, depending on the profession. All such terms denote the units which make up a practice, and they denote types of family-resembling examples. Thus, a physician may encounter many different 'cases of measles'; a lawyer, many different 'cases of libel'. As a practitioner experiences many variations of a small number of types of cases, he is able to 'practise' his practice. He develops a repertoire of expectations, images, and techniques. He learns what to look for and how to respond to what he finds. As long as his practice is stable, in the sense that it brings him the same types of cases, he becomes less and less subject to surprise. His knowing-in-practice tends to become increasingly tacit, spontaneous, and automatic, thereby conferring upon him and his clients the benefits of specialization.

On the other hand, professional specialization can have negative effects. In the individual, a high degree of specialization can lead to a parochial narrowness of vision. When a profession divides into subspecialties, it can break apart an earlier wholeness of experience and understanding. Thus people sometimes yearn for the general practitioner of earlier days, who is thought to have concerned himself with the 'whole patient', and they sometimes accuse contemporary specialists of treating particular illnesses in isolation from the rest of the patient's life experience. Further, as a practice becomes more repetitive and routine, and as knowing-in-practice becomes increasingly tacit and spontaneous, the practitioner may miss important opportunities to think about what he is doing. He may find that, like the younger children in the block-balancing experiment, he is drawn into patterns of error which he cannot correct. And if he learns, as often happens, to be selectively inattentive to phenomena that do not fit the categories of his knowing-in-action, then he may suffer from boredom or 'burn-out' and afflict his clients with the consequences of his narrowness and rigidity. When this happens, the practitioner has 'over-learned' what he knows.

A practitioner's reflection can serve as a corrective to over-learning. Through reflection, he can surface and criticize the tacit understandings that have grown up around the repetitive experiences of a specialized practice, and can make new sense of the situations of uncertainty or uniqueness which he may allow himself to experience.

Practitioners do reflect *on* their knowing-in-practice. Sometimes, in the relative tranquillity of a post-mortem, they think back on a project they have undertaken, a situation they have lived through, and they explore the understandings they have brought to their handling of the case. They may do this in a mood of idle speculation, or in a deliberate effort to prepare themselves for future cases.

But they may also reflect on practice while they are in the midst of it. Here they reflect-in-action, but the meaning of this term needs now to be considered in terms of the complexity of knowing-in-practice.

A practitioner's reflection-in-action may not be very rapid. It is bounded by the 'action-present', the zone of time in which action can still make a difference to the situation. The action-present may stretch over minutes, hours, days, or even weeks or months, depending on the pace of activity and the situational boundaries that are characteristic of the practice. Within the give-and-take of courtroom behaviour, for example, a lawyer's reflection-in-action may take place in seconds; but when the context is that of an antitrust case that drags on over years, reflection-in-action may proceed in leisurely fashion over the course of several months. An orchestra conductor may think of a single performance as a unit of practice, but in another sense a whole season is his unit. The pace and duration of episodes of reflection-in-action vary with the pace and duration of the situations of practice.

When a practitioner reflects in and on his practice, the possible objects of his reflection are as varied as the kinds of phenomena before him and the systems of knowing-in-practice which he brings to them. He may reflect on the tacit norms and appreciations which underlie a judgment, or on the strategies and theories implicit in a pattern of behaviour. He may reflect on the feeling for a situation which has led him to adopt a particular course of action, on the way in which he has framed the problem he is trying to solve, or on the role he has constructed for himself within a larger institutional context.

Reflection-in-action, in these several modes, is central to the art through which practitioners sometimes cope with the troublesome 'divergent' situations of practice.

When the phenomenon at hand eludes the ordinary categories of knowledge-in-practice, presenting itself as unique or unstable, the practitioner may surface and criticize his initial understanding of the phenomenon, construct a new description of it, and test the new description by an on-the-spot experiment. Sometimes he arrives at a new theory of the phenomenon by articulating a feeling he has about it.

When he finds himself stuck in a problematic situation which he cannot readily convert to a manageable problem, he may construct a new way of setting the problem – a new frame which, in what I shall call a 'frame experiment', he tries to impose on the situation.

When he is confronted with demands that seem incompatible or inconsistent, he may respond by reflecting on the appreciations which he and others have brought to the situation. Conscious of a dilemma, he may attribute it to the way in which he has set his problem, or even to the way in which he has framed his role. He may then find a way of integrating, or choosing among, the values at stake in the situation. [. . .]

In his mid-thirties, sometime between the composition of his early work *The Cossacks* and his later *War and Peace*, Lev Nikolayevitch Tolstoy became interested in education. He started a school for peasant children on his estate at Yasnaya Polanya, he visited Europe to learn the latest educational methods, and he published an educational journal, also called *Yasnaya Polanya*. Before he was done (his new novel eventually replaced his interest in education), he had built some seventy schools, had created an informal teacher-training programme, and had written an exemplary piece of educational evaluation.

For the most part, the methods of the European schools filled him with disgust, yet he was entranced by Rousseau's writings on education. His own school anticipated John Dewey's later approach to learning by doing, and bore the stamp of his conviction that good teaching required 'not a method but an art'. [. . .]

An artful teacher sees a child's difficulty in learning to read not as a defect in the child but as a defect 'of his own instruction'. So he must find a way of explaining what is bothering the pupil. He must do a piece of experimental research, then and there, in the classroom. And because the child's difficulties may be unique, the teacher cannot assume that his repertoire of explanations will suffice, even though they are 'at the tongue's end'. He must be ready to invent new methods and must 'endeavour to develop in himself the ability of discovering them'.

Researchers at the Massachusetts Institute of Technology (MIT) have undertaken a programme of in-service education for teachers, a programme organized around the idea of on-the-spot reflection and experiment, very much as in Tolstoy's art of teaching. In this Teacher Project,[5] the researchers have encouraged a small group of teachers to explore their own intuitive thinking about apparently simple tasks in domains such as mathematics, physics, music, and the perceived behaviour of the moon. The teachers have made some important discoveries. They have allowed themselves to become confused about subjects they are supposed to 'know'; and as they have tried to work their way out of their confusions, they have also begun to think differently about learning and teaching.

Early in the project, a critical event occurred. The teachers were asked to observe and react to a videotape of two boys engaged in playing a simple game. The boys sat at a table, separated from one another by an opaque screen. In front of one boy, blocks of various colours, shapes, and sizes were arranged in a pattern. In front of the other, similar blocks were lying on the table in no particular order. The first boy was to tell the second one how to reproduce the pattern. After the first few instructions, however, it became clear that the second boy had gone astray. In fact, the two boys had lost touch with one another, though neither of them knew it.

In their initial reactions to the videotape, the teachers spoke of a 'communications problem'. They said that the instruction giver had 'well-developed verbal skills' and that the receiver was 'unable to follow directions'. Then one of the researchers pointed out that, although the blocks contained no green squares – all squares were orange and only triangles were green – she had heard the first boy tell the second to 'take a green square'. When the teachers watched the videotape again, they were astonished. That small mistake had set off a chain of false moves. The second boy had put a green thing, a triangle, where the first boy's pattern had an orange square, and from then on all the instructions became problematic. Under the circumstances, the second boy seemed to have displayed considerable ingenuity in his attempts to reconcile the instructions with the pattern before him.

At this point, the teachers reversed their picture of the situation. They could see why the second boy behaved as he did. He no longer seemed stupid; he had, indeed, 'followed instructions'. As one teacher put it, they were now 'giving him reason'. They saw reasons for his behaviour; and his errors, which they had previously seen as an inability to follow directions, they now found reasonable.

Later on in the project, as the teachers increasingly challenged themselves to discover the meanings of a child's puzzling behaviour, they often spoke of 'giving him reason'.

In examples such as these, something falls outside the range of ordinary expectations. The banker has a feeling that something is wrong, though he cannot at first say what it is. The physician sees an odd combination of diseases never before described in a medical text. Tolstoy thinks of each of his pupils as an individual with ways of learning and imperfections peculiar to himself. The teachers are astonished by the sense behind a student's mistake. In each instance, the practitioner allows himself to experience surprise, puzzlement, or confusion in a situation which he finds uncertain or unique. He reflects on the phenomena before him, and on the prior understandings which have been implicit in his behaviour. He carries out an experiment which serves to generate both a new understanding of the phenomena and a change in the situation.

When someone reflects-in-action, he becomes a researcher in the practice context. He is not dependent on the categories of established theory and technique, but constructs a new theory of the unique case. His inquiry is not limited to a deliberation about means which depends on a prior agreement about ends. He does not keep means and ends separate, but defines them interactively as he frames a problematic situation. He does not separate thinking from doing, ratiocinating his way to a decision which he must later convert to action. Because his experimenting is a kind of action, implementation is built into his inquiry. Thus reflection-in-action can proceed, even in situations of uncertainty or uniqueness, because it is not bound by the dichotomies of Technical Rationality.

Although reflection-in-action is an extraordinary process, it is not a rare event. Indeed, for some reflective practitioners it is the core of practice. Nevertheless, because professionalism is still mainly identified with technical expertise, reflection-in-action is not generally accepted – even by those who do it – as a legitimate form of professional knowing.

Many practitioners, locked into a view of themselves as technical experts, find nothing in the world of practice to occasion reflection.

They have become too skilful at techniques of selective inattention, junk categories, and situational control, techniques which they use to preserve the constancy of their knowledge-in-practice. For them, uncertainty is a threat; its admission is a sign of weakness. Others, more inclined toward and adept at reflection-in-action, nevertheless feel profoundly uneasy because they cannot say what they know how to do, cannot justify its quality or rigour.

For these reasons, the study of reflection-in-action is critically important. The dilemma of rigour or relevance may be dissolved if we can develop an epistemology of practice which places technical problem solving within a broader context of reflective inquiry, shows how reflection-in-action may be rigorous in its own right, and links the art of practice in uncertainty and uniqueness to the scientist's art of research. We may thereby increase the legitimacy of reflection-in-action and encourage its broader, deeper, and more rigorous use.

NOTES

1 I first used this term in *Technology and Change* (New York: Delacorte Press, 1966).
2 Of course, the problem of the lack of agreement about ends has engaged the attention of many of the protagonists of the positivist epistemology of practice. Approaches to this problem have ranged from the search for an ultimate end, to which all others could be subordinated; to a 'universal solvent' for ends, as in the utility functions of the welfare economists; to the 'piecemeal social engineering' proposed by Karl Popper. For a discussion of these, their defects and merits, see Frankel, C. 'The relation of theory to practice: some standard views, in C. Frankel *et al.* (eds) (1968) *Social Theory and Social Intervention*, Cleveland: Case Western Reserve University Press.
3 The term is taken from Geertz, C. 'Thick description: toward an interpretive theory of culture', in Geertz, C. (1973) *The Interpretation of Cultures*, New York: Basic Books.
4 The whole of contemporary linguistics and psycholinguistics is relevant here – for example, the work of Chomsky, Halle, and Sinclair.
5 The staff of the Teacher's Project consisted of Jeanne Bamberger, Eleanor Duckworth and Margaret Lampert. My description of the incident of 'giving the child reason' is adapted from a project memorandum by Lampert.

REFERENCES

Birdwhistell, R. L. (1970) *Kinesics and Context*, Philadelphia: University of Pennsylvania Press.
Glazer, N. (1974) 'Schools of the minor professions', *Minerva*.
Goode, W. (1966) 'The Librarian: from occupation to profession', in: Vollmer and Mills (eds) *Professionalization*, Englewood Cliffs, NJ: Prentice-Hall.
Greenwood, E. (1966) 'Attributes of a profession', in: Vollmer and Mills (eds) *Professionalization*, Englewood Cliffs, NJ: Prentice-Hall.
Hughes, E. (1973) 'Higher education and the professions', in C. Kaysen (ed.)

Content and Context: Essays on College Education, New York: McGraw-Hill.

Inhelder, B. and Karmiloff-Smith, A. (1975) 'If you want to get ahead, get a theory', *Cognition*, vol. 3, no. 3: 195–212.

Maslow, J. E. (1981) 'Grooving on a baseball afternoon', *Mainliner*, May.

Moore, W. E. (1970) *The Professions*, New York: Russell Sage Foundation.

Ryle, G. (1949) 'On knowing how and knowing that', in *The Concept of Mind*, London: Hutchison.

Schein, E. (1973) *Professional Education*, New York: McGraw-Hill.

Schutz, A. (1962) *Collected Papers*, The Hague: Nijhoff.

Simon, H. (1972) *The Sciences of the Artificial*, Cambridge, MA: MIT Press.

Thorne, B. (1973) 'Professional education in medicine', in *Education for the Professions of Medicine, Law, Theology and Social Welfare*, New York: McGraw-Hill.

Veblen, T. (1962) *The Higher Learning in America*, New York: Hill and Wang (reprint of 1918 edition).

Chapter 2

Promoting reflection in learning
A model†

David Boud, Rosemary Keogh and David Walker

INTRODUCTION

We are now in a position to present our own model of reflection in learning. We have been led to this by an analysis of examples, by our own experience of the processes of learning and the work of a number of authors who have considered reflection as a part of learning.

We wish to restrict our scope to what Tough (1979) terms 'deliberate' learning. That is, learning which is intentional in which learners are aware that they are learning; learning with a definite, specific goal rather than generalized learning, for example, to 'develop the mind'; learning which is undertaken in order to pursue this goal; and learning which the individual intends to retain (Knapper and Cropley, in press). Of course, much of our discussion may also apply to other less conscious or less organized forms of learning, but these involve other considerations which would take us away from our main area of interest. Deliberate learning occurs within educational and training institutions, but a great deal takes place on a less formal basis away from these institutions (Tough, 1979). In addition we wish to focus primarily on experiential or experience-based learning (Boud and Pascoe, 1978) rather than what Coleman (1976) refers to as classroom learning which concerns symbolic or information assimilation, although we believe that similar considerations might also apply in these latter areas.

Reflection is a form of response of the learner to experience. In our model we have indicated two main components: the experience and the reflective activity based upon that experience. In the sense in which we are using the term, experience consists of the total response of a person to a situation or event: what he or she thinks, feels, does and concludes at the time and immediately thereafter. The situation or event could be part of a formal course, e.g. a workshop, a field trip, a lecture; or it

† This is an edited version of a chapter that appeared in *Reflection: Turning Experience into Learning*, London: Croom Helm, 1985.

could be more informal: an event arising from a personal study project or from the actions of a community group, or a totally unplanned occurrence in daily life. It could be provoked by an external agent or it could be an internal experience, arising out of some discomfort with one's present state. In most cases the initial experience is quite complex and is constituted of a number of particular experiences within it. In the case of the child care student the learning experience would consist of the time spent within the classroom, but within that there would be many observations, thoughts, perceptions, reactions, awkward moments, and interchanges which would make up the total experience.

After the experience there occurs a processing phase: this is the area of reflection. Reflection is an important human activity in which people recapture their experience, think about it, mull it over and evaluate it. It is this working with experience that is important in learning. The capacity to reflect is developed to different stages in different people and it may be this ability which characterizes those who learn effectively from experience. Why is it that conscious reflection is necessary? Why can it not occur effectively at the unconscious level? It can and does occur, but these unconscious processes do not allow us to make active and aware decisions about our learning. It is only when we bring our ideas to our consciousness that we can evaluate them and begin to make choices about what we will and will not do. For these reasons it is important for the learner to be aware of the role of reflection in learning, and how the processes involved can be facilitated. Some authors (for example, Taylor, 1981) present reflection as a stage in the learning process which occurs after substantial other activity has taken place, towards the latter part of a one-semester course, for instance. Although we accept that major periods of reflection may take place in this manner we also wish to include in our definition more modest reflective activities which may occur daily.

In our view, reflection in the context of learning is a generic term for those intellectual and affective activities in which individuals engage to explore their experiences in order to lead to new understandings and appreciations. It may take place in isolation or in association with others. It can be done well or badly, successfully or unsuccessfully. However, we wish to focus on what learners and teachers can do to ensure that it is a productive experience.

Probably, for adult learners, most events which precipitate reflection arise out of the normal occurrences of one's life. The impetus may arise from a loss of confidence in or disillusionment with one's existing situation. This could be provoked by an external event, or could develop from one's own reflection on a whole series of occurrences over time, causing a dissatisfaction which leads to a reconsideration of them.

Boyd and Fales (1983) refer to this experience as an 'inner discomfort', and Dewey writes of:

> a state of doubt, hesitation, perplexity, mental difficulty, in which [reflective] thinking originates, and . . . an act of searching, hunting, inquiring, to find material that will resolve the doubt, settle and dispose of the perplexity.
>
> (Dewey, 1933: 12)

Reflection may also be prompted by more positive states, for example, by an experience of successfully completing a task which previously was thought impossible. This may stimulate a reappraisal of other tasks and the planning of new experiences. For someone who has acquired some facility in reflection, the personal affective aspect would be a more frequent impetus rather than particular activities planned by others.

We believe that the more teachers and learners understand this reflective aspect of learning and organize learning activities which are consistent with it, the more effective learning can be. The model points to the starting point and objects of reflection: the totality of experiences of learners, the behaviour in which they have engaged, the ideas of which learners are aware and the feelings which they have experienced. It designates the outcomes of reflection, which may be a personal synthesis, integration and appropriation of knowledge, the validation of personal knowledge, a new affective state, or the decision to engage in some further activity. It also points to the various intellectual and affective processes involved in reflection. These may be facilitated by individual learners or, in some cases, by others assisting them in learning. Figure 2.1 presents this.

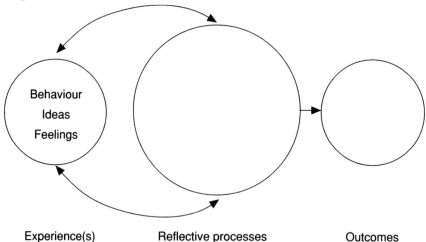

Experience(s)   Reflective processes   Outcomes

Figure 2.1 A model of reflection in the learning process

In discussing the model we will for the sake of simplicity refer to the initial learning experience as if it were a singular event; we will also assume in talking about reflection that a particular event has occurred which is the focus of reflection. Of course, in practice we all have a number of experiences over a period of time some of which will become the focus of reflection and some of which will not; often these will not be perceived as separate incidents and it may not be possible for us to identify a particular event which acts as a trigger. However, the general features of reflection in such circumstances are similar. Although we have defined the scope of what we term reflection, and we believe that this corresponds generally to current usage, other authors use different terms for this concept. For example, Van Manen (1977) following the German tradition uses the word 'experience', and More (1974) uses 'learning'.

Despite all that has been written about reflection it is difficult to be precise about the nature of the process. It is so integral to every aspect of learning that in some way it touches most of the processes of the mind. As yet little research has been conducted on reflection in learning and that which has been undertaken offers few guidelines for the practical problems which face us as teachers and learners. However, it is possible to extract some principles from those who have examined their own learning processes.

John Dewey wrote a great deal about what he referred to as reflective thought and, in common with a number of philosophers who have discussed reflection (cf Ryle), he assumed it was highly rational and controlled. He defined reflective thought as:

> Active, persistent, and careful consideration of any belief or supposed form of knowledge in the light of the grounds that support it and further conclusions to which it leads ... it includes conscious and voluntary effort to establish belief upon a firm basis of evidence and rationality.
>
> (Dewey, 1933: 9)

Dewey considered that reflection involves an integration of attitudes and skills in methods of inquiry; that neither attitudes nor skills alone will suffice (Zeichner, 1982). Although we acknowledge a great debt to Dewey, we do not fully follow his path. In particular, we give much greater emphasis to the affective aspects of learning, the opportunities these provide for enhancing reflection and the barriers which these pose to it.

In order to explore this model in more detail we shall consider each aspect of it in turn and focus on those issues which in our view are important in ensuring that the process of reflection is an effective one. First, we will examine some of the characteristics of learners and the significance of these for their response to the initial experience. As, by definition, the experience which will be processed has to be experienced by the individual, what the learner brings to the event is essential to an understanding of what occurs. Second, we will look at what we regard as the three major elements of the reflective process itself: returning to the experience, attending to feelings, and re-evaluating the experience. These elements are concerned with how the learner works on the experience, links new knowledge with old, re-examines the initial experience in the light of his or her own goals, integrates learning into his or her existing framework, and rehearses it with a view to subsequent activity.

THE LEARNER

The characteristics and aspirations of the learner are the most important factors in the learning process. The response of the learner to new experience is determined significantly by past experiences which have contributed to the ways in which the learner perceives the world. The way one person reacts to a given situation will not be the same as others and this becomes more obvious when learners from diverse backgrounds work together.

Those who approach the new learning experience from a history of success in similar situations may be able to enter more fully into the new context and draw more from it. The person who is adequately prepared in the particular area of learning can approach it with feelings of competence and confidence and is more likely to find it a rewarding experience at the time and will be drawn into it more easily. A history of positive associations with teachers can also contribute to productive involvements in new learning experiences. The building of a good climate in which to conduct learning activities is directed towards bringing these positive attitudes to the fore.

It is also necessary to take into account negative experiences from the past. An example of the unique response of an individual and how this can affect teaching plans is shown by a recent incident. In one of our classes a group of adults was shown a film about the life of the German theologian, Dietrich Bonhoeffer. It was intended that this should stimulate discussion on some of the values implicit in his work. After the film there was a period of discussion in small groups focusing on a series of questions provided to help each participant formulate his or her own response to the values presented. After the exercise was complete the group commented on the activity. Most of them had responded to the film in the way anticipated by the teacher. However, in one case the entire experience had been quite different. During the film there had been very brief flashes of atrocities inflicted in concentration camps: these appeared to have been included to provide a background for the issues presented in the film. However, they were sufficient to arouse in one participant a reaction quite unlike that of the others. This person, as a child, had experienced at first hand atrocities similar to those portrayed, and the film's brief flashes of them had caused her to relive those past events. Her response to the intellectual values presented in the film had been drowned in the emotional upsurge that had been triggered in her. The teacher's facilitation of reflection on the experience of the film in no way related to what this person had experienced, and, for her, the whole exercise was of a dramatically different nature from that of the others.

This example may appear a little atypical, but in all situations we find that our perceptions of events are conditioned by past experience which has shaped our response to the world around us, and that knowledge of how this has affected us in unknown or unknowable to a teacher. Less vivid examples of the above occur every day in other ways. A student who has had unpleasant experiences in, say, a mathematics or science class may, when exposed to similar situations in the future, experience again the same feelings of discomfort. These can interfere with the process of subject-matter learning as the student may become so pre-occupied with emotional reactions that the new information presented by the teacher is not clearly perceived. The learner does not relate to the mathematical or scientific content but rather responds covertly to the past humiliation and embarrassment. This emotional load can carry over into the learner's processing of the subject, and unless some way can be found of resolving these feelings there will be no new learning of the content in question. Such negative reactions to formal classroom situations are more common than we usually care to admit. Of course, there are also the mathematics students who have had enjoyable experiences and for whom maths is fun. After the particular class is over they continue holding their positive attitude; they may be good at mathematics not because of any special natural ability but because they feel comfortable about learning it.

George Kelly (1955) in his personal construct theory refers to the individual and unique perception of each person. He highlights the differences in individual perception and response to the one event and identifies the need for teachers to be aware that what is in their heads is not necessarily translated to the heads of their students. In Kelly's view objects, events or concepts are only meaningful when seen from the perspective of the person construing their meaning. This suggests that techniques to assist reflection need to be applied to the constructions of the learner, rather than those of the teacher. A similar emphasis can be found in the work of Paulo Freire (1970) although he stressed cultural rather than psychological factors in learning. His team of literacy workers adopted the view that learners have a personal perception of the world which is culturally induced, so that their personal meanings or constructs can only be comprehended in their unique social and political context.

Both Kelly and Freire highlight the centrality of individuals' perceptions in learning. As Abbs (1974) puts it, 'one must again and again return to the person before us'.

One of the most important areas of learning for adults is that which frees them from their habitual ways of thinking and acting and involves them in what Mezirow (1978, 1981) terms 'perspective transformation'. This means the process of becoming critically aware of how and why our assumptions about the world in which we operate have come to constrain the way we see ourselves and our relationships. He suggests that there are two paths to perspective transformation: one is a sudden insight into the structure of the assumptions which have limited or distorted one's understanding of oneself and one's relationships; the other is directed towards the same end but it proceeds more slowly by a series of transitions which permit one to revise specific assumptions about oneself and others until a stage occurs in which the assumptions become transformed. Freire (1970) has used the term 'conscientization' to describe the process by which one's false consciousness becomes transcended through education. In a similar context Reed (1981, cited in Cunningham, 1983) discusses what he calls 'the empowering learning process' which assumes that problems for individual learners may have their source in the structures of society. In Reed's view 'the essence of such an empowering process is the transformation of social conscious-ness' and this involves focusing on the social experience of learners and the historical development of society. Lessons are drawn from these in order to improve learners' own practice.

THE LEARNER'S INTENT

The intentions of the learner are particularly important; often a desire to learn for a particular purpose can assist in overcoming many obstacles and inhibitions. Intentions also influence a learner's approach to a situation and the ways which are chosen to process experience. When the activity being processed is one which is shared with others the intentions of the group may be paramount and it will then be necessary to take into account the potentially divergent goals within the group.

The learner can choose to direct reflective activity to a variety of ends. These intentions can influence both the manner of reflection and its outcome. They can be directed towards exploring organized knowl-edge, towards self-exploration, or examining the natural and human environment or context in which the learner is operating. For example, in the case of a geology field trip, the processing of the experience might be directed towards the study of geological strata, to the practicalities of working under field conditions, to the learner's response to these conditions or, indeed, to all of these. The outcomes of these might be an

improved conceptualization of particular rock features, a greater awareness of the use of certain surveying techniques, the development of a
lack of confidence in coping with the field environment, or a reappraisal
of the desire to become a field-based geologist. The intent of the learner
permeates every stage of the process from the choice to engage in a
particular activity to the ultimate results of the reflective process. Recollection of the event itself will be affected by it because, in the replaying
of the experience, particular attention may be given to those elements
which appear to be relevant to the goals of the learner.

Intentions vary both between individuals and within an individual
depending on the task at hand. Researchers who have studied university
students have identified approaches to learning which they have classified
as either deep or surface approaches. The deep approach is one in which
students seek an understanding of the meaning of what they are studying,
relate it to their previous knowledge and interact actively with the
material at hand. In contrast, those who adopt a surface approach tend
to memorize information and focus on the requirements of tests and
examinations (Säljö, 1981; Gibbs *et al.*, 1982). Entwistle and Ramsden
describe the deep approach as being characterized by an integration of
formal learning with personal experience, the formation of relationships
between parts of knowledge, and a search for meaning, and the surface
approach as the treatment of tasks as unrelated, an emphasis on memoriza-
tion and an attitude of unreflectiveness (Entwistle and Ramsden, 1983).
However, these approaches are not constant in any one student and
someone might adopt a deep or a surface approach depending on the
circumstances and their intentions at the time. The adoption of a reflective
approach is a choice which we can make or not as we wish, and is one
which can be associated with the deep approach to learning.

The importance of intent has been recognized in modern work on
reflection. For Dewey (1916) reflection is a process which perceives
connections and links between the parts of an experience. He thought
that the context of reflection is uncertainty in the environment and that
the learner's activity in that context is 'an intentional effort ... to
discover specific connections' which will improve certainty. For Jurgen
Habermas (1974) an important reflective process occurs in a context of
purpose which he calls 'critical intent'. He sees this as the disposition to
investigate and reconstruct an aspect of the social and moral environment
to achieve enlightenment and ultimately emancipation. In his view a
group of persons with critical intent bringing their informed judgement
to bear on the apparent issues or problem is an act of reflection. This
process generates critical ideas or theories about the validity of the
questions which are considered and the inferences which are drawn, and
the reconstruction of new ones. Reflective activity with critical intent is,
for Habermas, the heart of the process which frees the human mind.

Mezirow (1981) has used the framework of Habermas in his studies of adult learning and has given the concept of critical reflectivity a central role. Critical reflectivity plays a vital part in this demanding activity and Mezirow describes some of the major dimensions of this concept in his important theoretical paper.

At the first level there are the forms of reflectivity of our ordinary consciousness which Mezirow defines in the following way. *Reflectivity* is the act of becoming aware of a specific perception, meaning or behaviour of our own or of habits we have of seeing, thinking or acting; *affective reflectivity* is becoming aware of how we feel about the way we are perceiving, thinking or acting or about our habits of doing so. *Discriminant reflectivity* is assessing the efficacy of our perceptions, thoughts, actions and habits of doing things: identifying immediate causes; recognizing reality contexts (a play, game, dream, or religious, musical or drug experience, etc) in which we are functioning and identifying our relationships in the situation. There is also *judgemental reflectivity*, which is making and becoming aware of our value judgements about our perceptions, thoughts, actions and habits in terms of their being liked or disliked, beautiful or ugly, positive or negative.

There are also forms of reflectivity which pertain particularly to perspective transformation and to our critical consciousness. *Conceptual reflectivity* is becoming conscious of our awareness and critiquing it as, for example, when we question the constructs we are using when we evaluate another person. *Psychic reflectivity* is recognizing in oneself the habit of making precipitant judgements about people on the basis of limited information about them, and recognizing the interests and anticipations which influence the way we perceive, think or act.

These latter two aspects of critical consciousness may be differentiated from *theoretical reflectivity* which Mezirow believes is central to perspective transformation. *Theoretical reflectivity* is becoming aware that the reason for a habit of precipitant judgement or for conceptual inadequacy is a set of taken-for-granted cultural or psychological assumptions which explain personal experience less satisfactorily than another perspective with more functional criteria for seeing, thinking and acting.

PROMOTING REFLECTION

We want now to look at the process of reflection from the point of view of the learner and put special emphasis on the relationship of the reflective process to the learning experience and on what learners can do, with and without the aid of others, to enhance this activity.

In our view, one of the most important ways to enhance learning is to strengthen the link between the learning experience and the reflective activity which follows it. At the simplest level this link can be formed by incorporating into learning activities a specific allocation of time which can be used for reflection. This can be achieved, for example, by the scheduling of a debriefing period for a group or by setting specific time aside for keeping a diary of events and one's reactions to them. If we are exposed to one new event after another without a break we are unlikely to be able to make the most of any of the events separately. The link can also be formed through the application of various techniques to aid reflection during the time that has been set aside. We start from the position that it is useful for learners and teachers to have a model of reflection which points to some of the major processes which they should consider, for them to have their attention drawn to the importance of reflective activity, and for them to plan consciously for the reflective stage of the learning process.

Figure 2.2 lists the three elements which we believe are important in the reflective process. *Returning to experience* is simply the recollection of the salient events, the replaying of the initial experience in the mind of the learner or the recounting to others of the features of the experience. *Attending to feelings* has two aspects: utilizing positive feelings and removing obstructing feelings. Utilization of positive feelings involves focusing on positive feelings about learning and the experience which is subject to reflection. This may involve the conscious recollection of good experiences, attention to pleasant aspects of the immediate environment, or the anticipation of the possible benefits to be derived from the processing of events. Removing obstructing feelings is a necessary precursor to a rational consideration of events. This may involve expressing one's feelings when recounting an event to others by, for example, laughing through the tale of an embarrassing incident or through some other form of catharsis. It involves whatever needs to be done in order to remove impediments to a thorough examination of the experience.

This leads to the third stage of *re-evaluating experience* which, although it is the most important, is often not completed if the preceding two are omitted. Some form of evaluation might have taken place at the time of the experience and may in the learner's mind be part of the experience itself. Re-evaluation involves re-examining experience in the light of the learner's intent, associating new knowledge with that which is already possessed, and integrating this new knowledge into the learner's conceptual framework. It leads to an appropriation of this knowledge into the learner's repertoire of behaviour. This can involve a rehearsal in which the new learning is applied mentally to test its authenticity and the planning of subsequent activity in which this learning is applied in one's life. Although we have separated these elements and stages within each it is not possible to regard them as distinct and unrelated. In general, the process may tend to proceed in the sequence we have described, but this

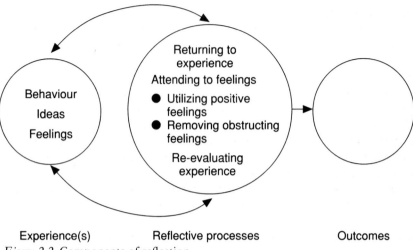

Experience(s)   Reflective processes   Outcomes

Figure 2.2 Components of reflection

may involve many cycles between stages, repetitions of important elements and lingering over particularly significant components.

Stage 1 Returning to experience

One of the most useful activities that can initiate a period of reflection is recollecting what has taken place and replaying the experience in the mind's eye, to observe the event as it has happened and to notice exactly what occurred and one's reactions to it in all its elements. It may be helpful to commit this description to paper, or to describe it to others. By whatever means this occurs the description should involve a close attention to detail and should refrain from making judgements. As one replays the experience chronologically, details usually begin to emerge which were ignored at the time of the experience, or only noted in passing. As we witness the events again they become available for us to reconsider and examine afresh; we realize what we were feeling and what responses prompted us to act as we did. This description provides the data for subsequent processing and can help to ensure that our reflection is on the basis of the actual events as we experienced them at the time, rather than in terms of what we wished had happened.

For example, the geology student may, at the end of the field trip, start to think about preparing a report and as a preliminary review her experience by recalling each day in the field. To aid her in this she may turn to her field notes to prompt her and help her reconstruct past events: 'why did I write this?', 'what was happening when I observed that?', 'I was really excited when that occurred'. Only part of this recollection will be of immediate use to her in writing her report, but the exercise helps her to focus on the experience and to extract from it what is important. Recollection may need to be repeated many times and from many perspectives; for example, once focusing on the external events, again noticing one's feelings, and again becoming aware of the ideas associated with it.

The simple replay of events and responses logically precedes any cogitation although in any given situation they may be interlinked. What takes place first is a clarification of the personal perceptions of the learner. The learner stands back from the immediacy of the experience and whatever personal challenge it may have been at the time and reviews it with the leisure of not having to act on it in real time. The learner can then start to view the experience from other perspectives, perhaps to see herself as others see her, or to stand back metaphorically to look at the wider context in which the event was situated. The review may not take long if it is done mentally; if it proves fruitful it can be developed to whatever length is desired.

The description of the experience should be, as far as possible, clear of any judgements as these tend to cloud our recollections and may blind us to some of the features which we may need to reassess. However, what can emerge in the descriptive process is the observation of judgements and interpretations which took place at the time of the experience itself or shortly thereafter. Often false perceptions can be detected by recollection alone. One of the main reasons for writing descriptions or reporting them to others is to provide a check on whether they are free from judgements. Debriefing is a technique which can be used for individuals or for groups which begins by a lengthy period of description and returns to the original experience before proceeding to any analysis.

Of particular importance within description is the observation of the feelings evoked during the experience. On occasions our emotional reactions can override our rationality to such an extent that we react unawarely and with blurred perceptions or they may foster the development of confidence and a sense of self-worth that can lead us to pursue paths which previously may have been unavailable to us. It is useful to recognize that this is occurring even though it may not be appropriate to focus further on these at this stage. Acknowledging feelings, whether experienced as positive or negative, can enable us to enter into the second and third phases of reflection more easily. Learners who do not observe this affective dimension of their experience may undermine the value of their reflections by restricting them to one aspect of their response to the world around them, thus placing artificial barriers on their response to experience.

At any stage insights might arise 'out of the blue'. They may be instantaneous or intuitive appreciations of an important truth, or enriched descriptions of the events. They cannot be planned, but they may signal the beginning of a new level of reflection which involves working with the insight as well as the recollections of experience and they may also involve re-evaluation and the making of judgements.

Stage 2 Attending to feelings

It has already been noted that describing events can bring us to an awareness of the feelings that were present during the initial experience. In the example given earlier about the reactions of a viewer of the Bonhoeffer film, the emotional response of the learner to the film, drowned the response which had been anticipated by the teacher. Even though our emotions and feelings are a significant source of learning, they can also at times become barriers. Depending on the circumstances and our intentions we need either to work with our emotional responses, find ways of setting them aside, or if they are positive ones retaining and enhancing them. If they do form barriers, these need to be recognized as such and removed before the learning process can proceed.

Utilizing our positive feelings is particularly important as they can provide us with the impetus to persist in what might be very challenging situations, they can help us see events more sharply and they can provide the basis for new affective learning. Unless we believe in ourselves and our own capabilities we can constrain ourselves to such an extent that we deny ourselves learning opportunities and fail to extract what is available to us in any given situation. Our geology student would not be able to go about all the technical tasks effectively if she did not feel that she could cope well with the basic requirements of living in the field. Positive feelings can be enhanced through attending to situations in which we have been successful or in which we have felt good about ourselves. We can focus on what we regarded as good about the experience and appreciate those things we did which were worthwhile, creative or stimulating. If we establish a positive affective state we are able to pursue both cognitive learning and to develop our emotional lives.

Sometimes in reflection we are not able to recollect events clearly, or we may be so rooted in one perspective or fixed on a given interpretation, that we give up reflection believing that we have reached an understanding of the experience. Commonly what has happened is that an affective barrier has been raised which has temporarily disabled us. Heron (1982) suggests that what is happening is that our 'human capacities' cease to respond flexibly and creatively to the current situation as it is'. When this occurs, the feelings in question need to be discharged or transformed in a way that enables us to regain our flexibility and creativity in responding to the current situation. It is not enough to repress these distorting feelings. Although this may remove them from our consciousness, it does not remove the potentially debilitating effects that they have on our mental processes.

These issues need to be handled sensitively. They need to be resolved in a way that will remove their undesirable influence and will facilitate continued support for future learning. They can be discharged by being expressed openly in a sustaining environment, for example on a one-to-one basis or within some kind of support group, so that an emotional obstacle can be removed through, for example, laughing, animated speech, anger or crying (Heron, 1982). Some people can discharge them, in the view of Rainer (1980), through forms of writing. Through such approaches learners can be freed from the mental bonds which were acting as constraints on them and they may be able to respond freely, flexibly and creatively once again. Not all authors, however, would regard discharge as the most appropriate avenue in the situations we can consider. An alternative way is through the transmutation of emotions through various meditative techniques (Heron, 1982).

We should acknowledge that most people are unaware of the internal processes that are active within them and cannot give sensible reports of what governs their learning (Nisbett and Wilson, 1977). The stages of description and attending to feelings are not intended to raise individuals' awarenesses of their own processes, although this may occur to a limited extent, but rather to draw attention to the role that these processes play in experiential learning and what individuals need to be able to do to manage their own reflective activities.

Stage 3 Re-evaluating experience

It might seem that this third stage, re-evaluating experience, should follow more closely on the learning experience itself. Surely it is natural to move straight from the experience to its evaluation? We have suggested two steps in between: returning to experience and attending to feelings. It is easy to jump from the initial experience to evaluation and judgements are often a part of the original experience. However, we suggest that, except in the special case of insights, it is usually not profitable to do so as we can potentially lose a great deal of value. We may find ourselves operating on false assumptions or reflecting on information which we have not comprehended sufficiently. Attention to description and feelings does not guarantee against this but it can help to minimize the possibility of it occurring.

We now proceed to examine some of the elements of the process of re-evaluation. We have distinguished four aspects which may need to be considered. These we believe can contribute to reflection and enhance its outcomes. They are: first, *association*, that is, relating of new data to that which is already known; *integration*, which is seeking relationships among the data; *validation* to determine the authenticity of the ideas and feelings which have resulted; and *appropriation*, that is, making knowledge one's own. These aspects should not be thought of as stages through which learners should pass, but elements of a whole. However, some elements would tend to follow others.

All of these stages are influenced by the intent of the learner. As learners, we do not wish to subject all of our experiences to the same level of reflective analysis. Indeed, there are some events in our lives which we would prefer to forget and others that we would like to cherish as simple memories. When we do desire to process our experience and to extract consciously some learning outcomes from it, the way in which we do so will be influenced by our goals and intentions. In many cases our intentions will be quite clear especially when we are involved in a formal learning task and these will guide both our experience and our forms of reflection. In others our intentions may be hazy and ill-defined and only become apparent to us as we proceed. Under these latter conditions close description becomes particularly important. We need to consider then what the experience has to offer to us as we are not able to select those aspects that are directly relevant to our purpose.

Association

Association is the connecting of the ideas and feelings which are part of the original experience and those which have occurred during reflection with existing knowledge and attitudes. It is necessary that the new ideas and information be related to, or associated with, those elements of the pre-existing knowledge relevant to it. Many learning theorists (e.g. Ausubel, Bruner), particularly those from the information processing school (Lindsay and Norman, 1972), regard this linking of new concep-tions to our existing cognitive structure as one of the central features of the learning process.

New associations are facilitated by positive attitudes and a responsive state. The new input linked with our existing knowledge and feelings can challenge us both intellectually and affectively. This aspect of reflection can lead us to the discovery that our old attitudes are no longer consistent with new ideas and feelings, that re-assessment is necessary and, in the cognitive area, that our earlier knowledge needs modifying to accommodate new ideas. It is useful that as many associa-tions be made as possible. Often it happens that an obvious connection sets us reflecting in a particular area with the result that we do not recognize or we neglect other, potentially more fruitful, associations. Immediate associations might not be the most profitable and might only pursue a well-worn path which does not lead to new conceptions. It is well known that many creative leaps in the sciences have occurred through previously unrecognized associations, but this process is also relevant in the more modest learning tasks which face all of us.

There are techniques which can assist us at this stage and help us ensure that we take time to search out those aspects of our prior knowledge and the new experience which may fruitfully be linked. The most common of these is the classic psychoanalytic technique of free association whereby we suspend our rational and analytical judgements and allow ourselves to explore freely whatever associations, whether images, thoughts or feelings, pass through our mind. We can do this in writing, through drawings, on tape, to another person or in whatever way seems to be the least constricting at the time. Rainer (1980) discusses a number of other approaches through writing which can be used. In groups working on similar problems this can be done through the technique of brainstorming (Osborn, 1953; Davies, 1971) in which ideas are generated without criticism, evaluation or comment prior to subsequent appraisal. The greater the number of associations which can be generated at this stage the greater will be the potential for integration.

Integration

Associations need to be processed to examine whether they are meaningful and useful to us. If they can be integrated into a new whole, a new pattern of ideas and attitudes develops. Association brings together ideas and feelings in an almost indiscriminate manner; integration begins the process of discrimination. There are two aspects to integration. The first of these is seeking the nature of relationships that have been observed through association. The second is drawing conclusions and arriving at insights into the material which we are processing. Synthesis is the characteristic of this integration phase in which we seek insight, which is the basis for further reflective activity. Boyd and Fales designate this phase as 'resolution':

> The individual experiences a 'coming together' or creative synthesis of various bits of the information previously taken in, and the formation of a new 'solution' or change in the self – what might be called a new gestalt.
>
> (Boyd and Fales, 1983: 110)

The methods which can be adopted to assist us in this phase depend on our circumstances, the particular issues we are considering and our preferences. The generation of brain-patterns (Buzan, 1982), concept maps (Novak, 1977), or Venn diagrams (White, 1982) may be useful when dealing with complex cognitive material. These involve portraying visually the links, interconnections and overlaps between ideas, concepts, and phrases. They provide a way to assist us to clarify our thoughts by writing them down and making connections between the perhaps disparate bits of knowledge we have so that we can visualize relationships between them. In areas of knowledge which do not lend themselves to visualization in this way, the use of analogies, similes and metaphors is more appropriate. In the domain of interpersonal relationships repertory grids have been extensively used to help individuals to identify their perceptions and constructions of others who affect them in their lives.

Validation

In validation we are subjecting what we have started to integrate to what we might call 'reality tests'. We are testing for internal consistency between our new appreciations and our existing knowledge and beliefs, for consistency between these and parallel data from others and trying out our new perceptions in new situations. If any contradictions present themselves we have to reappraise the situation and decide on what basis we should proceed. The results from these tests of truth or worth are not necessarily right or wrong. Just because a new perception is not consistent with that held by others it does not necessarily imply that we should reject our own. The idea may be breaking new ground and there will be little to contradict it or we may wish to hold a certain position regardless of conventional wisdom.

One of the techniques which can aid in validation is rehearsal. This can help us relate the knowledge which we believe we have integrated to its applications in our lives. It can take place internally or through literal enactment. At the simplest level we might think through the stages involved in putting our plan into practice. This can be quite a demanding activity which places great weight on concentration and discipline. It can be aided by making written notes, or through a more systematic form of mental rehearsal based on guided imagery. In guided imagery the learner is led by another through a series of steps which require the learner to visualize in detail all the steps required to enact the plan which is being pursued: who will be involved, what will be said, what will be written, what actions follow, what responses will be made, what will upset it and how distractions will be dealt with. As we visualize what might happen, we can correct discrepancies which might emerge and reorient our plans accordingly. This can give us confidence that our plan is capable of being implemented. Guided imagery requires no overt response on the part of the learner, but in some situations where action of a complex or interpersonal kind is required it is useful to rehearse it through various simulations and role-playing activities. These usually require someone to facilitate the process (e.g. van Ments, 1983), but may also be done in leaderless groups (e.g. Gibbs, 1983).

Appropriation

For some learning tasks it may be quite sufficient for us to have integrated the new knowledge which has arisen from the experience into our own conceptual framework, but in many areas a further step is required. The new information which has been integrated needs to be appropriated in a very personal way if it is to become our own. Some learning can become so related to the self that it enters into our sense of identity and can have a considerable importance and become a significant force in our lives. Significant feelings can come to be attached to this type of learning and any learning experience which touches this area can give rise to strong emotions that may need to be taken into account in future reflection. Tart has analysed this process and comments:

> adding the ego quality to information *radically* alters the way that information is treated by the system of consciousness as a whole.
>
> (Tart, 1975: 130)

Rogers also points to this reality when, in talking of the experiential character of learning, he writes of:

> the student who says 'I am discovering – drawing in from outside and making – that which is drawn in a real part of me' . . .
>
> (Rogers, 1969: 3)

Not all integrated and validated knowledge is appropriated in this fashion.

Appropriated knowledge becomes part of our value system and it is less amenable to change than other knowledge which we accept and work with but do not make our own to the same degree. Such knowledge people will express as their own and they may feel a strong degree of possessiveness about it. It has a special place within our integrated knowledge. This gives it a higher priority and other integrated material may be interpreted in the light of it.

Miller and others refer to this as an holistic approach, a unity of feeling and intellect. Appropriating new ideas and attitudes leads people to experience:

> a sense of wholeness; [they] can exercise [their] intuitive and imaginative faculties as well as [their] rational capabilities
>
> (Miller, 1976: 5)

which Bettleheim (1971) refers to as 'the informed heart'. We usually cannot predict which learning will become such a central part of ourselves. All that we can hope for is to select those experiences which are significant to us and ensure that we have processed them in the best way that we can find.

Outcomes and action

Whilst reflection is itself an experience (More, 1974) it is not, of course, an end in itself. It has the objective of making us ready for new experience. The outcomes of reflection may include a new way of doing something, the clarification of an issue, the development of a skill or the resolution of a problem. A new cognitive map may emerge, or a new set of ideas may be identified. The changes may be quite small or they may be large. They could involve the development of new perspectives on experience or changes in behaviour. The synthesis, validation and appropriation of knowledge are outcomes as well as being part of the reflective process. New links may be formed between previously isolated themes and the relative strengths of relationships may be assessed. Again, a significant skill in learning may be developed through an understanding of one's own learning style and needs.

Outcomes of an affective nature enable us to continue on to future learning as well as involve changes in our emotional state, our attitudes or sets of values. They could include a positive attitude towards learning in a particular area, greater confidence or assertiveness, or a changed set of priorities. In any given situation it will be difficult to distinguish between cognitive and affective outcomes and, at any point in time, it may not be possible to articulate what has been learned. In the case of the geology student the outcomes of that experience and reflection on it may have been a recognition of the complexity of the field situation and its conflicting personal and intellectual demands, increased skills in the recognition of various rock types, an awareness of the limitations of underground mapping in the field, and the identification of problems in delimiting boundaries of strata. The student might develop a negative attitude towards field work after experiencing some of the discomforts, but end up with an enhanced sense of his or her own personal capacity through having engaged in hard physical labour.

Some benefits of reflection may be lost if they are not linked to action. Although some of the outcomes are long term and often intangible, such as the appreciation of a work of art, others are more prosaic and can be consolidated by application. Application and action need not necessarily involve acts which can be observed by others. What is important is that the learner makes a commitment of some kind on the basis of his or her learning. What has been rehearsed must face the test of reality. Action ends the reflective process for the time being. Action can obviously occur at any stage of the learning process and it may itself precipitate a new phase of reflective activity.

Unfortunately, translating thoughts and ideas into action is not as straightforward a step as it might appear. Argyris (1976) has reported a study which makes gloomy reading for those interested in changing their own behaviour and in facilitating learning for others. He had developed a theory of experiential learning which emphasized the need for learners to question regularly their assumptions about how they act and the purposes they are pursuing, what he terms 'double-loop learning'. He had designed programmes which aimed to make people aware of the ways in which they act towards others and to help them modify their actions in order to achieve their goals more effectively. In two courses Argyris was successful in training the participants (architecture students and educational administrators) in recognizing the dysfunctional aspects of their own behaviour and in being able to identify what they needed to be able to do in order to respond effectively as double-loop learners. They were, however, unable to put this into practice in role-playing situations. Argyris and others have developed his idea in a number of publications and have identified some things which can be done to overcome the difficulties faced in the study above (Argyris, 1982; Argyris and Schön, 1974, 1978; Heller, 1982). What their work points to is the complexity of the learning process in real situations and the need for both teachers and researchers to acknowledge its complexity. Change is hard won; we can desire to do something and believe that it is possible, but still it is difficult to do. Maintaining a positive attitude towards ourselves as learners is a necessary prerequisite for us to overcome some of the problems that Argyris has identified.

The elements of reflection are not as clearly defined in practice as we have suggested earlier and as they are summarized in Figure 2.3. We have represented them diagrammatically as an aid to exposition. They do not proceed in a simple linear sequence and they are not independent of each other. We have separated them in order to draw attention to some of the features which we believe are often overlooked by both teachers and learners. To do justice to the full complexities of the process would involve a description which indicated the continual cycling back and forth between elements, the omission of some stages at times and the compression of some of the elements we have described. Nevertheless if learners are having difficulties in reflecting, it can be useful to think about the stages we have described and examine whether any of them have been omitted.

ASSISTING IN THE PROCESS OF REFLECTION

Most of the examples we have given in the description of stages have referred to what individuals can do for themselves. However, there are limits to what each of us can achieve unaided and often the learning process can be considerably accelerated by appropriate support,

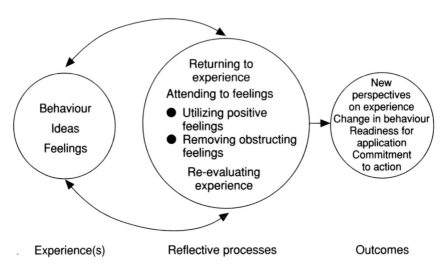

Experience(s)   Reflective processes   Outcomes

Figure 2.3 The reflection process in context

encouragement and intervention by others. Indeed, reflection alone has many challenges as Habermas recognizes:

> The self-reflection of a lone subject . . . requires a quite paradoxical achievement: one part of the self must be split off from the other part in such a manner that the subject can be in a position to render aid to itself . . . [furthermore] in the act of self-reflection the subject can deceive itself.
>
> (Habermas, 1974, cited in Grundy and Kemmis, 1982: 87)

We believe that if teachers and others assisting learners are to have an effective role in promoting learning that role is essentially to provide a stimulus for learning, to support the learner in the process and to assist the learner in extracting the maximum benefit from what occurs. Those who plan to set up a learning situation, whether it be formal or informal, cannot presume that the experience which they hope to elicit will actually take place. The nature of the experience will be determined largely by what the learner brings to the situation. Sometimes the outcome is different from what was planned and the teacher can be placed in the unenviable position of attempting to work with an experience which the student did not have. Teachers need to be conscious of the priorities of learners in the process of learning, and need to appreciate that what emerges from the learning activity will be determined more by the learner than by the person who designed the activity. [. . .]

Not only can teachers or facilitators adopt the important listening role but they can also suggest a variety of techniques which may be appropriate at each stage. To provide this assistance the helper need not be in a formal teacher–learner relationship with the learner, substantial benefits can be gained by peer-assisted learning at a formal or informal level (Cornwall, 1979), and from support groups within a profession or institution (Kirschenbaum and Glaser, 1978).

At the initial stage of returning to experience, facilitators can assist the learner to describe as objectively as possible what has taken place in the experience and to help him or her to avoid interpretations and analysis. This is directly analogous to the debriefing procedure for pilots after a mission. The facilitator asks for a detailed account of what happened, draws out events which at first may have gone unnoticed and draws attention to unacknowledged interpretations and speculations. Listening skills are important in this and the facilitator needs a keen awareness of the ways in which learners use language to describe or interpret their situation. It is vital that facilitators offer no interpretations or analyses of their own. Learners themselves can also check out the objectivity of their perceptions with their peers, especially those who have experienced the same event.

In the second stage, attending to feelings, learners can be assisted by being encouraged to be aware of the feelings that were present during the initial experience and to bring these to their consciousness. Because some feelings can be a barrier to learning they need to be clearly understood. Not only do they need to be identified but the learner needs to work with them to understand their significance and to find ways of discharging, transforming or celebrating them. The single most important contribution facilitators can make is to give free and undivided attention to the learner and what Rogers (1961) describes as 'unconditional positive regard'. If facilitators are more experienced and more confident they can also draw the attention of the learner to his or her behaviour: the non-verbal signs which betray emotions, the missing elements of a description and the repetitions which appear to punctuate the recollection. Facilitators should be aware of the limits of their own skill and be prepared to put learners in touch with those people who can assist in a more sophisticated way if needed. The particular approaches which appear to have most to offer at this stage are those which employ techniques such as those used in co-counselling in which learners assist each other, either on a one-to-one basis or in groups. For the unaided learner both writing (Rainer, 1980) and meditative (Heron, 1982) approaches have much to contribute.

At the re-evaluation stages facilitators have perhaps less to offer of their personal resources and need to draw on more of their technical skills than earlier in the process. They become a resource with access to various specialized techniques, but they must continue to offer their support and encouragement. They can help to clarify learners' intentions through the application of competency models (Knowles, 1980), providing criteria for performance, and generally through supportive questioning. They can provide technical assistance through the provision of repertory grids to clarify learners' constructs, through descriptions of free association methods, through leading brainstorming sessions to aid association and through introducing concept maps or the other devices mentioned earlier to aid integration. They can lead guided imagery sessions, initiate role-playing sessions and provide the context for applications.

Generally speaking, the role of those who assist the learner is to provide a context and a space to learn, give support and encouragement, listen to the learner and provide access to particular devices which may be of use. They may also at times act as a sounding board and help the learner clarify intentions and set goals. Of course, all this must be within the context of the learner's needs and interests. They also have roles to stimulate learning and initiate new experiences but these are beyond the scope of our present discussion. Perhaps one of their most important roles is to alert people to the nature of reflection in the learning process and provide ways whereby others can assist it at its various stages.

CONCLUSIONS

We have given an account of the reflective process which draws attention to what we regard as some of the areas of learning which have, until recently, been overlooked by researchers and under-emphasized by teachers and trainers. Although we have focused on the individual in this we hope that the implications for group reflection and for more formal learning situations are apparent. Learning theory, despite some hopeful signs, has yet to make any substantial contributions to the kinds of learning tasks with which we are normally faced. However, we hope we have offered some clues which may be pursued by those of us in the education profession.

Much research needs to be conducted in all of the areas we have considered. Many of our remarks cannot be underpinned by the kinds of research we would wish for. To date most research on learning has not sufficiently respected the unique perspective of the learner and has not taken into account the affective dimension to which we have referred. Nevertheless, considerable progress has been made in recent years on clarifying some of the issues involved. Dunlop (1984) is helpful in pointing to some of the issues involved in the education of feeling and emotion, and the forms of co-operative inquiry and action research discussed by Reason and Rowan (1981) offer ways in which we might be able to conduct research in this area. The importance of reflection in professional practice is beginning to be recognized. The important book, *The Reflective Practitioner*, by Schön (1983), which came to our attention after completing this chapter, offers some useful directions for exploring reflection-in-action. If professionals are to develop skills in reflective thinking it is important that they be encouraged to do so in their initial training. [. . .]

REFERENCES

Abbs, P. (1974) *Autobiography in Education*, London: Heinemann Educational.
Argyris, C. (1976) 'Theories of action that inhibit individual learning', *American Psychologist*, vol. 39: 638–54.
Argyris, C. (1982) *Reasoning, Learning and Action*, San Francisco: Jossey-Bass.
Argyris, C. and Schön, D. (1974) *Theory into Practice*, San Francisco: Jossey-Bass.
Argyris, C. and Schön, D. (1978) *Organizational Learning: A Theory of Action Perspective*, Reading, Mass: Addison-Wesley.
Bettleheim, B. (1971) *The Informed Heart*, New York: Avon.
Boud, D. and Pascoe, J. (1978) 'What is experiential learning?' and 'Conceptualizing experiential education', in D. Boud and J. Pascoe (eds) *Experiential Learning: Developments in Australian Post-Secondary Education*, Sydney: Australian Consortium on Experiential Education, 1–6, 61–4.
Boyd, E. M. and Fales, A. W. (1983) 'Reflective learning: key to learning from experience', *Journal of Humanistic Psychology*, vol. 23, no. 2: 99–117.
Buzan, T. (1982) *Use Your Head*, London: British Broadcasting Corporation, Revised Edition.
Coleman, J. C. (1976) 'Differences between experimental and classroom learning', in M. Keeton (Ed.), *Experiential Learning: Rationale, Characteristics and Assessment*, San Francisco: Jossey-Bass, 49–61.
Cornwall, M. G. (1979) *Students as Teachers: Peer Teaching in Higher Education*, Cowo-Publicatie 7906–01, Amsterdam: University of Amsterdam.
Cunningham, P. M. (1983) 'Helping students extract meaning from experience', *New Directions for Continuing Education*, vol. 19: 57–69.
Davies, I. K. (1971) *The Management of Learning*, London: McGraw-Hill.
Dewey, J. (1916) *Democracy in Education*, New York: Macmillan.
Dewey, J. (1933) *How We Think*, Boston: D. G. Heath, Revised Edition.
Dunlop, F. (1984) *The Education of Feeling and Emotion*, London: George Allen and Unwin.
Entwistle, N. and Ramsden, P. (1983) *Understanding Student Learning*, London: Croom Helm.
Freire, P. (1970) *Pedagogy of the Oppressed*, London: Penguin.
Gibbs, G. (1983) 'Using role plays in interpersonal skills training: a peer learning approach', *Simulation/Games for Learning*, vol. 13, no. 4: 147–55.
Gibbs, G., Morgan, A. and Taylor, E. (1982) 'A review of the research of Ference Marton and the Goteborg Group: a phenomenological research perspective on learning', *Higher Education*, vol. 11: 123–45.
Grundy, S. and Kemmis, S. (1982) 'Educational action research in Australia: the state of the art (an overview)', in S. Kemmis, *et al.* (eds), *The Action Research Reader*, Waurn Ponds, Victoria: Deakin University.
Habermas, J. (1974) *Theory and Practice*, London: Heinemann.

Heller, J. F. (1982) *Increasing Faculty and Administrative Effectiveness*, San Francisco: Jossey-Bass.

Heron, J. (1982) 'Education of the affect: the unexplored domain', in T. Habershaw (Ed.), *Three Ways to Learn*, Preston: Standing Conference on Educational Development Services in Polytechnics 31–46.

Kelly, G. A. (1955) *The Psychology of Personal Constructs, 1 and 2*, New York: Norton.

Kirschenbaum, H. and Glaser, B. (1978) *Developing Support Groups*, La Jolla, California: University Associates.

Knapper, C. K. and Cropley, A. J. (in press) *Lifelong Learning and Higher Education*, London: Croom Helm.

Knowles, M. S. (1980) *The Modern Practice of Adult Education*, Chicago: Follet, Revised Edition.

Lindsay, P. H. and Norman, D. A. (1972) *Human Information Processing*, New York: Academic Press.

Mezirow, J. (1978) *Education for Perspective Transformation: Women's Reentry Programs in Community Colleges*, New York: Centre for Adult Education, Columbia University.

Mezirow, J. (1981) 'A critical theory of adult learning and education', *Adult Education*, vol. 32, no. 1: 13–24.

Miller, J. P. (1976) *Humanizing the Classroom: Models of Teaching in Affective Education*, New York: Praeger Publishers.

More, W. S. (1974) *Emotions and Adult Learning*, Farnborough: Saxon House.

Nisbett, R. F. and Wilson, D. W. (1977) 'Telling more than we can know: verbal reports on mental processes', *Psychological Review*, vol. 84, no. 3: 231–59.

Novak, J. D. (1977) *A Theory of Education*, Ithaca: Cornell University Press.

Osborn, A. F. (1953) *Applied Imagination*, New York: Scribner.

Rainer, T. (1980) *The New Diary*, London: Angus and Robertson.

Reason, P. and Rowan, J. (eds) (1981) *Human Inquiry: A Source Book of New Paradigm Research*, Chichester: John Wiley.

Reed, D. (1981) *Education for a People's Movement*, Boston: South End Press.

Rogers, C. R. (1961) *On Becoming a Person*, Boston: Houghton Mifflin.

Rogers, C. R. (1969) *Freedom to Learn*, Columbus, Ohio: Merrill.

Säljö, R. (1981) 'Learning approach and outcome: some empirical observations', *Instructional Science*, vol. 10: 47–65.

Schön, D. A. (1983) *The Reflective Practitioner: How Professionals Think in Action*, London: Temple Smith.

Tart, C. T. (1975) *States of Consciousness*, New York: E. P. Dutton.

Taylor, M. (1981) 'The social dimensions of adult learning', in L. Salter (ed.), *Communication Studies in Canada*, Toronto: Butterworths, 133–46.

Tough, A. (1979) *The Adult's Learning Projects*, Toronto: Ontario Institute for Studies in Education, Second Edition.

Van Manen, M. (1977) 'Linking ways of knowing with ways of being practical', *Curriculum Inquiry*, vol. 6, no. 2: 205–28.

van Ments, M. (1983) *The Effective Use of Role-Play*, London: Kogan Page.

White, R. T. (1982) 'Two lessons in one: what you taught and what they learned in science', *Set: Research Information for Teachers*, 1, item 7.

Zeichner, K. M. (1982) 'Reflective teaching and field-based experience in teacher education', *Interchange*, vol. 12, no. 4: 1–22.

Chapter 3

Breaking the code
Engaging practitioners in critical analysis of adult educational literature†

Stephen Brookfield

In a body of recent work in our field, the development of critical thinking and critical reflection have been proposed by a number of writers as organising concepts to inform adult education practice (Mezirow, 1981, 1991; Brookfield, 1987; Marsick, 1987; Garrison, 1991, 1992), although the tensions between what have been called liberal and socialist interpretations of these ideas have been noted (Griffin, 1988, 1989). There has also been a spirited attempt to explore the connections between the intellectual movement known as critical theory, or critical social theory, and the field of adult education (Collard and Law, 1991; Collins, 1985; Collins and Plumb, 1989; Hart, 1990; Little, 1991; Welton, 1991). It is not surprising, then, that encouraging students to undertake a critical analysis of ideas embedded in adult educational literature is one of the most frequently espoused aims of programmes of university adult education and that many assignments in such a programme focus on this activity. Collins (1991: 110) is typical in his insistence that 'a critical practice of adult education needs to re-confirm the importance of writing as a means of careful expression'. For some of us who are lecturers and professors of adult education, written critical analysis is focused chiefly on deconstructing adult education texts for the political and social values which frame and inform research, philosophy and theory. This form of analysis draws on the Frankfurt school of critical social theory and neo-Marxism, and is concerned with identifying the dominant cultural values and hegemonic processes embedded in practice and the ways in which capitalist forms of organization are reflected in adult education provision. Practice, research and theory are scrutinized for the extent to which they do, or do not, pay attention to the variables of 'race', class and gender. Others, drawing primarily on traditions of progressive liberalism, see critical analysis as focusing essentially on exploring theory–practice connections and discrepancies, and on helping

† This is an edited version of an article that appeared in *Studies in the Education of Adults* (1993), vol. 25 (2).

adult educators clarify their own implicit, informal theories in use.

The concept of critical reflection informing my own work is one which draws on both of these perspectives and diverse intellectual traditions, and one which, therefore, runs the risk of being fatally flawed by 'bad eclecticism' or 'naive eclecticism' (Bright, 1989; Youngman, 1986). What seems to make sense as skilled critical practice may pose theoretical problems when educators draw from traditions that are epistemologically contradictory, and when insights regarding the nature of adult education are ripped out of the intellectual frameworks in which they are embedded. My own adult educational project has been to develop and live a practical theory of critical adult education – that is, a set of interpretations and evolved practices of critical adult education grounded in the context and autobiography of my own experience but subject to continuous critical analysis through a dialectical exchange with colleagues' reflections. Put concretely, the evolution of a practical theory of critical adult education has meant for me engaging in purposive experimentation with adults, checking the validity of my efforts through talking about them to colleagues engaged in similar work and learning from their insights and reactions, and interpreting and re-framing my emerging practice as a result of reading theoretical analyses of this form of adult education (see, for example, Shor, 1987; Shor and Freire, 1987; Usher and Bryant, 1989; Horton and Freire, 1990; Mezirow, 1990; Collins, 1991). Since working as an adult educator in the United States, I have sought deliberately to avoid grounding my own ideas explicitly within the Frankfurt school of critical social theory even though that tradition is pre-eminent in my own intellectual formation. My instinct is that critical adult education in the US must develop its own indigenous language and forms of critical analysis. Hence, part of my own practical theory of critical adult education in North America is that the language developed to describe this should spring from American intellectual traditions. What complicates matters inevitably is that some of the theorists, writers and activists who might serve as examples of how this might be done – for example Eduard Lindeman, C. Wright Mills and Myles Horton – are themselves strongly influenced by external traditions (seen, for example, in Horton's formational visit to the Danish Folk High Schools, Linderman's work on the labour academy in Frankfurt, and Mills' work on Marx). What is distinctive about these three writers and educators, however, is their ability to communicate to practising adult educators in language and conceptual categories which are critical yet recognizable. For me, Mills' essay on 'The Sociological Imagination' (1953) stands as one of the most potent (though largely ignored) manifestos for American graduate adult education. Given that I have struggled to avoid working within categories deliberately drawn from Habermas or Marcuse, and to speak in a voice which sounds recognizable to the great majority of adult educators who view political dimensions to practice as something beyond their ken, it is inevitable that I risk disavowing the political component to critical reflection.

Up to this point I have defined critical reflection as comprising two interrelated processes: (1) the experience of questioning and then replacing or reframing an assumption which is accepted as representing dominant commonsense by a majority; and (2) the experience of taking a perspective on social and political structures, or on personal and collective actions, which is strongly alternative to that held by a majority. There are, of course, problems which are immediately apparent with defining critical reflection in this way. For example, focusing so strongly on counting as 'critical' those assumptions and perspectives that challenge the mainstream could allow the development of far right assumptions (about, for example, the self-evident truth of notions of racial supremacy) to count as legitimate examples of critical reflection. After all, David Duke and Jean Le Pen have built their political constituencies by claiming to represent a challenge to conventionally espoused wisdom. Again, defined in the way described above, what count as episodes of critical reflection could focus exclusively on personal growth and miss entirely the political edge central to my own understanding of this process. Also, this definition of critical reflection risks separating reflection from action, of treating this process as a disconnected form of mental speculation with no requirement that the person concerned change herself, or her world, in any way. Consequently, a third dimension of analysis needs to be added to ensure the political edge to a concept which shows some danger of ending up mired in ineffectual acknowledgments of diversity, or becoming just one more example of technical rationality through its reduction to a set of processes and techniques. In effect, what I am trying to do is blend – in an informed and appropriate dialectic – universalist elements of the modernist valuing of rational analysis as a hedge against oppression with relativist elements of the postmodern emphasis on contextuality and multiplicity of perspectives. This fashioning involves extending the process of critical reflection to focus on the analysis of hegemony. Conceptualized with this additional dimension critical reflection focuses on the ways in which ideas, and their representations in actions and structures, are accepted as self-evident renderings of the 'natural' state of affairs. Applied to the field of adult education, this means that critical reflection analyses commonly held ideas regarding learning and educational practice for the extent to which they perpetuate economic inequity, deny compassion, foster a culture of silence and prevent adults from realizing a sense of common connectedness.

The literature and rhetoric of adult education provide rich examples of hegemonic concepts, with self-directed learning, meeting felt needs and valuing learners' experiences being particularly pervasive. A critical analysis of self-direction along the lines outlined above would point out how a concept which seems so bound up with liberty and freedom can end up serving repressive interests (see, for example, Hammond and Collins, 1991). Such an analysis would show how self-direction can serve to reduce our common connections, interdependence and interests, justify an obsessive focus on the self, and deny the validity of collective action. A critical analysis of the concept can also show how it can be used to justify the abandonment of public education – who needs publicly funded adult education if, on reaching adulthood, we are all self-directed? As an example of hegemony, then, the idea of self-direction can be seen to contain serious psychological and political dangers, leading people into a dissatisfied isolationism and stifling collective political action.

A critical analysis of the hegemonic force of the idea that meeting learners' felt needs is the hallmark of good adult education would show how serving adults' felt needs ends up reinforcing divisive competitive instincts, given that these needs are shaped in an entrepreneurial culture which values above all else the self-made man (sic) who has pulled himself up by his bootstraps. 'Needs' do not exist independently of culture in some kind of objective hierarchy, they are framed and con-structed by that culture. [. . .] Adult education which is premised on the felt-needs rationale almost inevitably leaves unchallenged the philosophy and culture of *laissez faire* capitalism in which individuals, communities, and 'races' are pitted against each other in a war for advantage which is portrayed as natural. [. . .]

UNDERSTANDING RESISTANCE TO CRITICAL ANALYSIS

In academic courses of adult education the choice of 'required' texts representing legitimate codified knowledge in the field, and the ways in which students are encouraged to read these texts, raise 'important questions about the ideological interests at work in forms of textual authority' (Aronowitz and Giroux, 1991: 105). Despite the existence of broad critical and postmodernist analyses of textual authority and the unproblematized nature of required texts (Apple, 1986; De Castell *et al.*, 1989; Apple and Christian-Smith, 1991), guidelines on how students can do the kind of critical reading of texts advocated above are rare. It is the provision of such guidance which is the chief purpose of this chapter.

Despite the enthusiasm with which the aim of critical analysis is proposed there are considerable barriers to its realization in programmes in adult education; ironically, the arena one might imagine would be the most receptive to this activity. Students complain of being exposed by professors and lecturers to a 'party line' on critical analysis, and to exhortations to 'write critically', without receiving any clear guidance. [. . .] One of the most important methodological insights for me as an adult educator (that was impressed upon me by reading my students' learning journals and evaluations) has been the importance of building a case to learners for ideas that in my own mind might be regarded as axiomatic. Central to this process is encouraging genuine critical analysis of the importance of the organizing idea itself.

The first barrier students speak about is the reverence they feel for what they define as 'expert' knowledge enshrined in academic publications. Most students on academic courses of study in adult education say that they regard themselves as practitioners rather than as theorists or academic thinkers. Although, as many have pointed out, it is impossible to practice without engaging in a form of informal theorizing, it is probably the case that graduate students' primary self-image is of themselves as activists, as people who make learning and education happen. [. . .] There is a feeling on students' part of impostorship, of their engaging in critical analysis as a rather unconvincing form of role-taking, even play acting. The assumption is that sooner or later any critique produced will be revealed to be the product of an unqualified and unfit mind. Overall, my experience has confirmed most strongly Usher's (1989: 88) contention that 'educational practitioners when they become students tend to be overawed; they find it difficult to question, given the status of formal theory as codified knowledge and the attached aura of "academic" legitimacy'.

The second problem students say that they face as they undertake critical analysis is that it is viewed as an abstract intellectual process that is too opaque and rarified. [. . .] The perceived remoteness of critical reflection as a form of analysis is not helped by the fact that much adult educational writing on its importance is informed by the Frankfurt school of critical social theory (Collins and Plumb, 1989; Collard and Law, 1991; Welton, 1991), particularly the work of Habermas (Mezirow, 1981; Collins, 1985), or by the ideas of the Italian political philosopher Antonio Gramsci (Ireland, 1987; Morgan, 1987; Armstrong, 1988). Works on critical social science (Fay, 1987), critical hermeneutics (Thompson, 1981) or critical pedagogy (Giroux, 1992) are sophisticated theoretical analyses requiring a familiarity with neo-Marxism and phenomenology.

Third, many of the writers and thinkers most commonly associated with a 'critical' perspective in adult education tend to interpret their practice as a form of left of centre social and political action. An important exception to this is Mezirow, whose concern with such action is made explicit but who has extended the analysis of critical reflection into the realm of personal relationships and the workplace (Mezirow, 1991). The largest portion of documented work on what most would call critical adult education tends to be located in case study descriptions of liberatory and emancipatory education within a social action frame-work (Thompson, 1980; Lovett *et al.*, 1983; Lovett, 1988; Youngman, 1986; Kirkwood and Kirkwood, 1989; Shor, 1987; Shor and Freire, 1987). Such work draws heavily on the ideas of Horton and Freire (Horton and Freire, 1990). Adult education students whose own backgrounds as practitioners seem to have no connection with community organizing or political action – such as those who run continuing education programmes, who are staff developers in hospitals or who are training managers for corporations – can quickly dismiss this body of work as 'outside our experience', 'interesting, but not for us' or 'irrelevant to our daily concerns'. Those educators for whom even liberalism represents a dangerous, left wing ideology, are likely to experience many difficulties in trying to engage seriously with books such as *Pedagogy of the Oppressed* or *We Make the Road By Walking*.

In trying to help students who see themselves primarily as practitioners come to terms with the task of undertaking a critical analysis of literature in adult education, I have found it most helpful to frame this task around certain critical questions each time they are confronted with a piece of writing. In this chapter I wish to present these questions directly as they are presented to students, so that interested readers can adapt any aspects of these that might be useful in their own practice of encouraging students' critical analysis. Questions are focused, direct and provocative, and students have told me that they sometimes use the questions discussed in this chapter as a benchmark, or a checklist, which they use as they first approach critical analysis. [. . .] I have found it important to keep emphasizing the fact that critical analysis focuses on positive as well as negative appraisal.

METHODOLOGICAL QUESTIONS

By methodological questions I mean those questions that have to do with the way in which evidence is obtained that underlies theoretical propositions, empirical descriptions and philosophical injunctions in the literature. To help students begin examining a text I suggest that they ask the following questions.

To what extent are the central insights of a piece of literature (whether these are framed as research findings, theoretical propositions or philosophical instructions) grounded in documented empirical evidence?

The literature of adult education abounds with uncontested claims about the nature of adult education (for example, that it is inherently empower-ing or that its quintessence is seen in small group discussion) or about the distinctive character of adult learning (for example, that critical reflection or self-direction are capacities experienced only in adulthood). A first step in encouraging students to take a more critical perspective on such claims is to suggest that every time they encounter them they search for the supportive empirical evidence discussed by the writer. So much writing in our field takes the form of speculative personal preference (which, if it is informed, is an entirely valid mode of expression) that asking the simplest questions regarding evidence for writers' assertions encourages students to take a more critical stance towards the printed word.

To what extent does the writing examined seem culturally skewed?

If there are confident claims made regarding 'the nature of adult learning' or 'the characteristics of adult learners', or if a 'theory of adult learning' is being advanced, students can be encouraged to ask whether the studies cited in support of these essential ideas involve learners from different social classes, cultures and ethnic groups. It is astounding how much theorizing about adult learning or the nature of adult educational practice is culturally blind, insensitive to gender and disturbingly ethnocentric. The idea that self-sufficient, individualistic, self-organized individuals represent the highest stages of adult development is distinctively American, strongly middle-class, male and white. Asking graduate students to look out for the number of times a writer talks about 'adult learners' as a generic group, or about 'adult learning' as a unitary process, and then encouraging these students to look for the kinds of adults the writer is discussing, and the kinds of cultures, classes and contexts in which these adults live, helps students to realize very quickly the blindness to issues of class, gender and ethnicity evident in so much professional writing. Again, asking students to undertake a simple content analysis of citations (who is mentioned most frequently, from what cultures are frequent citations drawn, what is the gender and ethnic balance of frequently cited authors and sources), and asking them to study the identities of contributors to volumes which stand as the public face of adult education, can help them to appreciate that the words that end up on printed pages in scholarly journals are produced by people in specific milieux with access to channels of communication.

To what extent are descriptive and prescriptive fused in an irresponsible and inaccurate way?

Much adult educational writing fuses descriptive and prescriptive elements in a dangerous way. Claims that adults exhibit innate standardized tendencies regarding learning, or that adult educational practice must exemplify certain essential features, can be taken apart and scrutinized by students for the extent to which they reflect the personal philosophical preferences of the writer. Writing which springs from deeply held philosophical and ideological convictions about what adult education should look like is often provocative and compelling – Freire's work is a good example of this – and students can be inspired to action (or intimidated) by such words. But such writing can also be imbued with a reading of the world, and adult education's place within it, which appears to be a self-evident, objective depiction of reality but which is unproblematized and open to multiple, and contested, interpretations. Asking students to read a piece for the extent to which prescriptive preferences are presented as generalized injunctions springing from an unproblematized depiction of adult educational reality gets them used to reading for unacknowledged meanings and buried assumptions. However, it is important to acknowledge the validity and desirability of openly polemical writing.

EXPERIENTIAL QUESTIONS

Experiential questions encourage students to view the depictions of adult learning processes and adult educational practices that are contained in the literature through the lenses of their own experiences, both as learners and educators. [. . .] One way students' experiences as adult learners can be used as a lens through which to view texts is by asking them to keep learning journals. Students who keep a learning journal over the course of their studies in which they document the rhythms of their learning and the episodes as learners that they find transformative (always assuming that there are some) can be encouraged to use these journals as the starting point for an emotive reading of formal models of transformative learning.

Before outlining some experiential questions students can be encouraged to ask about academic adult educational literature it is important to stress that I do not assume that students' experiences, by definition, possess such an innate validity that they make all formal theorizing seem sterile and pale by comparison. Neither do I believe that simply finding a connection, or discrepancy, between experience and texts means that critical analysis has occurred. The value of experiential questions lies chiefly in their ability to demystify texts for students, to bring them closer to home, to reduce the distance between what is often seen as codified academic knowledge and irrelevant personal histories. As such, getting students to raise experiential questions is often a useful and necessary precursor to getting them to consider some of the more pointed methodological, communicative and political questions.

Aronowitz and Giroux argue that the stress on honouring learners' experiences in the face of codified academic knowledge seems radical but contains some implicit dangers:

To take student voices at face value is to run the risk of idealizing and romanticising them. The contradictory and complex histories and stories that give meaning to the lives of students are never innocent, and it is important that they be recognized for their contradictions as well as for their possibilities

(Aronowitz and Giroux 1991: 130–1)

Since expressing and assessing experience is such a commonly stated aim of adult education, it is interesting to read what Aronowitz and Giroux see as its consequence:

Teaching collapses in this case into a banal notion of facilitation, and student experience becomes an unproblematic vehicle for self-affirmation and self-consciousness. Within this perspective it is assumed that student experience produces forms of understanding that escape the contradictions that inform them. Understanding the limits of a particular position, engaging its contradictory messages, or extending its insights beyond the limits of particular experiences is lost in this position. It overprivileges the notion of student voice, and refuses to engage its contradictory nature.

(Aronowitz and Giroux, 1991: 117)

One possible consequence of relying too strongly on the experiential approach is that this position lacks any sense of its own political project.

In their analysis of adult educators' practical theory development Usher and Bryant (1989) argue that without critical analysis the informal theories and pieces of practical knowledge derived from an analysis of educators' experiences risk remaining at the level of anecdotal, idiosyncratic reminiscence. Consequently, whereas experiential questions have the advantage of offering students a direct and accessible entry point into the analysis of academic literature, critical reflection requires that these experiences themselves, as well as theories of learning or models of practice, are scrutinized for their accuracy and validity. Usher and Bryant suggest two ways of doing this; first, the hunches, instincts and intuitions concerning learning and education deriving from students' experiences can be compared through a form of collaborative experiential scrutiny. Second, the hunches, instincts and intuitions found to have some commonality, recognition and generalizability can, in turn, be reviewed through the lens of formal theory. As described by Usher and Bryant, this process of coming to discriminate between wholly idiosyncratic and subjective aspects of experience, and aspects which, while embedded in individual experience are more generic, is a dialectic comprising forms of particular and universal analysis.

Notwithstanding the contradictions of honouring adult educators' experiences, there has been a spate of recent work on the importance of life history methods in adult education (Warren, 1982; Armstrong, 1987; Finger, 1989; Lainé, 1989) and on how this method can be used to encourage a reflective stocktaking of models for learning and practice. Students can be asked to keep a learning journal. The insights into learning contained within these journal entries can then be compared to prevailing models of self-directed learning, perspective transformation, critical thinking and so on. [. . .]

Some general questions that encourage a critical engagement with texts through experiential analysis are as follows:

What connections and discrepancies do you note between the descriptions of adult learning processes and adult educational practices contained in a piece of academic writing and your own experiences as an adult learner and adult educator?

This question needs to be made more specific and concrete. One way to do this is to ask students to note what metaphors academic writers most frequently use to describe learning and education, and then to encourage students to think about the metaphors they most frequently use when describing what they do, or how they think people learn, to their friends and colleagues. Since metaphors are shorthand encapsulations of how we perceive reality (for example, whether we talk of adult educators as midwives, gatekeepers or enablers says a great deal about the assumptions that frame our practice), any difference students note between their own metaphors and those contained in academic writings may be a useful starting point for the kind of experiential analysis I am suggesting. Another way to show how discrepancies between experience and es-poused ideas can be discussed is to locate case study examples which do this well. These can serve as recognition points, as triggers to students' discovery of comparisons between the case study described and their own experiences. [. . .]

What experiential omissions are there in a piece of literature that, to the student, seem important?

This question asks students to read descriptions of adult learning or adult educational practice for the extent to which important elements of students' own experiences as learners and educators are not present. If students have been encouraged to write critical incidents, to keep learning journals, and to participate in life history enquiry, then the central features of their own experiences as learners and educators are likely to be much clearer to them. Asking students to examine texts for the extent to which these central features are acknowledged is another way of stressing the situated, context-bound nature of academic writing.

Challenging dominant adult educational values and making a deliberate attempt to break with habitual and approved ways of practising adult education, are acts of learning that carry with them the real possibility of critical analysts being excluded from their former reference groups or sub-cultures. Feelings of anger or pain also figure largely in students' life histories as adult learners and as adult educators, yet are found to be conspicuous by their absence in the academic literature of the field. When students read theories of adult learning devoid of an emotional component, and when they study models of reflective practice or educational innovation that ignore the risk of educators' being ostracised by their colleagues for the vainglorious pretension that purposeful experimentation is seen as entailing, they can make some devastating criticisms of adult educational literature.

To what extent does a piece of literature acknowledge and address ethical issues?

Usher and Bryant (1989: 180) note that the kind of practical knowledge adult educators develop, 'since it is concerned with appropriate action in the world, must consider the rightness of the action'. Anyone who has followed what they see as the theoretical tenets of self-directed learning, andragogy, liberatory education, critical thinking and critical reflection, knows that embedded within such ideas, and the practice which flows from them, are painful and provocative ethical dilemmas. Writing on these ideas tends to acknowledge this fact but to give few concrete examples of these dilemmas and of the ways to work through them.

For example, much writing about transformative learning, or adult transitions, displays a tone of positive optimism. Transformation is portrayed as a break with distorted, constraining ways of thinking and acting and as the chief outcome of liberatory educational practices. As students examine their own transformations as learners they tend to stress the loneliness and isolation they experience as the stability of old support networks, friendships and even of the student's intimate relationships, become threatened by the changes the student is seen by others to be experiencing. Adults who come to interpret their actions, situations and cultures in changed and critical ways risk committing, in effect, a kind of cultural suicide. This poses an ethical dilemma for the educator who believes in the innate rightness of helping adults adopt a more critical perspective but who also believes that protecting the learner's physical safety and psychological self-esteem is a paramount principle of adult educational practice. Hence, formal academic analyses of critical thinking, and of the practices which flow from such analyses, can be scrutinized for the extent to which these dilemmas are recognized, and for the extent to which these writings explore how learners can minimize risks without destroying completely the desire to engage in critical thinking or to effect social change.

One useful way to explore the ethical dimensions to practice – and the extent to which these are acknowledged in academic literature – is to use a variant of the critical incident method. After students write critical incident descriptions of their most pressing ethical dilemmas, they can form small groups to read their vignettes out to each other and to look for commonalities. Having the groups identify common categories of ethical dilemmas gives individual students greater confidence in analysing texts for their ethical attentiveness, because each person no longer feels that the dilemma she experiences is contextually unique to her and, therefore, not worthy of being used as a point of departure for the critical analysis of academic writing.

COMMUNICATIVE QUESTIONS

Communicative questions focus on stylistic matters such as the voices present in academic writing, the use of a coded, private, specialized academic language and the connectedness between a piece of writing and adult educators' own lives. Although apparently concerned with matters of form, these questions are critical in that they prompt students to consider issues of power and control, such as whose definitions of importance are represented in research reports, whose voices are dominant, or the process by which some knowledge becomes officially codified and professionally approved and other knowledge is viewed as off limits, too radical, irrelevant, or imprecise.

Whose voices are heard in a piece of academic writing?

The concept of voice has recently gained a great deal of attention from writers in the critical practice and critical pedagogy movement. As Aronowitz and Giroux write:

> voice provides a critical referent for analyzing how people are made voiceless in particular settings by not being allowed to speak, or by being allowed to say what has already been spoken, and how they learn to silence themselves.
>
> (Aronowitz and Giroux, 1991: 101)

They, declare that textual authority:

> can be used either to silence students by denying their voices – that is, by refusing to allow them to speak from their own histories, experiences, and social positions – or it can enable them to speak by being

attentive to how different voices can be constituted within specific pedagogical relations so as to engage their histories and experiences in both an affirmative and critical way

Gilbert's (1989) categories of content, form and silence (silence being just as powerful a critical concept as voice, and one many students find more understandable) constitute a useful starting point for an ideological analysis of texts.

As students read a piece of academic writing – whether this be a report of research, conceptual analysis, policy appraisal or philosophical exhortation – they can be encouraged to develop the habit of asking whose voices are present in the words they are reading, and, by inference, whose voices are missing. On a broader level, students can be encouraged to study the production of adult education texts as political projects. In particular, mainstream adult education texts – those which purport to describe the current state of theory, philosophy, research and practice in adult education – can be analysed using the concept of voice to examine whose voices are mainstream in these texts and whose are marginalized or completely silenced. At the 1992 Adult Education Research Conference in Saskatoon, at which were gathered members of the American (AERC), British (SCUTREA) and Canadian (CASAE) adult education research communities, a heated debate erupted at a symposium on the significance of the newly published 'grey book' *Adult Education: Evolution and Achievements in a Developing Field of Study* (Peters and Jarvis, 1991). Participants found themselves in a political analysis of how the book was put together, whose voices were considered to be credible to speak for the field as a whole, what effect publishing the book with a commercial mainstream publisher had in terms of narrowing the terms of debate contained within its pages, and how authors were contacted and chosen. As a book presenting the public face of adult education in North America, much was made of the small number of female authors and of the absence of African-American, Hispanic-American, Asian American and Native American voices and concerns.

Finally, techniques drawn from media analysis, many of which are based in work on content analysis, can be applied by students to the discovery of voice and silence in adult educational literature. Adult educational writing on media literacy (Brookfield, 1986; Graham, 1989) contains suggestions on how to 'read' news broadcast from the point of view of how questions are constructed, how different background sets are framed for those speaking with voices to which different degrees of power are attached (for example, lounges and boardrooms for management, noisy picket lines for strikers) and what perspectives and voices are left out.

To what extent does the literature examined use a form of specialized language that is unjustifiably distanced from the colloquial language of adult learners and adult educators?

When specialized conceptual terminology is used in academic writing about adult learning and education, students can be asked to consider whether this use can be justified in terms of promoting clarity and understanding, or whether it is an example of jargon, of coded, scriptural signalling. Each time they encounter such language they can be encouraged to acquire the habit of checking the extent to which the writer provides an abundance of examples, analogies and metaphors that would help the reader to understand these specialized terms. Students can also be asked to do something as simple as checking that every time a new specialist term is introduced it is accompanied by a definition of what it embraces. When such generalized definitions are offered, students can check whether they can find in their own experiences specific examples or illustrations of the processes these definitions represent.

In their analysis of voice, Aronowitz and Giroux (1991: 90) reject the kind of claim for linguistic clarity made in the foregoing paragraphs, declaring that 'the call to write curriculum in a language that is touted as clear and accessible is evidence of a moral and political vision that increasingly collapses under the weight of its own anti-intellectualism'. They believe that those making the call for greater linguistic clarity:

> have missed the role that 'the language of clarity' plays in a dominant culture that cleverly and powerfully uses 'clear' and 'simplistic' language to systematically undermine and prevent the conditions from arising for a public culture to engage in rudimentary forms of complex and critical thinking.'
>
> (Aronowitz and Giroux, 1991: 91)

It is unfortunate that the terms 'clear' and 'simplistic' are brought together in this critique, since one refers to the communicative power of a set of words while the other refers to its analytical accuracy. Equating clarity of expression with crudely simplistic reasoning is a rhetorical trick which diverts attention from one of the most pressing needs of critical pedagogy; that is, to develop a language which takes this pedagogy outside a group of converts and justifies its relevance to the great mass of educators who see their practice as separate from politics.

[. . .] Myles Horton, in describing his work at the Highlander Folk School in Tennessee, provides perhaps the best example of how an accessible language of critical practice could be developed and fortunately some of this has been captured by his biographers and admirers (Kennedy, 1981; Kohl and Kohl, 1990). In his weaving together of stories, metaphors, strategic suggestions, parables, anecdotes and theoretical insights, Horton's speech is accessible, enlivening, inspirational and challenging. In this regard, it is interesting to note how another critical educator, Paulo Freire, now uses the talking book format (a series of transcribed and edited conversations) as the chief means for disseminating his ideas (Freire and Macedo, 1987; Shor and Freire, 1987; Freire and Faundez, 1989; Horton and Freire, 1990). Perhaps the best way to demystify the formal and overly academic language in this area is to insist that more people describe their ideas in conversations (that are then transcribed, edited and published), rather than starting with the idea of writing for scholarly publication. However this is achieved, the development of an accessible language to describe the processes of critical teaching and critical learning is a major tactical priority if these processes are ever to capture the attention of a majority of adult educators and learners.

To what extent does the piece of writing examined show a connectedness to practice?

In a field of practice such as adult education, research reports and theoretical explorations are much more likely to be attended to if their relevance to, and implications for, practice are clearly established. In adult education the self-concept which most people working in the field hold most prominently is that of practitioner or activist. Consequently, a strong case can be made that for a piece of writing to communicate itself to activists and practitioners the connections between theoretical, research and philosophical insights and adult educational practice must be explicitly addressed. In a field of practice 'academic' insights gain credibility (or come to be seen as irrelevant) through a process by which practitioners judge the accuracy and validity of these elaborations in a range of practical contexts. To propose such insights without exploring their connections to practice effectively renders them closed to the majority of adult educators working across the varied contexts in the field.

As students read academic adult education literature they can be asked to assess the extent to which a piece of writing has embedded within it insights, or even explicit suggestions, that would help them understand or change aspects of their practice. Connectedness in terms of enhanced understanding would mean that a practical tangle, ethical dilemma or methodological problem in the student's own life as an adult educator would be perceived more clearly as a result of reading a piece of academic literature.

POLITICAL QUESTIONS

Political questions about academic literature represent the application of a power analysis; that is, an analysis which focuses on the central issues of whose interests do the ideas in a piece of writing serve and how do the practices implied or advocated stifle or animate movements for social justice? To adult educators who see themselves as avowedly apolitical and above the fray of political action – as concerned with people not politics – these questions can be justified in adult educational terms because they spring from a concern with what many people have regarded as the central adult educational tradition, namely the creation of a democratic society. Collins (1991: 115) suggests beginning this kind of politically charged questioning 'in a deceptively naive way with the question: what is it about the way our society is arranged which stops us being kind to one another and acting together on behalf of our collective interests?' Concepts of kindness and collectivism, when linked together in the way Collins suggests, ease students into a form of ideological and political analysis that, if presented in a more orthodox way as 'radical' political critique would have little chance of gaining serious attention from those who see their classrooms as far removed from politics. When taken to the level of serious political analysis, asking what comprise collective interests and how kindness to each other is nurtured and killed in democracy are powerful political questions.

Depending on one's cultural context and ideology, of course, what actually comprises democracy in terms of its core philosophical values, preferred economic arrangements and models for political participation, varies widely. The American preference for liberal democracy – viewed by Fukayama (1992) as the endpoint of human social and political evolution – is one which emphasizes values of libertarian free speech rather than any socialization of the means or fruits of production. Rockhill (1985: 134), for example, has shown how Lindeman's emphasis on 'the socialization of power and the encouragement of critical reflection' as democratic processes have been pushed to the periphery in terms of his influence on American adult education, which pays much greater homage to the elements of his thought dealing with small group methods and the necessity to avoid mandating adult education attendance.

However, as we view the development of adult educational literature in the English speaking world during this century, it is possible to discern a concern for how adult education can help in the realization of democratic values. Writers such as Mezirow (1991) and Collins (1985, 1991) have found in Habermas' (1984, 1987) notion of communicative action a criterion that can be applied to judging the extent to which an adult educational activity can be regarded as fully democratic. Adult educational activities exemplifying the conditions of communicative action take the form of 'a kind of on-going, thoughtful conversation' in which:

> all participants anticipate that their individual contributions will receive serious consideration from others. At the same time they remain open to changing or reconstructing their own stance on the problem under consideration in the light of what others have to say and on the weight of all relevantly identified information.
>
> (Collins, 1991: 12)

Ideally, activities exemplifying this criterion will lead to the kind of inter-subjective understanding, 'that comes from individuals being open to what others have to offer while, at the same time, being willing to present their own viewpoints for critical assessment' (1991: 12). When social, economic and political forces prevent the realization of the conditions for communicative action, the adult educator is provided with a clear justification for encouraging, and engaging in, social action aimed at creating these conditions. Political questions that students can ask concerning academic adult educational literature are as follows.

Whose interests are served by the publication of a text?

Put more specifically, students can be encouraged to ask whether students' or educator's interests assume primacy. They can ask whether the educational practices advocated within a text are designed primarily to build adult educational empires – to accrue to adult education organizers larger enrolments, greater organizational visibility and political safety – or to increase students' sense of democratic agency? More particularly, students can be encouraged to read forewords, acknowledgements and prefaces closely for details of any foundation or organizational sponsoring of a text.

To what extent are models and ideal types of adult educational practice reified, presented as beyond human agency?

Although this question is, superficially, concerned with questions of methodology, it has a larger political significance. It asks students to read texts for the extent to which models of adult educational practice are presented as existing (and pre-existing) at a level above the actions of learners. Curricula and programmatic models which have the stamp of enduring authority on them and which appear to be independent of context and replicable across cultures and institutions have an understandable fascination for adult educators caught in intractable contextual dilemmas. Such models – whether they be of a behavioural objectives cast, a liberalized form of andragogy, or a more radical programme for conscientization – offer the seductive chimera of standardized formulaeic certainty. Searching for finality of this kind dampens people's sense of individual agency and encourages in them the idea that if they look long and hard enough they will find an expert, programme or model process that can solve their dilemmas and ease their pain. This habit, is devastating for the development of democratic action and for an engagement in critical conversation. [. . .]

What naturally assumed forms of curricular and programmatic provision are presented that stifle collectivism?

The predominant strain of adult educational analysis in the English speaking world is psychologistic; it focuses on the individual learner and regards the development of consciousness, cognitive growth or self-esteem as acts of individual volition. Students can be asked to read texts for indications that collectivism – the belief that individual and collective social or cultural advancement are inseparable – assumes a position of prominence. Does this book place models of learning squarely in a social context? Do accounts of learners' activities featured in this text focus primarily on renderings of internal experience (such as self-insights regarding learning style contained in a personal learning journal) or do they give equal attention to the role of social networks and cultural processes? Is learning, and the organization of education, cast in a self-directed or collective mode in this piece? To what extent does this text elevate the development of independence, of autonomy, of self-direction to the apex of adult educational goals?

How do texts prescribe adult educational roles which retain the professional distance between the field and learners?

Connected to questions concerning collectivism and the quest for programmatic and political saviours is the issue of how roles for adult educators are outlined in texts. I have asked my own students to write down sentences they find describing the educational roles suggested for adult educators in literature. Although I do not subscribe to the view that all members of learning groups learn in equal measure from each other, or that educators' actions within an adult educational group are accorded no greater significance than anyone else's, I do believe that texts, images and models of good practice within our field sometimes create an unnecessary, humiliating and anticollectivist distance between learners and educators. All too often renditions of critical practice create, often unwittingly, an unfortunate dichotomy between, on the one hand, the sophisticated critical pedagogue able to penetrate hegemony, dominant cultural values and structural distortions and, on the other the learner as unquestioning dolt, duped into an uncritical acceptance of distorted meaning perspectives which have made structural oppression, economic inequity, racism, sexism and the silencing of divergent voices seem wholly natural. Consequently, one habit students can acquire is of noting down the roles specified for educators (teachers, facilitators, enablers, animators, resources and so on) and the ways these roles are interpreted.

Do evaluative criteria and forms proposed to judge the merit of adult education programmes and adults' learning support the status quo and leave laissez fair capitalism as an educational and cultural as well as economic mode unchallenged?

This question focuses students' attention specifically on those parts of texts that deal with the evaluation of learning and adult educational programmes. As they discover criteria in literature they read – some of which are implicit, some of which are explicit – students are asked to estimate the extent to which these criteria bolster a culture of individual competitiveness. As they read about formats for evaluation (test scores, interviews, 'blind' peer review, observation, multi-choice questions and so on) they are asked to judge the extent to which these tear apart a spirit for collective work and pit student against student. More specific sub-questions ask students to look for examples, or absences, of evaluative forms that reward collective work – for suggestions of group grading, for recognition of group-authored documents, and for acknowledgments of group coordinated and researched dissertations as a proper form of doctoral study. As they read programmatic descriptions students are asked to note whether learners in those programmes will have their progress estimated through privately completed tests, the results of which are not publicized, or whether there is an acknowledgment of contributions to group efforts. If discussion formats are proposed in a text, I ask students to pay particular attention to the ways in which learners' participation is to be judged. Is participation equated with a survival of the linguistically fittest, so that those who speak the most and make the most sparkling contributions are the stars of the group? As students read such manuals critically they get into the habit of noting whether or not quieter actions which contribute to a discussion group's project of collective understanding and critical conversation (such as photocopying and distributing useful articles which introduce previously unnoticed perspectives on complex issues, or summarizing insights from personal learning journals which pertain to the group's dynamics) are considered as examples of 'participation'.

What contribution does a piece of writing make to the realization of democratic forms and processes?

Students can be asked to examine academic writing on adult learning and education with a view to considering how it connects to the central, defining tradition of adult education; that is, with the realization of democratic forms and processes. How does a piece of research, a philosophical statement or a theoretical exposition assist in the improvement of social and political conditions? One justification for doing academic writing is to help people come to an understanding of how aspects of the world work. For example, to what extent do analyses of self-direction, or research reports of this phenomenon, discuss the connections between self-direction, empowerment and social change (Hammond and Collins, 1991). Do studies of perspective transformation explain how this process assists in politicizing people so that they see the necessity for collective action (Cunningham, 1992)? Do analyses of adults' life histories as learners help them to interpret the personal troubles in their autobiographies in terms of wider social movements, and thereby reduce the tendency for them to blame themselves for their inadequacies and fecklessness (Mills, 1953)?

In writing on adult educational practice, to what extent are the political impediments to educational innovations addressed?

The literature of adult education is rife with heady exhortations to empowerment, liberation, emancipation and transformation. Yet the terrain between this inspirational rhetoric and successful social, political and educational action is pitted with landmines for the naive activist. Many years ago Freire (1970) warned of the dangers of unreflective activism, and in a recent dialogue he returned to the need for shrewd and informed tactical political action (Shor and Freire, 1987). One question students can raise regarding literature which contains suggestions for radical forms of adult educational action is the extent to which a piece of writing guides them through the impediments, barriers and sanctions that organizations and the wider political culture put in the way of such action.

Students can be encouraged to read liberatory treatises for the extent to which they provide recognizable scenarios of how their efforts as educators can have the maximum effect in the world with the least possible negative consequences for themselves. Do these treatises give advice on how to research a community or organizational culture, how to learn what symbolic forms and language organizations value so that they can be turned to the educator's advantage, and how to identify the most fruitful pressure points for change? Are exhortations to social change accompanied by a weighing of the risks and consequences involved (for learners and educators) in different courses of action, together with recognizable case studies and simulations of these alternatives? Are personal as well as professional risks acknowledged such as the possibility of burn-out, of committing cultural suicide, and of experiencing marital strife? And do these writings give suggestions as to how people can do their best to keep these personal risks manageable, so that their activism is not stillborn?

CONCLUSION

The questions offered in this chapter are one person's attempt to claw a path to clarity. Central to this project, as Usher and Bryant (1989) point out, is the presentation of embedded, situated practices for wider scrutiny by colleagues working in similar and allied contexts and for review through the lens of formal theory. This chapter represents such an effort. It is the phase in the continuous loop of practical theory development which involves presenting for public examination some grounded instincts regarding critical practice. Consequently, I do not regard the questions outlined as finite or fixed, but rather as my own best current attempt (undoubtedly flawed and distorted) at dealing with the problem of engaging adult education practitioners in a critical analysis of written texts in the field. Developing questions such as the ones I have outlined that appear to draw from epistemologically and politically incompatible liberal and radical traditions, that seek self-consciously to blend modernist and postmodernist elements, and that try to prompt an engagement in critical thinking without framing this, in its initial phases, as an overtly political process, is risky. One of the great dangers of this kind of educational project is that in stressing accessibility as a criterion for determining good questions one can denude critical reflection of its political 'edge'. Collins has pointed out how the relativistic tone of much adult educational writing on critical thinking has meant that:

> as adult educators operating within this overall text, we can spark debate and 'trip the light fantastic' with talk about critical thinking skills and a nod or two in the direction of 'radical adult educators' without any of it making a tangible difference to our own practice.
>
> (Collins, 1991: 50)

Hence, students could read the questions outlined and see in them only a form of intellectual gymnastics, critical reflection as cognitive muscle flexing. However, if the imperfections embedded within these questions suggest improvements, sharpenings, a honing of their critical edge, then they will have played some role in building a range of possibilities for critical questioning and they will have helped to give students some point of entry to the critical analysis of textual authority.

Finally, a comment about the relative importance of lists of questions, frameworks or other exercises for prompting written critique. Despite the stress placed on giving students categories of questions to help them in the critical analysis of academic literature, it is worth pointing out that commentaries on critical teaching (Shor, 1987), critical thinking (Brookfield, 1987, 1991), critical pedagogy (Smyth, 1988) and critical reflection (Mezirow *et al.*, 1990) emphasize the overwhelming importance to learners of their seeing the process of critical analysis modelled by educators. As Freire (Shor and Freire, 1987) notes, a crucial aspect of critical practice is the educator's public readiness to place his or her biases for learners' scrutiny. In education for critical reflection this means that the ideological outcome of a critical dialogue must always be open, and that educators must accept the possibility that engaging in this dialogue may cause them to alter some of their most strongly held, fundamental assumptions. [. . .] Stated simply (and somewhat inelegantly) critical teachers must be seen to be critical learners too.

REFERENCES

Apple, M. W. (1986) *Teachers and Texts: A Political Economy of Class and Gender Relations in Education*, London: Routledge.

Apple, M. W. and Christian-Smith, L. K. (eds). (1991) *The Politics of the Textbook*, London: Routledge.

Armstrong, P. F. (1987) *Qualitative Strategies in Social and Educational Research: The Life History Method in Theory and Practice*. Newland Papers, No. 14. Hull: University of Hull.

Armstrong, P. F. (1988) 'L'ordine nuovo: the legacy of Antonio Gramsci and the education of adults', *International Journal of Lifelong Education*, 6, 295–308.

Aronowitz, S. and Giroux, H. A. (1991) *Postmodern Education: Politics, Culture and Social Criticism*, Minneapolis: University of Minnesota Press.

Bright, B. (ed.). (1989). *Theory and Practice in the Study of Adult Education: The Epistemological Debate*, London: Routledge, Chapman & Hall.

Brookfield, S. D. (1986) 'Media power and media literacy: an adult educational interpretation', *Harvard Educational Review*, 56, 151–170.

Brookfield, S. D. (1987) *Developing Critical Thinkers*, Milton Keynes: Open University Press.

Brookfield, S. D. (1991) 'On ideology, pillage, language and risk: critical thinking and the tensions of critical practice', *Studies in Continuing Education*, 13, 1–14.

Collard, S. and Law, M. (1991) 'The impact of critical social theory on adult education: a preliminary evaluation', *Proceedings of the Adult Education Research Conference*, No. 32. Norman, Oklahoma: Center for Continuing Education, University of Oklahoma.

Collins, M. (1985) 'Jurgen Habermas' concept of communicative action and its implications for the adult learning process', *Proceedings of the Adult Education Research Conference*, No. 26. Tempe, AZ: Arizona State University.

Collins, M. (1991) *Adult Education as Vocation: A Critical Role for the Adult Educator*, New York: Routledge.

Collins, M. and Plumb, D. (1989) 'Some critical thinking about critical theory and its relevance to adult education practice', *Proceedings of the Adult Education Research Conference*, No. 30. Madison; University of Wisconsin-Madison.

Cunningham, P. (1992) 'From Freire to feminism: the North American experience with critical pedagogy', *Adult Education Quarterly*, 42, 180–191.

De Castell, S., Luke, A. and Luke, C. (eds). (1989) *Language, Authority and Criticism: Readings on the School Textbook*. Philadelphia: Taylor & Francis.

Fay, B. (1987) *Critical Social Science*, Ithaca: Cornell University Press.

Finger, M. (1989) 'The biographical method in adult education research', *Studies in Continuing Education*, 11, 33–42.

Freire, P. (1970) *Pedagogy of the Oppressed*, New York: Continuum.

Freire, P. and Faundez, A. (1989) *Learning to Question: A Pedagogy of Liberation*, New York: Continuum.

Freire, P. and Macedo D. (1987) *Literacy: Reading the Word and the World*, South Hadley, Massachussetts: Bergin and Garvey.

Fukuyama, F. (1992) *The End of History and the Last Man*, New York: The Free Press.

Garrison, D. R. (1991) 'Critical thinking and adult education: a conceptual model for developing critical thinking in adult learners', *International Journal of Lifelong Education*, 10, 287–304.

Garrison, D. R. (1992) 'Critical thinking and self-directed learning in adult education: an analysis of responsibility and control issues', *Adult Education Quarterly*, 42, 136–148.

Gilbert, R. (1989) 'Text analysis and ideology critique of curricular content' in S. de Castell, A. Luke and C. Luke (eds), *Language, Authority and Criticism: Readings on the School Textbook*, Philadelphia: Taylor & Francis.

Giroux, H. (1992) *Border Crossings: Cultural Workers and the Politics of Education*, London: Routledge.

Graham, R. J. (1989) 'Media literacy and cultural politics', *Adult Education Quarterly*, 39, 152–160.

Griffin, C. (1988) 'Critical thinking and critical theory in adult education', in M. Zukas (Ed.), *Papers from the Transatlantic Dialogue*, Leeds: School of Continuing Education, University of Leeds.

Griffin, C. (1989) 'Cultural studies, critical theory and adult education', in B. Bright (Ed.), *Theory and Practice in the Study of Adult Education: The Epistemological Debate*, London: Routledge, Chapman and Hall.

Habermas, J. (1984) *The Theory of Communicative Action. Vol. 1 Reason and the Rationalization of Society*, Boston: Beacon Press.

Habermas, J. (1987) *The Theory of Communicative Action. Vol. 2 Lifeworld and System: A Critique of Functionalist Reason*, Boston: Beacon Press.

Hammond, M. and Collins, R. (1991) *Self-Directed Learning: Critical Practice*, London: Kogan Page.

Hart, M. (1990) 'Critical theory and beyond, further perspectives on emancipatory education', *Adult Education Quarterly*, 40, 125–138.

Horton, M. and Freire, P. (1990) *We Make the Road By Walking: Conversations on Education and Social Change* (edited by Gaventa, J., Peters, J. and Bell, B.), Philadelphia: Temple University Press.

Ireland, T. D. (1987) *Antonio Gramsci and Adult Education*, Manchester: Centre for Adult and Higher Education, University of Manchester.

Kennedy, W. B. (1981) 'Highlander praxis: learning with Myles Horton', *Teachers College Record*, 83, 105–119.

Kirkwood, G. and Kirkwood C. (1989) *Living Adult Education: Freire in Scotland*, Milton Keynes: Open University Press.

Kohl, H. and Kohl, J. (1990) *The Long Haul: An Autobiography of Myles Horton*, New York: Doubleday.

Lainé, A. (1989) 'Two utilisations of life stories in adult education', *Studies in the Education of Adults*, 21, 117–131.

Little, D. (1991) 'Critical Adult Education: a response to contemporary social crisis', *Canadian Journal for the Study of Adult Education*, 5, 1–20.

Lovett, T. (ed.). (1988) *Radical Approaches to Adult Education: A Reader*, London: Routledge.

Lovett, T., Clarke, C. and Kilmurray, A. (1983) *Adult Education and Community Action*, London: Croom Helm.

Marsick, V. J. (1987) 'Learning in the workplace: the case for critical reflectivity', *Adult Education Quarterly*, 38, 187–198.

Mezirow, J. (1981) 'A critical theory of adult learning and education', *Adult Education*, 32, 3–24.

Mezirow, J. and Associates. (1990) *Fostering Critical Reflection in Adulthood*, San Francisco: Jossey-Bass.

Mezirow, J. (1991) *Transformative Dimensions of Adult Learning*, San Francisco: Jossey-Bass.

Mills, C. W. (1953) *The Sociological Imagination*, New York: Oxford University Press.

Morgan, W. J. (1987) 'The pedagogical politics of Antonio Gramsci – "Pessimism of the Intellect, Optimism of the Will"', *International Journal of Lifelong Education*, 6, 295–308.

Peters, J. and Jarvis, P. (1991) *Adult Education: Evolution and Achievements in a Developing Field of Study*, San Francisco: Jossey Bass.

Rockhill, K. (1985) 'The liberal perspective and the symbolic legitimation of university adult education in the USA', in R. Taylor, K. Rockhill and R. Fieldhouse (eds), *University Adult Education in England and the USA*, London: Croom Helm.

Shor, I. (1987) *Critical Teaching in Everyday Life*, Chicago: University of Chicago Press.

Shor, I. and Freire, P. (1987) *A Pedagogy for Liberation: Dialogues on Transforming Education*, South Hadley, Mass.: Bergin and Garvey.

Smyth, W. J. (1988) *A Critical Pedagogy of Teacher Evaluation*, Victoria, Australia: Deakin University Press.

Thompson, J. B. (1981) *Critical Hermeneutics: A Study in the Thought of Paul Ricoeur and Jurgen Habermas*, Cambridge: Cambridge University Press.

Thompson, J. L. (ed.). (1980) *Adult Education for a Change*, London: Hutchinson.

Usher, R. S. (1989) 'Locating adult education in the practical', in B. Bright (ed.). *Theory and Practice in the Study of Adult Education: The Epistemological Debate*. London: Routledge. Chapman and Hall.

Usher, R. S. and Bryant, I. (1989) *Adult Education as Theory, Practice and Research: The Captive Triangle*, London: Routledge, Chapman and Hall.

Warren, C. E. (1982) 'The written life history as a prime research tool in adult education', *Adult Education*, 32, 21–228.

Welton, M. (1991) 'Shaking the foundation: the critical turn in adult educational theory', *Canadian Journal for the Study of Adult Education*, 5, 21–42.

Youngman, F. (1986) *Adult Education and Socialist Pedagogy*, London: Croom Helm.

Chapter 4

Andragogy
An emerging technology for adult learning†

Malcolm Knowles

FAREWELL TO PEDAGOGY

Most of what is known about learning has been derived from studies of learning in children and animals. Most of what is known about teaching has been derived from experience with teaching children under conditions of compulsory attendance. And most theories about the learning–teaching transaction are based on the definition of education as a process of transmitting the culture. From these theories and assumptions there has emerged the technology of 'pedagogy' – a term derived from the Greek stem *paid-* (meaning 'child') and *agogos* (meaning 'leading'). So 'pedagogy' means, specifically, the art and science of teaching children.

One problem is that somewhere in history the 'children' part of the definition got lost. In many people's minds – and even in the dictionary – 'pedagogy' is defined as the art and science of teaching. Even in books on adult education you can find references to 'the pedagogy of adult education', without any apparent discomfort over the contradiction in terms. Indeed, in my estimation, the main reason why adult education has not achieved the impact on our civilization of which it is capable is that most teachers of adults have only known how to teach adults as if they were children.

Another problem with pedagogy is that it is premised on an archaic conception of the purpose of education, namely, the transmittal of knowledge. As Alfred North Whitehead pointed out a generation ago, it was functional to define education as a process of transmittal of what is known so long as it was true that the time-span of major cultural change was greater than the life-span of individuals. Under this condition, what a person learns in his youth will remain valid for the rest of his life. But, Whitehead emphasized, 'We are living in the first period of human history for which this assumption is false . . . today this time-span is

† This edited chapter originally appeared in M. Tight (ed.) *Adult Learning and Education*, London: Croom Helm, 1983. Original first published in 1970.

considerably shorter than that of human life, and accordingly our training must prepare individuals to face a novelty of conditions' (Whitehead, 1931: viii–xix).

Up to the early part of the twentieth century the time-span of major cultural change (e.g. massive inputs of new knowledge, technological innovation, vocational displacement, population mobility, change in political and economic systems, etc.) required several generations, whereas in the twentieth century several cultural revolutions have already occurred and the pace is accelerating. Under this new condition, knowledge gained by the time a person is 21 is largely obsolete by the time he is 40; and skills that made him productive in his twenties are becoming out of date during his thirties. So it is no longer functional to define education as a process of transmitting what is known; it must now be defined as a lifelong process of discovering what is not known.

Skilful adult educators have known for a long time that they cannot teach adults as children have traditionally been taught. For adults are almost always voluntary learners, and they simply disappear from learning experiences that don't satisfy them. So the practice of adult education has, in fact, been departing from traditional pedagogical practices for some time. And often this deviation has been accompanied by misgivings and guilt feelings over the violation of long-established standards, for adult educators have not had a coherent theory to justify their treating adults as adults.

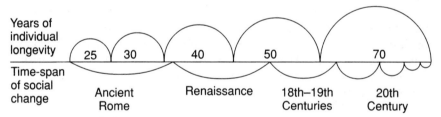

Figure 4.1 The relationship of the time-span of social change to individual life-span

This lack is now on the way to being remedied. For adult education theorists in both Europe (especially in Germany and [former] Yugoslavia[1]) and in North America are rapidly developing a distinctive theory of adult learning. And from this theory is evolving a new technology for the education of adults. To distinguish it from pedagogy, this new technology is being given a new name: '*andragogy*', which is based on the Greek word *anēr* (with the stem *andr*-), meaning 'man'. Andragogy is, therefore, the art and science of helping adults learn. [. . .]

SOME ASSUMPTIONS OF ANDRAGOGY AND THEIR TECHNOLOGICAL IMPLICATIONS

Andragogy is premised on at least four crucial assumptions about the characteristics of adult learners that are different from the assumptions about child learners, on which traditional pedagogy is premised. These assumptions are that, as a person matures, (1) his self-concept moves from one of being a dependent personality toward one of being a self-directing human being; (2) he accumulates a growing reservoir of experience that becomes an increasing resource for learning; (3) his readiness to learn becomes oriented increasingly to the developmental tasks of his social roles; and (4) his time perspective changes from one of postponed application of knowledge to immediacy of application, and accordingly his orientation toward learning shifts from one of subject-centredness to one of problem-centredness.

Each of these assumptions will be described briefly and some of its implications for the education of adults will be explored.

Self-concept

Children enter this world in a condition of complete dependency. Their every need, except for purely biological functions, must be taken care of by someone else. The first image a child gets of himself as a separate entity is that of a dependent personality whose life is managed for him by the adult world.

This self-concept of dependency is encouraged and reinforced by the adult world. In fact, society defines the normal role of a child as that of learner; this is his full-time occupation, the source of his rewards and self-fulfilment. And on the whole, this role is defined as the more or less passive one of receiving and storing up the information adults have decided children should have.

As the child's self-identity begins to take shape, he begins to see himself as having the capacity to start making decisions for himself, at first experimentally and in small matters that don't impinge on the adult world. But increasingly, as he matures, the child's self-concept moves in the direction of greater self-direction, and during adolescence his need to take significant responsibility for managing his own life becomes so strong that it often puts him in open rebellion against control by the adult world. [. . .]

But something dramatic happens to his self-concept when an individual defines himself as an adult. He begins to see his normal role in society no longer as being a full-time learner. He sees himself increasingly as a producer or doer. His chief sources of self-fulfilment are now his performance as a worker, a spouse, a parent, a citizen. The adult acquires a new status, in his own eyes and in the eyes of others, from these non-educational responsibilities. His self-concept becomes that of a self-directing personality. He sees himself as being able to make his own decisions and face their consequences, to manage his own life. In fact, the point at which a person becomes an adult, psychologically, is that point at which he perceives himself to be wholly self-directing. And at that point he also experiences a deep need to be perceived by others as being self-directing.

For this reason, adults have a need to be treated with respect, to make their own decisions, to be seen as unique human beings. They tend to avoid, resist, and resent situations in which they feel they are treated like children – being told what to do and what not to do, being talked down to, embarrassed, punished, judged. Adults tend to resist learning under conditions that are incongruent with their self-concept as autonomous individuals.

Often there is another ingredient in the self-concept of an adult that affects his role as a learner. He may carry over from his previous experience with schooling the perception that he isn't very smart, at least in regard to academic work. This fact about the adult psyche has several consequences for adult education. In the case of some adults remembering the classroom as a place where one is treated with disrespect is so strong that it serves as a serious barrier to their becoming involved in adult education activities at all. If these adults are to be enticed back to systematic learning, the rewards of learning must be made so great that they outweigh the anticipated pain of learning. But even adults who overcome this barrier typically enter an educational activity expecting to be treated like children, and this expectation is frequently so strong that adult students often put pressure on their teachers to behave toward them in this way. Once a teacher puts adult students into a dependent role, however, he is likely to experience a rising resistance and resentment.

On the other hand, when adult students are first exposed to a learning environment in which they are treated with respect, are involved in mutual inquiry with the teacher, and are given responsibility for their own learning, the initial reaction is usually one of shock and disorganization. Adults typically are not prepared for self-directed learning; they need to go through a process of re-orientation to learning as adults – to learn new ways of learning. Once an adult makes the discovery that he can take responsibility for his learning, as he does for other facets of his life, he experiences a sense of release and exhilaration. He then enters into learning with deep ego-involvement, with results that are frequently startling both to himself and to his teachers. Teachers who have helped their adult students to achieve this breakthrough report repeatedly that it is one of the most rewarding experiences of their lives.

Technological implications

Several implications for the technology of andragogy flow from this difference in assumptions about the self-concept of the child and the adult.

The learning climate

Certainly it has a strong implication regarding the nature of the environment in which adults learn. It suggests that the physical environment should be one in which adults feel at ease. Furnishings and equipment should be adult-sized and comfortable; meeting rooms should be arranged informally and should be decorated according to adult tastes; and acoustics and lighting should take into account declining audio-visual acuity.

Even more importantly, the psychological climate should be one which causes adults to feel accepted, respected, and supported; in which there exists a spirit of mutuality between teachers and students as joint inquirers; in which there is freedom of expression without fear of punishment or ridicule. A person tends to feel more 'adult' in an atmosphere that is friendly and informal, in which he is known by name and valued as a unique individual, than in the traditional school atmosphere of formality, semi-anonymity, and status differentiation between teacher and student. [. . .]

The behaviour of the teacher probably influences the character of the learning climate more than any other single factor. The teacher conveys in many ways whether his attitude is one of interest in and respect for the students or whether he sees them essentially as receiving sets for his transmissions of wisdom. The teacher who takes the time and trouble to get to know his students individually and who calls them by name (especially by first name) obviously conveys the first set of attitudes. But probably the behaviour that most explicitly demonstrates that a teacher really cares about a student and respects his contribution is the act of really listening to what the student says. [. . .]

Diagnosis of needs

The adult's self-concept of self-directivity is in direct conflict with the traditional practice of the teacher telling the student what he needs to learn. Indeed, it is even in conflict with the social philosophy that society has a right to impose its ideas about what he needs to learn on him. Of course, an adult will learn what others want him to learn if their power to punish him for not learning is strong enough. But he is more deeply motivated to learn those things he sees the need to learn.

In andragogy, therefore, great emphasis is placed on the involvement of adult learners in a process of *self-diagnosis* of needs for learning. This process consists of three phases:

1 Constructing a model of the competencies or characteristics required to achieve a given model of performance; it is in this model-building phase that the values and expectations of the teacher, the institution, and society are amalgamated with those of the learner into a composite picture.
2 Providing diagnostic experiences in which the learner can assess his present level of competencies in the light of those portrayed in the model.
3 Helping the learner to measure the gaps between his present competencies and those required by the model, so that he experiences a feeling of dissatisfaction about the distance between where he is and where he would like to be and is able to identify specific directions of desirable growth. This experiencing of self-induced dissatisfaction with present inadequacies, coupled with a clear sense of direction for self-improvement, is in fact a good definition of 'motivation to learn'.

The planning process

Every individual tends to feel committed to a decision (or an activity) to the extent that he has participated in making it (or planning it). Teachers of adults who do all the planning for their students, who come into the classroom and impose preplanned activities on them, typically experience apathy, resentment, and probably withdrawal. For this imposition of the will of the teacher is incongruent with the adult's self-concept of self-directivity.

Accordingly, a basic element in the technology of andragogy is the involvement of the learners in the process of planning their own learning, with the teacher serving as a procedural guide and content resource. When the number of students is small enough, they can all be involved in the planning directly; when the number gets much over thirty, adult educators make use of representative councils, committees, task forces, teams, or other devices through which the learners feel that they are participating in the planning by proxy.

The function of planning consists of translating diagnosed needs into specific educational objectives (or directions of growth), designing and conducting learning experiences to achieve these objectives, and evaluating the extent to which these objectives have been accomplished. In andragogy, responsibility for performing this function is a mutual one between the learners and the teacher.

Conducting learning experiences

In traditional pedagogical practice the function of the teacher is defined as 'to teach'. The teacher is expected to take full responsibility for what happens in the teaching–learning transaction. The learner's role tends to be that of a fairly passive recipient of the teacher's instruction.

In contrast, andragogical practice treats the learning–teaching transaction as the mutual responsibility of learners and teacher. In fact, the teacher's role is redefined as that of a procedural technician, resource person, and co-inquirer; he is more a catalyst than an instructor, more a guide than a wizard. Andragogy assumes that a teacher can't really 'teach' in the sense of 'make a person learn', but that one person can only help another person learn. [. . .] An andragogical learning situation, whether it be a course, an institute, a training programme, or a conference, is alive with meetings of small groups – planning committees, learning – teaching teams, consultation groups, project task forces – sharing responsibility for helping one another learn.

Evaluation of learning

Probably the crowning instance of incongruity between traditional educational practice and the adult's self-concept of self-directivity is the act of a teacher giving a grade to a student. Nothing makes an adult feel more childlike than being judged by another adult; it is the ultimate sign of disrespect and dependency, as the one who is being judged experiences it.

For this reason, andragogical theory prescribes a process of self-evaluation, in which the teacher devotes his energy to helping the adults get evidence for themselves about the progress they are making toward their educational goals. In this process, the strengths and weaknesses of the educational programme itself must be assessed in terms of how it has facilitated or inhibited the learning of the students. So evaluation is a mutual undertaking, as are all other phases of the adult learning experience.

In fact, what is happening in practice is that precisely the same procedures that are used for the diagnosis of learning needs are being employed to help the learner measure his gains in competence. For instance, by comparing his performance in solving a critical incident at the end of a learning experience with his performance in a similar critical incident at the beginning of the experience, a learner can quite precisely measure the changes produced by the experience. Because of the similarity of these two processes, I find myself now thinking less and less in terms of the evaluation of learning and more and more in terms of the *rediagnosis* of learning needs. And I find that, when my adult students perceive what they do at the end of a learning experience as rediagnosing rather than evaluating, they enter into the activity with more enthusiasm and see it as being more constructive. Indeed, many of them report that it launches them into a new cycle of learning, reinforcing the notion that learning is a continuing process.

This shift from evaluation to self-evaluation or rediagnosis places a heavy burden on the teacher of adults. He must set the example of himself being open to feedback regarding his performance. He must be skilful in establishing a supportive climate, in which hard-to-accept information about one's performance can be looked at objectively. And he must be creative about inventing ways in which students can get comprehensive data about their performance. [. . .]

Experience

Every adult enters into any undertaking with a different background of experience from that of his youth. Having lived longer, he has accumulated a greater *volume* of experience, but he also has had different *kinds* of experience.

There is, it seems to me, another rather subtle difference between children and adults as regards their experience. To a child, an experience is something that happens to him; it is an external event that affects him, not an integral part of him. If you ask a child who he is, he is likely to identify himself in terms of who his parents are, who his older brothers or sisters are, what street he lives on, and what school he attends. His self-identity is largely derived from external sources.

But to an adult, his experience *is* him. He defines who he is, establishes his self-identity, in terms of his accumulation of a unique set of experiences. So, you ask an adult who he is, he is likely to identify himself in terms of what his occupation is, where he has worked, where he has travelled, what his training and experience have equipped him to do, and what his achievements have been. An adult *is* what he has *done*.

Because an adult defines himself largely by his experience, he has a deep investment in its value. And so when he finds himself in a situation in which his experience is not being used, or its worth is minimized, it is not just his experience that is being rejected – he feels rejected as a person.

These differences in experience between children and adults have at least three consequences for learning:

1 Adults have more to contribute to the learning of others; for most kinds of learning, they are themselves a rich resource for learning;
2 Adults have a richer foundation of experience to which to relate new experiences (and new learnings tend to take on meaning as we are able to relate them to our past experience);

3 Adults have acquired a larger number of fixed habits and patterns of thought, and therefore tend to be less open-minded.

Technological implications

Several implications for the technology of andragogy flow from these differences in experience:

Emphasis on experiential techniques

Because adults are themselves richer resources for learning than children, greater emphasis can be placed on techniques that tap the experience of the adult learners, such as group discussion, the case method, the critical-incident process, simulation exercises, role playing, skill-practice exercises, field projects, action projects, laboratory methods, consultative supervision, demonstration, seminars, work conferences, counselling, group therapy, and community development. There is a distinct shift in emphasis in andragogy away from the transmittal techniques so prevalent in youth education – the lecture, assigned readings, and canned audio-visual presentation – toward the more participatory experiential techniques. Indeed, 'participation' and 'ego-involvement' are boldfaced words in the lexicon of the adult educator, with the assumption often being made that the more active the learner's role in the process, the more he is probably learning.

Emphasis on practical application

Skilful adult educators have always taken care to see that new concepts or broad generalizations were illustrated by life experiences drawn from the learners. But numerous recent studies on the transfer of learning and the maintenance of behavioural change indicate the desirability of going even further, and actually building into the design of learning experiences provision for the learners to plan – and even rehearse – how they are going to apply their learnings in their day-to-day lives.

Unfreezing and learning to learn from experience

A growing andragogical practice is to build into the early phases of a course, workshop, conference, institute, or other sequential educational activity an 'unfreezing' experience, in which the adults are helped to look at themselves more objectively and free their minds from preconceptions. Many diagnostic exercises help to serve this purpose, but the most effective technique of all is probably a sensitivity-training 'microlab', in which participants experience a short, intensive period of feedback on their behaviour. For one of the almost universal initial needs of adults is to learn how to take responsibility for their own learning through self-directed inquiry, how to learn collaboratively with the help of colleagues rather than to compete with them, and especially how to learn by analysing one's own experience.

Readiness to learn

It is well accepted in our culture now that children learn best those things that are necessary for them to know in order to advance from one phase of development to the next. These have been dubbed 'developmental tasks' by developmental psychologists:

> A developmental task is a task which arises at or about a certain period in the life of the individual, successful achievement of which leads to his happiness and to success with later tasks, while failure leads to unhappiness in the individual, disapproval by the society, and difficulty with later tasks.
>
> (Havighurst, 1961: 2)

Each of these developmental tasks produces a 'readiness to learn' which at its peak presents a 'teachable moment'. For example, parents now generally accept the fact that they can't teach a child to walk until he has mastered the art of crawling, his leg muscles are strong enough, and he has become frustrated at not being able to stand up and walk the way everybody else does. At that point, and only then, is he able to learn to walk, for it has become *his* developmental task.

Recent research suggests that the same phenomenon is at work during the adult years. Adults, too, have their phases of growth and resulting developmental tasks, readinesses to learn, and teachable moments. But whereas the developmental tasks of youth tend to be the products primarily of physiological and mental maturation, those of the adult years are the products primarily of the evolution of social roles. Robert J. Havighurst, one of the pioneers in this area of research, divides the adult years into three phases – 'early adulthood', 'middle age', and 'later maturity' – and identifies ten social roles of adulthood: worker, mate, parent, homemaker, son or daughter of aging parents, citizen, friend, organization member, religious affiliate, and user of leisure time. The requirements for performing each of these social roles change, according to Havighurst, as we move through the three phases of adult life, thereby setting up changing developmental tasks and, therefore, changing readiness to learn.

For example, in a person's role of worker, his first developmental task is to get a job. At that point he is ready to learn anything required to get a job, but he definitely isn't ready to study supervision. Having landed a job, he is faced with the task of mastering it so that he won't get fired; and at that point he is ready to learn the special skills it requires, the standards that are expected of him, and how to get along with his fellow workers. Having become secure in his basic job, his task becomes one of working up the occupational ladder. Now he becomes ready to learn to become a supervisor or executive. Finally, after reaching his ceiling, he faces the task of dissolving his role of worker – and is ready to learn about retirement or substitutes for work. [. . .]

Technological implications

At least two sets of implications for the technology of andragogy flow from these differences in readiness to learn.

Timing of learning

If the teachable moment for a particular adult to acquire a given learning is to be captured, it is obvious that the sequence of the curriculum must be timed so as to be in step with his developmental tasks. This is the appropriate organizing principle for an adult education programme, rather than the logic of the subject matter or the needs of the sponsoring institution. For instance, an orientation programme for new workers would not start with the history and philosophy of the corporation, but rather with real-life concerns of new workers: Where will I be working? With whom will I be working? What will be expected of me? How do people dress in this company? What is the time schedule? To whom can I go for help? [. . .]

Grouping of learners

The concept of developmental tasks provides some guidance regarding the grouping of learners. For some kinds of learnings, homogeneous groups according to developmental task are more effective. For instance, in a programme on child care, young parents would have quite a different set of interests from the parents of adolescent children. For other kinds of learnings, heterogeneous groups would clearly be preferable. For instance, in a programme of human relations training in which the objective is to help people learn to get along better with all kinds of people, it would be important for the groups to cut across occupational, age, status, sex, and perhaps other characteristics that make people different. In my own practice, I have adopted the policy of making provision in the design of any adult learning activity for a variety of subgroups so as to give the students a flexibility of choice; and I find that they quickly discover colleagues with similar developmental tasks.

Orientation to learning

Adults enter education with a different perspective from children, which in turn produces a difference in the way they view learning. Children tend to have a perspective of postponed application on most of their learning.

For example, most of what I learned in elementary school I learned in order to be able to get into high school; and most of what I learned there I learned to prepare me for college; and most of what I learned in college I hoped would prepare me for a happy and productive adult life. To a child, education is essentially a process of the accumulation of a reservoir of subject matter – knowledge and skills – that might be useful later in life. Children tend, therefore, to enter any educational activity in a *subject-centred* frame of mind.

Adults, on the other hand, tend to have a perspective of immediacy of application toward most of their learning. Education is a process of improving their ability to deal with life problems they face now. They tend, therefore, to enter an educational activity in a *problem-centred* frame of mind.

Technological implications

Several implications for the technology of andragogy flow from this difference in orientation to learning.

Orientation of adult educators

Where the youth educator can, perhaps appropriately, be primarily concerned with the logical development of subject matter and its articulation from grade to grade according to levels of complexity, the adult educator must be primarily attuned to the existential concerns of the individuals and institutions he serves and be able to develop learning experiences that will be articulated with these concerns. Andragogy calls for programme builders and teachers who are person-centred, who don't teach subject matter but rather help persons learn.

Organization of the curriculum

[. . .] Because adult learners tend to be problem-centred in their orientation to learning, the appropriate organizing principle for sequences of adult learning is *problem areas*, not *subjects*. For example, instead of offering courses on 'Composition I' and 'Composition II', with the first focusing on grammar and the second on writing style, andragogical practice would put in their place 'Writing Better Business Letters' and 'Writing Short Stories'. In the adult courses, matters of grammar and style would be treated in the context of the practical concerns of the learners.

Design of learning experiences

The problem orientation of the learners implies that the most appropriate starting point for every learning experience is the problems and concerns that the adults have on their minds as they enter. Whereas the opening session of a youth education activity might be titled 'What This Course Is All About', in an adult educational activity it would more appropriately be titled 'What Are You Hoping To Get out of This Course?' Early in the session there would be a problem census or a diagnostic exercise through which the participants would identify the specific problems they want to be able to deal with more adequately. This is not to suggest that a good adult learning experience ends with the problems the learners are aware of in the beginning, but that is where it starts. There may be other problems that the teacher or institution are expecting to be dealt with, and these are put into the picture along with the students' problems for negotiation between teacher and students.

SOME ASSUMPTIONS ABOUT LEARNING AND TEACHING

The critical element in any adult education programme is, of course, what happens when a teacher comes face-to-face with a group of learners. As I see it, the andragogical approach to the learning–teaching transaction is premised on three additional assumptions about learning and teaching.

Adults can learn

The central proposition on which the entire adult education movement is based is that adults can learn. One of the great moments in the history of the movement occurred at the annual meeting of the American Association for Adult Education held in Cleveland in 1927, when Edward L. Thorndike reported for the first time his findings that the ability to learn declined only very slowly and very slightly after age twenty. Until that moment adult educators had based their whole work on blind faith, in direct opposition to the prevailing belief that 'you can't teach an old dog new tricks'. But now their faith had been vindicated; there was scientific proof that adults can learn. [. . .]

The research to date on adult learning indicates clearly that the basic ability to learn remains essentially unimpaired throughout the life-span and that, therefore, if individuals do not actually perform as well in learning situations as they could, the cause must be sought in factors such as the following:

- Adults who have been away from systematic education for some time may underestimate their ability to learn, and this lack of confidence may prevent them from applying themselves wholly.
- Methods of teaching have changed since most adults were in school,

so that most of them have to go through a period of adjustment to strange new conditions.

- Various physiological changes occur in the process of aging, such as decline in visual acuity, reduction in speed of reaction, and lowering of energy levels, which operate as barriers to learning unless compensated for by such devices as louder sound, larger printing, and slower pace.
- Adults respond less readily to external sanctions for learning (such as grades) than to internal motivation.

Learning is an internal process

In our inherited folk wisdom there has been a tendency to look upon education as the transmittal of information, to see learning as an almost exclusively intellectual process consisting of the storing of accumulated facts in the filing drawers of the mind. The implicit assumption underlying this view of learning is that it is essentially an external process in the sense that what the student learns is determined primarily by outside forces, such as the excellence of the teacher's presentation, the quality of reading materials, and the effectiveness of school discipline. People holding this view even today insist that a teacher's qualifications be judged only by his mastery of his subject matter and clamour against his wasting time learning about the psychology of learning. For all practical purposes this view defines the function of the teacher as being to teach subject matter, not students.

A growing body of research into what really happens when learning takes place has put this traditional conception of learning in serious jeopardy. Although there is not yet agreement on the precise nature of the learning process (in fact there are many theories which seem to explain different parts of it), there is agreement that it is an internal process controlled by the learner and engaging his whole being – including intellectual, emotional, and physiological functions. Learning is described psychologically as a process of need-meeting and goal-striving by the learner. This is to say that an individual is motivated to engage in learning to the extent that he feels a need to learn and perceives a personal goal that learning will help to achieve; and he will invest his energy in making use of available resources (including teachers and readings) to the extent that he perceives them as being relevant to his needs and goals.

The central dynamic of the learning process is thus perceived to be the experience of the learner, experience being defined as the interaction between an individual and his environment. The quality and amount of learning is therefore clearly influenced by the quality and amount of interaction between the learner and his environment and by the educative potency of the environment. The art of teaching is essentially the management of these two key variables in the learning process – environment and interaction – which together define the substance of the basic unit of learning, a 'learning experience'. The critical function of the teacher, therefore, is to create a rich environment from which students can extract learning and then to guide their interaction with it so as to maximize their learning from it.

The important implication for adult education practice of the fact that learning is an internal process is that those methods and techniques which involve the individual most deeply in self-directed inquiry will produce the greatest learning. This principle of ego-involvement lies at the heart of the adult educator's art. In fact, the main thrust of modern adult educational technology is in the direction of inventing techniques for involving adults in ever deeper processes of self-diagnosis of their own needs for continued learning, in formulating their own objectives for learning, in sharing responsibility for designing and carrying out their learning activities, and in evaluating their progress toward their objectives. The truly artistic teacher of adults perceives the locus of responsibility for learning to be in the learner; he conscientiously suppresses his own compulsion to teach what he knows his students ought to learn in favour of helping his students learn for themselves what they want to learn. I have described this faith in the ability of the individual to learn for himself as the 'theological foundation' of adult education, and I believe that without this faith a teacher of adults is more likely to hinder than to facilitate learning. This is not to suggest that the teacher has less responsibility in the learning–teaching transaction, but only that his responsibility lies less in giving ready-made answers to predetermined questions and more in being ingenious in finding better ways to help his students discover the important questions and the answers to them themselves. [. . .]

There are superior conditions of learning and principles of teaching

It is becoming increasingly clear from the growing body of knowledge about the processes of adult learning that there are certain conditions of learning that are more conducive to growth and development than others. These superior conditions seem to be produced by practices in the learning–teaching transaction that adhere to certain superior principles of teaching as identified in Table 4.1 below.

Table 4.1 Superior conditions of learning

Conditions of learning	Principles of teaching
The learners feel a need to learn.	The teacher exposes students to new possibilities for self-fulfilment. The teacher helps each student clarify his own aspirations for improved behaviour. The teacher helps each student diagnose the gap between his aspiration and his present level of performance. The teacher helps the students identify the life problems they experience because of the gaps in their personal equipment.
The learning environment is characterized by physical comfort, mutual trust and respect, mutual helpfulness, freedom of expression, and acceptance of differences.	The teacher provides physical conditions that are comfortable (as to seating, smoking, temperature, ventilation, lighting, decoration) and conducive to interaction (preferably, no person sitting behind another person). The teacher accepts each student as a person of worth and respects his feelings and ideas. The teacher seeks to build relationships of mutual trust and helpfulness among the students by encouraging cooperative activities and refraining from inducing competitiveness and judgementalness. The teacher exposes his own feelings and contributes his resources as a co-learner in the spirit of mutual inquiry.
The learners perceive the goals of a learning experience to be their goals.	The teacher involves the students in a mutual process of formulating learning objectives in which the needs of the students, of the institution, of the teacher, of the subject matter, and of the society are taken into account.
The learners accept a share of the responsibility for planning and operating a learning experience, and therefore have a feeling of commitment toward it.	The teacher shares his thinking about options available in the designing of learning experiences and the selection of materials and methods and involves the students in deciding among these options jointly.

The learners participate actively in the learning process.	The teacher helps the students to organize themselves (project groups, learning–teaching teams, independent study, etc.) to share responsibility in the process of mutual inquiry.
The learning process is related to and makes use of the experience of the learners.	The teacher helps the students exploit their own experiences as resources for learning through the use of techniques such as discussion, role playing, case method, etc. The teacher gears the presentation of his own resources to the levels of experience of his particular students. The teacher helps the students to apply new learnings to their experience, and thus to make the learnings more meaningful and integrated.
The learners have a sense of progress toward their goals.	The teacher involves the students in developing mutually acceptable criteria and methods for measuring progress toward the learning objectives. The teacher helps the students develop and apply procedures for self-evaluation according to these criteria.

NOTE

1 See Dušan Savićević, 'Training adult educationists in Yugoslavia', *Convergence*, 1 (March 1968), p. 69.

REFERENCES

Havighurst, R. J. (1961) *Developmental Tasks and Education*, New York: David McKay Co.
Whitehead, A. N. (1931) 'Introduction', in W. B. Donham, *Business Adrift*, New York: McGraw-Hill.

Chapter 5

The search for a separate theory of adult learning
Does anyone really need andragogy?

Ann Hanson

Even before the increase in participation by adults in education and training in the mid-1980s in the United Kingdom and the development of access and other adult orientated schemes, there had been attempts to develop a professional perspective for 'adult education'. Embedded in the notion of adult education is often the belief that adult learners are different from children and that there needs to be a separate 'theory' underpinning the teaching and learning of adults. During the 1970s and early 1980s much debate revolved around the concept of andragogy as the organizing framework to substantiate claims about the different characteristics and needs of adult learners. However, despite many exchanges at both the level of theory and practice, there was little resolution of the question of differences between pedagogy ('the teaching of children') and andragogy ('helping adults to learn') (McKenzie 1977, 1979; Elias 1979; Knudson 1979; Knowles 1979a, 1979b, 1984; Cross 1981; Brookfield 1986). Some of these debates became lost in the realms of semantics. However, they were important in raising the consciousness of practitioners to the theoretical field of adult learning.

The focus of the debate surrounding the alleged dichotomy between pedagogy and andragogy had important consequences in practice, but as this chapter suggests, a closer examination of many of the theories does little to provide real evidence that adults and children are absolutely different in their learning. This is not to deny that differences of age and/or experience do exist, but their significance can be over-generalized and misleading. For instance, adults are not necessarily more experienced because they have lived longer.

Richer forms of analysis may lie in more specific examinations of the characteristics of specific individuals and their contexts with regard to what they are learning, the setting in which they learn and the relationships with those peers and tutors with whom they learn. All these considerations may contribute to how individuals learn – the learning process. This chapter therefore attempts to explore some of the major theories of adult learning and evaluate their assumptions and significance for practitioners working with diverse individuals in various settings for a range of purposes.

ANDRAGOGY: DESCRIPTION OR PRESCRIPTION?

It would seem to be of most relevance for practitioners to understand the practical basis for adult learning rather than engage in endless debates about the differences between pedagogy and andragogy. Such issues are not addressed by writers such as Knowles (1984). He outlines four components of adult status which come together as that point at which we arrive at a self-concept of being responsible for ourselves, of being 'self-directing'. Self-direction therefore becomes a dominant paradigm of what it means to be an adult and is therefore integral to the learning in which adults engage.

Knowles demonstrates he has a strong humanistic and individualistic commitment to his 'clients'. However, simply believing that adults are different from children as learners because they are adults is not sufficient grounds on which to construct a separate theory. Indeed it may dehumanize children and obscure real areas of similarity. More detailed work has been carried out (Allman, 1983), but the way the concept of andragogy is often used in the UK and North America often ignores the political and institutional constraints and even the day-to-day influences upon adult learners themselves.

Andragogy as a theory of learning and helping others to learn expounds a normative educational utopia. This can be seen in two ways. First, in how some practitioners like to think their institutions are providing learning opportunities for adults. Second, in how they would like to see adults behave – as autonomous, self-directed learners. These expectations may be at odds with actual experience. For some adults, for instance, acquiring knowledge may be a valid aim which reflective processes might hinder rather than help. The assumptions in theories of adult learning therefore need to be questioned. If the underlying claims of those who support andragogy are a set of normative humanist values, it would seem that they are as valid for children as for adults, in which case the andragogy/pedagogy debate is very artificial.

The search for a separate theory of adult learning thereby becomes problematic as wider questions are addressed; about the nature of education and training and the relationship between learners, what is taught, why, how and by whom. Issues of knowledge, power and control have to be addressed. To assume that an adult entering an institution will believe that things will be different from when they were at school, when in fact, due to external control on the institution and internal administration, they are not could be dangerous. In the context of subject areas increasingly pre-packaged in numbers of credits, pre-determined levels of achievement and final certificates, the possibility of exercising completely autonomous self-direction is, in many ways, severely curtailed. Any theory of adult learning which advocates the importance of each individual as an individual, but avoids issues of curriculum control and power does little to address the actual learning situations of adults. As Griffin (1983) argues:

> there is, as it were, a curriculum vacuum consequent upon a highly abstract model of both a 'learning system' and an adult learner, and no sense of what the system or the adult learns as a social, cultural and political construct.

Institutions may develop access courses and produce mission statements to justify increasing numbers of adults on their courses, but there is usually no clear distinction between pragmatic aims and ideological assumptions. It is possible to widen access, to increase mature student intake and ignore the social, cultural and political distribution of knowledge and skills. The paternalistic offering of courses for study, the certification ceremonies indicating success, the need to fit skills into particular levels of competence, are all legitimizing aspects of control of the learning environment. Without institutional and curriculum reform to stress autonomy, individuality and self-direction, are adults being offered anything other than what was available through schools? More importantly, is it always right that they should be? The assumed value of such goals need first to be foregrounded and discussed.

Writers, such as Rogers (1969), in relation to children and adults, and Knowles (1979a and 1979b) and Tough (1969), in relation to adults, promote the idea of the teacher as the facilitator of learning. This is meant to be a warm and open relationship. Yet, once again, constraints on the the actual learning setting may make such a relationship an aspiration more than an actuality. Curricula are primarily socially constructed prescribed areas of knowledge and skill external to the student. These provide targets to be achieved. Thus, the cultural constraints of formal curricula act upon the learners and tutors, and have an impact upon the relationship between them. The dehumanizing and mystifying effects of formal curricula and its role in reproducing the dominant culture and acting as a form of social control have been pointed out by many writers (Freire 1970; Green 1971). Theories of adult learning which do not take account of culture and power do adults little service, even if they aim to produce self-directed learners.

The discussion of power and control is thereby brought into debates surrounding a separate theory of adult learning. Knowles (1979a, 1979b) avoided these issues in the ideal type humanism of his early notion of andragogy. However, in his later writing (1984) he did start to recognize the prescriptive aspect of his notion of andragogy:

we as educators now have the responsibility to check out which assumptions are realistic in a given situation. If a pedagogical assumption is realistic for a particular learner in regard to a particular learning goal then a pedagogical strategy is appropriate, at least as a starting point. But there is one big difference between how an ideological pedagogue and an andragogue would go from there. The pedagogue perceiving the pedagogical assumptions to be the only realistic assumptions, will insist that the learner remain dependent on the teacher, whereas the andragogue, perceiving the movement towards the andragogical assumptions is a desirable goal, will do everything possible to help learners take increasing responsibility for their own learning.

(Knowles 1984: 62)

On this basis, of course, andragogy could be of equal relevance to children and adults.

Yonge (1985), Podechi (1987) and Griffin (1985) are among those who have criticized the assumptions of andragogy and its goal of self-direction. Making the latter a characteristic of adulthood seems to assume that becoming an adult is an all or nothing experience, when it may be necessary to relinquish certain aspects of adult status, including self-direction and autonomy, when learning something new. Others, most notably Mezirow (1981), have also used self-direction as a defining characteristic of andragogy, but attempted to situate it within an understanding of the context of culture, knowledge and power. However, the general perception persists among some of pedagogy as a form of 'powerlessness' and andragogy as a form of 'empowering'. This is despite the developing literature on feminist and critical *pedagogy* with its concerns with social change and emancipation.

The search for a separate theory of adult learning has largely comprised a debate about age and stage of development at the expense of questions of purpose, of how knowledge and skills are defined and valued and the relationship between individual and society. This has tended to produce research which looks for evidence to substantiate the assumptions about individual characteristics already in such theories. Rather than attempting to describe the various ways in which adult learn, there is the danger of andragogy prescribing how adults should learn. Adults should be self-directed, should be able to make use of their own experiences, should want to know or be able to do things for a particular reason at a particular time in their lives. The cultural assumptions underpinning such goals and the constraints upon their attainment are left unexamined.

ADULTS AS DIFFERENT; DIFFERENCES AMONG ADULTS

Knowles and his followers place great emphasis on the individuality of those adults returning to learn. However, it is a form of abstract individualism rather than an engagement with learners themselves within their real life situations. General characteristics are assumed rather than specific contexts and perceptions examined. To concentrate on these perceptions may tell us more about adult learners than making assumptions about the importance of experience, motivation or the need for self-direction. Indeed, in research carried out with mature students returning to study on full-time higher education courses (Hanson 1989), I found adults prepared to suspend their adulthood at the door of the institution and be only too willing to submit themselves to its constraints. However, this does not make them children again simply by their situational acceptance of the authority of the tutor. They accepted the unequal partnership in that particular situation, as long as the tutor had something to offer which justified the acceptance of their authority. Once this assumption no longer held good, the relationship of authority was broken. Here we see a difference in the power of education and training in relation to children and adults. Whereas the former are kept in schools through the power of coercion and reward, adults can normally vote with their feet. The authority of the tutor has therefore to be earned from their students; it cannot be assumed.

There is also, as suggested above, a danger of accepting a belief that experience is the key difference between children and adults in a learning context. Whilst it would seem apparent that by virtue of age, adults should have more experience upon which to base their learning and thereby provide more possibilities for active engagement in what they learn, such a distinction is ill-founded. Quantity of experience does not necessarily ensure quality of learning. Experience may even be a block to learning for adults who have become set in their ways. The range of experiences of some children in certain countries and situations may be far more extensive than that for adults elsewhere. Nor should we forget the gender differences that exist both in relation to forms of experience and self-reflection on experience.

One of the early learning experiences of my research with adult learners was the realization that mature students were not a homogeneous group and that there are dangers in treating them as such. A timetable between 10 am and 3 pm, aimed to assist those with child care responsibilities, alienated some who wanted a full working day as a student. Discrete groups to keep all mature students together were perceived as treating them differently from 'proper' students. Seeing someone early to enable them do their shopping later devalued students who used gaps in the day to take advantage of peace and quiet in the library. Within any group of adult learners therefore, there are significant differences regarding biographies, experiences, perceptions and, as a result, different expectations and approaches to learning.

An interesting part of my own research was also witnessing the coping strategies developed in the first term in full-time education. The straightforward explanation was that with experience the pressure of returning to study, fitting family life and study together, accommodating an existing social life with a new circle of friends and doing the work, all became easier. In fact, when asked, students did not focus on these issues, but were more concerned with knowing how they were progressing with their studies, as they had no yardstick to measure their performance in this new aspect of their lives. They had given work in, but not received any feedback. Once that was received they were able to cope. The individual perceptions of the adult returners therefore told a different story to what may have been assumed to be the case by those working with them. Notions of autonomy and independence are not substitutes for accurate feedback on progress.

PERSPECTIVE TRANSFORMATION AND REFLECTIVITY

Events take place in life which cannot be dealt with simply by extending previously used experiences. Personal biographies cannot simply be extended to cope with just any new experience. Even students who feel they have prepared themselves for new learning experiences, through access or preparatory study, enter new situations which may challenge assumptions and result in the re-assessment of beliefs and understandings, about themselves as well as what they are learning.

This can involve not simply a different way of looking at the same thing, but a change of perspective in which there is conscious recognition of the differences between one's old and new perspectives and a decision to adopt the newer as being of more use and value. This qualitative re-assessment is the process by which a transformation of perspective can occur. However, it is not always easy, as re-assessing beliefs and ideas may be threatening and can be resisted. It is often a specific situation – a personal crisis, a change in circumstances, a re-evaluation of lifestyle – which brings about a change in perspective. Moving to a new perspective may also require support in the process of transformation and in the capacity to sustain the change.

It was Mezirow (1978, 1981) who developed the theory of perspective transformation as central to adult learning. He saw 'meaning perspectives' as important for adults learning as they help to develop a critical awareness based on past experiences in a current context:

A meaning perspective refers to the structure of cultural assumptions within which new experience is assimilated to – and transformed by – one's past experience. It is a personal paradigm for understanding ourselves and our relationships

(Mezirow 1981: 4)

Through socialization we acquire the meaning perspectives of our culture but we have the propensity to become critically aware of our perspectives and of changing them. Mezirow claims that there is a difference between becoming aware of our awareness and being critical of that awareness. Perspective transformation involves becoming critically reflective on the cultural assumptions which govern the way adults think, feel and act. Mezirow sees critical reflectivity and particularly theoretical reflectivity as a distinctly adult capacity. This is achieved through perspective transformations which become the guiding paradigm for the practitioner with adults.

However, even here caution is necessary as different cultures and situations require different forms of socialization and the question of cultural assumptions has to be deployed against the notion of perspective transformation and critical reflectivity itself. Individual autonomy and self-direction are themselves very 'Western' goals. Indeed, even with 'the West' they may be gender-specific, dominantly reflecting male approaches to learning and life. For some cultures and situations conformity to the group may be more important than critical autonomy. Critical self-reflection is not always beneficial, as self-awareness and criticism are often the characteristics of seriously depressed people. Self-reflection and critical thinking may be reputed to be universal 'goods', but we need to be aware of their cultural specificity and power.

The theory of perspective transformation may be of less relevance therefore than may be apparent and be based on untested assumptions. In the pilot for my own research, part-time evening-only mature students demonstrated clearly instrumental attitudes towards learning. Self-direction and reflection was not part of their agenda and time and again they were critical of tutors who did not dictate notes and give handouts, and who expected them to look things up in the library and prepare work for the next session. Two hours per week of contact time and full-time jobs did not provide much time for self-direction and perspective transformation.

Although the latter has been of less influence in recent years, greater importance has been given to the promotion of reflection in learning. The literature is extensive. Boud et al. (1985) trace the notion of reflection back to Aristotle. They and Kolb (1984) comment on its use by writers such as Dewey, Lewin and Piaget. Brookfield (1987) admits to there being no one all-embracing approach to facilitating reflective learning, while giving practical insights into approaches that can be adopted to develop critical thinking which involves the emotions as well as cognitive activity.

For both Brookfield (1987) and Kolb (1984), reflection and critical thinking are processes rather than outcomes of learning. Kolb (1984) sees fixed outcomes as a form of non-learning, because they are a mark of rigid and persistent knowledge or beliefs not open to further change. This has implications for the certification of learning which purports to measure a fixed body of knowledge or skills at any one time. For Kolb, all learning is re-learning wherein the role of the facilitator is to not only to help the learner build new ideas, but more importantly re-evaluate old beliefs and perceptions of reality. However, the notion that outcomes are necessarily fixed is open to challenge, as is the view that reflection and critical thinking are solely processes. For some they can be both a process and an outcome of learning.

So, once again, for practitioners considerations creep in concerning the usefulness of such theoretical frameworks. Here perhaps the most important question is whether or how reflective learning can be fostered. There are those who would claim that such learning is very much an individual attribute, but this begs the question of the role of the tutor/ facilitator in fostering reflection. The role of the tutor may be one of providing conditions within which individuals become sufficiently 'empowered' to be able to reflect critically on a situation or piece of knowledge, to understand its meaning, to be able to incorporate the new concept into their own understandings sufficiently to transform perspectives. Brookfield (1987) talks of the need for a good facilitator of adult learning to take risks in achieving critical thinking as it is only by upsetting tacit understandings, even building up anger and frustration, that individuals can move forward.

However, when such a model of learning is put into practice, it tends to be subject to those criticisms I have already made of earlier notions of andragogy; it fails to address the context and people's active experience of the world. It is an ideal type and, by adopting it, there is the danger of replacing one form of prescription for another, one form of control with another. Adults returning to learning are faced with many threats, both positive and negative, to their identities. At what stage then will they feel confident enough to re-evaluate their beliefs? How are learning habits changed, experiences questioned and built? How much actual room is there for the self-directed, critically reflective, empowered learner in institutional structures largely governed by the policies and funding of the state? Could emphasizing reflectivity as a goal of learning actually result in failure elsewhere where it is not considered to be of value?

ANDRAGOGY IN CONTEXT

The search for a separate theory of adult learning is grounded in an abstract notion of the individual rather than the social context of learning, thereby raising more questions than answers. Clark and Wilson (1991) argue that to focus on particular issues such as perspective transformation fails to take account of the cultural context of learning. We need to remove many of the unsubstantiated assumptions based on almost utopian beliefs about the education and training of adults linked to uncontextualized views of learning and empowerment. In contextualizing learning within questions of culture and power we move away from the prescriptive humanist ideology and abstract individualism which has largely governed the attempts to distinguish between adults and children as learners. All-embracing theories only get in the way of developing an understanding of and the differing strategies necessary to enable diverse adults to learn different things in different settings in different ways. There are differences, but they are not based on the difference between children and adults, of pedagogy and andragogy. They are differences of context, culture and power.

REFERENCES

Allman, P. (1983) *Adult Development: An Overview of Recent Research*, Nottingham: University of Nottingham.

Boud, D., Keogh, R. and Walker, D. (1985) (eds) *Reflection: Turning Experience into Learning*, London: Kogan Page.

Brookfield, S. (1986) *Understanding and Facilitating Adult Learning*, Milton Keynes: Open University Press.

Brookfield, S. (1987) *Developing Critical Thinkers*, Milton Keynes: Open University Press.

Clark, M. and Wilson, A. (1991) 'Context and rationality in Mezirow's theory of transformational learning', *Adult Education Quarterly*, 41, 75–91.

Cross, K. P. (1981) *Adults as Learners*, San Francisco: Jossey-Bass.

Elias, J. (1979) 'Andragogy revisited', *Adult Education Quarterly*, 29, 252–6.

Freire, P. (1970) *Pedagogy of the Oppressed*, Harmondsworth: Penguin.

Green, M. (1971) 'Curriculum and consciousness', *The Record*, F3(2).

Griffin, C. (1983) *Curriculum Theory in Adult and Lifelong Education*, London: Croom Helm.

Griffin, C. (1985) *Recurrent and Adult Education: Policy or Discipline*. Sheffield; Sheffield City Polytechnic.

Hanson, A. P. (1989) 'Expectations and realizations: experiences of mature students returning to study in an institution of public sector higher education', CNAA. Unpublished PhD thesis.

Knowles, M. (1979a) *The Modern Practice of Adult Education: Andragogy versus Pedagogy*, N.Y.A. Press.

Knowles, M. (1979b) 'Andragogy revisited Part II', *Adult Education*, 30(1), 52–3.

Knowles, M. (1984) *The Adult Learner: A Neglected Species*, London: Gulf Publishing.

Knudson, R. (1979) 'Humanagogy anyone?', *Adult Education*, 29, 261–4.

Kolb, D. (1984) *Experiential Learning*, Englewood Cliffs; N. J.: Prentice-Hall.

McKenzie, L. (1977) 'The issue of andragogy', *Adult Education*, 27, 225–9.

McKenzie, L. (1979) 'A response to Elias', *Adult Education*, 29, 256–61.

Mezirow, J. (1978) 'Perspective transformation', *Adult Education*, 28(2), 100–10.

Mezirow, J. (1981) 'A critical theory of adult learning and education', *Adult Education*, 32, 1: 3–24.

Podechi, R. (1987) 'Andragogy: proofs or premises?', *Lifelong Learning*, 11, 3: 14–16.

Rogers, C. (1969) *Freedom to Learn*, Westerville, Ohio: Merrill.

Tough, A. (1969) *The Adults Learning Projects: A Fresh Approach to the Theory and Practice of Adult Learning*, Toronto: OISE.

Yonge, G. (1985) 'Andragogy and pedagogy: two ways of accompaniment', *Adult Education Quarterly*, 35(3), 160–7.

Chapter 6

On contemporary practice and research

Self-directed learning to critical theory†

Michael Collins

[. . .]

FOCUS ON THE LEARNER: SELF-DIRECTED LEARNING

In recent years the notion of self-directed learning has become virtually the guiding principle for the practice of adult education. It has emerged as a primary distinction, for many adult educators, between the modern practice of adult education and conventional schooling. The basis of this distinction, it is claimed, resides in the fact that with self-directed learning strategies the needs and activities of the learner take centre stage rather than those of the teacher, whose designated role is that of *facilitator*. Self-directed learning, in this sense, describes a context where the past experiences of adult learners and their natural inclination to undertake learning projects on their own initiative are taken into account.

The techniques and strategies associated with self-directed learning are said to constitute a distinctive practice of *andragogy*[1] in contrast to pedagogy, which characterizes the more teacher-directed approaches of conventional schooling. (Certainly, this is the prevailing perspective in contemporary North American adult education practice.) Whether or not a commonsense acknowledgement of adult learners' past experience and their ability to make significant contributions to the shape of all their learning experiences merits such a clear-cut distinction is, perhaps, debatable.[2] The intention in this context, however, is to raise questions about the extent to which self-directed learning as a guiding principle and methodology for the modern practice of adult education does, in fact, serve to foster the autonomously determined needs of adult learners.

† This is an edited version of a chapter that appeared in M. Collins, *Adult Education as Vocation*, London: Routledge, 1991.

There can be no doubt that self-directed learning has given credence to educational practices which are less overtly restrictive than those sustained within many formal education settings. In his book, *The Free University: A Model for Lifelong Learning*, William Draves places a high value on self-directed learning and describes the concept in these terms:

> Self-directed learning begins with the learner. It sees the learner as the primary impetus for and the initiator of the learning process. Teachers, classes, and other educational features are then put in a secondary light, as aids to the learning process rather than its central elements.[3]

And Malcolm Knowles, the best known advocate of self-directed learning, has this to say on the subject:

> As a person grows and matures his [*sic*] self-concept moves from one of total dependency (as is the reality of the infant) to one of increasing self-directedness.[4]

Malcolm Knowles's methodological approach, in particular, has attracted an enormous following from among professional adult educators. Hence, the methodology of self-directed learning, in one form or another, has been applied in many kinds of formal adult education settings from basic literacy training through to the professional preparation of medical doctors and Ph.D. students. From the insight that an individual is the primary source of her or his own learning experiences, an array of techniques (largely under the rubric of 'andragogy') has emerged for ready deployment on to the vast arena of formal and non-formal adult education.

While reification of the concept has been most remarkable within North American adult education practice, it is also called forth in the adult education literature and discourses of other countries. As a 'conceptual and methodological orientation'[5] self-directed learning seems to have opened up a considerable terrain for academic commentary and programme development.

The notion of self-directed learning as it is conceived, and deployed, in contemporary North American adult education can be traced most directly to the studies of Canadian adult educator, Allen Tough. However, in *Learning Without a Teacher: A Study of Tasks and Assistance during Adult Self-teaching*, first published in 1967, Tough acknowledged his debt to Cyril Houle, doyen of university adult education in the USA:

> It was Professor C. O. Houle of the University of Chicago who first focused attention on men and women conspicuously engaged in learning. The inquiry was then taken up and developed in a variety of studies by younger colleagues.[6]

[. . .]

The major achievement of Tough's work is to present the far from novel insight (a fact which he readily acknowledged) that adults learn on their own initiative, construing self-directed learning in such a way as to provide an arena for professional intervention by adult education practitioners. His studies are all preoccupied with the prospects for identifying strategies and pedagogical techniques from the perspective of the professional educator. They do not endeavour to explore the meanings, in context, and cognitive structures that adults bring to their learning endeavours. On the contrary, self-initiated learning, as conceptualized in these studies, has been reduced to a series of elements and tasks that are accommodative to institutionalized (especially professionalized) needs. This reductive manner of representation, characteristic of technocratic formulations, has tended to foreclose on the prospects in adult education encounters for levels of interpretation, critical analysis, and thoughtful conversations about how adults endow the learning projects of their everyday lives with meaning and structure. What it gives us, instead, is an explanatory framework that tells us more about the perspectives of professional educators than it does about autonomous learning.

In the wake of Allen Tough's initial publications on the adult's learning projects, Malcolm Knowles took up the task and, with the remarkable entrepreneurial panache characteristic of so many American academics, formulated self-directed learning into a readily deployable technique that has been evoked as a guiding principle and widely applied throughout the field of adult education. Among Knowles's numerous publications, *The Adult Learner: A Neglected Species, The Modern Practice of Adult Education: From Pedagogy to Andragogy,* and *Self-directed Learning: A Guide for Learners and Teachers*[7] are particularly noteworthy for the imprint they have on practice and research in contemporary adult education. *Self-directed Learning: A Guide for Learners and Teachers* is a how-to text which embraces without question an ideology of technique. It describes self-directed learning and then sets out, in formulaic terms, how it has to be done; directed self-directed learning, so to speak. Those practitioners who sense that the text is not sufficiently formulaic will find reassurance in Knowles's most recent book, *Using Learning Contracts.*[8]

For Malcolm Knowles the adult educator wedded to self-directed learning as andragogy becomes responsible for managing a pedagogic technique, usually in the form of a learning contract with a student client. Through a negotiation process, the client is expected to identify a learning project and to specify, at the outset, learning objectives, learning resources and strategies, evidence of accomplishment, and criteria for evaluation. One wonders whether Eduard Lindeman had this kind of formal reductionism in mind when he first advanced the notion of andragogy as the true method of adult learning.[9] In any event, self-directed learning as technique has been implemented in many institutional settings, including hospitals, business firms, colleges, public schools, and prisons.

The transformation of autonomous learning into a methodology for self-directed learning undoubtedly can work to the advantage of management in business and industry, professional organizations and large-scale institutions when individuals who depend upon them appear to be voluntarily directing their educational projects through formal learning contracts and in accordance with institutional purposes. In such contexts, the rhetoric of self-directed learning, often harnessed to a new-fangled notion of human resource development (human resources meaning people), supports a misleading scenario of adult men and women effectively shaping an important dimension of their everyday working lives while, in fact, the attendant methodology places the direction of their learning subtly, but firmly, in the hands of experts who serve predominantly institutionalized interests. Self-directed learning, systematically defined as it is in prevailing adult education practice, permits the learner to choose between options already defined by formal systems.

But is it the role of adult educators (whoever else's it may be) to provide, in a taken-for-granted manner, this kind of legitimation for society's organizations on behalf of individuals? Can they evade the issue with a claim that self-directed learning strategies bring institutional and individual needs together through the methodological device of the learning contract? Hardly. The distribution of power between formal institution and the individual is so manifestly unequal that it does not even have to be spelled out at the time 'self-directed' objectives are identified by the individual. In systematizing self-directed learning to become directed (though more or less subtly steered) self-direction in the form of individualized learning contracts, adult educators are working on behalf of institutional interests above those of individuals.

Recently, the self-directed learning motif has begun to absorb an important variation with two books by Stephen Brookfield. Both *Self-directed Learning: From Theory to Practice*, a selection of essays of which he is contributing editor, and *Understanding and Facilitating Adult Learning*[10] evince a critical awareness that institutional, socio-political, and cultural constraints influence the scope and quality of adult learning endeavours and should be openly addressed. The practical and ethical, rather than technocratic, intent of Brookfield's orientation to 'facilitating adult learning' is apparent from the following statement:

> The task of the educator becomes that of encouraging adults to perceive the relative, contextual nature of previously unquestioned givens. Additionally, the educator should assist the adult to reflect on the manner in which values, beliefs, and behaviors previously deemed

unchallengeable can be critically analyzed. Through presenting alternative ways of interpreting and creating a world to adults, the educator fosters a willingness to consider alternative ways of living.[11]

So, in addition to presenting adult educators with a very comprehensive synthesis of contributions to the stock of literature on self-directed learning, the two texts cited in the preceding paragraph do underscore the need for adult education practice to foster critical questioning of taken-for-granted assumptions. However, even though a 'critical philosophy of practice' is invoked,[12] the analysis remains at a level that permits an evasion of rational non-relativistic inquiry into the efficacy and ethics associated with the reification of self-directed learning as both technique and guiding principle for adult education practice.

Ivan Illich refers to the medieval 'commons' as a metaphor for drawing our attention to those accessible but precious parts of our personal and natural environment 'for which customary law enacted specific forms of respect'.[13] He writes in similar vein of 'vernacular values' to characterize meaningful and communal aspects of people's everyday lives that are continuously being eroded by the effects of what he would characterize as 'non-convivial' technological innovation and bureaucratic interventions.[14] Jürgen Habermas, who places a high premium on rationality and would abjure a romanticized anti-technology stand, concerns himself with the same theme when he refers to 'the colonization of the life-world'. His critical question, of immense pedagogical significance, yet to be confronted by adult education practice, is 'How can the relation between technical progress and the social life-world be reflected upon and brought under the control of rational discussion?'[15]

Such metaphors and images as these, together with the substantive theoretical works from which they emerge, point to the impairment of vital dimensions of everyday life in modern society. Formalized learning strategies and research protocols that emanate from professionalized notions such as the adult's learning projects and self-directed learning contracts represent further systematic intrusions on to personal and communal (inter-personal) events. Our capacity to learn on our own initiative, according to our own cognitive styles, is a vital part of the 'commons' of our everyday social life-world. Adult educators are remiss when they subvert their knowledge of this capacity to serve their own professionalized interests as teachers and researchers through the deployment of intrusive strategies.

Rather than formulating and implementing self-teaching frameworks that are indicative of professionalized orientations, adult educators could be working on strategies to identify and preserve valuable non-institutionalized (individual and community oriented) learning endeavours that are threatened by bureaucratized and professionalized interventions. Instead of deploying intrusive research designs based on independent learning project protocols, they might invite willing individuals to engage in exploratory conversations, as part of a pedagogical and hermeneutic process, to discover with what meanings adults endow their own learning experiences. This could be enacted without having recourse to pre-designed explanatory frames of reference.

Unhappily, preconceived protocol statements and components associated with adults' independent learning projects have led to technocratic formulations such as the learning contract. Self-directed learning is now subsumed under an ideology of technique to the extent that many adult educators and learners (and, presumably, adult educators as learners) are prepared to accept, on expert authority, specific directions on how to manage, and how to be, self-directed leaners. *Techniques that enable us to be what we already are.* To facilitate the process, adult educators can deploy a fifty-eight item multiple choice instrument entitled the Self-Directed Learning Readiness Scale.[16]

Techniques that are associated with self-directed learning, such as the learning contract, are essentially accommodative to prevailing institutional and societal needs. The adult educator becomes the mediator in a negotiation process where prospects for a critical engagement with coercive institutional requirements are overridden by a necessary preoccupation with technical aspects of the self-directed learning artifact. As a mediating technique, the learning contract relentlessly steers the learning experience within normative institutional parameters. In public schools, the learning contract is often used as a virtually last ditch technique to normalize recalcitrant and lazy students before more clearcut punitive measures are brought to bear. Self-directed learning methods have been enthusiastically accepted by management in such institutions as the military and prisons where structures of surveillance, normalization, and control are readily apparent. As an accommodative device, self-directed learning as technique readily blends into such settings where a willingness by individuals to monitor their own behaviour adds to the efficient management of the organization. So self-directed learning has emerged within a profession of adult education as an aspect of a constraining or disciplinary technology which forges, in the words of Michel Foucault, a 'docile body, that may be subjected, used, transformed, and improved'.[17] Learning experiences shaped by self-directed learning methods are individualized in a way that ensures learners become wrapped up in their own *contracted* learning project and the mediated relationship moulded by a facilitator. The possibilities for rational discourse with others that can lead to a disclosure of distortions and various forms of dominance within the immediate institutional context of the learning project are unattainable via this technocratic mediation. Prospects for rational communicative discourse, and the communicative competence required, cannot be realized by merely prompting learners to share with others learning projects they have structured on an individualized basis along lines marked out by a designated facilitator. Definable limits to learning, essentially accommodative to institutional norms, will prevail whatever variations on deploying self-directed learning techniques are adopted. The medium serves to shape the nature of any pedagogical discourse as well as the learning project itself. Facilitating self-directed learning and using learning contracts come to mean, above all, serving institutional needs.

Of late, the methodology of self-directed learning has been conveniently harnessed to large scale and clearly prescriptive curriculum development projects such as competency-based adult education. Within the managed learning environment which such overarching curriculum designs foster, 'self-directed learning' is bandied around almost interchangeably with such terms as 'individualized learning', 'computer assisted learning', 'standardized coping skills', and so on. At this level, it requires no critical analysis to comprehend that facilitating adult learning really means managing adult learning.

Self-directed learning as technique, then, serves to condition the individual into taken-for-granted acceptance of what is offered. Through the medium of the learning contract, as with other systematic curriculum frameworks, a pattern of communication is shaped in which individual needs are sublimated to institutional interests. Adult educators who subscribe to self-directed learning as technique are not only collaborators in effecting this sublimation, they become willing collaborators. The apparatus of self-directed learning as part of an ideology of technique is all the more pernicious because it is accompanied by the expression of an ethical concern with autonomous decision-making. Having trespassed upon an instinctual dimension of people's everyday lives which incorporates a vital capacity for individual and community oriented learning initiatives, the professional adult educator has deployed on to it a pedagogical technique. The capacity for autonomous learning becomes artificially construed and is effectively undermined. A preoccupation with promoting the kind of technocratic ethos embodied in such devices as the learning contract and the Self-Directed Learning Readiness Scale serves to obstruct the possibility for understanding contradictions and seeing the way to rational alternatives. The self-directed learning contract becomes an artifice in the service of institutional interests.

The most recent perspective on self-directed learning described in the preceding paragraphs does, however, allude to some of the deleterious consequences that stem from an excessive preoccupation with technique. It emphasizes the need for facilitating in adult learners the capacity for critical thought that can identify ambiguities, contradictions, normative stipulations, and so on. It makes brief reference to the kind of adult education settings and approaches which offer at least the possibilities for a rational, emancipatory practice of adult education. [. . .]

The most recent perspective on self-directed learning does endeavour to pause from a preoccupation with facilitating the adult learner as paramount theme for a consideration of the adult educator's situation when it refers to 'building a critical philosophy of practice'.[18] Yet it is here that the relativistic disposition becomes most apparent. In the end the best that can be offered is that adult educators 'develop a thoughtful rationale to guide their practice'. (Any rationale? A different rationale for every adult setting or encounter?) A comforting certainty can be extracted from a relativistic orientation. It ensures that a penchant for facilitating critical analysis can always be rationalized at a level that does not disturb the prevailing matrix of power relations within any particular institutionalized setting. The critical analysis need never have a cutting edge.

In *Understanding and Facilitating Adult Learning*, Stephen Brookfield refers to 'three modes of knowing' (the technical, the emancipatory, and the communicative) identified by the social theorist Jürgen Habermas.[19] Further exploration of these 'modes of knowing' as analysed by Habermas would have formed the basis for a critical edge in the assessment of self-directed learning strategies. An adherence to the rationality of a technical mode, as exemplified in the deployment of self-directed learning contracts, entirely usurps the prospects for a genuinely emancipatory practice of adult education that could emerge from rational communicative discourse.

It is from Habermas's most recent analysis of communicative action, in which he presents the pursuit of emancipatory interests as a rational generalizable project, that the prospects for a non-technocratic and non-relativistic guide to adult education practice can begin to emerge. A mere disposition to facilitate critical thinking leaves undisturbed the accommodative, intrusive, and coercive effects of a technical rationality that tends to be sustained by self-directed learning methods. On the other hand, the concept of communicative action that has evolved from Jürgen Habermas's extensive on-going theoretical work provides the rational grounds for an emancipatory practice of adult education of a kind envisaged by the prominent adult educator Paulo Freire. Habermas posits an ideal speech situation as the context for practical, genuinely democratic decision-making among groups of people focusing on a common area of concern. Integral to the communicative process is a commitment to grappling with identifiable distortions and coercive structures that impede rational discourse. In this way, relevant courses of action which stem from genuine democratic discourse become achievable.

Admittedly, the concept of communicative action, substantiated by lengthy theoretical research, envisages circumstances that would be difficult to enact given the prevailing socio-economic and political structures, and the inadequate levels of communicative competence which it reveals. Yet it does provide a rational standard to guide, and to assess, emancipatory adult education endeavours that are already the hallmark of some adult education study circles, residential adult education centres, and Freirean cultural circles. Adult educators, then, can look to pedagogical arrangements like these as the key to a rational practice of adult education intent on dissociating itself from the indoctrination, distortions, and manipulations of instrumentalized communicative strategies such as self-directed learning contracts. It is important to stress, however, that the rationality underlying communicative action does support the appropriate incorporation of technique. Technique, though, is subordinated to practical emancipatory interests derived from rational discourse. It is not allowed to steer the educative (decision-making) process. Only as the individuals involved begin to interpret relevant dimensions of the problem at hand,[20] with all the constraints and opportunities that this brings to light, will the question of what technique to use, if any at all, enter the discourse.

Although we will be addressing alternative strategies that lead towards an emancipatory practice of adult education, in the present context it is not possible to achieve even a brief sketch of Habermas's theory of communicative action that does justice to the complex nature of his entire research programme. And it would be a mistake, a disservice to the on-going theoretical project, to suggest that somehow a fully fleshed out concept of communicative action should be enshrined as the new sterling principle for adult education practice and research. (That would be subscribing to the established pattern exemplified by the reification of self-directed learning.) What the theory of communicative action provides is access to a realm of rational discourse, nourished by aspirations to genuine participatory democratic action, in which adult education practice and research can meaningfully participate. While the advantages of technique, and the prospects for efficient action which stem from them, are acknowledged, a paramount concern with ethical and practical interests establishes a context where the deployment of any innovative technique is the occasion for critical assessment rather than taken-for-granted acceptance. The perennial issue of freedom (autonomy) versus contingency (heteronomy) cannot be foreclosed by mere pedagogical techniques even if they are delivered under such labels as 'self-directed learning', 'learning how to learn', 'self-teaching', and so on. But the conditions for a pedagogy emanating from rational discourse that holds emancipation as an ultimate human goal are accessible.

The way is open, then, for the construction of a rationale that can sustain emancipation, and all that it entails in terms of a participatory democracy of educated people, at the core of adult education practice. The working out of such a project could bring discomfort for thoughtful adult educators, since it would clearly mark out practices and viewpoints that are accommodative to manipulative pedagogical strategies, especially those that come wrapped in the terminology of a humanistic orientation.

As a matter of fact, adults have always managed to learn on their own. This is a truism that serves to give pause for thought only inasmuch as we have become beguiled by the notion that learning, properly so called, can be achieved only through the mediation of an expert. However, self-evident though it may seem, the observation sustains a spurious basis from which professional educators deploy techniques associated with self-directed learning.

Learning is by definition self-directed. It denotes individual experiencing constituted by intentional (purposive) acts directed towards specific objects or events. Clearly, for nearly all adults, capable of experiencing in some way the events and objects of their everyday world (including the thought processes of their own inner mental world), learning takes place all the time. Learning is always done by the person involved. No one actually learns for anyone else. In this sense, the term 'self-directed' as applied to learning becomes redundant. However, there is a paradox at work here in that learning cannot take place in a complete vacuum. We could never learn without, at some time or other, interaction with something or someone in our environment. Mediation of some kind is inevitable. So there is no contradiction in the notion that learners do their learning on their own and their being taught by a teacher.

Recourse to a teacher, when an adult or group of adults identify a need for instruction and expert guidance, is quite in keeping with the rationale underlying a concept of communicative action and can be envisaged without a strategy to transform the role of teacher to that of facilitator. In fact, the vocation of teaching can just as readily be presented as a non-didactic undertaking, oriented towards process rather than content and, what is more, it carries with it more of an ethical force than can be conveyed by the term facilitator. Martin Heidegger's description of the teacher's role is instructive in this regard:

Teaching is more difficult than learning because what teaching calls for is this: to let learn. The real teacher, in fact, lets nothing else be learned than learning. His [*sic*] conduct, therefore, often produces the impression that we learn nothing from him, if by 'learning' we now suddenly understand merely the procurement of useful knowledge.

The teacher is ahead of his apprentices in this alone, that he has still far more to learn than they – he has to learn to let them learn.[21]

[. . .]. Though many educators would no doubt want to see a concrete reference to the transmission of specific subject matter in any definition of a teacher's role, opting for terms such as 'self-directed learner' and 'facilitator' merely to draw a distinction between public schooling and adult education is unnecessary. Unhappily, this terminology does have serious implications in that it leads adult learners to believe that they are making free choices when, in effect, they are being manipulated via pedagogic (andragogic) techniques into an accommodation with institutionalized and professionalized interests.   [. . .]

If the tenor of the analysis has been somewhat iconoclastic, it is because the only observations to date on the shortcomings of self-directed learning provide a level of critique, from a relativistic perspective, that has managed to incorporate itself as just another developmental phase of the self-directed learning enterprise. While calling for critical thinking on behalf of adult learners, it steers away from any direct confrontation with the artifacts and practices which militate against genuine prospects of realizing such aims.

While this critique launched against self-directed learning strategies could benefit from the support of more tightly construed subsequent analyses, an unequivocal focus on emancipation as a core concern would seem to offer a more profitable venture for critical theoretical research and practical discourse in adult education. With such an orientation, adult education might even begin to effect some unambiguous movement towards the aspirations of Thomas Hodgskin, the early nineteenth century adult educator and political economist, for 'the education of a free people'.[22]

RESEARCH TO PRACTICE IN ADULT EDUCATION

The kind of technicist and pseudo-scientific orientations that characterize approaches to the structuring of self-directed learning endeavours are discernible in professionalized adult education research. 'Professionalized' in this context refers to the research journal publications and conference presentations of academics and university graduate students in the field of adult education.

Along with researchers in other branches of education – behavioural psychology (which has shaped much of educational research in recent decades) and empirical sociology – many academicians and students of adult education have been inclined to emulate what they take to be the methodological approaches of the natural sciences. They are mistaken. Natural phenomena manipulated and examined through experimentation are essentially different from the artificial constructs reified by educational researchers (for example, 'cognitive styles', 'life-stage', 'intelligence quotient') as operational definitions. These reified operational definitions are the inventions of the researchers. They represent *their* particular order of social reality. They bring with them an aura of artificiality as they are deployed in the arena of human experience. Endeavours to measure these reified concepts, and to demonstrate causal connections between them, represent an entirely different concern from that of scientists whose commitment is to manipulating and demonstrating causal connections between natural phenomena.   [. . .]

Until recently, the adult education enterprise has definitely bestowed favour on academics who stress technique and methodological approaches considered to be in line with conventional scientific research. Instead of opting for the relevance, 'largeness of conception and freshness of approach'[23] required for meaningful investigations of human action, many adult education researchers deploying an instrumental statistical mode have been more preoccupied with displaying methodological muscle. This preoccupation, most apparent among North American adult education researchers, is guided by a conviction that emphasis on technique and quantification legitimizes their work, since it somehow corresponds closely to the way natural scientists carry out their investigations. However, natural phenomena are of quite a different order from the artificial, psychologistic, operational definitions which adult educators following a statistical mode concoct for the purpose of measurement and methodological manipulation While these operational definitions (e.g. cognitive styles, learning readiness indicators, motivational orientations, competences, intelligence quotients, etc.) are artificially construed and represent the interests, the order of reality, of researchers rather than those of the researched, they carry with them an aura of authority that permits the researchers with their methodological concerns to intrude upon, and define, the everyday life of adults. In this way, research becomes an imposition, a further invasion of the threatened and private domain of the adult's everyday life-world so graphically described by Illich as 'the commons'. Adult education researchers who confidently deploy techniques they believe to be based on the natural sciences foreclose on the prospects for responsive, sensitively construed, research that emerge relevantly to address problems conceived in a context of human interaction. They have sustained an ideology of technique which informs the way a great many adult educators go about needs assessment, instructional design, programme planning and evaluation, as well as the way they conceive of such burgeoning and profitable enterprises as continuing professional education and human resource development. Adult education becomes justified as technique, artificially and, often, coercively applied, rather than emancipatory practice.

More recently (since the early 1980s), the pre-eminence given in North American adult education to what is thought to be a natural science paradigm has subsided somewhat, more recognition being given to research studies of a qualitative and historical nature. While much of the former, under the rubric of such labels as grounded theory and naturalistic inquiry, is still bound in by methodological protocols and reified categories that restrict its investigative potential as human science, the signs are promising that the artificiality and intrusive characteristics associated with the deployment of a natural science paradigm in adult education can be viewed as problematic and resisted. Moreover, renewed interest in the history of adult education, especially when it is not confined to the mere chronicling of dates, facts, and events, is further reason for optimism that the foundations for an emancipatory practice of adult education can be retrieved from the technocratic framework of much that passes for modern practice. Technicist orientations, with their simplistic how-to formulations, tend to be non-reflective and decidedly ahistorical; that is, they are characterized by a general view that it is pointless to reflect and harp on the past. Carefully researched historical accounts of important adult education initiatives that have been overlooked to date are crucial to countering the narrowness of current technicist preoccupations in research and practice. The prevalence of the latter serves to obscure a necessity for critical reflection and analysis to conceptualize adult education as an emancipatory field of practice.

Outside the North American context a preoccupation with methodology, especially empirical – statistical technique, is not nearly so pronounced in the academic publications of adult education. Academic publication in Britain, for instance, is informed by historical, philosophical, and sociological orientations. It includes exemplary studies which attempt to combine practical relevance, originality, and an appropriate level of concern for method. From the perspective of some methodologically oriented North American researchers, however, much of this research takes the form of overly discursive, if exquisitely written, essays.

A somewhat marginalized alternative to the natural science paradigm has been apparent for some time in the work of a few adult educators whose practice involves participatory research.[24] The claims of critics that participatory research is nothing more than a relevant approach to community development merit consideration,[25] but do not serve to undermine the paramount concern of participatory research that researchers should not impose their own clearly identified investigative problems and categories on groups of other people while adopting the posture of detached scientific observers themselves. Participatory researchers envisage themselves as facilitators or 'animateurs' of a learning (research) process where new knowledge is created to address problems identified by community groups who also have a large say in determining the shape of research reports. Although the actual findings and reports of participatory research undertakings do not readily lend themselves to the formats of professional journals and research conference proceedings, they have constituted a form of rational resistance, in accordance with espoused adult education principles, to the intrusiveness and artificiality of conventional research. It is, perhaps, unfortunate that the original proponents launched participatory research on the field as a radical and new approach to research rather than as a form of action anthropology[26] that was already a somewhat more widely accepted genre of scientific research. The focus could then have been more on how well such research is done in helping adults learn to improve their circumstances rather than on whether or not it constitutes a legitimated research approach. After all, the emphasis of participatory research on the contextual relevance of problems identified within a community, and on reporting in terms that are acceptable to the subjects themselves, have long since been a matter of concern for anthropological research. Given the natural inclination to scepticism on the part of the research community, it was probably not fruitful to invoke a new research methodology that, to all intents and purposes, corresponds to an already established approach to research in the human sciences.

Sallie Westwood's article 'Learning and working: a study of women on the shopfloor'[27] is worthy of note here. It is informed by her background as an anthropologist as well as her commitment to adult education for social change and to the need for a researcher to share, in a significant way, the everyday experience of the people studied. Westwood's research was supported by a year's work on the shop floor. Although it is well theorized, she demonstrated that her research is not just a matter of theoretical analysis.

More academics in the field of adult education are beginning to recognize the prospects of non-empirical investigations, exploratory studies, and interpretative work as relevant approaches to research. Among the most promising studies of these research initiatives are those that draw on the disciplines of phenomenology and hermeneutics. Although a few studies along these lines have appeared in recent editions of the major research journals and as part of published conference proceedings,[28] they do not lend themselves conveniently to the standardized formats of these major outlets. Further, they tend to be more difficult to read than the usual fare prepared for adult educators.

Yet phenomenological perspectives can add significantly to adult education research and practice, since leading phenomenological concepts and orientations are very much akin to the major concerns and principles of adult education.[29] Further, philosophical phenomenology and hermeneutics provide the theoretical foundations for qualitative and interpretative studies as a vital human science free from the artificial restrictions of a technicist enterprise supposedly based on a natural science paradigm.

From phenomenology and hermeneutics adult education researchers can derive a rational basis for critical theory which has suddenly caught on, somewhat belatedly, among adult education academics in some quarters, as the poverty of reductionistic, or psychologistic, statistically possessed research becomes more apparent. Contemporary critical theory is associated with the Frankfurt School which emerged in Germany during the 1920s as a research centre for left wing, middle class, intellectuals who were profoundly disillusioned with Moscow's version of state communism and alarmed at the rising spectre of fascism.

In contrast to existing social science, critical theory aims to go beyond merely describing what is (an important enough task in itself, of course) to setting out what ought to be. This is to be realized through the unmasking and analysis of contradictions within the existing social structures. Herbert Marcuse, in the opening paragraph of *An Essay on Liberation*, offered an overall definition of critical theory within which the chief exponents felt it could sustain its scientific character:

> By logical inference from the prevailing conditions and institutions, critical theory may also be able to determine the basic institutional changes which are the prerequisites for the transition to a higher stage of development: 'higher' in the sense of a more rational and equitable use of resources, minimization of destructive conflicts, and enlargement of the realm of freedom.[30]

A touch utopian, perhaps, but surely not out of line with the primary commitments of adult education. And, unlike some of the recent adult educational writing informed by one kind of critical theorizing or another, it does hold out the possibility for social change as well as theoretical critique.   [. . .]

Exploratory and interpretative studies, which do not allow us to take prevailing political, socio-economic circumstances for granted, and critical analyses call for more nerve on the part of adult educators, especially those working in agencies which constitute formal adult education, than hitherto. Unlike adult education studies which purport to adopt a neutral stance supposedly based on natural science and avoid calling into question the motivating forces and structures sustaining modern political economies, they cut emphatically across the grain of contemporary society. However subtle may be the educational strategies which emerge from such research, a price will be exacted from those who endeavour to put the recommendations into practice.

If rational discourse alone cannot alter existing power relations (and this in itself does point to a relevant role for adult educators), the theoretical and empirical work of the most recent and pre-eminent critical theorist, Jürgen Habermas, though not without its critics among contemporary sociologists and social theorists, could well provide a very significant reference point for adult educators committed to emancipatory practice and to research that is not totally under the sway of instrumental reasoning. Jürgen Habermas's carefully worked out notion of communicative action as we have described, envisages consensual interactions between adults, free of coercive elements and various forms of distortion, that lead to decision-making based on rational discourse. (In view of the way an ideology of technique, or cult of efficiency, entices us into taking for granted elements of coercion and distortions of communication in our everyday lives, the educative task envisaged is a formidable one.) The theoretical underpinnings of Habermas's notion of communicative action can be brought to bear on the pedagogy of adult educator Paulo Freire, which merits further analysis, and needs retrieving entirely from the transfigurations of those professional educators who have packaged it for American consumption.

In bringing both the chapter and this discussion on adult education research to a close, it is appropriate to tie in again to one of the concepts addressed by Ivan Illich. Illich draws a distinction between research *in* education and *on* education.[31] Research *in* education, the prevalent paradigm, is conducted by the professionalized expert who defines the problems to be researched as well as the methodologies and the nature of the discourse through which they will be addressed. The professionalized concerns of the educator take centre stage, with any other critical concerns, emanating perhaps unpredictably from community needs, as supporting cast. In this way, the professional educators' definitions of needs to be satisfied and outcomes to be achieved become a legitimized paramount reality, which is only reinforced by psychologized strategies under the rubric of self-directed learning. Thus vernacular (non-professionalized) learning is debased. Until they can be defined according to the normative criteria of the professionalized educator, such vital initiatives as home schooling, self-help groups, and non-formal adult education which seek to retrieve, and preserve, vernacular values are viewed by the experts as either idiosyncratic or as the preserve of a privileged minority. To the extent that such initiatives are defined according to criteria of conventional research and professionalized practice, they become institutionalized and more amenable to bureaucratic interventions. It is not surprising and, in view of our theme, to some extent heartening, that researchers following conventional research designs often encounter resistance, or studied non-cooperation, when intruding upon the kind of voluntaristic initiatives that connect us to vernacular values.

Research *on* education, on the other hand, envisages a less narrowly defined, professionalized, orientation to research and practice. Rather than placing the institutions of professionalized practice and the concerns of the professionalized expert at the centre of research projects, research *on* education endeavours to 'relate the spheres of education, health, welfare, research, finance, economics, politics'.[32] It is not confined to licensed experts (those with doctorates in one or other of the pedagogical disciplines, for example) and eschews prescriptions in favour of any particular research paradigm to the exclusion of others. Research *on* education acknowledges the interconnectedness between research and practice, drawing no hard-and-fast lines (which is *not* the same thing as relinquishing rigorous and recognizable standards) between the two, and inviting educators to reflect carefully on what it is they do and what it is they are, without recourse to the constructs, constraints, and basic assumptions of professionalized pedagogues. This calls for a continuing reflection on everyday educational practice and its relevant implications for people acting· within the various contexts identified in preceding paragraphs. The kind of thoughtful commitment required is not to be found in the technocratic stipulations of a professionalized pedagogy characterized by contracts for self-directed learning, formal needs assessments, instructional design, behavioural objectives, centralized curriculum formats, and protocols for communication through bureaucratically determined channels. It resides, rather, in a sense of vocation that forms the basis of a rational and emancipatory practice of adult education.

The obsession with technique, or technical rationality, has induced modern adult education to evade serious engagement with critical, ethical, and political issues. It has effectively sidelined adult education as a social movement and supports initiatives that tend to de-skill the practitioner's pedagogical role. Thus, the distinctiveness of adult education as a field of practice has been seriously eroded. Therein lies the deepening crisis. A renewed sense of vocation in adult education is invoked as a prelude to the orchestration of technique on a more humane scale and for the shaping of a genuinely reflective, emancipatory practice.

NOTES AND REFERENCES

1 In *The Modern Practice of Adult Education: From Pedagogy to Andragogy* (New York: Cambridge, 1980), Malcolm Knowles connects the notion of self-directed learning to the idea of *andragogy* first advanced by Eduard Lindeman in 1927 as 'the true method of adult learning' (Brookfield, *Learning Democracy: Eduard Lindeman on Adult Education and Social Change*, Croom Helm, Beckenham, Kent, 1987, p. 27.). Knowles has presented a method of adult learning (andragogy) as an array of techniques in *Self-directed Learning: A Guide for Learners and Teacher* (New York: Cambridge, 1980).

2 After all, some school teachers do aspire to take into account the experience of their students and recognize the need to encourage self-directedness.

3 W. Draves, *The Free University: A Model for Lifelong Learning* (Chicago: Association Press, 1980), p. 191.

4 M. Knowles, *The Adult Learner: A Neglected Species* (Houston, Texas: Gulf Publishing, 1973), p. 45.

5 S. Brookfield, 'Self-directed learning: a conceptual and methodological orientation', *Studies in the Education of Adults*, vol. 17, no. 1: April 1986, 19–31.

6 A. Tough, *Learning Without a Teacher: A Study of Tasks and Assistance during Adult Self-teaching Projects* (Toronto: Ontario Institute for Studies in Education, 1981), p. iv.

7 M. Knowles, *The Adult Learner: A Neglected Species; The Modern Practice of Adult Education; Self-directed Learning: A Guide for Learners and Teachers* (New York: Cambridge Book Co., 1980).

8 M. Knowles, *Using Learning Contracts: Practical Approaches to Individualizing and Structuring Learning* (San Francisco: Jossey-Bass, 1986).

9 S. Brookfield, *Learning Democracy: Eduard Lindeman on Adult Education and Social Change*, p. 27.

10 S. Brookfield (ed.), *Self-directed Learning: From Theory to Practice*, and *Understanding and Facilitating Adult Learning* (San Francisco: Jossey-Bass, 1985).

11 S. Brookfield, *Understanding and Facilitating Adult Learning*, p. 284.

12 S. Brookfield, p. 287.

13 I. Illich, 'Silence is a commons', *Co-Evolution Quarterly*, winter, 1983, p. 6.

14 I. Illich, *Tools for Conviviality* (New York: Harper & Row, 1973). See also 'Vernacular values and education', *Teachers College Record*, vol. 81, no. 1, 1979.

15 J. Habermas, *Toward a Rational Society: Student Protest, Science, and Politics* (Boston, Mass.: Beacon Press, 1971), p. 53.

16 L. and P. Guglielmino, *Learning Style Assessment* (Boca Raton, Fla.: Guglielmino & Associates, 1982).

17 M. Foucault, *Discipline and Punish* (New York: Vintage Books, 1979), p. 198.

18 S. Brookfield, *Understanding and Facilitating Adult Learning*, pp. 287–90.

19 S. Brookfield, p. 115.

20 M. Collins, *Competence in Adult Education: A New Perspective* (Lanham, Md: University Press of America, 1987), pp. 4–12.

21 M. Heidegger, *What Is Called Thinking?* (New York: Harper & Row, 1968), p. 15.

22 Thomas Hodgskin tied his aspirations for an emancipatory pedagogy to the mechanics' institutes which increased in number throughout Britain at an impressive rate during the 1820s and 1830s. See M. Collins, 'The Mechanics' Institutes – education for the working man?' *Adult Education: Journal of Research and Theory*, vol. xxiii, no. 1, 1972, pp. 37–47.

23 C. Houle, 'Ends and means in adult education research', *Adult Education*, **12**, (4) 1962, p. 218.

24 Budd Hall of the International Council for Adult Education was largely responsible for bringing participatory research to the attention of adult educators. He has published a number of papers on the subject. Perhaps the most relevant in this context is 'Participatory research: breaking the academic monopoly', in J. Niemi (Ed.), *Viewpoints on Adult Education Research* (Columbus, Ohio: ERIC Clearing House, 1979), pp. 43–71. ICAE in Ontario has printed a number of papers on participatory research projects and an annotated bibliography of 100 articles, books, and essays covering Africa, Asia, Europe, Latin American, and North America.

25 W. Griffith, 'Participatory research: should it be a new methodology for adult educators?' in J. Niemi (ed.), *Viewpoints on Adult Education Research*, pp. 15–42.

26 See, for example, S. Tax, 'The people versus the system – dialogue in urban conflict', in *Proceedings, Community Service Workshop* (Chicago: Acme Press, 1969), and *Horizons of Anthropology* (Chicago: Aldine Publishers, 1964).

27 S. Westwood, 'Learning and working: a study of women on the shopfloor', *Studies in the Education of Adults*, 16, October 1984, pp. 3–20.

28 See, for example, M. Collins, 'Major Constituents of Two Successful Prison Education Programs: A Phenomenological Study', and S. Stanage, 'Learning How to Learn: A Phenomenological Analysis of Adult Educative Learning', *Adult Education Research Conference Proceedings* (New York: Syracuse University Press, 1986), pp. 66–72, 267–73. Examples of studies on hermeneutics include A. Chené, 'Hermeneutics and the Educational Narrative', and A. Chené, M. Collins and J. Theil, 'The Relevance of Hermeneutics for Research and Practice in Adult Education', *Adult Education Research Conference Proceedings* (Tempe, Ariz.: Arizona State University Press, 1985), pp. 76–81 and 96–108. For a text on phenomenology in adult education, refer to S. Stanage, *Adult Education and Phenomenological Research* (Malabar, Fla.: Krieger, 1987).

29 M. Collins, 'Phenomenological perspectives: some implications for adult education', in S. Merriam (ed.), *Selected Writings on Philosophy and Adult Education* (Malabar, Fla.: Krieger, 1984), pp. 179–89.

30 H. Marcuse, *An Essay on Liberation* (Boston, Mass.: Beacon Press, 1969), p. 3.

31 I. Illich, 'Vernacular values and education', pp. 72–4.

32 I. Illich, p. 73.

Chapter 7

Freire and a feminist pedagogy of difference†

Kathleen Weiler

We are living in a period of profound challenges to traditional Western epistemology and political theory. These challenges, couched in the language of postmodernist theory and in postcolonialist critiques, reflect the rapid transformation of the economic and political structure of the world order: the impact of transnational capital; the ever more comprehensive integration of resources, labour, and markets; the pervasiveness of media and consumer images. This interdependent world system is based on the exploitation of oppressed groups, but the system at the same time calls forth oppositional cultural forms that give voice to the conditions of these groups. White male bourgeois dominance is being challenged by people of colour, women, and other oppressed groups, who assert the validity of their own knowledge and demand social justice and equality in numerous political and cultural struggles. A major theoretical challenge to traditional Western knowledge systems is emerging from feminist theory, which has been increasingly influenced by both postmodernist and cultural-identity theory. Feminist theory, like other contemporary approaches, validates difference, challenges universal claims to truth, and seeks to create social transformation in a world of shifting and uncertain meanings.

In education, these profound shifts are evident on two levels: first, at the level of practice, as excluded and formerly silenced groups challenge dominant approaches to learning and to definitions of knowledge; and second, at the level of theory, as modernist claims to universal truth are called into question.[1] These challenges to accepted truths have been raised not only to the institutions and theories that defend the status quo, but also to the critical or liberatory pedagogies that emerged in the 1960s and 1970s. Feminist educational critics want to retain the vision of social justice and transformation that underlies liberatory pedagogies, but they find that their claims to universal truths and their assumptions

† This is an edited version of an article that appeared in *Harvard Educational Review*, vol. 61(4) 1991.

of a collective experience of oppression do not adequately address the realities of their own confusing and often tension-filled classrooms. This consciousness of the inadequacy of classical liberatory pedagogies has been particularly true for feminist educators, who are acutely aware of the continuing force of sexism and patriarchal structures and of the power of race, sexual preference, physical ability, and age to divide teachers from students and students from one another.

Paulo Freire is without question the most influential theorist of critical or liberatory education. His theories have profoundly influenced literacy programmes throughout the world and what has come to be called critical pedagogy in the United States. His theoretical works, particularly *Pedagogy of the Oppressed*, provide classic statements of liberatory or critical pedagogy based on universal claims of truth.[2] Feminist pedagogy as it has developed in the US provides a historically situated example of a critical pedagogy in practice. Feminist conceptions of education are similar to Freire's pedagogy in a variety of ways, and feminist educators often cite Freire as the educational theorist who comes closest to the approach and goals of feminist pedagogy.[3] Both feminist pedagogy as it is usually defined and Freirean pedagogy rest upon visions of social transformation: underlying both are certain common assumptions concerning oppression, consciousness, and historical change. Both pedagogies assert the existence of oppression in people's material conditions of existence and as a part of consciousness; both rest on a view of consciousness as more than a sum of dominating discourses, but as containing within it a critical capacity – what Antonio Gramsci called 'good sense'; and both thus see human beings as subjects and actors in history and hold a strong commitment to justice and a vision of a better world and of the potential for liberation.[4] These ideals have powerfully influenced teachers and students in a wide range of educational settings, both formal and informal.

But in action, the goals of liberation or opposition to oppression have not always been easy to understand or achieve. As universal goals, these ideals do not address the specificity of people's lives; they do not directly analyse the contradictions between conflicting oppressed groups or the ways in which a single individual can experience oppression in one sphere while being privileged or oppressive in another. Feminist and Freirean teachers are in many ways engaged in challenging accepted meanings and relationships that occur at 'political or more often micropolitical' levels. But in attempting to challenge dominant values, feminist and Freirean teachers raise conflicts for themselves and for their students, who also are historically situated and whose own subjectivities are often contradictory and in process. Attempting to implement these pedagogies without acknowledging the conflict not only of divided consciousness but also the conflicts among groups trying to work together to name and struggle against oppression – among teachers and students in classrooms, or among political groups working for change in very specific areas – can lead to anger, frustration, and a retreat to safer or more traditional approaches.[5] The numerous accounts of the tensions of trying to put liberatory pedagogies into practice demonstrate the need to reexamine the assumptions of the classic texts of liberatory pedagogy and to consider the various issues that have arisen in attempts at critical and liberatory classroom practice.[6]

As a White feminist writing and teaching from the traditions of both critical pedagogy and feminist theory, these issues are of particular concern to me. In this chapter I examine and critique the classic liberatory pedagogy of Paulo Freire, particularly as it is presented in *Pedagogy of the Oppressed*. I then examine the development and practice of feminist pedagogy, which emerged in a particular historical and political moment in the US, and which provides an example of some of the difficulties of putting these ideals into practice and suggests at the same time some possible theoretical and practical directions for liberatory pedagogies in general. I argue that an exploration of the conflicts and concerns that have arisen for feminist teachers attempting to put into practice their versions of a feminist pedagogy can help enrich and re-envision Freirean goals of liberation and social progress. This emerging pedagogy does not reject the goals of justice – the end of oppression, and liberation – but frames them more specifically in the context of historically defined struggles and calls for the articulation of interests and identity on the part of teacher and theorist as well as student. This approach questions whether the oppressed cannot act also as oppressors and challenges the idea of a commonality of oppression. It raises questions about common experience as a source of knowledge, the pedagogical authority of the teacher, and the nature of political and pedagogical struggle.

THE PEDAGOGY OF PAULO FREIRE

Freire's pedagogy developed in particular historical and political circumstances of neocolonialism and imperialism. Freire's methods developed originally from his work with peasants in Brazil and later in Chile and Guinea–Bissau.[7] Freire's thought thus needs to be understood in the context of the political and economic situation of the developing world. In Freire's initial formulation, oppression was conceived in class terms and education was viewed in the context of peasants' and working people's revolutionary struggles. Equally influential in Freire's thought and pedagogy were the influence of radical Christian thought and the revolutionary role of liberation theology in Latin America. Freire's pedagogy is thus founded on a moral imperative to side with the oppressed that emerges from both his Christian faith and his knowledge and experience of suffering in the society in which he grew up and lived. Freire has repeatedly stated that his pedagogical method cannot simply be transferred to other settings, but that each historical site requires the development of a pedagogy appropriate to that setting. In his most recent work, he has also addressed sexism and racism as systems of oppression that must be considered as seriously as class oppression.[8] His most commonly read text still is his first book to be published in English, *Pedagogy of the Oppressed*. In this classic text, Freire presents the epistemological basis for his pedagogy and discusses the concepts of oppression, conscientization, and dialogue that are at the heart of his pedagogical project, both as he enacted it in settings in the developing world and as it has been appropriated by radical teachers in other settings.

Freire organizes his approach to liberatory pedagogy in terms of a dualism between the oppressed and the oppressors and between humanization and dehumanization. This organization of thought in terms of opposing forces reflects Freire's own experiences of literacy work with the poor in Brazil, a situation in which the lines between oppressor and oppressed were clear. For Freire, humanization is the goal of liberation; it has not yet been achieved, nor can it be achieved so long as the oppressors oppress the oppressed. That is, liberation and humanization will not occur if the roles of oppressor and oppressed are simply reversed.

> Because it is a distortion of being more fully human, sooner or later being less human leads the oppressed to struggle against those who made them so. In order for this struggle to have meaning, the oppressed must not, in seeking to regain their humanity (which is a way to create it), become in turn oppressors of the oppressors, but rather restorers of the humanity of both.[9]

The struggle against oppression leading to humanization is thus utopian and visionary. [...] Freire presents a theoretical justification for a pedagogy that aims to critique existing forms of oppression and to transform the world, thereby creating new ways of being, or humanization.

Radical educators throughout the world have used *Pedagogy of the Oppressed* as the theoretical justification for their work. As an eloquent and impassioned statement of the need for and possibility of change through reading the world and the word, there is no comparable contemporary text.[10] But when we look at *Pedagogy of the Oppressed* from the perspective of recent feminist theory and pedagogy, certain problems arise that may reflect the difficulties that have sometimes arisen when Freire's ideas are enacted in specific settings. The challenges of recent feminist theory do not imply rejection of Freire's goals for what he calls pedagogy for liberation; feminists certainly share Freire's emphasis on seeing human beings as the subjects and not the objects of theory. A critical feminist rereading of Freire, however, points to ways in which the project of Freirean pedagogy, like that of feminist pedagogy, may be enriched and re-envisioned.

From a feminist perspective, *Pedagogy of the Oppressed* is striking in its use of the male referent, a usage that was universal in the 1960s, when this book was written.[11] Much more troublesome, however, is the abstract quality of terms such as humanization, which do not address the particular meanings imbued by men and women, Black and White, or other groups. The assumption of *Pedagogy of the Oppressed* is that in struggling against oppression, the oppressed will move toward true humanity. But this leaves unaddressed the forms of oppression experienced by different actors, the possibility of struggles among people oppressed differently by different groups. This assumption also presents humanization as a universal, without considering the various definitions this term may bring forth from people of different groups. As Freire writes. 'Their ideal is to be men; but for them, to be men is to be oppressors. This is their model of humanity'.[12] What is troubling here is not that 'men' is used for human beings, but that the model of oppressor implied here is based on the immediate oppressor of men – in this case, bosses over peasants or workers. What is not addressed is the possibility of simultaneous contradictory positions of oppression and dominance: the man oppressed by his boss could at the same time oppress his wife, for example, or the White woman oppressed by sexism could exploit the Black woman. By framing his discussion in such abstract terms, Freire slides over the contradictions and tensions within social settings in which overlapping forms of oppression exist.

This usage of 'the oppressed' in the abstract also raises difficulties in Freire's use of experience as the means of acquiring a radical literacy, 'reading the world and the word'. At the heart of Freire's pedagogy is the insistence that all people are subjects and knowers of the world. Their political literacy will emerge from their reading of the world – that is, their own experience. This reading will lead to collective knowledge and action. But what if that experience is divided? What if different truths are discovered in reading the world from different positions? [. . .] The nature of their perception of the world and their oppression is implicitly assumed to be uniform for all the oppressed. The possibility of a contradictory experience of oppression among the oppressed is absent. [. . .]

The assumption again is that the oppressed are submerged in a common situation of oppression, and that their shared knowledge of that oppression will lead them to collective action.

Central to Freire's pedagogy is the practice of conscientization; that is, coming to a consciousness of oppression and a commitment to end that oppression. Conscientization is based on this common experience of oppression. Through this reading of the world, the oppressed will come to knowledge. The role of the teacher in this process is to instigate a dialogue between teacher and student, based on their common ability to know the world and to act as subjects in the world. But the question of the authority and power of the teacher, particularly those forms of power based on the teacher's subject position as raced, classed, gendered, and so on is not addressed by Freire. There is, again, the assumption that the teacher is 'on the same side' as the oppressed, and that as teachers and students engage together in a dialogue about the world, they will uncover together the same reality, the same oppression, and the same liberation. [. . .] In fact, of course, teachers are not abstract: they are women or men of particular races, classes, ages, abilities, and so on. The teacher will be seen and heard by students not as an abstraction, but as a particular person with a certain defined history and relationship to the world. In a later book, Freire argues that the teacher has to assume authority, but must do so without becoming authoritarian. [. . .]

Freire acknowledges the power of the teacher by virtue of the structural role of 'teacher' within a hierarchical institution and, under the best of circumstances, by virtue of the teacher's greater experience and knowledge. But Freire does not go on to investigate what the other sources of 'antagonism' in the classroom might be. However much he provides a valuable guide to the use of authority by the liberatory teacher, he never addresses the question of other forms of power held by the teacher by virtue of race, gender, or class that may lead to antagonisms. Without recognizing more clearly the implicit power and limitations of the position of teacher, calls for a collective liberation or for opposition to oppression slide over the surface of the tensions that may emerge among teachers and students as subjects with conflicting interests and histories and with different kinds of knowledge and power. A number of questions are thus left unaddressed in *Pedagogy of the Oppressed*: How are we to situate ourselves in relation to the struggles of others? How are we to address our own contradictory positions as oppressors and oppressed? Where are we to look for liberation when our collective 'reading of the world' reveals contradictory and conflicting experiences and struggles? [. . .]

Calling into question the universal and abstract claims of *Pedagogy of the Oppressed* is certainly not to argue that Freire's pedagogy should be rejected or discarded. The ethical stance of Freire in terms of praxis and his articulation of people's worth and ability to know and change the world are an essential basis for radical pedagogies in opposition to oppression. Freire's thought illuminates the central question of political action in the world increasingly without universals. [...] But in order better to seek the affirmation of our own humanity and to seek to end suffering and oppression, I am arguing for a more situated theory of oppression and subjectivity, and for the need to consider the contradictions of such universal claims of truth or process.

In the next section of this chapter I explore feminist pedagogy as an example of a situated pedagogy of liberation. Like Freirean pedagogy, feminist pedagogy is based on assumptions of the power of consciousness raising, the existence of oppression and the possibility of ending it, and the desire for social transformation. But in its historical development, feminist pedagogy has revealed the shortcomings that emerge in the attempt to enact a pedagogy that assumes a universal experience and abstract goals. In the attempt of feminist pedagogy to address these issues, a more complex vision of a liberatory pedagogy is being developed and explored.

FEMINIST PEDAGOGY, CONSCIOUSNESS RAISING, AND WOMEN'S LIBERATION

Feminist pedagogy has developed in conjunction with the growth of women's studies and what is inclusively called 'the new scholarship on women'. These developments within universities – the institutionalization of women's studies as programmes and departments and the challenge to existing canons and disciplines by the new scholarship on women and by feminist theory – are reflected in the classroom teaching methods that have come to be loosely termed feminist pedagogy. Defining exactly what feminist pedagogy means in practice, however, is difficult. It is easier to describe the various methods used in specific women's studies courses and included by feminist teachers claiming the term feminist pedagogy than it is to provide a coherent definition.[13] But common to the claims of feminist teachers is the goal of providing students with the skills to continue political work as feminists after they have left the university.

The pedagogy of feminist teachers is based on certain assumptions about knowledge, power, and political action that can be traced beyond the academy to the political activism of the women's movement in the 1960s. Women's studies at the university level have since come to encompass a wide variety of political stances and theoretical approaches. Socialist feminism, liberal feminism, radical feminism, and postmodern feminism all view issues from their different perspectives. Nonetheless, feminist pedagogy continues to echo the struggles of its origins and to retain a vision of social activism. Virtually all women's studies courses and programmes at least partially reflect this critical, oppositional, and activist stance, even within programmes now established and integrated into the bureaucratic structures of university life. [. . .] Despite tensions and splits within feminism at a theoretical level and in the context of women's studies programmes in universities, the political commitment of women's liberation continues to shape feminist pedagogy. Thus, like Freirean pedagogy, feminist pedagogy is grounded in a vision of social change. And, like Freirean pedagogy, feminist pedagogy rests on truth claims of the primacy of experience and consciousness that are grounded in historically situated social change movements. Key to understanding the methods and epistemological claims of feminist pedagogy is an understanding of its origins in more grassroots political activity, particularly in the consciousness-raising groups of the women's liberation movement of the late 1960s and early 1970s.

Women's consciousness-raising groups began to form more or less spontaneously in northeastern and western US cities in late 1967 among White women who had been active in the civil rights and new left movements.[14] In a fascinating parallel to the rise of the women's suffrage movement out of the abolitionist movement in the mid-nineteenth century, these activist and politically committed women came to apply the universal demands for equality and justice of the civil rights movement to their own situation as women.[15] The unique organizational basis for the women's liberation movement was grounded in the small groups of women who came together for what came to be known as consciousness raising. Early consciousness-raising groups, based on friendship and common political commitments, focused on the discussion of shared experiences of sexuality, work, family, and participation in the male-dominated left political movement. Consciousness raising focused on collective political change rather than on individual therapy. The groups were unstructured and local – they could be formed anywhere and did not follow formal guidelines – but they used the same sorts of methods because these methods addressed common problems [. . .]

Perhaps the clearest summary of consciousness raising from this period can be found in Kathie Sarachild's essay, 'Consciousness raising: a radical weapon'.[16] [. . .] Fundamental to Sarachild's description of consciousness raising is its grounding in the need for political action. She describes the emergence of the method of consciousness raising among a group of women who considered themselves radicals in the sense of demanding fundamental changes in society. [. . .] A second fundamental aspect of consciousness raising is the reliance on experience and feeling. According to Sarachild, the focus on examining women's own experience came from a profound distrust of accepted authority and truth. These claims about what was valuable and true tended to be accepting of existing assumptions about women's 'inherent nature' and 'proper place'. In order to call those truths into question (truths we might now call hegemonic and that Foucault, for example, would tie to structures of power), women had nowhere to turn except to their own experience. Sarachild describes the process in her group:

> In the end the group decided to raise its consciousness by studying women's lives by topics like childhood, jobs, motherhood, etc. We'd do any outside reading we wanted to and thought was important. But our starting point for discussion, as well as our test of the accuracy of what any of the books said, would be the actual experience we had in these areas.[17]

The last aspect of consciousness raising was a common sharing of experience in a collective, leaderless group. As Michelle Russell points out, this sharing is similar to the practice of 'testifying' in the Black church, and depends upon openness and trust in the group.[18] The assumption underlying this sharing of stories was the existence of commonality among women: as Sarachild puts it, 'we made the assumption, an assumption basic to consciousness raising, that most women were like ourselves – not different[19] [. . .]

Consciousness raising shared the assumptions of earlier revolutionary traditions: that understanding and theoretical analysis were the first steps to revolutionary change, and that neither was adequate alone; theory and practice were intertwined as praxis. As Sarachild puts it, 'Consciousness raising was seen as both a method for arriving at the truth and a means for action and organizing'.[20] What was original in consciousness raising, however, was its emphasis on experience and feeling as the guide to theoretical understanding, an approach that reflected the realities of women's socially defined subjectivities and the conditions of their lives. 'When we think of what it is that politicizes people it is not so much books or ideas but experience'.[21]

While Sarachild and other early feminists influenced by a left political tradition explored the creation of theory grounded in women's feelings and experiences, they never lost the commitment to social transformation.[22] In their subsequent history, however, consciousness raising and feminist pedagogy did not always retain this political commitment to action. As the women's movement expanded to reach wider groups of women, consciousness raising tended to lose its commitment to revolutionary change. This trend seems to have been particularly true as the women's movement affected women with a less radical perspective and with little previous political involvement. Without a vision of collective action and social transformation, consciousness raising held the possibility of what Berenice Fisher calls 'a diversion of energies into an exploration of feelings and "private" concerns to the detriment of political activism'.[23] The lack of structure and the local nature of consciousness-raising groups only reinforced these tendencies toward a focus on individual rather than collective change. The one site in which the tradition of consciousness raising did find institutional expression was in academia, in the growth of women's studies courses and programmes stimulated by the new scholarship on women. The founders of these early courses and programmes tended to be politically committed feminists who themselves had experienced consciousness raising and who, like Friere, assumed that education could and should be a means of social change.

The first women's studies courses, reflecting the growth of the women's movement in what has come to be called the second wave of feminism, were taught in the late 1960s.[24] [. . .] By the late 1980s, respected journals such as *Signs* and *Feminist Studies* were well established, and women's studies programmes and courses were widespread (if not always enthusiastically supported by administrations) in colleges and universities.[25] At the same time, feminist research and theory – what has come to be called 'the new scholarship on women' – put forth a profound challenge to traditional disciplines.[26] The growth of women's studies programmes and feminist scholarship thus provided an institutional framework and theoretical underpinning for feminist pedagogy, the attempt to express feminist values and goals in the classroom. But while feminist scholarship has presented fundamental challenges to traditional androcentric knowledge, the attempt to create a new pedagogy modelled on consciousness raising has not been as successful or coherent a project. Serious challenges to the goal of political transformation through the experience of feminist learning have been raised in the attempt to create a feminist pedagogy in the academy. The difficulties and contradictions that have emerged in the attempt to create a feminist pedagogy in traditional institutions such as universities raise serious questions for all liberatory pedagogies and echo some of the problems raised by the unitary and universal approach of *Pedagogy of the Oppressed*. But in engaging these questions, feminist pedagogy suggests new directions that can enrich Freirean pedagogies of liberation.

Feminist pedagogy has raised three areas of concern that are particularly useful in considering the ways in which Freirean and other liberatory pedagogies can be enriched and expanded. The first of these concerns the role and authority of the teacher; the second addresses the epistemological question of the source of the claims for knowledge and truth in personal experience and feeling; the last, emerging from challenges by women of colour and postmodernist feminist theorists, raises the question of difference. Their challenges have led to a shattering of the unproblematic and unitary category 'woman', as well as of an assumption of the inevitable unity of 'women'. Instead, feminist theorists have increasingly emphasized the importance of recognizing difference as a central category of feminist pedagogy. The unstated assumption of a universal experience of 'being a woman' was exploded by the critiques of postmodern feminists and by the growing assertion of lesbians and women of colour that the universal category 'woman' in fact meant 'White, heterosexual, middle-class woman', even when used by White, heterosexual, socialist feminists, or women veterans of the civil rights movement who were committed to class or race struggles.[27] [. . .]

The role and authority of the teacher

In many respects, the feminist vision of the teacher's authority echoes the Freirean image of the teacher who is a joint learner with students and who holds authority by virtue of greater knowledge and experience. But as we have seen, Freire fails to address the various forms of power held by teachers depending on their race, gender, and the historical and institutional settings in which they work. In the actual practice of feminist pedagogy, the central issues of difference, positionality, and the need to recognize the implications of subjectivity or identity for teachers and students have become central. Moreover, the question of authority in institutional settings makes problematic the possibility of achieving the collective and nonhierarchical vision of early consciousness-raising groups – an emphasis on feeling, experience, and sharing, and a suspicion of hierarchy and authority – continue to influence feminist pedagogy in academic settings. But the institutionalized nature of women's studies in the hierarchical and bureaucratic structure of academia creates tensions that run counter to the original commitment to praxis in consciousness-raising groups. Early consciousness-raising groups were homogeneous, antagonistic to authority, and had a commitment to political change that had directly emerged from the civil rights and new left movements. Feminist pedagogy within academic classrooms addresses heterogeneous groups of students within a competitive and individualistic culture in which the teacher holds institutional power and responsibility (even if she may want to reject that power).[28] The very success of feminist scholarship has meant the development of a rich theoretical tradition with deep divisions and opposing goals and methods.[29] Thus the source of the teacher's authority as a 'woman' who can call upon a 'common woman's knowledge' is called into question; at the same time the feminist teacher is 'given' authority by virtue of her role within the hierarchical structure of the university. [. . .]

Feminist educators have attempted to address this tension between their ideals of collective education and the demands of the university by a variety of expedients: group assignments and grades, contracts for grades, pass/fail courses, and techniques such as self-revelation and the articulation of the dynamics of the classroom.[30]

Another aspect of institutionalized authority, however, is the need for women to *claim* authority in a society that denies it to them. As Culley and Portuges have pointed out, the authority and power of the woman feminist teacher is already in question from many of her students precisely because she is a woman.[31] [. . .]

Thus the issue of institutional authority raises the contradictions of trying to achieve a democratic and collective ideal in a hierarchical institution, but it also raises the question of the meaning of authority for feminist teachers, whose right to speak or to hold power is itself under attack in a patriarchal (and racist, homophobic, classist, and so on) society. The question of asserting authority and power is a central concern to feminists precisely because as women they have been taught that taking power is inappropriate. From this perspective, the feminist teacher's acceptance of authority becomes in itself liberating to her and to her students. [. . .] It is instructive for students to see women assert authority. But this use of authority will lead to positive social change only if those teachers are working also to empower students in a Freirean sense.[32] [. . .]

The authority of the intellectual raises issues for feminists in the academy that are similar to those faced by other democratic and collective political movements, such as those described by Freire. There is a contradiction between the idea of a women's movement including all women and a group of what Berenice Fisher calls 'advanced women'.[33] Feminists who question the whole tradition of androcentric thought are deeply suspicious of women who take a position of 'experts' who can translate and interpret other women's experiences. Fisher articulates these tensions well:

> Who are intellectuals in relation to the women's movement? . . .
> Are intellectuals sorts of leaders, sage guides, women who give voice to or clarify a broader urge toward social change? Is intellectual work essentially elitist, a matter of mere privilege to think, to write, to create? Is it simply a patriarchal mode of gaining and maintaining power, a way of negating women's everyday experience, a means of separating some women from the rest of the 'community'?[34]

Fisher argues that feminist intellectuals are struggling with these questions in their scholarship, teaching, and roles within the universities and the wider women's movement. She does not reject the authority of the feminist intellectual, but she also does not deny the need to address and clarify these contradictions.

In terms of feminist pedagogy, the authority of the feminist teacher as intellectual and theorist finds expression in the goal of making students themselves theorists of their own lives by interrogating and analysing their own experience. In an approach very similar to Freire's concept of conscientization, this strategy moves beyond the naming or sharing of experience to the creation of a critical understanding of the forces that have shaped that experience. [. . .] Thus feminist educators such as Fisher and Bunch accept their authority as intellectuals and theorists, but they consciously attempt to construct their pedagogy to recognize and encourage the capacity of their students to theorize and to recognize their own power.[35]

Feminist concerns about the authority of the feminist teacher address questions of classroom practice and theory ignored by Freire – in his formulation of the teacher and student as two 'knowers' of the world, and in his assertion that the liberatory teacher should acknowledge and claim authority but not authoritarianism. The feminist exploration of authority is much richer and addresses more directly the contradictions between goals of collectivity and hierarchies of knowledge. Feminist teachers are much more conscious of the power of various subject positions than is represented in Freire's liberatory teacher. An acknowledgment of the realities of conflict and tensions based on contradictory political goals, as well as of the meaning of historically experienced oppression for both teachers and students, leads to a pedagogy that respects difference not just as significant for students, but for teachers as well.

Personal experience as a source of knowledge and truth

As feminists explore the relationship of authority, theory, and political action, they raise questions about the categories and claims for truth underlying both consciousness raising and feminist pedagogy. These claims rest on categories of experience and feeling as guides to theoretical understanding and political change. Basic to the Freirean method of conscientization is the belief in the ability of all people to be knowers and to read both the word and the world. In Freirean pedagogy, it is through the interrogation of their own experiences that the oppressed will come to an understanding of their own power as knowers and creators of the world; this knowledge will contribute to the transformation of their world. In consciousness-raising groups and in feminist pedagogy in the university, a similar reliance on experience and feeling has been fundamental to the development of a feminist knowledge of the world that can be the basis for social change. Underlying both Freirean and early feminist pedagogy is an assumption of a common experience as the basis for political analysis and action. Feeling is looked to as a guide to a deeper truth than that of abstract rationality. Experience, which is interpreted through ideologically constructed categories, also can be the basis for an opposition to dominant schemes of truth if what is experienced runs counter to what is set forth and accepted as 'true'.

Feminist educators have explored both experience and feeling as sources of knowledge, and both deserve closer examination.

In many ways, feeling or emotion has been seen traditionally as a source of women's knowledge about the world. As we have seen, in the early consciousness-raising groups, feelings were looked to as the source of a 'true' knowledge of the world for women living in a society that denied the value of their perceptions. Feelings or emotions were seen as a way of testing accepted claims of what is universally true about human nature or, specifically, about women. As feminist pedagogy has developed, with a continued emphasis on the function of feelings as a guide to knowledge about the world, emotions have been seen as links between a kind of inner truth or inner self and the outer world – including ideology, culture, and other discourses of power.[36] However, as feminist educators have explored the uses of feeling or emotion as a source of knowledge, several difficulties have become clear. First, there is a danger that the expression of strong emotion can be simply cathartic and can deflect the need for action to address the underlying causes of that emotion. Moreover, it is not clear how to distinguish among a wide range of emotions as the source of political action. At a more theoretical level, there are contradictions involved in claiming that the emotions are a source for knowledge and at the same time arguing that they are manipulated and shaped by dominant discourses. Both consciousness-raising groups and feminist theorists have asserted the social construction of feelings and their manipulation by the dominant culture; at the same time, they look to feelings as a source of truth. Berenice Fisher points to the contradiction implicit in these claims:

> In theoretical terms, we cannot simultaneously claim that all feelings are socially conditioned and that some feelings are 'true'. We would be more consistent to acknowledge that society only partly shapes our emotions, leaving an opening where we can challenge and change the responses to which we have been socialized. That opening enables the consciousness-raising process to take place and gives us the space in which to reflect on the new emotional responses that our process evokes.[37]

[. . .]

Perhaps the most eloquent argument for feelings as a source of oppositional knowledge is found in the work of Audre Lorde. Lorde, a Black lesbian feminist theorist and poet, writes from the specificity of her own socially defined and shaped life. For her, feeling is the source of poetry, a means of knowing that challenges White, Western, androcentric epistemologies. She specifically ties her own feelings as a Black woman to a non-Western way of knowing. She writes:

As we come more into touch with our own ancient, non-European consciousness of living as a situation to be experienced and interacted with, we learn more and more to cherish our feelings, to respect those hidden sources of power from where true knowledge and, therefore, lasting action comes.[38]

[. . .]

For Lorde, then, feelings are a guide to analysis and to action. While they are shaped by society and are socially constructed in that sense, Lorde insists on a deeper reality of feeling closer in touch with what it means to be human. This formulation echoes the Freirean vision of humanization as a new way of being in the world other than as oppressor and oppressed. Both Freire and Lorde retain a Utopian faith in the possibility that human beings can create new ways of being in the world out of collective struggle and a human capacity to feel. Lorde terms this the power of the erotic; she speaks of the erotic as 'a measure between the beginnings of our sense of self and the chaos of our strongest feelings', a resource 'firmly rooted in the power of our unexpressed or unrecognized feelings'.[39] Because the erotic can challenge the dominant, it has been denied as a source of power and knowledge. But for Lorde, the power of the erotic provides the basis for visionary social change.

In her exploration of feelings and of the erotic as a source of knowledge about the world, Lorde does not reject analysis and rationality. But she questions the depth of critical understanding of those forces that shape our lives that can be achieved using only the rational and abstract methods of analysis given to us by dominant ideology. In Foucault's terms, she is seeking a perspective from which to interrogate dominant regimes of truth; central to her argument is the claim that an analysis framed solely in the terms of accepted discourse cannot get to the root of structures of power. That is what her well-known phrase, 'The master's tools will never dismantle the master's house' implies. As she argues:

> Rationality is not unnecessary. It serves the chaos of knowledge. It serves feeling. It serves to get from this place to that place. But if you don't honor those places, then the road is meaningless. Too often, that's what happens with the worship of rationality and that circular, academic analytic thinking. But ultimately, I don't see feel/think as a dichotomy. I see them as a choice of ways and combinations.[40]

Lorde's discussion of feeling and the erotic as a source of power and knowledge is based on the assumption that human beings have the capacity to feel and know, and can engage in self-critique; people are not completely shaped by dominant discourse. The oppressor may be within us, but Lorde insists that we also have the capacity to challenge our own ways of feeling and knowing. When tied to a recognition of positionality, this validation of feeling can be used to develop powerful sources of politically focused feminist education.

For Lorde and Fisher, this kind of knowing through an exploration of feeling and emotion requires collective inquiry and constant re-evaluation. It is a contingent and positioned claim to truth. Similar complexities arise in the use of experience as the basis for feminist political action. Looking to experience as the source of knowledge and the focus of feminist learning is perhaps the most fundamental tenet of feminist pedagogy. This is similar to the Freirean call to 'read the world' to seek the generative themes that codify power relationships and social structures. The sharing of women's experiences was the touchstone of early consciousness-raising groups and continues to be a fundamental method of feminist pedagogy. [. . .] As became clear quite early in the women's movement, claims about experience as a source of women's knowledge rested on certain assumptions about commonalities in women's lives. Women were conceived of as a unitary and relatively undifferentiated group. Sarachild, for example, spoke of devising 'new theories which . . . reflect the actual experience and feelings and necessities of women'.[41] Underlying this approach was the assumption of a common woman's experience, one reflecting the world of the White, middle-class, heterosexual women of the early feminist movement. But as the critiques of lesbians, women of colour, and postmodernist feminist theorists have made clear, there is no single woman's experience to be revealed. Both experience and feeling thus have been called into question as the source of an unproblematic knowledge of the world that will lead to praxis. As Diana Fuss comments: '"female experience" is never as unified, as knowable, as, universal, and as stable as we presume it to be'.[42]

Challenges to the concept of a unitary women's experience by both women of colour and by postmodern critics has not meant the abandonment of experience as a source of knowledge for feminist teachers. Of course experience, like feeling, is socially constructed in the sense that we can only understand it and speak about it in ideas and terms that are part of an existing ideology and language. But in a stance similar to that of Lorde in her use of the erotic, feminist teachers have explored the ways in which women have experienced the material world through their bodies. This self-examination of lived experience is then used as a source of knowledge that can illuminate the social processes and ideology that shape us. As Fuss suggests, 'Such a position permits the introduction of narratives of lived experience into the classroom while at the same time challenging us to examine collectively the central role social and historical practices play in shaping and producing these narratives'.[43] One example of this approach is found in the work of Frigga Haug and the group of German feminists of which she is a part.[44] Haug and this group use what they call collective memory work to explore their feelings about their own bodies in order to uncover the social construction of their selves. [. . .] This collective exploration of 'the point where . . . chains chafe most' recalls the Freirean culture circles, in which peasants would take such examples as their personal experiences with the landlord as the starting point for their education or conscientization. Basic to their approach is a belief in reflection and a rejection of a view of people as 'fixed, given, unchangeable'. By working collectively on 'memory work', a sharing and comparison of their own lives, Haug and her group hope to uncover the workings of hegemonic ideology in their own subjectivities. [. . .]

For Haug and her group, the early consciousness-raising groups, and the Freirean culture circles, collective sharing of experience is the source of knowledge of the forces that have shaped and continue to shape them. But their recognition of the shifting meaning of experience as it is explored through memory insists on the profoundly social and political nature of who we are.

The question of difference

Both women of colour writing from a perspective of cultural feminism and postmodernist feminist theorists converge in their critique of the concept of a universal 'women's experience'. Although the idea of a unitary and universal category 'woman' has been challenged by women of colour for its racist assumptions, it has also been challenged by recent analyses of feminist theorists influenced by postmodernism, who point to the social construction of subjectivity and who emphasize the 'unstable' nature of the self. Postmodernist feminist critics such as Chris Weedon have argued that socially given identities such as 'woman' are 'precarious, contradictory, and in process, constantly being reconstituted in discourse each time we speak'.[45] This kind of analysis considers the ways in which 'the subject' is not an object; that is, not fixed in a static social structure, but constantly being created, actively creating the self, and struggling for new ways of being in the world through new forms of discourse or new forms of social relationships. Such analysis calls for a recognition of the positionality of each person in any discussion of what can be known from experience. If we view individual selves as being constructed and negotiated, then we can begin to consider what exactly those forces are in which individuals shape themselves and by which they are shaped. [. . .]

Both women of colour and lesbian critics have pointed to the complexity of socially given identities. Black women and other women of colour raise challenges to the assumption that the sharing of experience will create solidarity and a theoretical understanding based upon a common women's standpoint. Lesbian feminists, both White and of colour, point to the destructive nature of homophobia. As is true of White, heterosexual, feminist educators, these theorists base their analysis upon their own experiences, but those experiences reveal not only the workings of sexism, but of racism, homophobia, and class oppression as well. This complex perspective underlies the Combahee River Collective Statement, a position paper written by a group of African-American feminists in Boston in the 1970s. This statement makes clear what a grounded theory of experience means for women whose value is denied by the dominant society in numerous ways. For African-American women, an investigation of the shaping of their own identities reveals the ways in which sexism and racism are interlocking forms of oppression:

> As children we realized that we were different from boys and that we were treated differently. For example, we were told in the same breath to be quiet both for the sake of being 'ladylike' and to make us less objectionable in the eyes of white people. As we grew older we became aware of the threat of physical and sexual abuse from men. However, we had no way of conceptualizing what was so apparent to us, what we *knew* was really happening.[46]

The investigation of the experiences of women of colour, lesbian women, women whose very being challenges existing racial, sexual, heterosexual, and class dominance leads to a knowledge of the world that both acknowledges differences and points to the need for an 'integrated analysis and practice based upon the fact that the major systems of oppression are interlocking'.[47] The turning to experience thus reveals not a universal and common women's essence, but, rather, deep divisions in what different women have experienced, and in the kinds of knowledge they discover when they examine their own experience. The recognition of the differences among women raises serious challenges to feminist pedagogy by calling into question the authority of the teacher/theorist, raising feelings of guilt and shame, and revealing tensions among students as well as between teacher and students. In classes of African-American women taught by African-American teachers, the sharing of experience can lead to the same sense of commonality and sharing that was true of early consciousness-raising groups. But in settings in which students come from differing positions of privilege or oppression, the sharing of experience raises conflicts rather than building solidarity. In these circumstances, the collective exploration of experience leads not to a common knowledge and solidarity based on sameness, but to the tensions of an articulation of difference. Such exploration raises again the problems left unaddressed by Freirean pedagogy: the overlapping and multiple forms of oppression revealed in 'reading the world' of experience.

CONCLUSION

Both Freirean and feminist pedagogies are based on political commitment and identification with subordinate and oppressed groups; both seek justice and empowerment. Freire sets out these goals of liberation and social and political transformation as universal claims, without exploring his own privileged position or existing conflicts among oppressed groups themselves. Writing from within a tradition of Western modernism, his theory rests on a belief of transcendent and universal truth. But feminist theory influenced by postmodernist thought and by the writings of women of colour challenges the underlying assumptions of these universal claims. The recognition of our own histories means the necessity of articulating our own subjectivities and our own interests as we try to interpret and critique the social world. This stance rejects the universalizing tendency of much 'malestream' thought, and insists on recognizing the power and privilege of who we are. As Biddy Martin and Chandra Mohanty comment:

> The claim to a lack of identity or positionality is itself based on privilege, on the refusal to accept responsibility for one's implication in actual historical or social relations, or a denial that positionalities exist or that they matter, the denial of one's own personal history and the claim to a total separation from it.[48]

Fundamental to recent feminist theory is a questioning of the concept of a coherent subject moving through history with a single essential identity. Instead, feminist theorists are developing a concept of the constant creation and negotiation of selves within structures of ideology and material constraints.[49] This line of theoretical analysis calls into question assumptions of the common interests of the oppressed, whether conceived of as women or peasants; it challenges the use of universal terms such as oppression and liberation without locating these claims in a concrete historical or social context. The challenges of recent feminist theory and, in particular, the writings of feminists of colour point to the need to articulate and claim a particular historical and social identity, to locate ourselves, and to build coalitions from a recognition of the partial knowledges of our own constructed identities. Recognizing the standpoint of subjects as shaped by their experience of class, race, gender, or other socially defined identities has powerful implications for pedagogy, in that it emphasizes the need to make conscious the subject positions not only of students but of teachers as well. These lines of theoretical analysis have implications for the ways in which we can understand pedagogy as contested, as a site of discourse among subjects, teachers, and students whose identities are, as Weedon puts it, contradictory and in process. The theoretical formulation of the 'unstable self', the complexity of subjectivities, what Giroux calls 'multi-layered subjects', and the need to position ourselves in relation to our own histories raise important issues for liberatory pedagogies. If all people's identities are recognized in their full historical and social complexity as subject positions that are in process, based on knowledges that are partial and that reflect deep and conflicting differences, how can we theorize what a liberatory pedagogy actively struggling against different forms of oppression may look like? How can we build upon the rich and complex analysis of feminist theory and pedagogy to work toward a Freirean vision of social justice and liberation?

In the complexity of issues raised by feminist pedagogy, we can begin to acknowledge the reality of tensions that result from different histories, from privilege, oppression, and power as they are lived by teachers and students in classrooms. To recognize these tensions and differences does not mean abandonment of the goals of social justice and empowerment, but it does make clear the need to recognize contingent and situated claims and to acknowledge our own histories and selves in process. One significant area of feminist work has been grounded in the collective analysis of experience and emotion, as exemplified by the work of Haug and her group in Germany. In many respects, these projects look back to consciousness raising, but with a more developed theory of ideology and an acute consciousness of difference. As Berenice Fisher argues, a collective inquiry 'requires the slow unfolding of layers of experience, both the contradictory experiences of a given woman and the conflicting experiences of different women'.[50] Another approach builds on what Bernice Reagon calls the need for coalition building, a recognition and validation of difference. This is similar to what has come to be known as identity politics. [. . .] This is a validation of both difference and conflict, but also an attempt to build coalitions around common goals rather than a denial of differences.[51] It is clear that this kind of pedagogy and exploration of experiences in a society in which privilege and oppression are lived is risky and filled with pain. Such a pedagogy suggests a more complex realization of the Freirean vision of the collective conscientization and struggle against oppression, one which acknowledges difference and conflict, but which, like Freire's vision, rests on a belief in the human capacity to feel, to know, and to change.

NOTES AND REFERENCES

1 See as representative Henry Giroux, ed., (1991) *Postmodernism, Feminism and Cultural Politics*, Albany: State University of New York Press; Cleo Cherryholmes, (1988) *Power and Criticism: Poststructural Investigations in Education*, New York: Teachers College Press; Henry Giroux and Roger Simon, (eds). (1989) *Popular Culture, Schooling and Everyday Life*, Westport, CT: Bergin & Garvey; Deborah Britzman, (1991) *Practice Makes Practice*, Albany: State University of New York Press; Patti Lather (1991) *Getting Smart: Feminist Research and Pedagogy With/in the Postmodern*, New York: Routledge.

2 Paulo Freire, (1971) *Pedagogy of the Oppressed*, New York: Herder & Herder, p. 28.

3 Margo Culley and Catherine Portuges. 'Introduction', in *Gendered Subjects* (1985) Boston: Routledge & Kegan Paul. For comparisons of Freirean and feminist pedagogy, see also Frances Maher, 'Classroom pedagogy and the new scholarship on women', in *Gendered Subjects*, pp. 29–48, and 'Toward a richer theory of feminist pedagogy: a comparison of "liberation" and "gender" models for teaching and learning', *Journal of Education*, vol. 169, no. 3 (1987), 91–100.

4 Antonio Gramsci (1971) *Selections from the Prison Notebook*, New York: International Publishers.

5 Audre Lorde (1984) *Sister Outsider*, Trumansburg, NY: The Crossing Press.

6 See, for example, Elizabeth Ellsworth, 'Why doesn't this feel empowering? Working through the repressive myths of critical pedagogy,' *Harvard Educational Review*, 59 (1989), 297–324; Ann Berlak, 'Teaching for outrage and empathy in the liberal arts', *Educational Foundations*, vol. 3, no. 2 (1989), 69–94; Deborah Britzman. 'Decentering discourses in teacher education: or, the unleashing of unpopular things' in *What Schools Can Do: Critical Pedagogy and Practice*, ed. Candace Mitchell and Kathleen Weiler, Albany: State University of New York Press, in press.

7 Freire's method of codifications and generative themes have been discussed frequently. Perhaps the best introduction to these concrete methods can be found in Paulo Freire (1973) *Education for Critical Consciousness*, New York: Seabury Press.

8 See, for example, Paulo Freire (1985) *The Politics of Education*, Westport, CT: Bergin & Garvey; Paulo Freire and Donaldo Macedo (1987) *Literacy: Reading the Word and the World*, Westport, CT: Bergin & Garvey; Paulo Freire and Ira Shor (1987) *A Pedagogy for Liberation*, London: Macmillan; Myles Horton and Paulo Freire (1990) *We Make the Road by Walking: Conversations on Education and Social Change*, (eds) Brenda Bell, John Gaventa, and John Peters, Philadelphia: Temple University Press.

9 Freire, *Pedagogy of the Oppressed*, p. 28.

10 Freire and Macedo, *Literacy: Reading the Word and the World*.

11 See Simone de Beauvoir (1953), *The Second Sex* (New York: Knopf), for a more striking use of the male referent.

12 Freire, *Pedagogy of the Oppressed*, p. 30.

13 When definitions of feminist pedagogy are attempted, they sometimes tend toward generalization and such a broad inclusiveness as to be of dubious usefulness. For example, Carolyn Shrewsbury characterizes feminist pedagogy as follows:

It does not automatically preclude any technique or approach. It does indicate the relationship that specific techniques have to educational goals. It is not limited to any specific subject matter but it does include a reflexive element that increases the feminist scholarship component involved in the teaching/learning of any subject matter. It has close ties with other liberatory pedagogies, but it cannot be subsumed under other pedagogical approaches. It is transformative, helping us revision the educational enterprise. But it can also be phased into a traditional teaching approach or another alternative pedagogical approach. (Shrewsbury (1987) 'What is feminist pedagogy?', *Women's Studies Quarterly*, vol. 15, nos. 3–4: 12.)

Certain descriptions of feminist pedagogy show the influence of group dynamics and interractionist approaches. See, for example, Nancy Schniedewind, 'Feminist values: guidelines for teaching methodology in women's studies', *Radical Teacher*, *18*, 25–8. Methods used by feminist teachers include cooperation, shared leadership, and democratic process. Feminist teachers describe techniques such as keeping journals, soliciting students' responses to readings and to the classroom dynamics of a course, the use of role playing and theatre games, the use of self-revelation on the part of the teacher, building leadership skills among students by requiring them to teach parts of a course, and contracting for grades. For accounts of classroom practice, see the articles in the special issue on feminist pedagogy of *Women's Studies Quarterly*, vol. 15, nos. 3–4 (1987); Culley and Portuges, *Gendered Subjects*; Charlotte Bunch and Sandra Pollack, (eds.) (1983) *Learning Our Way*, Trumansburg, NY: The Crossing Press; Gloria Hull, Patricia Bell Scott, and Barbara Smith, (eds.) (1982) *But Some of Us Are Brave*, Old Westbury, NY: The Feminist Press; and numerous articles in *Women's Studies Newsletter* and *Radical Teacher*.

14 A discussion of the relationship of the early women's liberation movement to the civil rights movement and the new left can be found in Sara Evans (1980) *Personal Politics*, New York: Vintage Press. Based on extensive interviews as well as pamphlets and private documents, Evans shows the origins of both political goals and methods in the earlier male-dominated movement, particularly the model of Black student organizers and the Black church in the South.

15 While mid-nineteenth century suffragists developed their ideas of human equality and justice through the abolitionist movement, by the late nineteenth century, White suffragists often demonstrated racist attitudes and employed racist strategies in their campaigns for suffrage. This offers another instructive parallel to the White feminist movement of the 1960s. Here, once again, feminist claims emerged out of an anti-racist struggle for civil rights, but later too often took up the universalizing stance that the experiences and issues of White women represented the lives of all women. See bell hooks (1981), *Ain't I a Woman?*, Boston: South End Press and (1984) *Feminist Theory from Margin to Center*, Boston: South End Press for powerful discussions of these issues.

16 Kathie Sarachild (1975) 'Consciousness raising: a radical weapon', *Feminist Revolution* (ed.) Red-stockings, New York: Random House.

17 Sarachild, 'Consciousness raising', p. 145.

18 Michele Russell, 'Black-eyed blues connection: from the inside out', in Bunch and Pollack, *Learning Our Way*, 272–84.

19 Sarachild, 'Consciousness Raising,' p. 147.

20 Sarachild, 'Consciousness raising', p. 147.

21 Irene Peslikis, 'Resistances to consciousness', in *Sisterhood Is Powerful*, Robin Morgan (ed.), (1970) New York: Vintage Books, p. 339.
22 See, for example, Kathy McAfee and Myrna Wood (1970) 'Bread and roses', in *Voices from Women's Liberation*, (ed.) Leslie Tanner, New York: New American Library for an early socialist feminist analysis of the need to connect the women's movement with the class struggle.
23 Berenice Fisher, 'What is feminist pedagogy?', *Radical Teacher*, 18, 20–25. See also bell hooks (1989) 'on self-recovery', in *Talking Back, Thinking Feminist, Thinking Black*, Boston: South End Press.
24 Marilyn Boxer, 'For and about women: the theory and practice of women's studies in the United States', in *Reconstructing the Academy: Women's Education and Women's Studies*, (eds) Elizabeth Minnich, Jean O'Barr, and Rachel Rosenfeld (1988) Chicago: University of Chicago Press, p. 71.
25 Boxer estimates there were over 300 programmes and 30,000 courses in women's studies given in 1982. See 'For and about Women', p. 70.
26 The literature of feminist challenges to specific disciplines is by now immense. For general discussions of the impact of the new scholarship on women, see Ellen DuBois, Gail Kelly, Elizabeth Kennedy, Carolyn Korsmeyer, and Lillian Robinson, (eds), (1985) *Feminist Scholarship: Kindling in the Groves of Academe*, Urbana: University of Illinois Press and Christie Farnhum (ed.), (1987) *The Impact of Feminist Research in the Academy*, Bloomington: Indiana University Press.
27 See, for example, Diana Fuss (1989) *Essentially Speaking*, New York: Routledge; hooks, *Talking Back*; Britzman, *Practice Makes Practice*.
28 Susan Stanford Friedman, 'Authority in the feminist classroom: a contradiction in terms?', in Culley and Portuges, *Gendered Subjects*, 203–8.
29 See Alison Jaggar (1983) *Feminist Politics and Human Nature*, Sussex: The Harvester Press, for an excellent discussion of these perspectives.
30 See, for example, Evelyn Torton Beck (1983) 'Self-disclosure and the commitment to social change', *Women's Studies International Forum*, 6, 159–64.
31 Margo Culley and Catherine Portuges, 'The politics of nurturance', in *Gendered Subjects*, p. 12. See also Margo Culley, 'Anger and authority in the introductory women's studies classroom', in *Gendered Subjects*, pp. 209–17.
32 See Davis, 'Teaching the feminist minority', for a thoughtful discussion of the contradictory pressures on the feminist teacher both to nurture and challenge women students.
33 Fisher, 'What is feminist pedagogy?', p. 22.
34 Fisher, 'Guilt and shame in the women's movement', p. 202.
35 See Berenice Fisher (1982) 'Professing feminism: feminist academics and the women's movement', *Psychology of Women Quarterly*, 7, 55–69, for a thoughtful discussion of the difficulties of retaining an activist stance for feminists in the academy.
36 See Arlie Russell Hochschild (1983) *The Managed Heart*, Berkeley: University of California Press, for a discussion of the social construction of emotions in contemporary society. Hochschild argues that emotion, is a 'biologically given sense . . . and a means by which we know about our relation to the world' (p. 219). At the same time she investigates the ways in which the emotions themselves are manipulated and constructed.
37 Berenice Fisher (1987) 'The heart has its reasons: feeling, thinking, and community building in feminist education', *Women's Studies Quarterly*, vol. 15, nos. 3–4, 48.
38 Lorde, *Sister Outsider*, p. 37.

39 Lorde, *Sister Outsider*, p. 53.
40 Lorde, *Sister Outsider*, p. 100.
41 Sarachild, 'Consciousness raising', p. 148.
42 Fuss, *Essentially Speaking*, p. 114.
43 Fuss, *Essentially Speaking*, p. 118.
44 Frigga Haug, (1987) *Female Sexualization*, London: Verso Press.
45 Chris Weedon (1987) *Feminist Practice and Poststructuralist Theory*, Oxford: Basil Blackwell, p. 33.
46 Combahee River Collective, 'Combahee river collective statement', p. 274.
47 Combahee River Collective, 'Combahee river collective statement', p. 272.
48 Biddy Martin and Chandra Mohanty (1986) 'Feminist politics: what's home got to do with it?', in *Feminist Studies/Critical Studies*, (ed.) Teresa de Lauretis, Bloomington: University of Indiana Press, p. 208.
49 See, for example, Flax, 'Postmodernism and gender relations in feminist theory'; Sandra Harding (1986) *The Science Question in Feminism*, Ithaca: University of Cornell Press; Dorothy Smith (1987) *The Everyday World as Problematic*, Boston: Northeastern University Press; Haraway (1985) 'A manifesto for cyborgs', *Socialist Review*, 80, 64–107; Nancy Hartsock (1983) *Money, Sex, and Power*, New York: Longman; Mary O'Brien (1981) *The Politics of Reproduction*, Boston: Routledge & Kegan Paul; Irene Diamond and Lee Quinby, (eds.), (1988) *Feminism and Foucault*, Boston: Northeastern University Press; Linda Alcoff (1988) 'Cultural feminism versus post structuralism: the identity crisis in feminist theory', *Signs*, 13 405–37; Special Issue on Feminism and Deconstruction, *Feminist Studies*, vol. 14, no. 1 (1988); Judith Butler (1990) *Gender Trouble*, New York: Routledge; Linda Nicholson, (Ed.), (1990) *Feminism/Postmodernism*, New York: Routledge.
50 Fisher, 'The heart has its reasons', p. 49.
51 Bernice Reagon, 'Coalition politics: turning the century', in Smith, *Home Girls*, 356–69.

Chapter 8

The British adult education tradition
A re-examination

Bob Bell

One of the most enduring characteristics of British political discourse is its love of dichotomies. Any suggestion that our national life could be better organized on the basis of compromise and the pragmatic blurring of ideological differences is not just seen as a betrayal by the doctrinally pure, but infuriates the tabloid press who thrive on clear-cut enmity and what they dubiously claim are choices between good and evil. Coalition government, so common among our economically successful European partners, is seen as a recipe for weakness and, while third parties are tolerated in the name of democracy, they are seen by the press as a nuisance, amusing and newsworthy in by-elections but to be firmly squashed at 'real' election times.

Unfortunately this love of emotionally charged dichotomies is equally characteristic of much British educational discourse. Those engaged in battles over the existence of independent schools or over the curricular autonomy of the teaching profession seem to get so much emotional satisfaction out of being committed to ideological purity that they cherish the clash of extremes. This ignores completely the successful development of a mixed school economy and a moderate national curriculum in most of the other educationally advanced countries of Europe.

One unhelpful dichotomy in particular has retained its virulence in the UK despite many well-argued challenges and wide evidence of its increasing abandonment elsewhere. There remains a staunch belief that education and training are quite different animals and that the former, being 'liberal', is more spiritually exalted and worthy of greater respect than the latter. This assumption still runs through many a newspaper article and many a political speech, despite what so much of our personal experience tells us: that much of what is still labelled 'education' consists, like much industrial training, of little more than a search for vocationally orientated certification.

Indeed, vocationally linked training, by exciting the curiosity and uncovering the latent talents of a hitherto unsuccessful student, may be just as personally liberating for the student as many a 'pure' course in the arts or sciences. It can sometimes indeed motivate and stimulate that individual to an extent not found amid the academically more prestigious but nevertheless mechanical learning of French grammar or the reproducing of history notes in a course, not overseen by City and Guilds, but by a university board.

However, the old suspicions linger, especially in a period such as this when financial priority in the field of adult learning seems increasingly to be given to occupational training. There is a great eagerness on the part of those who see their professional task as more than 'mere' training to see this as yet another manifestation of governmental philistinism and materialism, favouring the needs of industry (not to say capitalism) at the expense of the workers' human development. The purpose of this chapter is to question whether such an approach is as much out of line with British tradition as many people suggest.

In 1990 the Education Department of the Scottish Office decided to end government support for Newbattle Abbey College in Dalkeith and thus bring to an end a commendable and widely praised attempt to provide Scotland with its only real equivalent to a Nordic folk high school. Newbattle Abbey was a small residential establishment where those who had missed out on the benefits of secondary school certification could catch up in a dignified way, free from the pressures of the cramming establishment and tutored on a personal basis that no correspondence college could ever achieve. It was a well-loved institution that had been of enormous value to its alumni and its enforced closure was seen as a key event, a cold-blooded decision by government to end a liberal tradition which it clearly did not value or, at least, value sufficiently to justify the expenditure of further public funds.

It could just as easily have been argued that the vulnerability of Newbattle Abbey College was really a consequence of its uniqueness and isolation, and of the failure of successive governments of all persuasions to follow the example of most other north European countries in encouraging the founding of such establishments on a very wide scale. However, it was far easier to see its closure as yet another example of a tendency on the part of government to regard all forms of institutional adult learning not related to the labour market as personal luxuries to be financed in the future by the participants themselves. As evidence of this, the government's opponents cited not just changes in the funding of the so-called recognized bodies, the University Extra-mural Departments and the Workers Educational Association (WEA), but also the ever-spiralling charges for 'liberal' activities which hard-pressed local authorities were having to impose as a result of financial restrictions imposed by central government.

The new emphasis on work-related courses provided a field-day for critics from a wide range of ideological standpoints. Marxists discerned a straight sell out to the imperatives of capitalism. 'Progressive' education-ists readily saw in it an obvious return to the world of Dickens and the crude instrumentalism of Gradgrind schooling. More moderate main-stream figures simply warned of the danger of possibly neglecting our more intangible national needs. Those who saw adult education as having primarily a social mission to the disadvantaged saw no virtue in facilitating the career enhancement for those already able to stand on their own two feet at the expense of the political and economic empower-ment of those oppressed by the present social system.

For many people, therefore, the government's new priorities were a betrayal, a reversal, they believed, of all that adult learning provision in Britain had traditionally stood for. But was this really so? Perhaps underlying the entire discussion of such matters there has been a misconception of the real nature of mainstream British adult education as well as of the perceptions and wishes of most of the educators' clients themselves.

Such a misconception has arisen, at least in part, from the fact that much discussion of the history of British adult education has been distorted by two factors. First, there has been too obsessive an interest in the doings of specific organizations with an easily charted history, such as the university extra-mural departments and the Workers Educa-tional Association (WEA). Neither of these ever commanded a mass audience. Second, there has been an increasing and quite unjustified assumption that the really influential figures in the development of adult learning provision have been those concerned with the political empower-ment of the disadvantaged. The fact that many of these crusaders are skilled writers and have been involved in useful and fascinating work has convinced all too many students that their work is mainstream rather than exceptional. Yet the patronage accorded by international bodies to Freire, for example, should not deceive us into thinking that his methods are those most often used by the majority of modern literacy pro-grammes. The prominence given by standard textbooks to the pioneering community work of figures such as Cody or Lovett should not make us assume that their ideas, however sensible and useful, are necessarily being widely implemented. Even less should we believe that many of the directly political analyses provided by sociologists of adult learning during the last thirty years have had much of an influence outside certain circles.

Moreover, we must beware of the prevailing dichotomy tricking us into believing that the 'liberal' educators of the extra-mural departments and the WEA have always been the allies of the radical crusaders. For many years a famous struggle raged between the WEA, attempting to raise workers' horizons to those of the 'educated' middle classes, and the

Plebs League who sought to establish forms of education more related to what they, in Marxist terms, saw as the true situation of the working class and who castigated their WEA rivals as the tools of a capitalist-dominated university establishment (Kelly 1970). It was only the radicalization of academia during the 1960s and 1970s that brought the two sides closer together so that by the 1980s they had become natural allies against Thatcherite policies that threatened the funding of both groupings.

Most British adults remain blissfully unaware of all these developments. Even those conscious of the ideological issues raised by matters such as secondary school selection or the curricular challenges posed by gender, would probably be astonished to discover that the nature and provision of adult learning facilities has any general political importance. Much of their most significant adult learning has been informal and highly personal, in the middle of a family crisis, for example, on moving to a new job or on losing an old job. Their most formative and informative experiences will have occurred while awaiting a child or while serving in the army. If they have encountered institutional learning arrangements at all it will most probably have been at work, in 'evening classes' connected with DIY or other skills, at a village gardening club or in the Women's Institute. Only a minority will have been involved in adult education of the WEA kind and even fewer will have been under the influence of political empowerers.

For most politicians and leaders of opinion, therefore, adult learning has until recently never needed to be organized in the same urgent sense as primary or secondary schooling. It was regularly assumed that most of the provision would either be made by industry which would make its own arrangements, by voluntary bodies or by the local authorities who would provide evening classes staffed by secondary teachers and other local subject experts, all working for pin money. It was therefore hardly an area requiring a system of proper teacher training. What diploma courses there were in the subject were very much undersubscribed and often depended on overseas students to keep them in existence. Most universities contented themselves with organizing extramural classes and took little interest in developing theoretical courses on the subject. Indeed, there was widespread doubt about whether any significant body of theory actually existed in relation to adult learning. When, as recently as the early 1980s, a group of Open University (OU) sociologists first mooted the idea of launching a course on the theory of adult education, considerable scorn was poured upon the proposal even by many of the keenest and most enlightened teachers among the OU professoriate, a remarkable reaction within what was generally regarded as the major adult education institution in the country.

This lack of a training base has had a profound effect on the

professional status of adult educators and on the general public perception of the field. Child schooling has now been compulsory for over a
century and has depended on a teacher training system that from the
start took on board the great body of pedagogical theory, then readily
available from Germany and America. In the case of adult education, the
lack of a compulsory element and the consequent belief that no general
training system was needed meant that there was no great interest in or
wide diffusion of adult education theory. Indeed, the serious academic
study of adult learning only began to penetrate the British universities
on a discernable scale once adult educators were seen as having a social
mission. Certainly most of the early diploma courses seem to have had
such a mission in mind and had close affinities with social work training.
This inevitably distanced many of the new professional training courses
from the actual world of adult education as experienced by the majority
of the population and indeed narrowed the view of those training
courses.

The absence of a major state presence in the adult learning field not
only meant that no overall system of provision ever emerged to parallel
that in child education. It also meant that there never was a feeling that
the provision of adult learning facilities was a human right which every
government must guarantee. Certainly moral pressure, along with
common sense and economic considerations, did produce expenditure on
a literacy programme but any payments made to voluntary bodies, such
as the WEA, remained acts of grace and favour like grants to the arts or
to sport, gestures that could be withheld by hard-pressed governments
at any time. For the government to embark on massive support for
occupation-related training in the name of social welfare and economic
development does not therefore represent a change of policy. It simply
represents a new choice of area in which to dispense grace and favour.
Indeed, it can be seen merely as a development of the previous Labour
government's decision to establish the Manpower Services Commission
and to finance on an unprecedented scale adult activities not hitherto so
widely supported from public funds.

The strength of the traditional British belief that adult learning is not
an area appropriate for major government intervention has over the
years been amply demonstrated by the response of all the main parties to
major international challenges in this field. The report 'Learning to Be'
published by UNESCO in 1972 pressed upon all governments the
notion of each individual's *entitlement* to organized life-long education,
emphasizing not just the human rights involved but also the national
economic advantages to be gained from the implementation of such a
programme. It gave not only hope to the individual but also a realistic
means of dealing with rapid technological change and new patterns of
demography. Even so, it never made a real impression with any British

political party. Some individual politicians espoused the cause of life-long learning but those compiling the party manifestos paid little attention to what was not even seen as a minor issue. It was only after Harold Wilson had created a rhetorical vision of a Britain transformed economically by the 'white heat of technology' that he finally pledged his support for the Open University. This was certainly a major government commitment to adult learning but it was only acceptable to many of his parliamentary colleagues because what was being proposed *was* a university with clearly defined standards and status and not merely an agent of general adult education. Moreover, because of its close links with the broadcast media the OU also gave the impression of being technologically advanced and far removed from what were increasingly seen as the old-fashioned classrooms of the evening institute or the WEA.

Certainly, adult learning was beginning to be viewed in a far wider light. The introductory television programme of the OU course E355 *Education for Adults*, compiled in the mid-1980s, provided a definition of adult education that seemed to cover virtually every process of adult self-improvement or disimprovement, whether conscious or half-conscious, physical or mental. It embraced not merely a highly formal class in Sanskrit, half an hour spent jogging while listening to an instructional tape as well as an insightful pub conversation but even the reading of inscriptions on public monuments! On the other hand, most academic writers on the subject continued to confine their attention to more formal encounters, especially to those being organized by new-style 'facilitators', a term seen as less authoritarian in tone than 'teachers' or even 'tutors'.

Even so, as the Newbattle Abbey College dispute demonstrated, a great deal of emphasis was and is still laid by its adherents on the classroom based 'liberal' traditions of Mansbridge, a figure whose face-to-face tutorial system had become widely known abroad as a peculiarly British contribution to the field but has had a strictly limited influence in its country of origin. Certainly his affect on individual adult lives has been meagre compared with that of Grundtvig, whose folk high schools have catered for hundreds of thousands of his fellow Danes as well as for many more in the other north European countries which adopted his philosophy and institutional model. The truth is that most British adults have remained largely untouched by any such elaborate institutional provision. In so far as they seek organized learning opportunities at all, they make their arrangements in a highly personal, not to say idiosyncratic way. They shop around, mixing the formal and the informal in a totally pragmatic manner and are just as likely to turn to the public library or to the correspondence colleges, so despised by the advocates of face-to-face tuition, as to Mansbridge-style study groups.

This individualist and eclectic approach is far from uniquely British.

The Canadian, Tough (1976), also sees the individual adult rather than the institution or the government as the chief planner of conscious adult education. Most adults intent on learning, he suggests, employ institutional providers simply in the way that *any* consumer uses suppliers, whether these are adult learning centres or supermarkets. Although his views have been noted and have made their way into some adult education training courses, they have on the whole attracted less attention than the liberation theology of the political empowerers. True, those concerned with access to higher education strike a more realistic note, being mainly concerned with certification and smoothing the way of the individual into what is still an institution-dominated situation. But Tough's message has largely been swept aside amid justifiable objections to his sampling procedures. On the whole he has come to be regarded as a curiosity rather than a central thinker.

Most British adult education practitioners however, like the majority of British politicians of all parties, have in other ways tended to take Tough's position for granted – that organized, conscious adult learning outside the workplace is usually something that adults plan and choose for themselves. They also assume that, unless you are unwaged, it is something that you will normally be expected to pay for unless the government or your employer sees some gain for themselves in making it available free. For this reason, the vast majority of the population react to changes in the financial priorities of adult learning much as they would react to any of the other changes they have long expected from government, such as increases in train fares or taxation: assaults that may affect them personally but have eventually to be accepted philosophically. Indeed, a survey conducted by MORI (NIACE 1994: 2) had as its 'most surprising finding' the discovery that there was 'agreement across all social classes, among current participants and non-participants, rich and poor, old and young, that the taxpayer should be asked to bear a smaller share of the cost of study, and that individuals and their employers should bear more'.

The common belief that institutional adult education is an extra, a luxury that has to be paid for by the individual is partly the result of, but also one of reasons for, the fact that educational policymakers have never marked it out as a primary concern. The 1944 *Education Act* enjoined local authorities to provide it but made no detailed mandatory provisions about the form it should take or the scale on which it should be mounted. The Russell Report of 1973, *Adult Education: A Plan for Development*, led to precious little development of a major kind, largely accepting as it did the current structure of the system and calling in vain for new financial commitments that no British government of any complexion has ever been prepared to make. The later insightful and far more challenging 1982 report of the Advisory Council for Adult and

Continuing Education (ACACE), *Continuing Education: From Policies to Practice*, sought to move English and Welsh institutional provision far more into the European main-stream, advocating for the first time a comprehensive truly national system of continuing education. It was discarded by Keith Joseph at its very launch, even though he was then in the throes of making major changes in the provision of primary, secondary and even tertiary education.

The ACACE report did in fact recommend many things that might have been expected to appeal to a government intent on rationalization and the pursuit of industrially relevant training objectives. It was even pragmatic enough in its approach to recommend specific means for overcoming the interdepartmental disputes which it said 'can lead to unhelpful administrative and policy divisions between education and training which [were] now being further divided as education budgets [were] cut and training resources [were] increased' (ACACE 1982: 183). It also called upon government to follow the example of its European partners by regarding all education as something to be planned as a continuing process throughout life. Clearly, in Joseph's eyes to have accepted such notions would have been simply to surrender to faddists. Instead he abolished the Council and turned to other things.

Only in Scotland did government take any real notice of such a national survey. There a number of the key recommendations of the Alexander Report of 1975 were accepted, though in retrospect the effect of the major changes were probably cosmetic rather than profound. Virtually all adult provision in the non-occupational sector was suddenly labelled 'community education' though how far that affected its real nature is still a matter for debate.

The generally negative attitude of the Thatcher government towards any proposals for setting up a proper adult education system was, however, in no way exceptional. In the face of economic difficulties the far-reaching clauses of the 1918 *English and Welsh Education Act*, making part-time education compulsory for school-leavers up to the age of 18, were set aside far more readily than similarly important clauses affecting schools. In the 1944 *Education Act* the adult sections were the least detailed and the least mandatory. Adult education remained the optional extra, a topping up process for individual citizens to take or leave. For most people the archetypal adult education institution remained not the extra-mural classes or the WEA meetings that so dominate historical perception, but the night classes where you topped up the lessons of your apprenticeship with a bit of theory, topped up your efficiency as a householder by gaining a few extra useful skills, topped up your experience of elementary or secondary schooling by brushing up a language for the holidays or, more rarely, launched into some hitherto unexplored area such as art appreciation or the history of ship-building.

Such attitudes prevailed regardless of whether the activities involved were job-related or merely personal pleasures. Indeed, many of the courses could have fallen into either category depending on the individual's motivation. Personal satisfaction justified the choice and few people saw choosing a 'liberal' activity as inherently superior to a job-related activity. If local government parsimony made fewer liberal courses available, this was seen as a restriction of consumer choice rather than a deliberate ideological attack on defenders of opposing values.

It is perhaps for such reasons therefore that we have seen no real public outcry over moves to give clearly vocational provision financial priority, certainly none to equal that from the adult education professionals themselves, and from that still small band of political enthusiasts who see adult educational provision as a key factor in the general shaping of society. Indeed, the most effective protests have come not so much from those with an anti-capitalist political commitment as from those who are merely concerned that any damage to adult opportunities to study the arts or the social sciences adversely affects a market in which all tastes should be catered for. That such prioritizing will take us all in a materialistic direction and towards a less humane society seems to have been a less important consideration than whether it offends consumerist principles and, a crucial issue for local politicians, whether a significant number of voters are being alienated by being cut off from their favourite pastimes.

Moreover, the government could legitimately argue that this shifting of priorities in the public provision of facilities is itself justified on consumerist grounds now that non-vocational 'topping up' has become far more widely and cheaply available outside the walls of educational institutions. As the twentieth century began, the only access most people had to the views and inspiration of leading experts was via books and newspaper articles. Given the literary style of the day, many of these did not make easy reading and remained closed to those with only an elementary education. Hence the need for classes and tutorials, for lantern lectures or epidiascope shows followed by a discussion or questions, often provided in an uncomfortable classroom approached through dark and wet streets. Now, the simple exposition of ideas is far more readily available within the home itself through the mass media and often in a far more palatable form than the pioneers could ever have imagined, as well as at far less cost to the individual. It is hardly surprising therefore that the provision of subsidized instruction in such areas as art history and economics should now be in less demand. Indeed, the cheap public provision of instruction in such subjects is increasingly restricted to certificated courses, whereas those attending non-certificated classes are increasingly seen as sociable enthusiasts who, unless they are unwaged, are naturally expected to pay for their pleasures like everybody else. The decision of Birmingham City Council to merge its remaining non-vocational provision into an actual leisure department, hitherto dealing with sport and entertainment, was a clear example of how politicians in England's second largest city viewed such adult provision. Any objections to an increase in price or decrease in provision was, with some justification, likely to be categorized alongside objections to an increase in the price of swimming bath admissions or the hiring of halls for youth club discos.

This Birmingham decision was greeted with horror by many adult education professionals who saw it as degrading to their calling which, though strictly secular, had increasingly taken on the air of a religious mission. Yet it was a decision that caused no general public outcry, because the public probably really did see non-vocational educational provision as just another leisure activity and saw it as equally logical to balance expenditure on heating rooms and hiring leaders for local history discussion groups against the cost of providing equipment for pole-vault practice or space for tap-dancing displays. Any official attempt to categorize non-vocational adult learning as 'liberal' or 'leisure' has in fact become impossible. By a further irony, certain activities hitherto thought of as belonging strictly to the leisure category, such as rock-climbing and sailing, have suddenly begun to play a role in industrial training and selection, thus making them also, despite their sporting origins, an integral part of the government's now favoured occupation-related sector of adult learning.

Much of that sector was, of course, meant to concern itself with the needs of the unemployed. One might therefore have expected those with the interests of the 'deprived' in mind to have been pleased with a government decision to concentrate funding on the very forms of provision most likely to be of direct value to and to be most desired by at least the younger 'deprived'. It is, after all, the fact that so many adults are usually working or seeking immediate work that most obviously differentiates them from school pupils. In secondary school there is a respectable argument for imposing a balanced curriculum and there is a real danger that too great a concentration on job-related skill acquirement will crowd out of the curriculum subjects required for more general personal development. But to extrapolate any such danger to the post-compulsory sphere is to forget that there never can be any controlled balance of the curriculum where adults are concerned. Even if vocational provision were cut and funds diverted to provision that was less obviously vocational, there is absolutely no guarantee or indicative evidence that more than a handful of students would avail themselves of it, given the limited enthusiasm for institutional general studies tradition-ally to be found among British workers.

The curriculum of one group of students, however, needs to be protected, whether one is using vocational or non-vocational criteria. Those with inadequate school certification who are seeking access to further education, those indeed who usually formed the core of Mansbridge's 'liberal' students, may well need to be provided with courses that have no obvious job-relevance but which are extremely expensive in the full fee-paying sector.

This was a justifiable concern of those opposing the closing of Newbattle Abbey College, though the situation in Scotland had been eased by the growth in the number of access courses available to mature students not just in further education colleges but also in the upper classes of the secondary schools. However, the position of such students does not yet seem critical given that, according to official figures for 1993, mature students aged over twenty-one then made up 52.46% of university entrants and the total number of mature university students (excluding postgraduates) had increased by 48% over the previous four years. Indeed access, far from being the victim of some war on 'liberal' studies, can be seen as one of the great adult education successes of recent years. Moreover, as Tight (1993) has emphasized, not just formal access classes but a whole new set of processes including the assessment of prior experiential learning and the more common provision of money-saving advanced standing, have eased the road to university for many of those who would hitherto have been excluded from higher education. The fact that many such students choose to study arts and social science subjects at least suggests that in supporting access arrangements the authorities are hardly displaying a ruthless insistence on financing only industry-orientated study.

No doubt there are those who believe that in emphasizing certification and examination success the expansion of adult participation in higher education and the access movement have themselves altered the nature of 'liberal' adult education for the worse. Everyone knows that the search for marks can all too readily turn the study of poetry into a soul-destroying rote-learning of notes from some cramming booklet or the study of history into a mere question-spotting exercise. But if these objections are taken too far and we begin deploring a quest for certification that is often linked to job aspirations, indeed mistrust any intrusion of occupation-led considerations into adult learning, we are in danger of embracing an educational puritanism that is all too akin to those Victorian élitist notions that saw applied science as inferior to pure science and being 'in trade' as socially inferior to being a professional or living on inherited wealth. Those dedicated to 'pure' adult education can all too easily lose touch with the bulk of the population who, in accordance with British tradition, still see adult provision as either job-related, DIY-related or pure leisure. This is how they and their politicians have been trained to see it and any body of educators which scorns such a view is likely in the short term to lose much of its audience as well as its subsidies.

At the same time it would be foolish to claim that more lofty aims are beyond the reach of adult educators. Evidence from other parts of the European Union (EU) constantly reminds us that the British are almost certainly wrong to assume that institutional adult education is not a national essential like primary or secondary schooling. Certainly, in most north European countries, governments of all persuasions have usually adopted a much more committed approach to adult provision. For them it is not an optional luxury. As one Dutch Conservative minister observed in the early 1980s, he and his fellow politicians in all parties saw adult education not just as a topping up process towards which people could adopt a 'take it or leave it' attitude but as what he called 'a kind of necessity' without which Western democracies could not function properly. Moreover, the Dutch see it as equally related to both personal and vocational life and, in relation to the needs of both home and work, both liberal and job-related elements are equally important.

As a result, Dutch educational law encourages and even presses individuals into seeking formal learning within a balanced curriculum without necessarily seeing the liberal elements simply as an antidote to oppressive industrial influences. Indeed some Dutch industrialists have regularly encouraged liberal studies in work-time as a way of developing personal confidence and initiative among employees at all levels. The economic strains of the late 1980s and early 1990s may well have caused some modifications in the scale of such provision. However, immigrants wishing to embark on a period of major vocational training are still expected to spend an equivalent preliminary period pursuing a general education course as a basis for comfortable citizenship before being subjected to more detailed job-related instruction.

This notion of readily available, compensatory all-round education as a basis for both national and industrial life is one that has also been widely accepted in other north European countries. In Sweden, for example, the hierarchy of the employers' association, was as long ago as the 1970s, quite willing to encourage trade union recruitment of workers for subsidized general studies classes. A visiting British employer poured scorn on this notion and enquired why they and their government were willing to waste money on polishing non-executive 'pebbles' when they might more profitably, in British fashion, have concentrated on polishing their 'diamonds'. The Swedish employers' spokesman calmly replied that their 'diamonds' received a pretty good education anyway and as they had to use the 'pebbles' they preferred them also to be polished.

Even in times of recession, such underlying national assumptions with regard to adult learning remain, assumptions that firmly include the legitimacy of job-related training, not as separate from, but as an integral part of general education. At the same time, enterprises and trades unions have also made non-vocational education a natural part of their own activities. In many of the German *lander* it has been the norm for government to distribute funding widely for the encouragement of general adult learning not only among the churches and political parties but also among trades unions which, like their counterparts in the Nordic countries, have been more than willing to provide academic education in the style of the folk high schools – or Newbattle Abbey College. Most British unions, on the other hand, have been less keen on providing liberal studies for the mass of their members. Instead they have usually chosen to sponsor the studies of a comparatively small group of exceptional students at centres such as Ruskin College, Oxford or the Cooperative College at Loughborough, while focusing their own colleges' attention on the minimal task of instruction related to the day-to-day running and development of the union itself. This was a policy that left many of their educationists in despair (Lowe 1970). One or two unions are now belatedly trying to put things right. UNISON, for example, has now set up an Open College for its members. In fairness, however, one has to accept that British Union leaders were in the past simply reflecting the general attitude to 'liberal' adult education. Had they attempted to set up folk high school style establishments as many of their Nordic counterparts did, it would never have been certain, given the prevailing national attitudes to formal adult learning, that many of their members would have patronised them without extra job-related inducements.

The attitudes of both employers and employees in Britain have, however, shown some recent signs of change. The UNISON proposals and the scheme introduced by Ford (UK) whereby it finances its employees' participation in learning schemes specifically unrelated to their occupational needs, have helped to start an as yet small-scale discussion of such issues, and a number of other unions and enterprises have already decided on action. However, the general mass of British employers and employees remain largely unaware that elsewhere in our own continent gestures of the Ford type are not seen as altruistic (and therefore a probable waste of money) but as eminently practical procedures closely related to economic success.

It is, of course, in this instrumental and pragmatic perception of liberal education that the secret of general European attitudes lie. Certainly Grundtvig saw his folk high schools as relevant not merely to the personal development of farmers but also to the improvement of their farming. As the Finnish educational philosopher Toukonen puts it:

Values stressing personal development may once have been behind the idea of continuing education, but a closer look reveals that the

original idea has become increasingly utilitarian . . . Continuing education is (now) mostly defined on the basis of an individual's needs and
interests . . . Education must continuously adapt itself to the needs of
industries and even correct their mistakes.

(Toukunen 1993: 45)

Toukunen even goes on to quote the claim of one of Finland's most
celebrated educational pioneers, J. V. Snellman, that an individual becomes a real person to the extent that he or she possesses property.
'Thus it is a man's duty', he said, 'to acquire property so as to become a
person, whose personality other people can recognize. The principle of
continuing education supports this pattern'.

Such an assertion does remind us that not all educational reformers
have been opposed to linking continuing education with work. Indeed
one explanation of Britain's failure to interest as high a proportion of its
citizens in continuing education as Finland has succeeded in doing may
well lie in the traditional embarrassment of the British adult education
establishment when it sees its own activities being linked too closely to
industry or when they are seen as forming a business in their own right.
Some educators have recently been willing to show more open financial
enterprise. The university departments of continuing education at Sheffield and Lancaster, for example, have built up summer leisure programmes that would do a private sector entrepreneur proud. Too often,
however, there has been a refusal to accept that the attraction of funds
from customers is not a degradation but a natural characteristic of an
educational sector which always was and will continue to be in the
marketplace and for which governments will only provide funding when
it proves to be worth their while.

There are, in fact, sufficient exciting experiments in train, both in the
mass media and in the field of open learning, to suggest that far from
being oppressed, British adult education is now entering something of a
golden age. Moreover, if the Ford scheme and others like it gain a real
grip, then in time the British also will learn that too rigid an insistence on
a vocational/liberal dichotomy will be a destructive act rather than a
guarantee of 'pure' education. As the Swedish observer, Rubenson, puts it:

in a learning society the borderlines between various forms of education, as well as between the world of work and the world of
education, are becoming fuzzy. What will happen in this situation
with regard to who gets access to what kind of education-learning
opportunities will . . . to a large extent depend on the balance of
power between the two major collectives, capital and labour.

(Rubenson 1993: 60)

It will also depend, as he himself admits, on the current economic situation and, in any case, any strictly maintained liberal education/ training distinction is an irrelevance.

If, since 1979, there has been an erosion of 'traditional' adult education provision in Britain it may simply be that the market has moved elsewhere. There is certainly good evidence that the public desire for self-improvement is as lively as ever, even if it is less dependent on a professional body of adult educators. The 1994 MORI survey mentioned earlier revealed that only 10 per cent of the British population aged seventeen and over was actually 'studying' at that time and only 3 per cent people over sixty-five, those with the greatest amount of leisure, were doing so. Less than 50 per cent claimed to have done any studying since they left school. Yet more than 60 per cent of the respondents refused to say that they were uninterested in any kind of study and one is left with the suspicion that what was being rejected was formal adult education of the traditional kind and that other forms of adult self-improvement and cultural development are continuing on a major scale.

The fact that book sales of all kinds are booming, that art exhibitions attract larger crowds than ever before and (so it is claimed), that more Scots go to the opera in a year than go to League football matches must say something about the present state of adult learning. Even if professionals retort that these are largely middle class activities, then we must at least rejoice in having a better educated middle class and at least one less philistine than in Matthew Arnold's day. The defenders of traditional formal adult education would do well also to remember that the WEA, even in its subsidized heyday, was mainly supported by this same middle class or by working class students only too anxious to rise in the world by means of middle-class style education and the acquiring of middle-class cultural tastes.

These last observations do, however, beg a further perennial question, often asked but never taken seriously: is the sudden liberation that can often be produced by 'liberal' adult education always a constructive contribution to the student's life? It is certainly a question raised by Willie Russell in his *Educating Rita* where he makes it abundantly clear that the widening of Rita's intellectual and cultural horizon is made at considerable cost, destroying her marriage and alienating her from her family and friends. The OU authorities certainly rejoiced in the power of her liberation into middle class values and awarded the actress who played the part in the film an honorary degree. But can those who see education as a power for good really rejoice in a process that leaves her still-disadvantaged husband and family even more disgruntled and distanced from their middle class neighbours? Perhaps if Rita's intellectual awakening had taken place more gradually and organically, through learning processes more naturally related to her family's daily needs, including even their work needs rather than through a traumatic introduction to D. H. Lawrence and heady literary criticism at the hands of an alcoholic university lecturer, she might well have become a cultural bridgehead for her community rather than a free-ranging intellectually intoxicated melancholic.

It is perhaps their instinctive suspicions of such a process that has led the British working class to be wary of middle class adult educators bearing cultural gifts, especially when those gifts are unrelated to their daily lives and have no occupational pay-off. Sometimes their memory of compulsory schooling has been too grim. Sometimes the middle class nature of the experience being offered to them is so undisguised that they feel in danger of being patronized. In the absence of a Swedish-style sense of living in a learning society, British people are naturally suspicious of activities with none of the obvious practical outcomes that their own self-arranged or employer-arranged programmes of adult learning provide. Only in isolated pockets, such as West Belfast, have inspiring practitioners such as Lovett gathered enthusiastic students around them, usually in a community setting, and established the embryo of a learning society. The atmosphere of a formal course dedicated to 'cultural' values is usually too off-putting.

Elsewhere in Europe, where adult educators have not been ashamed to link liberal education to occupational advancement or to the working life of the immediate neighbourhood, the folk high schools and union-sponsored certificate classes in the arts subjects have boomed along with the uncertificated discussion conducted in study circles, significantly meeting in people's homes and undominated by 'experts'. In Britain, access classes clearly linked to social and professional advancement have also succeeded. The old war between 'liberal' and 'job-related' has been both unnecessary and destructive, a mere clash of false images.

Indeed, this is an artificial war that has diverted attention from all too many of the real educational tragedies of the last fifteen years – the oppression of the public library system, the gradual erosion of television standards as a consequence of the ratings war, the increasingly prohibitive cost of our greatly underestimated correspondence courses and teach yourself systems. These developments hit right at the heart of self-organized study systems in the Tough mould. But most determined adults still find their way round such obstacles. The marketplace still offers worthwhile bargains – the University of the Third Age, for example, or those small community study groups which meet in each other's houses and incur hardly any expenses at all. They might even be experiencing a truly liberal awakening at the hands of a work-related open learning course. If their finances allow it they may already have embarked on the great information highway, no small thing at a time when the British Library is contemplating a total end to the publication of printed books.

With all its faults the traditional, pragmatic British form of adult education continues. Its strengths are its adaptability and its encouragement of individual and local enterprise. Its weaknesses are its lack of coherence and its failure to be recognized as a national asset worthy of greater encouragement. It can only be strengthened therefore by the input of extra funding for any constructive purpose. It can only be weakened by a continuing, destructive and ultimately pointless insistence on making too clear a distinction between what is training, what is leisure and what is liberal enlightenment.

REFERENCES

ACACE (1982) *Continuing Education: From Policies to Practice*, Leicester: ACACE.

Alexander Report, (1975) *Adult Education: The Challenge of Change*, Edinburgh: HMSO.

Faure, E. *et al.* (1972) *Learning to Be: The World of Education Today and Tomorrow*, Paris: UNESCO.

Kelly, T. (1970) *A History of Adult Education in Great Britain: From the Middle Ages to the Twentieth Century*, Liverpool: The University Press.

Lowe, J. (1970) *Adult Education in England and Wales: A Critical Survey*, London: Michael Joseph.

NIACE (1994) *What Price the Learning Society?* Leicester: NIACE.

Rubenson, K. (1993) 'Adult education policy in Sweden, 1967–91', in Edwards R., Sieminski S. and Zeldin D., (eds) *Adult Learners, Education and Training*, London: Routledge.

Russell Report, (1973) *Adult Education: A Plan for Development (The Russell Report)*, London: HMSO.

Tight, M. (1993) 'Access, not access courses: maintaining a broad vision', in Edwards R., Sieminski S. and Zeldin D. (eds) *Adult Learners, Education and Training*, London: Routledge.

Tough, A. (1976) 'Self-planned learning and major personal change', in R. M. Smith (Ed.) *Adult Learning: Issues and Innovations*, North Illinois University: ERIC.

Toukunen, M. L. (1993) 'The continuing education principle: a paradox of adult education', *Life and Education in Finland*, Issue 2/93, Helsinki.

Chapter 9

Concepts, organization and current trends of lifelong education in Sweden†

Kenneth Abrahamsson

THREE PERIODS OF SWEDISH ADULT EDUCATION

In a historical perspective, Swedish adult education can be divided into three major periods. The first period from the late nineteenth-century to the early 1960s reflects the great contribution of popular adult education to the modernization of the Swedish nation. Study circles and folk high schools provided alternative learning options for adults being neglected in their young years. The concept of self-education symbolizes this period.

'Self-education' comprised a collective social value implying that it was the movement that played the major role for educating its members. With some overstatement you could say that education is too important a societal responsibility to be handed over to the education sector itself. In practice, however, popular adult education did play a complementary or compensatory role. The late Olof Palme once labelled Sweden a 'study circle democracy', thereby paying tribute to the role of active citizenship and collective learning in the development of modern Sweden.

The second period started in the late 1960s and lasted for almost two decades. In short, it can be characterized by the 'building up of the Swedish adult education model'. During the 1970s especially a number of political decisions were taken in order to create a diversified system of publicly organized adult education. Access and outreach activities to cater for new learners were important components of this model.

A new system of municipal adult education was made available all over the country to meet the needs from the seventh grade of formal schooling. New educational options were also created to combat adult illiteracy and to support adult studies for individuals with evident reading and writing problems. Special initiatives were taken in order to

† This is an edited version of an article that appeared in *International Journal of University Adult Education* vol. xxxii, (3), 1993.

secure the options of adult learning through a new law of educational leave of absence in combination with a new system of study finance for adults. Special attention was also given to broadening the options for adults with short prior education to study during working hours. Special training allowances were made available for trade union members. A significant expansion of adult learning activities in a broad sense is a sign of this period.

A comprehensive view of adult learning was elaborated through the concept of recurrent education. The idea was to promote adult learning in a lifelong perspective by alternating periods of work, education and leisure activities. During this period the policy of paid parental leave of absence was also set into practice. In fact, adult education in Sweden was almost transformed into a women's movement. Men came to form the minority in most forms of adult education with the exception of employment training and on-the-job learning. Women and men also had different priorities concerning the possible use of shortened work time. Women preferred shorter working days while men wanted longer vacations. The interest in using time for learning was rather limited.

The third period starts in the mid 1980s. At that time a number of policy decisions were taken in the Swedish Parliament, Riksdagen, to open up for other financial sources and for a more flexible organization of adult education. Employment training was separated from the national educational administration and was transformed into the National Employment Training Board. It used to be a step-daughter taken care of by the Swedish National Board of Education and the National Labour Market Board.

The second decision taken was to open up a number of new options of commissioned or customized adult education. Finally, Parliament decided to create the so-called renewal funds, by cutting 10% off the extra-profit of the bigger enterprises or companies. The total sum added up to between five and six billion kronor, around £600 million, to be used for corporate learning strategies during five years starting from 1986. This policy had a strong impact on work-oriented learning strategies. Even though the employers were very sceptical about this method of using their profits, it is obvious that the interest in employers' sponsored adult education has increased strongly during the late 1980s.

SWEDEN – A NATION OF ADULT LEARNERS?

Study circles in Sweden have their roots in popular movements, other fora for civic participation, community actions and adult learning. Staff-development programmes and various forms of workplace learning are today as frequent as study circles. The Swedish adult education family also comprises folk high schools (residential colleges for adults), formal education for adults (a parallel school for adults), employment training and distance education. Higher education can also be seen as a part of adult education. During the early 1980s almost half of the new entrants were aged twenty-five or more. Today, young students are again in a majority, but many of them have acquired life and work experience prior to higher studies.

The fact that almost one out of two adults in Sweden are joining some kind of organized adult learning each year raises the following question: are people in Sweden 'sentenced' to lifelong education or is it a free and voluntary activity? Youth education is compulsory in almost every country. The number of years of obligatory school attendance varies from eight to twelve years. But what about the rest of your life?

Adult education in Sweden is, of course, not formally compulsory. There is no adult education court authorized to sentence people to enduring educational activities. No authority or public agency could say 'Due to your obvious lack of knowledge and skills needed in our modern society, I hereby sentence you to lifelong education . . .!' The common argument is instead 'adults not having basic skills or not being literate in their society, will run a higher risk of suffering from unemployment or social exclusion. In short, 'if you don't join the education brigade, you will be a loser'.

The social impact is, of course, that many adults have to join adult education to cope better with present or future skill requirements. People belonging to the growing number of unemployed adults will be offered a variety of different training options. Employees risking redundancy due to the closing down of factories or public services will also have to respond to various educational programmes. [. . .]

Civic education to enhance citizen participation more and more is being replaced with competence development and workplace learning. The development of adult education in Sweden is characterized by shifting ideals and the formation of new institutional patterns to meet changing needs in society. At present 'the market' has taken the initiative away from 'the popular movements'. The state still has to spend a lot of money, due to unemployment. The mandate of the current governmental one-person commission on adult education is first to reduce costs and second to make the system more cost-efficient. Not surprisingly, the interest in open learning and distance education is growing in a restrictive financial climate.

SWEDISH ADULT EDUCATION – GOALS AND PROFILE

Popular movements, state interests and market incentives have played different roles in the development of modern adult education in Sweden. Popular movements gave birth to the idea of adult learning. The state took care of the 'adult learning child' and gave it bread and money to develop and grow. Today, when the state has overspent its resources, everybody is looking for a helping hand from the market. So far, however, the state seems to balance cuts and fresh money between different ministries. Support from the Ministry of Education and Culture is strongly declining. Due to a growing input of employment-oriented education supported by grants from the Ministry of Labour, adult education is expanding against the 'political wind'.

All adult education organized or subsidized by the State, whether credential or non-credential, has been subject to goals of educational policy defined by the Riksdag during the 1980s.

Adult education, then, has the following aims:

- to bridge the education gaps and in this way promote greater equality and social justice;
- to increase the ability of adults to understand, critically appraise and take part in cultural, social and political life and in this way contribute towards the development of a democratic society;
- to train adults for various duties, to contribute towards the transformation of working life and to help achieve full employment, in this way promoting development and progress in society;
- to cater to individual adult preferences with respect to wider opportunities of study and education, and to give them an opportunity of supplementing the education received in their formative years.

In principle, adult education is open to all adults and to groups spontaneously turning to it, either as a means of improving their general knowledge of one or more fields or because they find it necessary to improve their competence in the community or at work. These studies are often of a wide-ranging, basic character, and above all they provide persons whose youth education was brief and insufficient with an opportunity of raising their general level of knowledge.

ADULT EDUCATION PROVISION AT COMMUNITY LEVEL

Formal adult education comprises municipal adult education, which is provided at two levels. All municipalities are obliged by law to respond to the need for adult education corresponding to the whole nine year compulsory school (*grundskolan*). The *School Act* adopted in May 1991 also stresses the need for municipal adult education at upper secondary level. The public school system for adults also includes basic Swedish language instruction for immigrants. Formal adult education is, above all, aimed at giving adults a chance of making up for deficiencies in their previous schooling and of qualifying for further studies, for vocational education or for employment.

Popular adult educational activities, comprising studies at folk high schools or under the aegis of adult educational associations, are partly State-subsidized. To qualify for subsidies, the education has to meet certain general conditions, but otherwise the mandators are at complete liberty to decide the emphasis and content of educational activities for themselves.

The abundant variety and generous availability of popular education also makes it possible to reach those who would otherwise not go in for educational activities. Popular education has the declared objective of developing basic democratic values in society. This education confers knowledge and skills, but perhaps its main importance lies in strengthening the self-confidence of the participants, increasing their understanding and respect for other people's opinions and in this way contributing towards the democratization of society.

Sweden has a very active labour market policy, aimed at sustaining full employment. Labour market training is an important measure for the prevention and solution of unemployment problems. Mostly it takes the form of specially organized vocational training, but it can also make use of the regular educational system.

Personnel education or in-service training, in the present context, can be defined as the education which concerns employees and is organized on the employer's term and at his expense in companies and national and local authorities. Decisions relating to personnel education, then, are made by the employer, but the trade union organizations are able to exert various degrees of influence. Sweden does not have any legislation governing entitlement to or influence on personnel education, but agreements on the subject have begun to develop between the labour market parties. There are great differences between categories of employees. [. . .] The already well-educated receive twice as much personnel education as others.

ACCESS, PARTICIPATION AND NEW TARGET GROUPS

Equity as a widened access to all kinds of adult learning opportunities has been a key characteristic of Swedish adult education during the last two or three decades. The system of municipal adult education or in Swedish 'komvux' was at first created to cater for the pool of talented adults wanting to add to their already acquired education. In the early 1970s the trade unions and the working-life oriented study associations reacted strongly and claimed that *komvux* should be directed to adults with only six or seven years' formal schooling.

It is, of course, not possible to rank priority groups in Swedish adult education. The list below can be seen as groups that all have been given a high level of priority in the policy process.

- Adults with no more than seven or eight years of formal schooling due to the fact that they did not have the opportunity to benefit from the modern nine-year compulsory school (*grundskolan*).
- Adults in the work force either being made redundant or being employed in a sector subject to major structural transformation. Labour market education and employment training programmes have permanently had a high policy priority and has represented the largest financial investment in the adult education sector over the years.
- Adults with reading and writing difficulties or being functional illiterate in contemporary Swedish society and working life. Swedish for immigrants as well as adult basic education have been provided extensively for over fifteen years.
- Adults wanting to enhance their civic capacities are also an important group in Swedish policies and especially within the framework of popular adult education through study circles and folk high schools.
- Another group of adults receiving more policy attention in the last years are employees that have been excluded from the labour market due to bad work environment and mis-match between work requirements and human capacities. Special resources have been ear-marked for rehabilitation of former members of the work force and education and training as well as work design have been used as tools for these 'come back to work' projects.
- Older adults do not form a priority group as such but they are a growing component in popular adult education. The arena of post-retirement learning represents a crucial challenge to any system of lifelong education.
- Young individuals not starting or completing upper secondary education are also important target groups for adult education. A special group in this respect is upper secondary students who become 'tactical drop-outs' with the aim of getting better marks in *komvux*.

The most significant shift regarding target is reflected in the increasing numbers of unemployed adults. The new pattern is that they no longer represent only unskilled or semi-skilled labour but also white-collar workers and professionals with a high level of prior education. The ongoing transformation of the public sector within the framework of decentralization and increasing efficiency has contributed to the high level of white-collar worker unemployment. Another major factor is the financial restrictions and cut-backs at the municipal level.

The reforms of the 1970s in adult and higher education led to a growth in adult participation in all kinds of programmes and courses in higher education. In the mid-1980s adults were in a majority in short-cycle courses and also in some degree programmes. In general, 50 per cent of the population took part in some kind of adult education study, mainly study circles and employer-sponsored training.

Thus, the system of higher education was subject to a process of 'adultification' giving less opportunities to young students than adults. Every political decision in the field of higher education during the last decade has aimed at giving young students better or at least equal opportunities in comparison with adults. [. . .] In general, however, adults in higher education is not a strong policy field for the new government. Youth education and the idea of Sweden developing 'the best school in Europe' is receiving much higher priority.

HOW IT USED TO BE – SOME GENERAL CHARACTERISTICS

The Swedish model of adult education can be characterized by the following aspects:

- Adult education has been provided in almost all local municipalities through study circles, folk high schools, formal adult education and employment training.
- Study assistance has been available both for short-time and long-time studies. The most common form is a combination of a grant and a loan. For employment training students, however, there is a training allowance which is not repayable.
- All gainfully employed persons are entitled by law to educational leave, without any restriction as regards its duration or the choice of studies. An employer can only postpone, not reject an employee's request to study.
- Adult studies and learning also have occupied a prominent position in the reform of working life. The *Shop Stewards Act*, the *Co-determination Act* and various collective agreements entitle trade union representatives to devote time to studies during paid working hours.
- Finally, adult education can be viewed as an important element of general welfare policy. A high level of knowledge and education benefits both the individual and society.

Sweden, then, has had a working model of wide high-ranging adult education. The means exist for achieving an ambitious objective of this kind. This is not to say that all the problems have been solved and that genuine educational opportunities have been created for everybody. The ongoing reorientation of educational policies in Sweden comprises all the five points listed above. The pattern of local provision is shifting in a variety of ways. Formal adult education at the upper secondary level is much more organizationally linked to youth education. There is also an increasing pattern of mixed or mingled provision due to the ideas of customized training.

Study assistance for adults has been subject to heavy cut-backs, whereas training allowances for the unemployed have expanded at a speed almost impossible to control. The law of educational leave of absence is subject to further reflection and change within a new governmental commission. The learning rights for trade unionists have been drastically down-graded. The idea of a general welfare policy is genuinely shifting its face and function in a public service system more dependent on private provisions, privatization and market incentives.

SHIFTING IDEALS AND NEW PRIORITIES

At the end of 1991 *Newsweek* nominated Sweden to have the best adult education in the world. A few weeks after this recognition, the new government presented its first Education Bill to Riksdagen in January 1992. It comprised very heavy cuts in both municipal adult education and popular adult education. The total reductions were about £50–60 million and almost 20 per cent of the total expenditures for public service adult education. Within a few days there were a number of demonstrations and much criticism put forward in the public debate. Many interest groups asked why the government wanted to cut and hold back adult education in times of a dramatically increasing unemployment level.

The media activities gave *komvux* and municipal adult education a public face. When the Bill was dealt with in Education Committee in the Parliament, the cuts were reduced by 50 per cent. The political decision taken underlined the importance of municipal adult education as a tool to counter unemployment. Thus, municipal adult education began to play an important role as employment training and work qualification. The extra money was not channelled through the education budget, but within the framework of labour market policies. The field that suffered the most severe cuts was trade union education and subsidies for short-time leave of absence.

The downgrading of adult education has been commented upon in a current OECD-examination of Swedish education policies.

Adult education, traditionally considered as one of the 'jewels' in the educational crown of Sweden, is not a priority for the new government. The need for infusing greater coherence into the manifold activities that are going on in this field is generally recognized. But we could detect no signs of a concern for setting in motion steps in this direction and it would be useful to know the reasons for this. All the more so as the need for adult training and life-long learning will be even stronger in the future and will call for closer coordination between the education and employment sectors. Is the Ministry's policy to leave the initiative for this to its employment counterparts, the municipalities, the firms and individual themselves? What is the Ministry's reaction to the proposal made in Section II of our report that, rather than let adult education erode continuously, an assessment should be undertaken of the present state of affairs and of future needs as a basis for redefining the direction for the future development of the entire adult education sector?

(OECD 1992)

The conservative–liberal government replied that adult education has a higher priority due to the fact that the *School Act* (adopted in Riksdagen during the social democratic government in the spring of 1991) states that all adults have the legal right to education corresponding to nine years of schooling (*grundskolan*). Furthermore attention was given to the increasing option to let adults and young students participate in the same courses and programmes at the upper secondary level. Finally, the government pointed at the one-person commission on 'a more efficient adult education'. This effort, in the governments view, could be a good point of departure to evaluate the role of adult education in Sweden.

In spite of this answer it is quite obvious that the conservative–liberal government gives much higher priority to youth education than to adult education. Raising the quality standards of higher education and research is a top priority, which also is reflected in the number of initiatives in that field. [. . .]

'THE MORE YOU CUT, THE MORE WE GROW . . .'

In spite of the various efforts to limit the role of adult education it has, paradoxically enough, expanded significantly in the last year. The explanation is, of course, the role of *komvux* as the new employment training scheme. In this respect, *komvux* has been more flexible to meet the needs of unemployed white-collar workers from public administration or the service sector in need of a theoretical platform, with basic skills in Swedish, English and Mathematics.

[1992–3] could be described as an economic catastrophe for Sweden. There has been an ongoing decline of the industrial sector. Many banks have had extremely high deficits and should have had to close if the government had not secured guarantee money. Productivity development has also been negative. Large amounts of currency began to move out from the country. A political legitimation crisis came closer and closer. 'The market' expected a strong and firm political intervention from the four-party minority government. It could not, however, seek political support from the new populistic party, New Democracy. The only solution was to make a political agreement with the social democrats.

The outcome of this historic agreement between, the two blocks of Parliament was labelled the 'Rosenbad agreement'. It was compared with the historic 'Saltsjobad's agreement' from the late 1930s showing the way for the collaborative spirit between the unions and the employers in the creation of the modern Sweden. The new agreement implied heavy reductions in public expenditures and a forthcoming transformation of the social security system from the public sector to the trade unions. The government had to withdraw a number of suggestions to privatise publicly owned enterprises.

One week after this agreement another package of crisis management appeared with new cuts in the public sector. During the period of the negotiations between the two blocks, there was an enormous escalation of political energy in order to save the Swedish crown and to present a firm and confident public image to the market. Education investments turned out to be a very important dimension in the new national agreement on how Sweden's financial disease and low productivity temperature should be cured. The result of this historic agreement was presented in a new Bill to the Riksdag 1992/93:50 'on different measures to stabilize the Swedish economy'.

ACCESS, EQUITY AND THE FUTURE SWEDISH ADULT EDUCATION MARKET

In total £60 million has been earmarked to promote adult education at various levels. [. . .] At present, it is very difficult to anticipate how the new system of study assistance will be developed in the future. Some of the conservative critics say that the former policy had too much of a 'spoon-feeding-function' for adults with little prior education. Education grants and study assistance were provided without really checking their motivation and learning interests. According to these ideas education resources should be allocated to gifted people with high aspiration and a significant amount of prior learning.

These ideas are quite foreign to the value climate of access and equity that coloured the Swedish adult education reforms of the 1970s. At that time, adults with short education should have the best resources. Society and the public sector should do their very best to facilitate adult learning over the life span. Educational leave of absence, options to study during working hours, outreach activities by active study organizers, a broad provision of adult education, open college policies for higher education were tools used to enhance lifelong learning.

The volume, structure and context of Swedish adult education is not just a question of political priorities. The future of the Swedish learning society is also dependent on the tax-payers' views and priorities regarding the public service sector as such. No country with a declining productivity curve can afford to have a strong public sector without living on loans from foreign countries or future generations of citizens. Thus, it seems likely that a social democratic government also should have to make cuts in various parts of the education system.

The next decade will be a crossroads for Swedish adult education. The former Swedish model of recurrent education still seems to have a high reputation in the OECD and the EC. It is, however, regarded as a bureaucratic construction within the neo-liberal culture of the present government. [. . .]

From a progressive policy point of view, it is important to ensure that adults will be able to use their rights to learn and develop across the lifespan. Supposedly this need does not just reflect domestic needs in Sweden. It is, in fact, a crucial component in the development of a future European citizenship with or without the formation of a European Union.

CONCLUDING REMARKS ON 'LIFELONG EDUCATION SOCIETY'

The title of the Swedish background report for the recent OECD-examination of educational policies in Sweden is *The Swedish Way Towards a Learning Society*. The metaphor of a learning society or a study circle democracy is much more common than a 'lifelong education society'. Sweden as a learning society can be characterized in the following way considering the post-war development:

- a growth in the average number of years of education for different age cohorts from 6–7 years to 11 or 12 years;
- an almost continuous growth in the percentage of the population studying full-time, from 12 per cent in 1950 to nearly 20 per cent in 1990;
- a broad provision of education at all levels throughout the country in order to increase access and equity;
- a systematic effort to use training and retraining of the labour force as an instrument to implement policies of full employment and to adapt the labour force to new needs.

A retrospective look at education in Sweden also has to consider the fact that:

- the level of unemployment in Sweden has been very low in international terms over than last few decades. The low unemployment

level, at best between 1 and 2 per cent has, however, shifted dramatically the last two years (and is now up to around 7 per cent);

- female participation around 80 per cent in the labour force is very
  high in international terms;
- education has two functions in relation to the public sector which are
  particularly worthy of note. First, almost all education is provided
  within the public sector. Second, the public sector has been more
  efficient than the private sector in absorbing individuals with a higher
  education background.

It is obvious that investments in education and training for young
individuals and adults have been integral components in the formation
of the Swedish welfare model. It is also evident that Swedish experiences
in the field of manpower development and labour market education
have been recognized in many countries. Equality of opportunity and a
broadened access to learning and competence development across the
life span also signify Swedish public policies. The last two or three years
have dramatically changed the conditions of implementing Swedish full
employment policies. The rejection of young individuals without sufficient education and the exclusion of older blue and also white collar
workers have strong repercussions on the needs for future education and
training of the work force. The strong focus on introductory courses
during the 1980s has been replaced by the growing interest of outplace-
ment and learning to leave your job instead of job-related competence
development.

The ageing population expands the span of lifelong education, but it
also implies growing needs in the field of social and medical care of
citizens over 80 years of age carrying various functional disabilities. The
threat of social exclusion of minorities may not be as evident in Sweden
in comparison with other countries with a strong ethnic and multi-
cultural mix. It is a problem, however, that cannot be neglected. The
immigration during the last decade has mainly comprised refugees from
third world countries and the former Yugoslavia. Many refugees have
very short if any formal schooling from their home countries.

The ethnic, cultural and educational gap reflected above calls for
substantial educational and social measures in order to avoid the risk of
future social exclusion. It is not a challenge, however, that can be met by
a one-sided strategy educating and adapting new immigrants to the
Swedish society. It is as important to initiate learning processes among
Swedish citizens in order to deepen the cultural understanding, increase
the social dialogue and last but not least to counteract racism and
hostility against immigrants.

It is not true to talk about the decreasing role of trade unions in
Sweden. Some of the major trade unions have, in fact, increased their

number of members in the last year. It is more relevant to discuss the changing context of trade unions due to increasing decentralization and privatization of society. My anticipation is that the trade unions will survive the ongoing organizational and structural transformation and also expand their role in promoting adult education and learning at the work place. Today, as in the early 1970s, trade unions tend to be among the strongest speakers for adult education and competence development. They also focus on the role of workplace learning as well as the learning impact of production technology, division of work and work design as such.

The arrows of change seem to move in a number of complementary, contradictory and also conflicting directions at the same time. The increasing decentralization is reflected through the hierarchical arrow from the centre to the periphery. The strong and bureaucratic state intervention is withdrawing and thereby opening up new options at the local and community-oriented level. The horizontal arrow is hitting the strong public service sector by providing more private initiatives and incentives. Within this transition it is possible to observe the confusing and contradictory impact of a diagonal arrow symbolizing the dramatically changing international context with particular reference to the new European setting.

It is not easy to anticipate the impact of these new conditions on the notion of a lifelong education society. From a Swedish perspective, it is possible to conclude, however, that the 'grand plan' of a coherent strategy of recurrent education has seen its best days. Collectively organized solutions backed up by overall organizationally pre-fabricated patterns are no more in service.

Today there is more focus on finding matching areas connecting individual needs and sets of incentives to stimulate and facilitate active adult learning projects. With some oversimplification, it is possible to conclude that Sweden is taking a big step from recurrent education to recurrent learning and is thereby getting closer to the concept of lifelong learning used in many Unesco settings. The latest evidence in this process of value change is represented by a commission on the future of Swedish labour market education.

The main proposal is to change the legal status of the employment training board from a public agency to a free enterprise in the competence market. In order to support the individual adult learner in this new context, the task force has outlined an individually based competence insurance. By the use of this tool each citizen could accumulate learning time that could be used for different lengths and also various learning stations across the life span.

With such an insurance, it would be possible for every citizen and employee to start new life and work learning projects independent of social, cultural and economic background. It would also be a way to reorient the current provision of adult learning options to meet the needs of competence up-grading and education on behalf of the individuals instead of contributing to the survival of the existing institutions of adult education. The great challenge or threat of this model is of course, the issue of access and participation of adults with a low level of prior education. [. . .]

It is up to the reader to interpret the adult learning impact of all these changes. Among the possible alternatives to discuss are (i) the preservation or conservation of the adult education reforms from the 1970s; (ii) giving adult education policies in Sweden a new and second chance in a system of education more dependent on decentralization and privatization, thus aiming at a new balance between public and private in Sweden, or (iii) the search for a new and alternative model stressing the needs of self-directed and active citizens and not considering the need for survival of the existing institution of adult education.

Issues of access, participation and equity will, however, determine the future learning context of all three alternatives. Unemployment, immigration and the risk of social exclusion in a more market oriented society may produce a new educational underclass. Thereby, it transforms the idea of lifelong education from a right for all citizens to a mechanism to sort, select and reject adult citizens during their life cycle development.

REFERENCES

Ministry of Education and Science (1992) *The Swedish Way Towards a Learning Society. Report to OECD.* Sweden: Ministry of Education and Science.
OECD (1992) *Review of Education Policy in Sweden. Examiner's Report and Questions,* Paris: CERI.

Chapter 10

The second chance

The vital myth of equal opportunities in adult education†

Risto Rinne and Osmo Kivinen

INTRODUCTION

[. . .] Adult education has often been marketed as a 'second chance' system, offering the opportunity of a second beginning for those who have been held back in social status through inadequate education and training. Indeed, it is in accordance with the ideals of democracy that adult education can provide students with a means of enhancing their social status, participation and liberation. Nonetheless its emancipatory effect is largely dependent upon the structural conditions imposed by society. It has been queried by Courtney (1992, p. 146), for instance, whether present forms of education are primarily designed for those who need it most, and whether their needs will really be met by an expansion of current forms of education, since in the long run these needs derive from basic social problems anchored in the economy and polity. [. . .] He argues that a comprehensive theory of participation in adult education does need to take into account a wider range of explanatory factors than are found in the received life cycle, motivational orientation or decision models. The theory needs to incorporate other sociological factors as well, and to recognize that for adults, learning is a 'discretionary' activity, competing with their other activities both customary and non-customary. The objective of the theory must be to explicate adult education in its wider societal context.

This chapter offers an examination of adult education in Finland as a 'second chance' route, on the basis of interview material relating to the year 1990, gathered with the aid of Statistics Finland from a representative sample of the adult population of the country ($n = 3990$; for further details see Rinne *et al.*, 1992).

† This is an edited version of an article that appeared in *Scandinavian Journal of Educational Research*, vol. 37(2), 1993.

THE CUMULATIVE CHARACTER OF ADULT EDUCATION

In research into participation in adult education, very similar observations have been repeated ever since the 1920s (Brunner *et al.*, 1959; Courtney, 1992). In the United States, for instance, the typical participant in adult education has been characterized as male or female, white, middle-class, relatively well-educated and relatively young. The picture is drawn of typical adult education students during the 1960s in the massive classic 600-page survey by Johnstone and Rivera:

> The participant is just as often a woman as a man, is typically under forty, has completed high school or better, enjoys an above-average income, works full-time and most often in a white-collar occupation, is typically white and Protestant, is married and a parent, lives in an urbanized area (more likely in the suburbs than a large city), and is found in all parts of the country, but more frequently on the West Coast than would be expected by chance.
>
> (Johnstone and Rivera, 1965, p. 78)

David Riesman's rule, familiar in many other fields of life – 'the more, the more' – applies equally appositely to participation in adult education as well. The irony is that those who participate most in continuing education are those who in a sense need it least; one of the heaviest impacts of accumulated educational capital, in fact, is found in the adult education participation rate (Johnstone and Rivera, 1965, p. vi, p. 103).

In the Nordic countries, one of the major objectives for adult education has been to promote greater democracy. Nordhaug (1983, 1989) has examined public adult education policy in terms of social, generational, gender and regional equality, and his finding is that overall the policy being applied is one of welfare state egalitarianism, i.e. one where the main thrust is to encourage maximum take-up of the services available – in this case, adult education. Despite the desire to support participation by adults from lower-income groups, however, their participation rate has not in fact significantly risen, and Nordhaug (1983, p. 36) suggests that in Norway the gap between participants and non-participants may even be increasing.

Courtney (1992, p. 50) has emphasized that one of the most frequent and significant findings in the research into participation in adult education is that adults are more likely to study for 'continuity' than for 'compensation', and more probably for occupational and career reasons than out of a pure love of learning. What adult education represents for many people is primarily an extension of their formal education. Adult education can also be examined as a form of 'cultural consumption', offering considerable potential status value and contributing to the formation of cultural capital (cf. Bourdieu, 1985).

Until the 1970s, at least, participation in adult education was typically studied in terms of presumed information needs. The basic assumption was that in situations where individuals experienced information deficits, e.g. in relation to the requirements encountered in their work or life, demand for adult education would quasi-automatically materialize. The societal factors promoting or hindering participation in adult education were reduced to a few variables phrased in terms of the satisfaction of needs arising from informational conflicts. This view, with its emphasis on good intentions, can easily be recognized in the early Finnish investigations into participation in adult education (see Lehtonen and Tuomisto, 1972, p. 35). It fits well with the ideology of the second chance, and with the attempt to guarantee the egalitarian availability of adult education benefits.

The idea of information deficits triggering educational needs fitted very comfortably with an expansionist ideology of vocational adult education, founded on the fear of rapid obsolescence of workers' qualifications in the rush of scientific and technological progress. Society's interests were seen as including both the satisfaction of information deficits experienced by individuals at work, and also the upgrading of educational inadequacies among the older generations in the labour force. A well-intentioned ideology of the satisfaction of individuals' educational needs was complemented by the concept of conflicting 'structural imperatives' which adult education could be used to resolve. In Finland, towards the end of the 1980s educational policy began to be focused around this kind of thinking, and vocational adult education came to be seen as the core for 'new' educational policies aimed at bringing processes of structural change in the economy and society under control (see Kivinen and Rinne, 1992). In the context of a distinctly hardening mood in public debate, talk of the second chance gave way to seeing adult education simply as a means for the implementation of labour policy, in the attempt to reconcile demand and supply on the labour market.

ADULT EDUCATION IN FINLAND, 1990

In absolute numbers, participation in adult education in Finland has risen drastically during the 1970s and 1980s; by 1990 there were 1.6 million people taking part in adult education: over 40 per cent of the adult population, and almost a million more than in 1970. Only 15 per cent of adults had never participated in adult education in any form. Table 10.1 sets out participation in the different forms of adult education in Finland in 1990.

The largest category is very clearly that of workplace training provided by employers. During 1990, one in five of the total Finnish population, and one in four of the adult labour force, had been involved in training at work (cf. KO, 1991, p. 10).

Table 10.1 Number of adults participating in different forms of adult education in Finland, 1990

Form of adult education	Number of adults
Training arranged at work by employers	693,500
Courses at Institutes of Adult Education	469,000
Courses arranged by trade unions and other associations	346,100
Courses at Centres for Continuing Education	291,600
Courses at vocational institutes	179,000
Manpower Training courses	45,200
Summer university courses	44,400
Vocational courses provided by universities	43,700
Open university degree-level	41,500
Language schools	34,200
Short-term courses at Folk High Schools	18,300
Courses provided by Study Centres	16,500
Apprenticeships	9,800
Miscellaneous	81,900

The second place in the statistics is taken by the municipal institutes of adult education (Citizens' Institutes and Workers' Institutes), which form the largest organized adult education network in Finland, with almost 300 institutes covering the entire country (see Rinne *et al.*, 1991, p. 57). Other major providers of organized adult education were trade unions, voluntary associations, and similar organizations, together with the universities' Centres for Continuing Education, and the vocational institutes.

Figure 10.1 shows the distribution of adult education courses by major objective (work/leisure) over 20 modes. At the Adult Education Institutes, only a sixth of the courses were linked to the participants' work, the overwhelming majority being leisure activities, whereas workplace training, naturally, was primarily job-oriented. [. . .] In the Finnish context, the lowest levels of general education are to be found among the older generations, unskilled workers and the unemployed, people on low incomes, and the population of the peripheral regions. [. . .]

Gender and generations

In Finland, women form a majority of those studying in all forms of education except postgraduate university training (see Isoaho *et al.*, 1990),

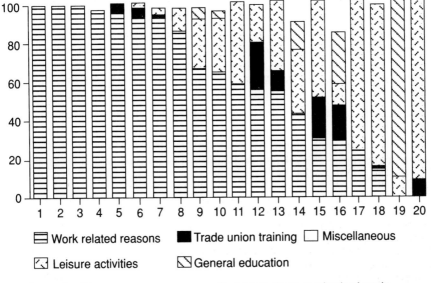

Figure 10.1 Distribution of adult education courses, by mode of education and major objectives (%)

Work related reasons   Trade union training   Miscellaneous

Leisure activities   General education

1 Apprenticeships
2 Skilled vocational qualifications
3 Training provided by employers
4 Manpower Training
5 Universities Centres for Continuing Education
6 Other continuing education institutions
7 Mature students' courses at vocational institutes
8 Language schools
9 Summer universities
10 Open University extramural courses
11 Adult students at schools of music
12 Training provided by trade unions and other associations
13 Short-term courses at Folk High Schools
14 Correspondence colleges
15 Courses provided by Study Centres
16 Long-term courses at Folk High Schools
17 Courses for adults at sports institutes
18 Institutes of Adult Education
19 Evening schools (including evening senior secondary schools)
20 Dancing schools, etc.

Table 10.2 Participation in adult education, by sex (%)

Sex	Participation		
	Never	Sometimes	During 1990
Men	18	82	38
Women	13	87	46
Total	15	85	43

but as is the case in other modes of education, significant gender-conditioned differences are found between educational pathways and in choice of content (see Table 10.2).

The group with no participation whatsoever in adult education included more men than women. During the year 1990, approximately half of the women, but only a third of the men had participated. On leisure-oriented courses, women form a solid majority, but in a significant change from earlier patterns, women nowadays, are also participating in vocational adult education. Women's choices are clearly focused on arts and skills, health, and welfare, whereas men dominate in management and business courses and on courses for adults in natural sciences and technology.

The average time spent by men on training per year is 6.4 days, whereas the figure for women is 9.2 days. Training provided by employers is markedly directed more towards men. Over half of the women had paid for themselves for at least one of the courses they had taken, whereas only just over a quarter of the men had done so.

Women were more motivated than men by self-development while for the men improved salary was a more important motive. Many of the men did not in fact recognize the necessity for adult education. Two reasons more significant for women than for men were the desire to retain their jobs, or to change occupation; but altogether four men in ten, compared with only just over a quarter of the women, stated that as a result of adult education they had moved into more demanding tasks.

The age group making most use of adult education services were those aged 25–49, well over half of whom took part in some kind of course each year. Immediately above the age of 50, however, the participation rate falls to below 40 per cent and continues to fall steadily thereafter, to no more than one in ten among the over-60s.

Examination of the lifetime patterns of participation in adult education reveals a peak in the age group 30–34. This group, born in the late 1950s, and living through the main expansion in adult education, has succeeded in accumulating the largest deposit of educational capital.

In terms of numbers of students, the largest numbers in adult education are found in the middle generations; if the average duration in days is taken into account, however, there is a steady decrease with rising age. In Finland, the adult education stronghold is to be found among the working population, and is linked to employment and career prospects. Maintaining the level of occupational or professional skills emerges as the most important motivation for studying, except in the youngest age group (18–24), for whom the major motivation for study is improved salary, followed by the desire to obtain or secure a job (both reasons being more significant than with older generations).

The age group 25–39 are most likely to report hindrances to their studies especially (for the women) problems of childminding. For the younger age groups, these problems are not yet serious, and for the older groups they are no longer relevant. The problems of the oldest groups concerned illness, transport, clashing with other leisure activities, or lack of interest; these also partially applied to the middle-aged (40–49), whereas the youngest respondents are more likely to mention financial difficulties.

The best results in terms of coping better with tasks at work, or obtaining transfer to more demanding work, are found among those in the middle stages of their working careers (40–49), whereas the youngest had not yet had time to see the realization of these benefits.

Social status and educational background

Among white-collar workers, virtually everyone had participated in adult education at some stage during his or her life; among managerial and professional employees the rate of those taking part in some form of course during the year was four-fifths; and among administrative and clerical personnel two-thirds. The difference between these and the other groups is a sharp one (see Figure 10.2).

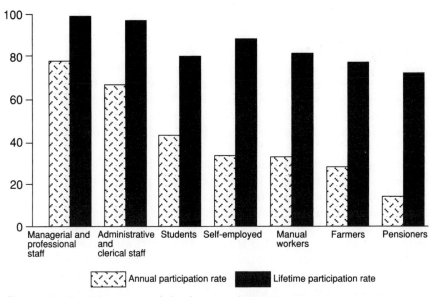

Figure 10.2 Participation in adult education, by socio-economic status (%)

In relative terms, the socio-economic grouping with the third highest lifetime participation rate were the self-employed; their annual participation rate, however, was only one in three. For manual workers, the lifetime participation rate was four-fifths, but during the sample year, less than half. Farmers, who by economic criteria are also self-employed, display much lower participation rates, only just over a quarter having taken part during the sample year.

In terms of occupational groupings, in the category including school-teachers, school principals, and junior academic staff, every individual had taken part in some form of adult education during the preceding year. Other occupational groupings with very high participation rates included physicians, senior public officials, systems analysts, social workers, various categories of nurses, bank and insurance clerks, special education staff, and senior sales personnel; in all of these categories, more than four in five had taken part in some form of adult education during 1990.

At the opposite extreme, the marginal groups for participation in adult education include various categories of construction labourers, stone and metal workers, decorators, joiners, and labourers in the timber industry; in each of these groups, less than one in five had participated in adult education during 1990. In other words, the high participants in adult education are drawn from the white-collar professions, and over half of them are university graduates, whereas the marginal groups in terms of participation in adult education come from industrial occupations in the manual working-class.

Despite a historical decline in the effect of wealth and income on overall participation in education, the influence of money on educational choice has by no means disappeared (cf. Pöntinen, 1990), and it continues to affect participation in adult education as well. There is a close link between income and levels of adult education activity: the higher the income, the higher the participation rate. Below a monthly income of 5000 marks (US$ = about 5 marks), only one in three takes part in adult education; at high income levels of 19,000 to 20,000 marks per month, four in five do so.

The highest levels of participation in adult education for work-related reasons were reported among managerial and professional workers (92 per cent), and among administrative and clerical staffs (88 per cent). These two categories of white-collar workers stand out clearly from other occupational groupings. By contrast, farmers and pensioners are more likely to be studying for leisure or pleasure. Moreover, the higher the income, the closer is the link between adult education participation and work; it would appear that the acquisition of a high income, and the consolidation of the status which makes this possible, require a constant investment in work-related training, cutting into the time, energy and opportunities needed for taking part in leisure-oriented education. In terms of adult education, too, therefore, high incomes reinforce work-centredness.

Almost the same pattern emerges if the level of financing supplied by employers is compared with income levels: the higher the income bracket, the more funding employers put up for training. The poor must pay for their own education and training, whereas the rich have it paid for them. A relevant factor, of course, is the fact that people in high-income groups are more likely to be studying for work-related reasons, meaning that employers will have a stronger motive to provide funding.

Previous educational background is another factor closely linked with participation in adult education: the higher the level of education, the higher the participation rate (see Figure 10.3). Among those who had attended only elementary school, one in five had never participated in adult education at all during their lifetimes, and three quarters had taken part in no adult education course during 1990. Among those holding the Matriculation Examination, on the other hand, only 6 per cent had never participated in adult education at any point during their lives, and only a third had not done so during 1990. The contrast is reinforced by the figures for those with no vocational qualifications: over one in five with no participation in adult education at all during their lifetime, and only one in four participating during 1990.

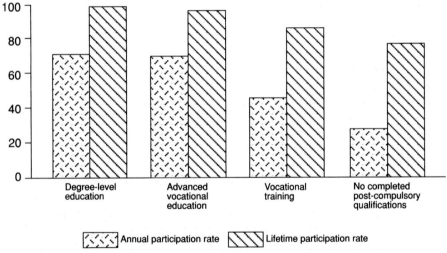

Figure 10.3 Annual and lifetime participation rates in adult education, by previous level of education (%)

Similarly, among those completing senior high school, higher participation rates in adult education are found among those going on to complete university degrees and lower rates among those who had only taken more modest vocational qualifications. Persons who have achieved senior positions through degree-level or advanced vocational education are in later life more likely to be found in the classroom again, whereas – despite generous grants available – the most marked lack of interest in on-going education is found among those holding basic postcompulsory vocational training: over one in five had taken no further part in education, while six in ten were only willing to enter upon full-time study if they could receive at least three-quarters of their normal salary.

High participants and non-participants: YUPs and ORLs

It is thus clear that the second chance applies to only a minority of the students taking part in adult education in Finland; the heaviest consumers of adult education services are drawn from highly privileged groups.

Let us therefore now concentrate our analysis on those adults who have participated especially intensively in adult education in Finland. The criteria used to define 'high participants' are a minimum annual total duration of two weeks, and a minimum of at least ten participations during their lifetime (YUPs; Young, Urban, Professional). The opposite extreme, naturally, will consist of those Finnish adults who had not participated in adult education at all (ORLs; Old, Rural, Labourer).

Between them, these two groups established for comparison contained altogether 654,000 persons. High participants in adult education amounted to 184,000, i.e. approximately one-tenth of the total labour force while non-participants amounted to 470,000, or almost a fifth of those in employment. Although high participants provide only around one-tenth of the total number of adults taking part in adult education annually, they account for almost a quarter of the total student-days spent on courses.

Adult education can be described today as a 'quaternary' level of education. If adult education were genuinely a second chance route, then at least some high participants ought to consist of people with relatively modest educational back-grounds, engaged in improving their status on the labour market, ensuring their continued employment, and/or improving their working skills and their cultural capital.

The majority of the high participants in 1990 were women, whereas among the non-participants the majority were male. The strongest age group among the high participants was 40–49, whereas non-participants were more likely to be young (below 25) or elderly (over 60). In geographical terms, high participants were found in the cities, especially in Greater Helsinki, but also in the far north of Finland while the non-participants tended to come from the middle of the country.

There is a very clear link between previous educational background and participation in adult education: the convergence between higher levels of general education and higher participation rates can be seen in Table 10.3. Similar systematic trends can also be confirmed in terms of levels of vocational training.

As income rises, the chances of becoming a high participant steadily increase; correspondingly, with falling income the likehood of non-participation rises. Below monthly incomes of 6000 marks, 97 per cent

Table 10.3 High participants and non-participants in adult education, by
previous levels of education (%)

General educational level	High participants	Non-participants	Total
Senior secondary/ matriculation (12 yrs)	62	38	100
Comprehensive or senior elementary (9 yrs)	31	69	100
Elementary (<9 years)	14	86	100

do not take part in adult education at all; three-quarters of those with
monthly salaries in excess of 11,000 marks belong to the high
participants. Thus socio-economic status exercises a very wide-based
influence on the probability of self-selection either as a heavy consumer
or nonconsumer of adult education services (see Table 10.4).

Table 10.4 High participants and non-participants in adult education, by
socio-economic status

Socio-economic status	High participants	Non-participants	Total
Managerial and professional staff	89	11	100
Administrative and clerical staff	55	45	100
Self-employed	11	89	100
Farmers	10	90	100
Manual workers	3	97	100

The overwhelming majority of people in management and professional
positions are high participants, and half of those in administrative and
clerical work, but only a tiny minority of manual labourers; low socio-
economic status is strongly linked to the likelihood of non-participation.
Like the manual labourers, both the self-employed and farmers are
characterized by non-participation (see Figure 10.4).

Non-participants are thus typically people with low levels of vocational training, on low incomes, in labouring and agricultural occupations,
or unemployed or on pensions; usually, moreover, male, and typically
either very young or elderly.

The bias revealed in Figure 10.4 is further accentuated by the fact that
the adult education services enjoyed by the high participants tend to
consist of personnel training or of courses provided by the Centres of
Continuing Education at the universities: high-status education for
career builders.

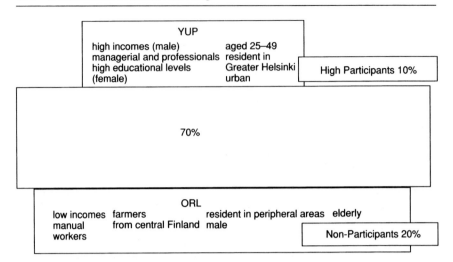

YUP
high incomes (male)   aged 25–49
managerial and professionals resident in
high educational levels   Greater Helsinki
(female)   urban   High Participants 10%

70%

ORL
low incomes farmers   resident in peripheral areas elderly
manual   from central Finland male
workers   Non-Participants 20%

Figure 10.4 Characterization of the labour force in relation to participation rates in adult education

CONCLUSION

An adult's probability of participation in adult education is thus heavily influenced by social status, cultural capital, sex, region of residence, and generation. Like other forms of education, adult education emerges as a mode of cumulative cultural capital, and the adult education market in Finland in 1990 as highly segmentalized. For those whose formal educational career finished in elementary school, or in basic post-compulsory vocational training, adult life is unlikely to foster either the traits of character, interest, or the perceived need to participate in adult education other than by compulsion or in the face of the threat of unemployment.

In the past, education was a privilege of a small upper class, and helped to distinguish the élite from the masses through mechanisms closely linked with social class (cf. Kivinen *et al.*, 1989; Pöntinen, 1990). Today it is still the case that education selects people in the context of societal status, and contributes to cultural differentiation in their ways of life. The drive for social differentiation characteristic of the highly educated YUPs emerges clearly in their career-oriented approach to adult education, and stands in stark contrast to the passive, or educationaly immune world of the ORLs.

Conventional educational policies seem to be almost too powerless to change these fundamental conditions of social and cultural existence.

REFERENCES

Bourdieu, P. (1985) 'The genesis of the concepts of habitus and of field', *Sociocriticism*, 2, 11–24.

Brunner, E., Wilder, D., Kirchner, C. and Newberry, J. (1959) *An Overview of Adult Education Research*, Chicago: Adult Education Association.

Courtney, S. (1992) *Why Adults Learn: Towards a Theory of Participation in Adult Education*. New York: Routledge.

Isoaho, H., Kivinen, O. and Rinne, R. (1990) *Education and the Family Background of the Young in Finland*, Studies, No. 172, Helsinki: Central Statistical Office of Finland.

Johnstone, J. and Rivera, R. (1965) *Volunteers for Learning: A Study of the Educational Pursuits of American Adults*, Chicago: Aldine.

Kivinen, O. and Rinne, R. (eds) (1992) *Educational Strategies in Finland in the 1990s. Research Report, No. 8*, Turku: Research Unit for the Sociology of Education, University of Turku.

Kivinen, O., Rinne, R. and Ahola, S. (1989) *Koulutuksen rajat ja rakenteet* (Boundaries and Structures of Education; in Finnish), Helsinki: Hanki ja Jää.

KO (1991) *Aikuiskoulututstukimus 1990* (Research on adult education 1990; in Finnish), Helsinki: Tilastokeskus.

Lehtonen, H. and Tuomisto, J. (1972) *Aikuiskoulutukseen osallistuminen. Toereettinen prosessimalli*. Tampereen yliopiston aikuiskasvatuksen laitoksen tutkimuksia ja selvityksiä (Participation in adult education; in Finnish), Tampere: Tampereen yliopisto.

Nordhaug, O. (1983) 'Distribution of adult education: the Norwegian case', *Adult Education Quarterly*, 34, 29–37.

Nordhaug, O. (1989) 'Equality and public policy: ideals, realities and paradoxes', *International Journal of Lifelong Education*, 8, 289–300.

Pöntinen, S. (1990) 'Koulutuksen kehityslinjoja' (Development trends in education in Finnish), in: O. Rijhinen (toim.) *Suomi 2017*, Jyväskylä: Gummerus.

Rinne, R., Kivinen, O. and Naumanen, P. (1991) *Aikuiskoulutuksen yhteiskunnalliset lähtököhdat* (Social foundations of adult education; in Finnish). Turun yliopston täydennyskoulutuskeskus. Avoimen korkeakouluopetuksen julkaisuja, Turku: Center for Extension Studies.

Rinne, R. Kivinen, O. and Ahola, S. (1992) *Aikuisten kouluttautuminen Suomessa. Osallistuminen, kasautuminen ja preferenssit* (Schooling of adults in Finland; in Finnish). Turun yliopiston koulutussosiologian tutkimusyksikön tutkimusraportteja 10, Turku: Research Unit for the Sociology of Education, University of Turku.

Chapter 11

Learning and 'leisure'

Naomi Sargant

Much more is understood now than twenty-five years ago about what adults are interested in learning, how and where they choose to learn and for what reasons. We are indebted to the work of a number of key researchers for these understandings, which make it clear that adult learning is not confined within conventional institutions or conveyed only by qualified teachers. Much adult learning is self-planned and quite deliberate. It may be, as Tough noted in 1971 'initiated for highly practical reasons' and be motivated by 'curiousity, interest and enjoyment'. The learning that goes on in public places, whether it is described as education, training or community development, is only the tip of the iceberg.

To attempt to map all such learning is, by definition, a daunting if not impossible task. Some obvious and orthodox research techniques are not available – observation, for example. Neither is it possible to rely on information collected through institutions since many non-conventional or disadvantaged learners will not have had access to them. The main option that remains, though an expensive one, is to survey a sample of the adult population as a whole, and ask them directly to provide details of their own experience. The first such national population study covered England and Wales and took place in the winter of 1980. The report, funded by the Department of Education and Science (DES) and carried out by the Advisory Council for Adult and Continuing Education (ACACE), appeared as *Adults: Their Educational Experience and Needs* (ACACE, 1982).

The mischance of the demise of the Inner London Education Authority (ILEA) in 1990 was to provide the first opportunity, happily exactly a decade later, to use the report of 1980 survey (ACACE, 1982) as a benchmark against which to measure future change. The ILEA commissioned the National Institute for Adult Continuing Education (NIACE) to carry out a study to document the ILEA's contribution to adult learning and it was possible to ensure that comparisons could be made in *Learning and 'Leisure'*[1] (Sargant, 1991) with key sections of the

1980 survey, and extend the sample to cover Scotland. Even a sample of 2500 people was not large enough to produce useful numbers of minority ethnic groups and the Employment Department, as a contribution to Adult Learners' Week 1992, commissioned a further study of the education and training experience of six selected minority ethnic groups resident in Great Britain, published as *Learning for a Purpose* (Sargant, 1993).

Drawing on these two surveys, this chapter looks at participation in education and training by adults, their interest in current study and in future learning. Patterns of participation in adult learning are strongly related to educational advantage and to age, but also vary significantly across regions of Great Britain. Some types of provision are more accessible to particular groups and individuals than others. It is clear that the ability to take up educational opportunities is affected not just by people's own motivation and circumstances, but by their knowledge of and the availability of learning opportunities. Informal learning also plays a significant role, particularly among minority ethnic groups, and whether this is from choice or necessity is an important question. There are interesting variations in cultural and educational activities in different parts of Great Britain. And there are greater differences in participation between the different minority ethnic groups than there are between those groups as a whole and the general British population.

THE USE OF LEISURE TIME

Children learn automatically and have already been learning for many years before we put a label round part of their lives and call it 'schooling'. Our habit of placing learning within schools is a relatively recent one in historical terms, and is being challenged not just by some educators but also by newer technologies and many of the young themselves. The custodial function that schools provide for parents and the community is, however, a useful one, and as a society we are unlikely to decide that we wish schools to stop providing it. The formal framework within which children learn is therefore not a voluntary one: attendance at school is compulsory between the ages of five and sixteen. The phrase 'post-compulsory' is an ugly but correct one to cover all the education that goes on after sixteen. The important point is that most learning after the age of sixteen is voluntary. It is also true that for young people following the tidy academic track through A levels to college or university it may well not feel voluntary.

Workplace-determined education and training is another grey area which may or may not feel voluntary. When it takes place at work and is organized by the employer, it is effectively compulsory. However, much vocational learning is determined by individuals rather than employers and is often aimed at job change rather than current work.

Most adults interweave their learning with the rest of their lives, their work and their family and use some of their leisure time for their studies. The *Oxford English Dictionary* definition of leisure makes the point neatly: 'Freedom or opportunity to do something specific or implied' and in the narrower sense: 'opportunity afforded by freedom from occupation'. For some people the boundaries between leisure and learning are virtually invisible. Frequently, leisure activities provide a bridge into active learning. On the other hand, many people learn from their leisure activities without realizing the knowledge or skills they are gaining.

Gardening is a classic example of this, involving soil chemistry, the climate, botany, plant genetics and issues of chemical pollution. The continued active membership of local horticultural and allotment societies, with their programmes of lectures and competitive flower and vegetable shows, involves a high level of learned theoretical and practical knowledge and organization, which for some people also turns into profitable employment. Alternatively, there are people who choose actively to construct their learning as leisure, often providing a different perspective to the rest of their lives.

It is not, as the Government has increasingly suggested, that there are subjects which are vocational and work-related and other topics which are 'leisure' subjects. The same subjects may be vocational for some people and of general interest to others. Such distinctions rest on the motivations of the learners, not on the subject of the course or the form of its provision.

Demands on people's leisure and their leisure activities change over their life-time, often in relation to family position and ownership of property. The varying activities of the age-groups are interesting (Table 11.1). Not surprisingly, social activities and sport figure high on the list for the young, whereas interest in gardening and handicrafts (including DIY) increases only as people get older. Voluntary service and committee work also become increasingly important as people get older: they seem to replace some of the time previously spent on social activities. Languages appeal across the age-range though at a low level as a 'leisure' activity. They emerge more strongly as a 'learning' activity.

Comparisons between main leisure interests in 1980 and 1990 show remarkable stability. Despite general fears that reading would diminish as television viewing became more dominant, reading has maintained and slightly increased its position at the top of the list: from 48 per cent in 1980 to 51 per cent in 1990. This increase is, however, among women, who read much more than men, and may well be partly

Table 11.1 Main leisure interests and activities, by age

	Age (%)							
	17–19	20–24	25–34	35–44	45–54	55–64	65 +	Total (%)
Reading	38	45	43	56	49	55	60	51
Social activity	69	70	55	50	40	30	26	46
Sports	47	50	49	44	36	37	25	40
Garden	3	9	23	35	44	53	49	34
Handicrafts	12	23	32	38	38	42	36	34
Indoor games	11	13	12	12	9	11	11	11
Voluntary service	4	4	5	10	9	13	12	9
Committee work	1	2	4	10	7	11	9	7
Play	5	8	5	4	4	5	3	5
Music collecting	2	5	4	6	6	5	4	5
Listen music	3	2	3	3	4	5	5	4
Foreign languages	2	2	3	4	3	3	3	3

accounted for by the increase in the proportion of older women in the population as a whole. Both sexes record an increase in physical sports, a category which includes non-competitive sports such as walking and fishing. One-half of all men list physical sports as a main activity compared with one-third of women. It is interesting that sport, which featured strongly as a 'learning' activity in the 1980 survey, now shows an increase as a leisure activity and a major drop as a learning activity. The trend over the last decade for sports provision to be made through leisure centres rather than through adult education appears to have affected people's definition of it as leisure rather than learning.

The only area to have shown a marked drop as a leisure activity, somewhat surprisingly, is the general area of handicrafts and DIY, including activities such as sewing and woodwork. This has always been a stronger area of interest among women, where the proportion is still high, though it has dropped from 51 per cent in 1980 to 43 per cent in 1990. The figure for men is down to 24 per cent and a possible inference, for men at least, is that doing up the house is no longer seen as 'leisure', but as a necessity about which they have little choice. This is confirmed by the very small numbers who now include such subjects in their current study.

CURRENT PARTICIPATION IN STUDY

The ACACE survey (ACACE, 1982) adopted a wide-ranging definition of education and used a question designed to include study in its broadest sense, whether full or part-time, at work or elsewhere since the completion of full-time education. The 1990 survey used effectively the same question: 'Are you studying currently, or have you done any kind of study, learning or practising, part-time or full-time, at work or elsewhere since you completed your full-time education?' In addition, everyone was asked a question designed to elicit information about informal learning along the lines of the theories implicit in the work of Tough (1971): 'Are you trying to learn about anything (else) at the moment, or trying to teach yourself anything, at work, at home, with friends or in a club – for example, cooking, how to use a computer, photography, etc.?'

The 1990 survey shows one in ten adults as engaged in some form of current study. A further 16 per cent have been studying within the past three years. Therefore one-quarter of all adults describe themselves as current or recent students. At the same time 17 per cent of adults indicate that they are learning something informally, the most of whom (10 per cent out of the 17 per cent) are not also studying formally. So over one-third (36 per cent) of the adult population is or has been studying or learning informally in the past three years. Three per cent of the sample interviewed, (who were all 17 or over) were still at school or in some form of full-time education.

Whereas the overall proportion studying now or recently has increased by 7 per cent since 1980, the proportion of men studying has increased more than that of women (by 9 per cent compared with 4 per cent). The sex differences in participation are similar to those quoted in *Training in Britain* (Rigg, 1989) which also shows a higher proportion of men receiving vocational education and training in the last three years.

Though the participation of women in post-school education has increased over the last decade, in particular in degree courses in higher education, they are still in a significant minority in much of the lower level education and training provision. More detailed research (Woodley *et al.*, 1987) shows that men predominated on courses leading to qualifications in polytechnics (now new universities), specialist colleges and in university postgraduate courses. Women formed the majority in art colleges and in colleges of further and higher education. On courses not leading to qualifications, the proportion of women was very high: almost eight out of ten in LEA classes and in the sector as a whole. Even in the non-LEA classes there were virtually two women to every one man. LEA classes have always been particularly important for younger women who are at home caring for children and have few other options.

It is for this reason that the proposals in the 1991 White Paper *Education and Training for the 21st Century* (HMSO, 1991) to separate further education from local authority provision and to provide national funding only for specified areas of mainly vocational and qualifying provision were seen as likely to do serious damage to opportunities for women, many of whom use such opportunities to keep in touch and return to learning and thence to paid employment as their children get older. The lack of protection for general adult education funding since the 1992 *Act* has indeed led either to a reduction in LEA provision or an increase in costs in many areas.

An increasing number of women are now working part-time, and indeed the main increase in new jobs is in part-time service industry jobs, usually taken by women. In addition, training opportunities are more widely available to full-time rather than part-time workers, and to higher rungs of the employment ladder, i.e. to men rather than to women. Women, often coping with a double agenda of paid work and family management, are doubly disadvantaged. They are particularly dependent on local part-time learning opportunities and have been traditionally the greatest users of adult education, often as a means of re-entry to vocational opportunities. Neither are many of them well-placed to pay additional fees.

REGIONAL DIFFERENCES IN PARTICIPATION

There are marked differences between Scotland, Wales and English regions in leisure habits, cultural activities, religious attendance, and awareness of and participation in learning and study. There is no obvious pattern to these differences, and there is a paucity of information nationally about provision and expenditure which would enable proper regional comparisons to be made.

However, the range of variation between the regions is much less in relation to cultural and leisure activities than it is in relation to educational activities. Some areas emerge positively, recording high proportions of the different indicators. For example, East Anglia has the highest awareness of use of local adult education centres, the highest regular use of libraries, and the highest number learning at work, while the south-west has a high level of reading, the highest proportion of informal learners and the highest expressed desire to learn in the future. Other areas emerge negatively, although not usually in all respects. Some clearly do present a mixed profile, or indeed no clear profile at all.

What is curious about Scotland, a country which is proud of its educational tradition, is that whilst it shows the highest level of knowledge of providers, it also records the lowest level of current/recent participation and the lowest proportion wanting to learn something new in the future. Wales records low proportions of awareness of provision and of attendance at local centres, but expresses a high desire to learn.

Although differences in provision and participation will to some extent have developed in relation to local circumstances and local needs, the degrees of difference do raise the question as to whether access to continuing opportunities for education and training for adults are being made available on an equitable and accessible basis over the country, particularly since much provision is nationally funded and controlled, and relates to national and not just local and personal needs. Recent changes in legislation and funding structures are affecting provision locally. The major decision under the 1992 *Further and Higher Education Act* to move the funding of further education away from local authorities, to give independence to further education and sixth form colleges, encourage competition between individual colleges, and to place the funding of a large part of post-sixteen education under a Further Education Funding Council (FEFC) has both positive and negative effects on provision.

What is at risk in many areas is the provision of general (mainly uncertificated) adult education in its traditional sense. Although local education authorities have an obligation to 'secure adequate provision' for 'further education', there is no laid-down definition of adequacy, the definition is quaint, being spelled out as meaning 'in such organized cultural, training and recreative activities as are suited to their requirements' and the calculation of the amount that the government has allowed for the provision of adult education in the Standard Spending Assessment for an individual local authority is not published and its expenditure can, therefore, not be monitored. In some areas, notably those which have had their expenditure capped, adult education has been cut back or is no longer provided.

On the encouraging side, there has over recent years been a marked increase in mature students entering higher education – they are indeed now in a majority – often studying part-time, and mainly through the new universities. There is also an increase in the number of adults entering further education. Of more concern is the pressure on provision, usually not accredited, that relates to personal and social needs. Parent and health education, English for speakers of other languages, training for school governors, and computer studies are all examples. Also under pressure are courses for women to return to learning, or to take up science and engineering and courses for older people to prolong their active citizenship. More flexible working arrangements, early retirement and longer life, as well as increased unemployment and the reduction of public transport, all argue for an increase in a wide variety of locally available part-time provision.

DEMOGRAPHIC DIFFERENCES IN PARTICIPATION

Another major discriminating factor is, of course, age. The educational system has been designed to provide front-end education rather than continuing education or lifelong learning and young adults clearly dominate the formal system. One half of adults aged 20–24 were studying or had studied in the past three years compared with one-third of 25–34 year olds and 35–44-year-olds. Over forty-five, the proportion dropped to one-quarter. The 1991 White Paper (HMSO, 1991) focused its discussion on the young even though there had been general debate and agreement about the impact of the decline in the birthrate and the likely requirement that more older people, particularly women, would be required to rejoin or stay longer in the work-force over the coming decades. The recent White Paper *Competitiveness: Helping Business to Win* (DTI, 1994) again focuses far more attention on the young than on adults, arguably a limited view since the young form a very small proportion of the total work-force.

The major factor affecting participation continues to be social class. The upper and middle classes stay at school longer, go on to post-school education at a higher rate and are then much more likely to return to continue their education as adults than the working classes. The proportions of people studying recently in the 1990 survey were 42 per cent of ABs (upper and upper-middle classes), 37 per cent of C1s (lower middle-class, 29 per cent of C2s (skilled working-class) and 17 per cent of DEs (unskilled working class). Two-and-a-half times as many ABs are or have been studying in the past three years as DEs and twice as many C1s as DEs.

SUBJECTS OF STUDY

People study an incredible variety of subjects, many of them clearly vocational and others of general interest. The desire to differentiate between vocational and non-vocational subjects has its roots in the philosophy and politics of adult education as well as in the ideology and economics of government policy rather than in learning needs. The judgement as to whether a subject is vocational is ultimately made by the learners who know what they want to learn and why they want to learn it. Examples of this are two of the currently most popular subjects: foreign languages and computer studies.

Vocationally related subjects do, in fact, dominate the 1990 list:

vocational qualifications (9 per cent), foreign languages (9 per cent) computer studies (8 per cent), engineering and electronics (7 per cent), shorthand/typing/office skills (6 per cent), business administration and management (6 per cent). Engineering, though had halved its numbers since 1980, as had science. Subjects which have increased in popularity since 1980 tend to be in the harder, more vocational, areas, which are also traditionally male ones and the ones that government policies have mainly supported in the last few years. Subject areas which have decreased include the arts and social sciences, academic and domestic subjects, and some vocational areas which were traditionally occupied by women.

Sports and physical activities have also dropped dramatically, but only, as noted earlier, in the sense of being thought of as subjects of study. As leisure activities, they are more popular, reflecting both the increase in interest and, probably, the increase in provision through leisure centres rather than through adult education.

SUBJECTS OF STUDY CHOSEN BY LEARNERS OF DIFFERENT BACKGROUNDS

There are clear differences in subjects of study between working women and non-working women. Working women are studying shorthand/typing/office skills (16 per cent), computer studies (9 per cent), other vocational qualifications (9 per cent), business administration/management (8 per cent), and social work (6 per cent). Women not working or working part-time are studying languages (18 per cent), shorthand/typing/office skills, English language/literature (7 per cent) social work (6 per cent), handicrafts (6 per cent), cookery (6 per cent), and arts and cultural subjects (6 per cent). The current emphasis on vocational training is likely to disadvantage women who are not working, whether they are young mothers or older or retired women.

Men who are not working or are retired study across the conventional subject divide – 14 per cent are studying foreign languages, 12 per cent engineering, 12 per cent computer studies and 12 per cent the arts and cultural subjects.

In terms of social class, the lower middle class (C1s) are particularly motivated to pursue vocational studies/qualifications, as is the group (some of whom are the same people) who left school at 16 or 17. Languages are more attractive to the upper and middle classes, as are arts and cultural subjects. The caring areas show a flat class profile, whereas home skills, both male and female, are of more appeal to the working class.

Minority ethnic groups surveyed in 1992 (Sargant, 1993) are far more vocational in their choice of subjects studied than the GB sample:

overall summary comparisons for main subjects studied are shown in Table 11.2

Table 11.2 Main subjects studied – the surveys compared

	Minority ethnic sample (%)	Learning and 'leisure' (%)
English language/skills	18	3
Business/management	11	6
Computer studies	8	8
Social work/sciences	8	6
Other professional quals	7	5
Science/maths/statistics	6	3
Foreign languages	6	9

SUBJECTS OF INFORMAL STUDY

As noted earlier, we do not know whether informal learning is a preferred choice for many learners or whether they choose it for some subject areas rather than others. The fact that most informal learners in the 1990 survey are *not* also learning formally would seem to indicate a conscious preference, but may also indicate the inaccessibility of conventional provision. More people from the minority ethnic groups overall were studying informally (23 per cent) than from the 1990 sample (17 per cent), and this figure rises to 31 per cent among the African group, with the Chinese next (27 per cent).

Many of the subjects of informal learning are instrumental in their use and may well relate to vocational purposes, as well as assisting in personal development and life enhancement. Learning about or how to use a computer is a clear example of this and ranks as the subject most often mentioned by one in five (19 per cent) of all informal learners in the 1990 sample. Ten years ago, although many people had bought home computers, few people were actively using them. Over the decade the situation has clearly changed. Among the minority ethnic sample, the proportion of people learning about computers informally is even higher (27 per cent). Learning foreign languages is also mentioned by a higher proportion of informal learners in the 1990 survey (12 per cent) than formal students (9 per cent).

The minority ethnic sample is again more vocational in its choice of subjects of informal learning and it is interesting to compare some of the main subjects in both modes (Table 11.3).

The main subjects which appear in only one list are for *informal learning*: photography, handicrafts and childcare/parenting; and for *formal*

Table 11.3 Comparison between main subjects both being studied and learned informally

Ethnic minority weighted sample	All studying now/recently (%)	All learning informally (%)
English	18	11
Business/management	11	6
Computer studies	8	27
Foreign languages	6	5
Cookery	2	11
Religion/theology	2	4
Typing/word-processing	5	2

study: other professional and vocational qualifications of all sorts as well as a range of academic subjects. There is obviously scope, particularly with English, computer studies and business studies to offer more provision or support to those now learning these subjects informally. There may also be scope for engaging people in more formal study of the subjects which they now engage in informally, for example, photography.

WHERE CURRENT OR RECENT STUDY OR LEARNING TOOK PLACE

Where people are actually studying, as opposed to at what type of institution, becomes a more significant question with the increase in open and distance learning and of informal learning. In the 1990 survey, more than one-half of learners were not studying at an educational institution. While formal educational institutions were the dominant provider (39 per cent) in the 1990 survey, just over one-quarter said they were learning at home from a book and 11 per cent at home from a prepared course. An even higher proportion of minority ethnic groups were learning at educational institutions (48 per cent). This choice of place appears to be confirmed by their answers to a question about preferred styles of learning: by far the largest group (42 per cent) said they would prefer to learn in a class with a group of other learners, the most familiar method of education for most people.

In terms of work-related locations, 7 per cent of both surveys say they are learning at a training centre, but double the number in the GB sample are learning at work (15 per cent) than in the minority ethnic sample (8 per cent). More men (18 per cent) than women (12 per cent) are learning at work in the GB sample. In the minority ethnic sample, similarly, more men than women from the Indian sub-continent are studying at work (11 per cent of men compared with 6 per cent of women.) With the Afro-Caribbean group, however the position is reversed with 11 per cent of women studying at work compared with 5 per cent of men.

These figures raise two important issues. First, that although most of the subjects minority ethnic groups are studying are vocational in nature and their reasons for studying are work- or qualification-related, only a small proportion of them are studying *at work*. There are implications here for Training and Enterprise Councils, Local Enterprise Companies and for employers. Second, that minority ethnic groups are more reliant on conventional provision than the GB population. It is, therefore, particularly important, as the new FEFC funding arrangements begin to affect the nature of local provision, for colleges to ensure that they really are accessible to learners from ethnic minorities, since in many areas local authority provided community and adult education is being cut back.

SUBJECTS PEOPLE WOULD LIKE TO LEARN ABOUT

Nearly one-half (47 per cent) of the adult population in Great Britain said thay would like to learn about something they had not previously studied. This figure is substantially lower than ten years earlier. In the country as a whole, interest in learning about new subject areas increases as terminal age of education increases. In terms of age, it peaks at 25–34 and decreases thereafter (Table 11.4).

Table 11.4 Main groupings of 'new' subjects people would like to learn about, by age-group

	17–19	20–24	25–34	35–44	45–54	55–64	65 +	Total
Foreign languages	17	21	23	24	21	24	21	22
Arts/culture	14	13	19	21	24	30	26	22
Home skills	10	16	19	23	22	21	19	19
Science/maths	14	12	12	11	7	9	7	10
Business/ professional	7	12	17	14	8	2	4	10
Sports	7	6	4	5	4	6	6	6
Computers	4	5	7	4	6	3	1	5
Social sciences	4	3	5	5	3	1	3	4
Want to learn	50	52	55	51	45	46	35	47

The subjects that have remained stable or increased are mainly vocational, for example, computer studies and work-related subjects. The decreases are much more marked in leisure and other non-vocational subjects. It is possible that some people are re-defining 'leisure' to include some activities they would previously have thought of as 'learning', as indeed the Government suggested in the White Paper, *Education and Training for the 21st century*. (HMSO, 1991) It is also possible that they are excluding some domestic functions which are now thought of necessary activities rather than pleasurable leisure.

People as learners do not easily differentiate between what is vocational and what is non-vocational. These are terms used by politicians, funders and some providers. The breadth of peoples' interests and motivations cuts across such boundaries.

The desire to learn something new tends to take on a broader form as people get older and to be less narrowly confined to short-term vocational concerns. There is a clear need for a generous range and variety of provision to be maintained, without unreasonable financial barriers, as the social and demographic trends of increased early retirement, unemployment and active old age are likely to increase need and demand. The most recent national survey (MORI, 1994) shows even fewer people of age sixty-five and over to be engaged in current or recent study (6 per cent) compared with the 1990 survey (9 per cent). There is concern that the changes in funding arrangements which leave the provision of most general adult education to be funded under already straitened local authority budgets has already diminished the very provision which is most accessible to older people; in particular older women.

The proportion of people wanting to learn something new among minority ethnic groups is higher than among the British population (58 per cent compared with 47 per cent), though it is not surprising that many of the subjects are the same. There is, of course, the obvious difference that English (for speakers of other languages) ranks as the highest subject, mentioned by one in five (21 per cent) who wish to learn. Additionally, nearly as many from these groups (17 per cent) wish to study other foreign languages. Groupings of subjects which are clearly vocationally-related are nearly all ranked higher by the minority ethnic sample than the 1990 sample: professional/work-related subjects (12 per cent compared with 5 per cent) computer studies (9 per cent compared with 5 per cent), social studies (8 per cent compared with 4 per cent).

NON-PARTICIPANTS: IDENTITY AND LEARNING NEEDS

Educators continue to be concerned and challenged by those people who do not participate or do not appear to wish to participate in adult learning. Those with minimum initial education, manual workers and the elderly are consistently under-represented in education as adults. The general pattern of participation recorded over the last twenty years, including the *Adequacy of Provision Study* (NIAE, 1970) and the ACACE study (1982) has, as McGivney (1990) notes in her valuable review of the literature of non-participation, shown little change. It is important, however, to note that in order to keep the project to manageable proportions, her review did not include any private providers, employers or distance education schemes, but was confined to the main statutory and some voluntary providers of organized educational activities for adults. This means that her review omits any reference to the significant body of research into the large body of adult students at the Open University (OU), the National Extension College and other correspondence colleges, as well as much work-oriented learning.

In particular, using, as both ACACE (1982) and McGivney (1990) did, the useful terminology of Cross (1978), it means that the two major 'situational' barriers to access – time and place – may tend to be underestimated in comparison with 'dispositional' and 'attitudinal' barriers. There are clearly good reasons why thousands of adults apply every year to study with the OU rather than through their local university or college. It is highly likely that the same inflexible barriers of time and place which prevent them studying locally also prevent many from participation in *any* form of education as adults. The reasons given for not studying by the minority ethnic groups confirm time pressures as just such a reason, both due to work (28 per cent) and due to family pressures (28 per cent). Relatively few people from these groups mention lack of money (3 per cent) or other typical barriers to access.

Nearly two-thirds of people interviewed in 1990 were 'not studying now, or recently', or 'not learning now' 62 per cent of men and 62 per cent of women. More than half of them did not want to learn about anything new, ranging from 47 per cent of 17–24 year olds to 85 per cent of people aged 65 and over. One-quarter of the minority ethnic sample says 'there is nothing I want to study'. Evidence from recent studies on individual commitment to adult learning provides clear evidence that many people's motivation to study is directly related to its relevance to their current or future work.

A major difficulty has been the success of the Government over the last fifteen years in focusing attention and funding only on those learning activities which contribute to enhancing narrowly defined vocational skills. For many people who have no job in view, and limited financial means for study, study options which appear relevant are genuinely more limited. It must be remembered that the education of adults is a goal of social policy as well as of economic policy. It is therefore necessary to return to a more generous notion of the relevance and scope of adult learning if we are to provide for the needs of adults throughout their lives, let alone if we are to meet the national training and education targets!

NOTE

1 The survey published under the title *Learning and 'Leisure'* is referred to, for convenience, as the 1990 or GB survey, since it covered England, Wales and Scotland.

REFERENCES

ACACE (1982) *Adults: Their Educational Experience and Needs*, Leicester: ACACE.

Cross, K. P. (1978) 'A critical review of state and national studies of the needs and interests of adult learners', in: C. B. Stalford (ed.), *Adults' Learning Needs and the Demand for Life-long Learning*, Washington: National Institute for Education.

DTI (1994) *Competitiveness: Helping Business to Win*, White paper, London: HMSO.

HMSO (1991) *Education and Training for the 21st Century*, Cm 1536, London: HMSO.

McGivney, V. (1990) *Education's for other people*, Leicester: NIACE.

NIAE (1970) *Adequacy of Provision*, Leicester: NIAE.

Rigg, M. (1989) *Training in Britain: Individuals' Perspectives*, London: Training Agency/HMSO.

Sargant, N. (1991) *Learning and 'Leisure'*, Leicester: NIACE.

Sargant, N. (1993) *Learning for a Purpose*, Leicester: NIACE.

Tough, A. (1971) *The Adult's Learning Projects*, Toronto: Ontario Institute for Studies in Education.

Woodley, A., Wagner, L., Slowey, M., Hamilton, M. and Fulton, O. (1987) *Choosing to Learn*, Milton Keynes: SRHE/Open University Press.

Chapter 12

Part-time: whose time?
Women's lives and adult learning†

Marlene Morrison

INTRODUCTION

> Feminists agree that any understanding of human beings that excludes
> women is inaccurate . . . there is no faith, however, in the 'add
> women and stir' recipe . . . An understanding of the world through
> the eyes of women alters both the method and the vision . . . Finding
> a way of learning to see the invisible and bring to a conscious,
> reflected, and discursive level those aspects we take most deeply for
> granted, necessitates phenomenological action.
>
> (Adam 1989: 464)

In this chapter I attempt to bring assumed aspects of women's lives to a
conscious level of understanding. This is couched within the framework
of a research project which explored the meanings of part-time education
as experienced by staff and students in a college of further education.
This chapter focuses on students, most of whom were women. At one
level it reflects a burgeoning of writing on women's issues; at another
it places time in the central research frame. Only recently have writers
such as Adam (1990) renewed the connections developed by early social
scientists between time and social theory.

The research lens is focused on a specific group; no claims are made
as to the general applicability of their experiences, either to all women or
to adults in general. Instead it is hoped that among the issues raised will
be those considered worthy of attention in other sectors, and/or with
other student groups experiencing education on a temporary or part-
time basis.

† This is an edited version of a paper that appeared in *Managing Time for Education*,
CEDAR Paper 3, Centre for Educational Development, Appraisal and Research, University of Warwick, 1992.

TIME: WHOLE AND PART, PUBLIC AND PRIVATE

Time is a basic element of human experience. Intuitively we know it is experienced in multiple and complex ways. Driving to work each day along a busy motorway, I experience a passage of time and space which includes planning for future work and home-related activities, is interwoven with a mixture of reminiscences about past actions, and a kaleidoscope of short-term reflections on the landscape, other vehicles, and other drivers. Such times are important and precious to me; rarely do I afford them conscious thought and reflection.

Yet, in modern Western society, time has acquired a scarcity of commodity value; with the emergence of industrial time, life rhythms have revolved increasingly around work times. Provonost, however, cautions us against placing too much emphasis on industrialization as the only determinant of modern time, reminding us that current conceptions of time result from an amalgam of:

> economic changes, the gradual secularisation of certain sectors of activity, the introduction of increasingly accurate measurements of time, a transformation of the family environment, and the increasing importance of school obligations.
>
> (Provonost 1989: 28)

As attention is focused on ways of scheduling, synchronizing and prioritizing time, humans are increasingly directed towards finding ways of organizing time in order to save or win it. The organization of time becomes a problematic, even frantic activity.

Building on the work of earlier writers, Hassard introduces the problem in terms of attempts by humankind to meet three needs. These are:

> firstly, the need for time schedules, to enable us to make reliable predictions of times when certain events will occur;
> secondly, the need to synchronize human actions so there is coordination between them; and
> thirdly, the need for time allocation, so that the activities which consume it will be done in a rational way.
>
> (Hassard 1988: 84–90)

Rationality involves value judgments and is frequently externally imposed. In our society valued time is organized 'rationally' in linear time schedules. This may be neither rational nor efficient for all humans, specifically those assigned caring and domestic roles. Nonetheless, such scheduling remains largely the norm for temporal organization in the tertiary sector of education, and builds on structures already well developed in secondary education.

The term part-time assumes that whole time is divisible into parts into which individuals can compartmentalize different aspects of their life schedules, in this case for part-time study. In relation to the research project, college-based part-time education, which offered opportunities for adults, mainly women, to study for credentials in relatively short, intensive time-slots, appears to meet the needs referred to above.

What it tends to ignore, however, is the potential and actual tensions facing female students who need to organize time in terms of study-based and/or work-orientated careers, and in terms of traditional and multiple patterns of socially organised and sexually stratified divisions of labour. The structure of the part-time courses investigated did not explicitly challenge traditional assumptions about women's domestic roles; neither did they bring about any radical change in the way the college was organized.

TIME FOR EDUCATION: AN ICEBERG MODEL

A key feature of part-time educational experience is that it takes place in at least two time spheres. A time 'iceberg' is perhaps an appropriate metaphor to describe a programme of educational study whose visible and invisible parts present part-time students with differing challenges. A recent analysis of perspectives on self-direction in adult learning applies the same metaphor (Brockett and Hiemstra 1991: 37–83). In relation to the research project, college attendance at classes constituted the visible part, a period of intensive group study in fixed time slots. The invisible part was the period of private study engaged in by students in their own time, when it was assumed that they, rather than the college, would take greater responsibility for decisions about scheduling, planning and implementing their learning experiences. [. . .]

The advantage of intensive periods of visible college time, namely its convenience and brevity, generated additional study burdens in that part of educational experience which remained essentially private and under-taken at home. In a study situation where college time was half that offered to full-time students, the effective use of private study time was expected to be critical in relation to course outcomes.

Thus the research problem was to investigate the complex negotiation of time engaged in by part-time students. This would extend beyond college attendance into private spheres of educational experience, and would examine the organization of time between its private and public spheres, specifically its relationship to institutions like the school and family. [. . .]

At the heart of the complex relationship between women and part-time education lies the relationship between women and the family . . . and between the family and time dimensions of each of its members.

> The family is at the crossroads of three different time dimensions: the life-cycles of each of its members, the professional paths of husband and wife and the family life-cycle itself . . .
>
> (Provonost 1989: 46)

Despite recent changes, many women remain central to the coordination of family activities. As feminist researchers have pointed out (for example, Davies 1989) the gender-laden and time consumptive nature of that role has frequently been ignored, with issues of time management and organization being viewed individualistically and/or asexually.

WOMEN AND PART-TIME: MAKING CONNECTIONS

The majority of part-time students were women. Attempts to accommodate visible college-based time with invisible and private study time reflects women's lives at a more general level, especially those with dual responsibilities in the public sphere of paid employment and the family sphere of home and family. Similarly, it was anticipated that blurred boundaries between public and private activities would also be features of part-time study, particularly the overlapping of leisure with study or work time.

Whilst writers have focused on the problematic aspects of combining dual roles (Yeandle 1984), and on ideologies which underpin perceptions of male and female lives (Morgan 1985) we should, perhaps, be cautious in not over-emphasizing the extent to which women perceive the balancing of 'parts' as endemically problematic or experienced in similar ways. This reflects a blurring between choice and necessity in adult lives, made more complex by differential adaptations to sexually stratified divisions of labour.

Nevertheless, whilst the ideologies underpinning male and female lives might not always be recognized, their organizational contexts, including the timing of multiple activities, are increasingly seen as problematic, or at least, open to challenge.

> But if we look at how women use their time, it is obvious that it is rather a question of 'collective' time which others, for example, their families, have a right to lay claim to . . . The time that she is able to use for paid work is adjusted to other family members' needs of time. The time she needs for herself and her own interests is often given very little, if any space.
>
> (Gunnarsson and Ressner 1985: 110)

For a 'minority' male respondent in the project, women 'drop-outs' and erratic attenders were viewed as poor managers of time. In contrast, he organized 'a daily/weekly time plan with the aid of a personal organiser' [. . .] Perhaps a solution to the acknowledged higher 'drop-out' rate among part-time students (Woodley *et al.* 1987) would be to equip them with personal organisers?!

METHODOLOGY

[. . .]

The main research questions posed were:

- What role did part-time study play in women's lives, and to what extent was it possible to schedule it in a compartmentalized way?
- What priority over other activity was it given, and to what extent could it be synchronized to withstand any encroachment on it by other demands? Did simultaneity of timed experienced offer any clues to 'coping'?
- Was part-time study the most appropriate way of organizing learning and for whom?
- Did students respond to other people's assumptions about what it meant to be a part-time student? If so, who or what were the most significant influences?

The routes to data collection and analysis included:

- verbal and written accounts by students of their initial attempts to organize returning to learn;
- a questionnaire survey to investigate the extent to which part-time education was a choice or a necessity;
- an analysis of diaries completed by students to investigate the organization of part-time study, including private study;
- follow-up interviews; and, as importantly, frequent conversations throughout the period of the research (an academic year).

For the period of study, I was a Sociology lecturer for two groups of part-time day and evening class students and a tutor for the part-time day group. Initial tutor strategies were to establish a basis for year long student/tutor collaboration. The initial research strategy was to gain an early appreciation of college days for students and to establish a rapport with those who would be the main subjects of the study.

This was facilitated by a complementarity in the part-time(s) being experienced by the researcher and researched. Whilst similarities in gender, race, age, domestic circumstances, and geographical area in which we lived and worked, were important dimensions of the researcher/researched relationship, differences in educational experience and status constituted a barrier to my 'going native'. Nevertheless, mutual connivance in rule-breaking activities, such as bringing convalescing off-spring to classes when child care was unavailable, helped to foster an atmosphere which encouraged ongoing explorations about educational experience in ways which transcended the segmentation of women's lives as staff, students, domestic partners, or mothers (discussed, for example, by Adam 1989: 470).

RETURNING TO LEARN

For most of the students, returning to learn occurred after long periods of absence from education. In the following extract, a student records her feelings as she prepares for her first days in college:

> Must get myself ready. What have I committed myself to? It is now exactly thirty years since I sat an examination. Have I left it too late?

I considered that one of the crucial points at which the boundaries between private and public time would become most challenging would be the early period of returning to learn. At this point in time, it might be expected that attempts would be made to establish identities as students, alongside other identities which might hitherto have been prioritized. Moreover, the initiation period would also require skills of time scheduling, coordination and allocation. Verbal and written accounts by women during these early days were discussed as they were experienced, and later in hindsight. College-based time was discussed as part of a whole day's events as well as a distinct category of educational time.

Findings indicated that 'being placed at the centre of the coordination of family activity' (Provonost, 1989: 45) impinged heavily on initial stages of returning to learn. Several accounts offered important indicators of the ways in which women were attempting to push and pummel time schedules into shapes which would allow college times to make the least disturbance to family schedules. A student recalled her activity schedule before college:

> We usually get up about 7.00 am. I come down first . . . feed the cats, get the packed lunches ready . . . We have breakfast in stages so we stagger bathroom times. Extra organizing to do today as my husband is going on a course. I like to get most of the housework done before 9.00 am.

The organization of time was also seen in offering reassurance to other family members that college time would not threaten the collective time women used for their families. A student commented:

> I got up at six and cleaned downstairs. I didn't want the family to think I was neglecting them just because I was going to the tech.

That student left at the end of the first term, reflecting on her inability to cope with the guilt and frustration at doing less than before in relation to domestic activity and 'less than enough' in relation to her studies. Role playing made her exit from the course predictable; the quality of written work and out of class conversations provided a sharp contrast to the role played in class.

An interesting aspect of routinizing and scheduling college time during the early stages was to make it a distinctive experience from the multiplicity of heterogeneous activities engaged in. For several students this included attempts either 'to look different' or to look the part of 'student'.

> I had a shower and a hairwash . . . I thought about what to wear. I didn't want to look different from anybody else.

Another student took:

> some time to decide what to wear. I'd like to have dressed outrageously to make a good impression; instead I dressed in jeans and a sloppy jumper, because I feel comfortable and younger like that and behaved more or less as usual, i.e. rather quiet and shy.

Such strategies had time implications which extended beyond class time into early morning schedules.

A sense of college identity, as distinct from usual identity, was also facilitated by the 'timed space' that the journey provided. A student recalled pre-college strategies on the first two mornings:

> I drove to college with plenty of time to spare, just as well because the car park was full and I had to find somewhere to park. . . . I checked my pens and books were in order. I did this a few times.

For the following student, the convenience of attending college when children were at school was, in the early days, tempered by feelings of disorientation:

> Having taken the children to school, I felt totally alone and found great difficulty in concentrating on which direction I was heading for.

The trepidation felt in initial stages was frequently accompanied by emotions which invaded other time. A student who was very aware of 'leaving' her 'housewife hat behind' discovered that the early days of study made her 'irritable and snappy towards the children' during the post-college period. Another recalled her first two attendances:

> After college I went to work. Quite frankly when I arrived I was not in a fit state to work so I did a few routine things which didn't require much thought.

What was interesting about first impressions of learning was that comments tended to relate, not only to the content of the subject matter to be studied, but also to events which were incidental to the courses chosen. Attention was therefore given to appearing 'the capable student'. Recollections were about seating; when, and how, to speak and look.

In the following extract, for example, a student chooses to recall little about the content of the early sessions, concentrating instead on her entrance:

> I was a little bit late and felt that everybody was looking at me as I walked in. I try to sit down where I would cause the least disturbance. Then we had to introduce ourselves. I didn't listen to the first ones, I was so busy thinking about what I'd say. I sat near a window which was causing a draught. I thought whether the other people in the class would mind if I closed it . . . after a little while I asked.

Another recalls her 'ordeal' at being asked to introduce herself:

> When having to introduce myself to other members of the Sociology group I silently rehearsed every word and I must admit, was very relieved, not to be the first to speak.

Lying was a strategy used by another student to establish an identity which it was hoped, would fit more closely to expectations of the student role:

> When asked to introduce myself I made up a few hobbies, I didn't want to seem too boring.

Towards the end of the course, students tended to reflect on their part-time experiences in terms of teaching, learning and subject content. Contrasted with early accounts, hindsight reflections illustrated ways in which educational experiences become re-negotiated and re-interpreted over time.

The end of the college day or part-day marked the beginning of the next time phase and was, without exception for the women studied, packed with continuous overlapping activities. The following example provides an illustration:

> After college I
> Cleaned out the rabbit
> Did the housework, i.e. made the beds
> Hoovered, dusted
> Cooked a meal, washed up
> Read the hand-out from college
> Collected children from school
> Got tea ready
> Fed dog

Read with the children
Watched TV
Got children washed
Read
Said prayers together
Tidied up
Saw to dog
Had a drink
Bed

Hassard (1988: 85–87) has noted that in Western societies status is frequently given to those (usually men?) who acquire expertise in specific fields, and then pursue careers which might be judged according to the timing of accomplishments within their areas of specific expertise. Initial impressions of those returning to learn were illustrative of those who considered their skills to be 'natural', heterogeneous, and of low esteem:

> When a mother has been at home with her children . . . it can be very refreshing – if I can pass an exam, I'll know I can actually retain information . . . staying at home can make a person self-centred and unable to communicate.

These were illuminating starting points at which to begin to analyse adults' attempts to acquire specific credentials, via a changed use of time.

EXPERIENCING COLLEGE TIME

In the particular research context, a specific relationship between study and time was expected since students were on time-intensive courses. Expectations therefore excluded finding students who would be taking courses 'to pass the time' in a casual recreational mode. Moreover, in the questionnaire no attempt was made to codify study as work or as leisure; this was to ascertain how study was perceived by the students themselves.

Respondents distinguished between college, private study, paid employment, domestic-related and leisure time. When coordination between areas broke down or became problematic, study time moved into leisure time. Viewed negatively, a student noted that:

> part-time study gives me no time for leisure or I feel guilty when I take some.

Viewed positively, part-time education was equated with leisure and/ or a sense of fulfilment.

A part-time day student discussed her college attendance in the following way:

> People suddenly assume I'm very brainy, and remark on how intelligent and confident I must be. This is really embarrassing but I do feel more confident.

Choosing to view part-time study as leisure time was not without its problems. An evening class student compared it with her partner's leisure time:

> I've had to give up a lot of things that I enjoy to come and enjoy this – but it's quite pressurized enjoyment especially nearer the exam. When my husband does things, it's his enjoyment, out of work, and he classes this as my enjoyment, but it's hard work as well . . . it's a real struggle sometimes.

Most responses indicated that the organization of their children's time, in relation to starting or leaving school had been a key consideration in enabling respondents to deflect a slot of time away from family and towards study.

> I am able to organize my time in a disciplined way because my son is at school all day. I can set aside time to study during the day fitting it in with my housework and shopping. Also I can study when my son has gone to bed.

Whilst school and family schedules provided timed spaces during the day, there was a sense in which this was marginalized time. Sometimes this compression of activities broke down altogether. In which case, several respondents recorded that first, study times, and second, college times, were the movable or removable schedules.

> Being a single parent and self-employed means that there isn't time for everything. Something has to go, usually it's study.

Another student commented that:

> Study is difficult because there are other activities I am committed to like housework. Perhaps I do more housework than other women?

The importance of external support and encouragement in sustaining motivation to 'stay the course' was frequently commented on by respondents. When adults, mainly women, made decisions to study part-time those decisions became enmeshed into networks of support from significant others. Evidence suggested that the significant others upon whom students depended were also those who made the most demands on available time. Moreover, whilst motivation could be collectively generated, the ownership of part-time study was individual and less amenable to sharing with others.

Why was the need for external support so strong? One reason appeared to be that at that time the supportive influence of college, apart from immediate classmates and/or tutor, was minimal. Evidence showed that few part-time students availed themselves of the services used by full-time students, namely catering, recreational or social facilities. Moreover, the latter were not specifically geared to the needs of part-time students. College time was, therefore, class contact time. Once college time had become routinized then students tended to stay the course. Vulnerable periods were three to four weeks after the start of term and the beginning of the second term. Responses illustrated the ways in which college time became incorporated into life schedules:

I get quite excited on a Tuesday evening at the thought of coming in on a Wednesday. On Wednesdays I tell people I'm a student (laughter)!

Again, another student reflected:

I felt strange at first. I'd gone straight from school, more or less, to marriage. But the feelings went. We saw people (other students) in the town and we stopped and chatted . . . There were only a few of us – we rang each other up . . . I liked the coursework . . . much better than exams. I write like I talk, it was easy.

Towards the end of the course, college time was reflected upon again using group discussion to facilitate what has been described as 'conversations with purpose' (Burgess 1988:137). At this point in time reflections were linked more closely with styles and strategies for teaching and learning.

I don't think there was enough time to go through all the materials. We don't have as much time as other students and we don't get as much interaction with other students . . . I suppose courses are designed to be intensive to keep them cheap and allow us to fit them in between school times. I don't think it would put me off coming again.

Of equal interest were moments during those conversations when, as lecturer, I was gently chastized for not imposing a time discipline upon students which would link college and private study time:

Look, I don't find coming in on Wednesday night a problem. I accept it and I come, but I needed something more concrete for homework. Treat me like a school child. Because when you gave me reading I just panic. I know I won't discipline myself with other things I do.

We went on to discuss, as we had on previous occasions, the extent to which self-guided reading was not the optional extra but an essential part of discovering sociology which could not be accommodated in two-hour weekly sessions either by learners or by mentors. Without the 'stick' of the 'telling-off' several women were expressing doubt about the timed self-discipline relevant to studying in privately negotiated ways. [. . .]

INVISIBLE TIME

The questionnaire responses were useful in illustrating the range and variation in time spent by students outside college on private study. Whilst it was expected that students would have different abilities, experiences of academic courses, and propensitites to be truthful about private study, there were, however, wide variations in time spent as Table 12.1 illustrates:

Table 12.1 Time spent in study

Student respondents	Range in study time (hours/week)*
Taking 1 GCSE	1–10
Taking 2 GCSEs	3–15
Taking 3 GCSEs or 1 'A' level	6–15
Taking 2 'A' levels	6–25

* These are written estimates of time spent studying outside class contact time by twenty-one part-time day and evening students.

One of the emerging issues was that women without paid employment did not spend more time on private study than those in employment. It tended to be the perception of those in employment that if they did not work they would spend more time studying.

Evidence also suggested that the ways in which individuals organized their time led to variations in amounts of free and/or study time; the time diary analysis allowed me to pursue this in more detail.

TIME DIARIES

These were used to map activities over time. I was aware of methodological and theoretical criticisms about their use; both have been well documented (for example, Provonost 1989: 76–80).

The contribution of time schedules was open to possible accusations of descriptive banality, that diaries would merely illustrate what was already known, that is, that women led 'busy' lives. My response was that whilst knowledge of the complex nature of women's lives might be considered commonplace, less was known about the mechanisms used by women to coordinate that complexity. Moreover, the term 'busy' has value implications. If it was related to certain kinds of activity, it would be useful to discover whether study time was considered to be legitimate 'busy' activity. Unravelling some of these mechanisms would be expected to have implications for those organizing part-time study.

A second criticism is gender based, namely that the use of time diaries assumes a male view of time, in which time is divided simplistically into linear 'time parcels' (discussed, for example, by Davies 1989). Certainly, time diaries tended to overlook overlapping times, including those described in the project as 'emotional times'. The latter might have delayed and/or prolonged time consequences for men and women, and specifically for those assigned caring, expressive roles. The term referred to events which occurred in a previous time slot and yet were brought to other time, for example, when concerns about previous events 'invaded' students' private study times. Time, viewed in this multi-faceted way, linked the past, present and future, and suggested a complexity which included a simultaneity as well as sequencing of time. An attempt was made to take account of this complexity. Space was given for diarists to record main and secondarily prioritized activities within time-slots as short as fifteen minutes. Diarists were able to record what Davies (1989) called 'waiting time', respondents noting 'thinking', 'worrying', 'meditating' and 'wasting' time, whilst engaged in other activities.

To summarize, the study recognized that life schedules could not be reduced to quantitative measures only. However, it is argued that they offered further insights into the organization of time and the prioritization of daily tasks, including study.

Time diary returns illustrated ways in which students were attempting to weave college and study times into a complex web, in which domestic-related/child care time remained dominant. Time spent on housework tended to vary according to personal identification with the role rather than time available for it. Women with part-time employment commitments tended to squeeze more into short time-slots, especially at peak times; both ends of the day were used as study periods. (One student used study as a sleep-inducing mechanism!)

Overall, the diaries suggested that those who work in adult education may seriously over-estimate the amount of time many students give to out-of-college, home study activities. This was underpinned by the problematic notion of taking 'time out' to study. For several students, feelings of guilt were shown to accompany time taken on activity which was not perceived as concrete (or 'busy'?). The following examples from diaries illustrated this:

'*Just* thinking'.
'*Wasting* time reading a trashy novel'.
'*Wasted* time watching Eastenders'. [my emphasis]

It was not difficult to understand why study time which involved 'just' thinking or 'just' reading might be negotiated away.

In relation to study times, diarists tended to prioritize them as main activities or not prioritize them at all. Where they were itemised, they provided fascinating snapshots of home-based study, as the following examples indicate.

Jan Green comes home from her part-time job at 3.00 pm. In the following hour she writes:

MAIN ACTIVITY	SUPPLEMENTARY ACTIVITY(IES) WERE YOU DOING ANYTHING ELSE?
3.00 pm make lunch answer telephone eat lunch children home children out	STUDYING
3.45 pm ironing	
4.00 pm STUDYING 4.45 pm	Turn on cooker for dinner

Pat Coleman has spent from 6.00 pm to 7.00 pm cooking, laying the table, eating dinner, filling the washing machine, and listening to the radio. Then she writes:

MAIN ACTIVITY	SUPPLEMENTARY ACTIVITY(IES) WERE YOU DOING ANYTHING ELSE?
7.00 pm MATHS HOMEWORK ASSESSMENT 5	empty washing machine chat to family
7.45 pm	let the cat out

If women were already snatching time from categories incorporating personal care and domestic task related time, from where might private study time be taken especially when college attendance had already made inroads into whole time?

Joan: I don't seem to have a lot of choices in my life. A lot of choices are imposed on me. If Jonathan (her son) doesn't want to sleep till 10.00 then I've a problem. I don't feel I'm relaxed till the children are asleep. Then that's the time I have to start sociology . . .

MM: That's interesting isn't it? Your bit of the day starts when others are over . . .

Joan: Yes, I know, I can't help it (background chorus of agreement among the evening class group).

The diaries reflected the fragmentation in the lives of respondents. That fragmentation was shown to exist mainly in the private sphere, where it remained largely unrecognized and arguably, undervalued. As Hughes and Kennedy have commented:

The adaptability of women is in a contradictory way both over-exploited in the home and under-used in the world outside . . . Woman's life-lines tend to be crisis-crossed, blurred . . .

(Hughes and Kennedy 1985: 15 and 19)

Hopefully research strategies, like time diaries, did take first steps in recognizing the diversity of women's roles in ways which might encourage the development of such diversity as a possible model for change, inside and outside education. Meanwhile, most of those who 'stayed the course' would eventually produce coursework of a standard which equalled or surpassed that of their full-time counterparts. For others, success would relate to outcomes which were not necessarily exam-related.

NO TIME FOR STUDY? DROPPING OUT

Decisions by students to embark on courses of part-time study are voluntary as is their decision to continue. On the courses where I was lecturer, 40 per cent of part-time day students and 50 per cent of evening class students did not complete their studies. Reasons given included external and internal factors. The common denominator for both reasons tended to be given as lack of time. Earlier writers have noted that:

In one sense a person's decision to drop out, just like the decision to enrol, will be unique to the individual. It will be the result of a complex interplay of personal and social factors.

(Woodley *et al.* 1987: 147)

Possible patterns in 'dropping out' were examined by the latter. Their evidence suggests that a lack of time might be a rationalization of other factors. Students:

who have found a course too difficult or who fail to put much effort
into them may seek to protect their self-esteem by attributing their
withdrawal to external pressure, such as lack of time.

(Woodley *et al.* 1987: 161–62)

Yet tentative evidence from my research suggested that the converse
was also applicable. I decided to explore what participation and dropping
out meant to an individual in the context of life schedules. This required
an exploration of how people explained their use of time to themselves
and to others. Contact was made with one of the students who had not
completed the course, and an interview was arranged.

Its focal point would be the interplay of positive and negative factors,
encouraging or discouraging a student from completing a part-time
course. In the following account, pseudonyms are used.

INTRODUCING JULIE GRAYSON

Julie Grayson had enrolled for the part-time day course intending to
take GCSEs in two subjects. Thirty-eight years old, with an eighteen-
year-old son and sixteen-year-old daughter, she was married to an estates
gardener, and lived in the grounds of the estate near a small village in
the midland shires. To get to college she needed transport, and she
shared car lifts with two students who came from the same area (and
who subsequently left the course before completion). Julie attended
eleven out of thirteen sessions in the first term; at the beginning of the
second term she called in twice to collect hand-out materials. Thereafter
she did not return to the course.

She enrolled for Sociology and English and paid for both examinations; she sat neither, but did complete some of the course-work.
In the middle of the autumn term, she obtained part-time employment
at a large supermarket in town. At the beginning of February she
contacted me to explain that her mother-in-law had been taken ill;
this was taking up a lot of time in terms of caring support and
travelling. She was giving up the course as she no longer had time
to study. In May, I telephoned Julie to thank her for participating
in the questionnaire; she informed me that her mother-in-law had
died.

In several ways, then, Julie was not untypical of women students in
the locality of the investigation. The college was situated in a market
town with a potentially large rural catchment area. Some villages had
irregular or no public transport. Like a number of other students, she
had postponed a return to study until her children were 'almost off her
hands'. Julie had spent two years in office work, when she left school.

Married at eighteen, she then prioritized her domestic caring role till she started the course in September 1988.

We met in June, at the college where she had enrolled the previous autumn. In relation to earlier information, I half expected to find a somewhat disheartened student 'drop-out'. I was mistaken. Julie began telling me how much she had enjoyed the course.

> *JG*: When I enrolled, everything seemed just right. The children were settled and preparing for the next stage in their lives. My daughter's got a place at college and my son's got a good job and a steady girlfriend, and so the time was right . . . then my mother-in-law took ill, and then she died. I seemed to move from one thing to another, still now it's over.

Julie had moved from one part of her life cycle, hopefully into a period of personal, free time. She then found herself caught up in a renewed cycle of caring in relation to her in-law.

> *MM*: You came with two other students. They stopped coming fairly early on. Did that matter to you?
>
> *JG*: No, it didn't. I was going to come on my own anyway, and then Sally and Thelma decided to come. As you know, where we live, Wakebridge, is a long way out. We've got cars because we have to. There are no buses, so we shared lifts, that's how we did it. Thelma wanted to do something new.
>
> *MM*: Why did they stop coming?
>
> *JG*: Well, Thelma was a nervous kind of women. It was no good telling her not to be worried about everything, the classes. It got on top of her and she decided to leave. And then Sally had problems – well, work's her problem – she's a cook at the big house. Wednesday was her day off, then all of a sudden, they (her employers) said Wednesday was hunting day, so, she had to work.
>
> I didn't have that problem. Wednesdays were alright and then things started to happen. First, Peter (her son) went for a job interview and I had to drive him, and then something else happened, I can't remember what, and then we were called to my mother-in-law's. I stayed over there (another part of the country) for three weeks. My husband stayed there and I came back. I couldn't come back to classes – there was so much to do at home, and I helped with my husband's gardening.

From this data, one gets a glimpse of the complexity of the female life-cycle and the way in which events and tasks have taken over Julie's study and college time. In Thelma's case, it would appear that a lack of confidence combined with anxiety over the course she had embarked upon precipitated dropping out. Sally was using her one day a week off to attend college; a change in plans by her employers, left her without a 'free' day to attend college.

> *MM*: You got a part-time job in the autumn term. Could you explain what effect that's had?
>
> *JG*: Getting a job didn't affect my ability to study but it did affect me. It's given me confidence, and I was promoted from shop to office and last Friday was made Section Manager. I used to work in an office when I left school. I married at eighteen and moved here. That was a long way to move in those days. I didn't do anything except bring up the children – and then I did cleaning – because you can fit that in with school hours. I lost a lot of confidence not seeing anyone. My husband didn't really like me doing cleaning. He said I could do better, and was pleased when I went for the shop job. 'You'll be among people', he said. I needed to see how other people think – it's really interesting and to see how people have different priorities.
>
> *MM*: So lots of things have happened this year?
>
> *JG*: Oh yes. My whole life's turned round this year – with the children, college, the job, mother-in-law. And coming to classes made me see things differently. It's really made me look at things in new ways.
>
> *MM*: That's great . . . I wonder . . . would you have any suggestions as to how we might improve things here for adults like yourself?
>
> *JG*: No – not really. The times were quite good. You have to fit into time slots – it's like at school, isn't it. Teachers can't be expected to teach at any time, can they . . .
>
> I want to take 'A' level English Literature next year. I know I can cope with it, because I've seen the syllabus. But my problem is now the job . . . I might do it at evening classes . . . I work different hours on different days.

In the last extract, it is seen that enrolling for college courses had pre-empted a paid employment application. By doing both, Julie considered herself to have gained in self-esteem. Ultimately, when family illness struck, study became the necessary sacrifice. At one point in the interview Julie had said:

> . . . coming to classes isn't just about education is it, it's also about meeting people.

Julie now had another means of accomplishing the latter. Had I not met the interviewee on this occasion, it would have been easy to write Julie off as another 'wastage' or 'drop-out' statistic. Lack of time to study would have been the given reason.

For the college and for lecturers, dropping-out has negative implications in terms of college numbers, organization, teaching staff contracts, and, ultimately, calculations of examination successes. Yet, as the interview suggested, Julie had clearly interpreted, her time spent at college, not in terms of failure, but as a first stage in gaining confidence to be with other people, getting a job, coping with renewed caring, and ultimately to consider returning for more study. In which case, the usual criteria for success did not apply.

In her questionnaire, Julie had prioritized the acquisition of qualifications in order to get a job. She had achieved the latter goal, and considered that attending the course had contributed towards gaining confidence to do this. Course attendance was not seen by Julie as personal or intellectual failure, but as a timely opportunity to develop communication and study skills.

She had gained what she wanted. Even when travel and care time intensified, she retained that which she considered more important – her job. Decisions had become interwoven with a complex web of activities over time.

CONCLUSIONS

Time has been a central focus for this chapter as it was for the research investigation. Management decisions to provide part-time courses in intensive day and evening time slots were considered to be both market-led and an institutional response to traditional patterns of sexually stratified divisions of labour.

Evidence suggested that part-time, which was organized in terms of both linear progression and discontinuous discrete activities, was both a solution and part of the recurring female dilemma of fragmented and collective time over which others could lay claim.

Opportunities and problems were open to a variety of interpretations and reflections over time; moreover, what was viewed as problematic for some interested parties, for example by college management in relation to 'dropping out', was not necessarily seen as problematic for others. Value judgements about the learning experience also changed . . . over time. [. . .]

WAYS FORWARD

Research findings suggested a number of recommendations for improving part-time educational experience:

- Returning to learn for mature students may include feelings of vulnerability and insecurity. In which case, there ought to be a friendly programme of induction and familiarization for all part-time students. This might take the form of: familiarization mornings or days before term started, a Saturday family or open day, and an induction programme.

- The importance of time management skills, as one aspect of study skills, was highlighted. These need to be integral to the structures, planning and implementation of courses, and not seen as ad hoc responses to individual deficiencies.

- There were early indications that college time would take up much of the free time available to students for study. This suggests the need for learning strategies which lean less heavily on front-led sessions and more on grouped learning experiences within and beyond the classroom, supported by active tutorial assistance.

- Research emphasized the costs and benefits of studying part-time, and a blurring between choice and necessity in the time mechanisms chosen. If study time is replacing leisure time, it needs to be seen as meaningful, enjoyable, and purposeful if it, rather than the leisure time which has been forfeited, is to be sustained. This has implications for pedagogy, content, and the physical environments in which courses and study take place.

- There were wide variations in the amount of time considered appropriate study time. Some students found it easier to organize time than others; some lacked an awareness of the skills they already possessed. This suggests the need for other access routes to knowledge and skills, including those which build on qualities already possessed by students and are specifically utilized in 'private time'.

- In the absence of credible examination alternatives, adults were continuing to take examinations which 'tested' knowledge that, in some cases, showed little relevance to their adult lives. This ought to be challenged; Access and pre-Access courses are part of that challenge.

- The study highlighted the complex and fragmented nature of women's lives. Implications might be that in periods of social, economic and educational change, such fragmentation could become positive and valued if actively encouraged by: flexible learning systems, drop-in support networks, rolling programmes, workshop activities, and learning programmes which emphasized student and group centredness. Consideration might also be given to a coherent outreach policy, so that alternative venues might be considered. In other words, we need to reinforce the view that self-directed learning for women, while flexible, need not occur in isolation (see also Brockett and Hiemstra 1991: 11–12).

- Questions were posed regarding the traditional evaluation of successful adult learning in terms of examination passes and completion rates achieved after 'set' periods of time. In relation to the latter, women, rather than institutions, would continue to be seen as 'the problem'. Policies were needed which included an acceptance that adults would move into, and out of, learning situations when they considered goals were achieved and desired, or were unachievable and undesirable.

Continuing education does not have to perpetuate existing or earlier educational experiences. Adults, male and female, staff and students, should be able to challenge policy and practice. Parts of that reality are linear schedules which place women into what have been described as 'temporal straitjackets which are not of their own making' (Davies 1989). Moreover, in times of changing employment patterns, such 'straitjackets' may become as ill-fitting for men as for women.

If we can create roles for men and women where fragmented time is considered positively rather than negatively, then family, part-time education, and employment, could become complementary institutions. At the very least, we could question the order in which 'education, work . . . and leisure come over the course of a lifetime' (Provonost 1989: 8). [. . .]

REFERENCES

Adam, B. E. (1989) 'Feminist social theory needs time: reflections on the relation between feminist thought, social theory and time as an important parameter in social analysis'. *The Sociological Review*, 37, 458–73.

Adam, B. E. (1990) *Time and Social Theory*, Cambridge: Polity Press.

Brockett, R. G. and Hiemstra, R. (1991) *Self-direction in Adult Learning: Perspectives on Theory, Research and Practice*, London and New York: Routledge.

Burgess, R. G. (1988) 'Conversations with a purpose' in R. G. Burgess (ed.), *Studies in Qualitative Methodology*, vol.1, New York: JAI Press.

Davies, K. (1989) *Women and Time. Weaving the Strands of Everyday Life*, Sweden: University of Lund.

Gunnarsson, E., and Ressner, U. (1985) *Frutunniers gora, Kvinnor pa Kontor och Verkstadsgolv*, Stockholm: Prisma, quoted in K. Davies, 1989, Sweden: University of Lund.

Hassard, J. (1988) 'Time and organization', in P. Blyton, (ed.) *Time, Work and Organization*, London: Routledge and Kegan Paul.

Hughes, M., and Kennedy, M. (1985) *New Futures, Changing Women's Education*, London: Routledge and Kegan Paul.

Morgan, D. H. J. (1985) *The Family, Policies and Social Theory*, London: Routledge and Kegan Paul

Provonost, G. (1989) *The Sociology of Time: Current Sociology*, vol. 37, no. 3, Winter. London: Sage Publications for the International Sociological Association.

Woodley, A., Wagner, L., Slowey, M., Hamilton, M., and Fulton, O. (1987) *Choosing to Learn: Adults in Education*, Milton Keynes: SRHE.

Yeandle, S. (1984) *Women's Working Lives*, London: Tavistock.

Chapter 13

Learner autonomy in a changing world

Stephen McNair

The idea that education exists to develop individual autonomy is a very old one. Traditionally the arguments rested on an appeal to fundamental rights, but in recent years it has been argued, from both ends of the political spectrum, that there are new economic and social reasons for promoting autonomy in individuals. A number of recent policy initiatives have some bearing on this issue, including moves to describe the outcomes of learning more explicitly, which has been presented as a means of extending individual autonomy by giving individuals more informed choice about the management of their lives and learning.

Interest in autonomy and its relationship to social and economic change in the late twentieth century create strange bedfellows. From the political right, individual autonomy is attractive because it reduces the individual's dependence on state and employer. Individuals are encouraged to stand on their own feet interacting in an endless series of market transactions. Education helps them to do this more effectively. From the left comes a tradition of empowerment, either of individuals or groups. Here autonomy is about the redistribution of power, of a more equal society, in which individuals or disempowered groups can exert more influence. It is possible that, at the end of the twentieth century, new technological and economic conditions are bringing these together in a fundamentally new configuration. Alternatively, we may be seeing merely a temporary or superficial conjunction which will rapidly pull apart again.

This chapter explores some of these arguments. It is in three parts: the first explores why learner autonomy matters, and why this is changing, the second explores the definition of autonomy, and the third considers the relationship between these issues and the 'learning outcome movement'.

ARGUMENTS FROM PRINCIPLE

For some people, autonomy is a fundamental value. From this standpoint, it is as immoral to restrict another person's autonomy as it is to restrict their freedom of movement, and one would wish to promote it whether or not this had any measurable effect on the health of society or the economy. This approach sits comfortably with the notion that education seeks to liberate the individual from prejudice and misconception, through the pursuit of 'knowledge for its own sake', and progression in education can be seen in the learner's increasing ability to think and act autonomously. Not only is extrinsic justification not needed it may be positively unwelcome, since it confuses the fundamental argument of principle.

However, in practice, most societies have restricted the range of people who are encouraged to become autonomous. This notion of rationing autonomy leads to the conventional distinction between 'education' which is open-ended and leads to autonomy, and 'training' which leads to competent performance within defined roles, and it has fitted well with social and economic structures based upon hierarchy and control. Members of élites get more education, and those with more education are gradually absorbed into those élites. Thus, those with access to power were provided with the means to become autonomous while those without it were relegated to dependent roles, economically and socially.

INSTRUMENTAL ARGUMENTS

A combination of factors have led to a shift of attention in the late twentieth century away from the idea that autonomy is an absolute value, to its promotion for instrumental reasons. The historical experience of the twentieth century, developments in philosophy and the social sciences, and the acceleration of global communication have all strengthened the sense that many apparently absolute values are relative. We are now less confident in speaking for the human race from a northern European perspective when it is evident that individual autonomy is not given such priority in many parts of the world, where people appear to be willing to see the individual's relationship to the community in quite different ways. This may partly explain the search in recent years for more instrumental arguments for individual autonomy – educational, social and economic.

The educational argument is concerned with the efficiency of the learning process itself, proposing that 'autonomous learners' are more efficient learners. It has its roots in the psychology of learning and proposes that the autonomous learner has a strong sense of self, of who she is and why she is learning, and a confidence that she is capable of achieving the result. Teaching strategies which feed these qualities will lead to the fastest and most fundamental learning, whereas those which do not recognize the self, or fail to reinforce the individual's intrinsic motivation and sense of ownership and competence, will discourage learning, or render it superficial.

The social case is a more pragmatic one: that a democracy cannot function without individuals who are capable of some degree of independent thought and action. From this perspective the notion of autonomy is linked to citizenship, rights, and responsibilities as a member of a community. Again, the concept is not value free, and not all cultures give a very high status to such principles. Nevertheless, the notion of an educated democracy is a powerful one in most northern European cultures, and has figured large in the movements for adult education which followed the two world wars, associated with the need to re-establish a stable society.

THE ECONOMIC CASE FOR AUTONOMY

It is the economic case for promoting individual autonomy which has changed most dramatically in the late twentieth century, as a result of changes in the nature of work itself, its organization, and the nature of lifelong careers.

The first of these is the shift towards a knowledge-based economy. A growing proportion of work is concerned with the creation and management of knowledge, rather than physical artifacts. As a result, for a growing number of people, work is requiring more individual creativity and self-management. In the world of mass production and hierarchical management, autonomy and creativity were not qualities to be valued in most workers. The organization rarely needed new ideas, and survived by continuing to work the old ones consistently for long periods, with workers whose role was to keep doing the same thing reliably and without question. Conformity was highly valued, often at the expense of autonomy. Now, however, economic survival for firms and nations depends increasingly on new ideas and products, developed rapidly, tailored to very specific needs, with a high knowledge content, and often requiring customer training and ongoing support. Firms which allow their rate of innovation and improvement and their levels of personal customer support to fall are rapidly overtaken by competition, which may be local, regional or global. This calls for a different kind of worker, who can produce ideas faster, both to conceive of new products and services, and to find new ways of organizing, producing and marketing them.

Individual working careers are becoming more complex and unpredictable, and external support for the individual is becoming less reliable. As organizations and industries are shrinking, their lifespan is shortening. Most individuals will, during their lifetimes, move between jobs, employers and industries, usually needing some education and training to assist with the transition. Multiple careers will become the norm as industries rise and die. Planning and managing one's own life must become a skill which all have, in a world where all decisions and choices have become more complex and unpredictable.

This is not a world for those who wait to be told what to do. Amin Rajan has defined the qualities of these new 'knowledge workers'.[1] They will be highly qualified, with good problem-solving and decision-making skills and the ability to take on a range of responsibilities in the workplace. They will also have:

> a high sense of self worth, individualism, autonomy and enterprise, a greater loyalty to their 'craft' than to their employer, and a higher propensity for job and career change, which will make training for them an uneconomic proposition for their employers.
>
> (Rajan 1993)

EQUITY

This world of the autonomous and creative individual, fully in control of her own career decisions and strategies, learning continually and adapting to a rapidly changing environment sounds exciting. However, not all will welcome the challenge, and it is far from clear what proportion of the new workforce will be engaged in these kinds of activities. To date we have signally failed to find socially acceptable ways of sharing out the apparently limited supply of employment, and the social and psychological benefits which go with it. Although the experience of paid work is becoming richer, more diverse and creative, albeit more stressful for those in employment, the actual numbers involved are declining.

After a long period when technology seemed not to be destroying jobs, its impact is now being felt very forcefully, and not only in traditional manufacturing activity where people have been replaced directly by machines. Developments in materials are also reducing demand for traditionally labour intensive work in the maintenance, repair and servicing roles, whereas in professional and white-collar fields where the work remains, and may, indeed, be growing in volume, the same technologies make it possible to export services such as accountancy or publishing to parts of the world where labour costs are lower and educational levels are rising. Whilst to date the creation of new jobs has broadly kept pace with the disappearance of old ones,[2] it is far from certain that this will continue to be the case, and many factors have combined to make the change uncomfortable for many people.

The people who occupy the new roles will certainly be more autonomous, and there may be more of them than formed the traditional élites, but they are likely to remain a minority. Alongside them will remain a body of low skill, low autonomy work. In principle, one can conceive of two distinct strategies to deal with this dilemma. The first is to try to preserve the status quo, by educating a minority of the population for high skill, high autonomy roles, and the mass of the population for low skill work or 'leisure'. The option offers little prospect of economic growth, and is politically unstable, because the low skill work is likely to be eroded by technology and overseas competition, leaving a shrinking minority generating the wealth to support a growing dependent population. The former will increasingly resent paying, and the latter will resent being trapped in a life which offers few rewards.

The second option is to seek to educate the whole population, either in the hope that newly empowered individuals will find entirely new ways of using their talents, generating new and unexpected sources of wealth, or that fiercer competition between autonomous individuals will lead to the most efficient winning the race for work, making the economy more efficient, even if no additional jobs are created. The former route underpins policies in a growing number of countries, and countries as diverse as Singapore and Finland have explicitly committed themselves to pursuing the high skills, high investment approach. Others are less clear.

Although Government policy on these issues in the United Kingdom is sometimes ambiguous, there appears to a be a growing consensus in favour of the active promotion of individual autonomy. An example is the espousal of the cause by the CBI in its 1989 report *Towards a Skills Revolution*, which argued for the first time (at least in such explicit terms) that the collective economic interest will be better served by encouraging individuals to pursue their own particular interests and enthusiasms, than by engaging them in learning programmes dictated by their employers. This reflects two distinct agendas. On one hand, there is a political resistance to the idea of labour market planning at the level of government or enterprise. The future is too uncertain, and it suits many employers to leave the burden of coping with structural change on the individual. On the other hand it recognizes that the resulting individuals will be much more powerfully motivated to act on what they have learned when they feel that they own it. If the resulting skills match those of the employer, they will be much more productive; if not, they will be better placed to find alternative employment or uses for their time.

The same principles underlie some of the Employee Development schemes developed since the mid-1980s, of which the Ford EDAP scheme is the first and best known.[3] Here, funds are created on which individuals can draw to pay for education and training programmes of their own choosing, regardless of their employers' training needs. A recent study of such schemes[4] is revealing – industrial relations improved markedly because of the signals about employers' commitment to their employees as people, and participation among the socio-economic groups who normally do not participate in education rose to the levels of those who normally do.

Both these examples show major players in the labour market seeking ways of encouraging individuals to make their own decisions about priorities for learning, opening possibilities for new occupations in or out of employment, extending control over their lives and identities, as well as extending their own competence in specific fields. The skills reserve in the economy and community is extended, people's ability to make productive use of their time, and control their own lives was extended. All these are benefits to the community, and some will be starting points for new kinds of economic activity.

WHAT DO WE MEAN BY AUTONOMY?

Although there may be a growing consensus that we wish to see greater individual autonomy, it does not follow that we have a consensus about what that means. The notion is a complex one, and the subject of debate in several distinct academic fields. The definition below aims to represent the broad common ground across a range of academic fields, although almost anything on this subject can be contentious. I would suggest that autonomy is:

- positive motivation – not merely a freedom from constraint, or having a range of choice, although greater choice provides more scope to exercise autonomy;
- an internal quality of the individual – a quality of self-directedness which is evident in intrinsic (rather than extrinsic) motivation, commitment and growth;
- a matter of degree – one is not either autonomous or not autonomous, one is more or less autonomous;
- a quality which can develop, and be deliberately developed;
- demonstrated in a context – we recognize autonomy through what people do or think in the real world;
- demonstrated in a sense of self, which enables the individual to make decisions and act to change her world, however large or small that may be. This is closely linked to a sense of control over circumstances,

and competence in addressing the relevant tasks;
- not necessarily individualistic – the autonomous individual can choose whether to act with or against others – autonomy embraces collective and individual action;
- distinct from isolation – an autonomous person may choose to live as a hermit, but living alone is not the same as being autonomous.

An educational programme to support this notion of autonomy would begin with how the individual sees and understands herself. Autonomy is at least as much about attitude and motivation as about circumstances. Furthermore, it would emphasize progression in terms of increasing control over knowledge and skill, and ability to make sound and independent decisions. It would also incorporate an ability to reflect on one's own interests and those of others, and to relate these where appropriate.

The key questions are 'Who am I?' 'Who do I want to be?' (rather than 'what') and 'How will this learning help me to become this?' This is true not only of those learning tasks which are clearly directed to personal fulfilment, but also of learning with more practical and instrumental purposes. This is widely recognized in the practice of trainers working with adults, and in the processes of mentoring, coaching and supervision which are characteristic of much adult learning in the workplace. However narrow and specific the learning objectives may be, learning will increase autonomy most if it recognizes and builds on the individual's sense of self. In the strict sense, adult learning is about the 're-creation' of the individual. In Eraut's terms[5] it begins with 'personal knowledge', which starts with impressions, and uses reflection and synthesis to build this into a 'scheme of experience' – an internal map of the self and its relationship to the world. Unless it begins with personal knowledge (knowledge *why*), it will never arrive at process knowledge (knowledge *how*), let alone propositional knowledge (knowledge *that*).

This view is supported, from a different direction, by the body of literature on adult learning which points to the notion of 'self-confidence', which is often the term used in the English literature of adult education to describe how adults change in the course of learning. Jones and Charnley, for example, drew attention to how much more highly this was rated by adult literacy students than measurable performance in reading.[6] It was clear that for learners and teachers there was an inner quality, of how people felt about themselves, which was of central importance to them. Similar issues are addressed by work on 'personal effectiveness' and 'personal transferable skills', which have formed the central part of much work by the CBI and Government in reshaping the curriculum to the needs of employment.[7]

A LANGUAGE OF OUTCOMES

In recent years policymakers have sought to address individual ownership and responsibility in post-school education and training by attempting to make the outcomes of learning more explicit, enabling 'purchasers
in the education and training market' to make better informed choices
about routes and options. I now turn to an exploration of how far this
movement is, in reality, capable of supporting the development of
autonomy, and how it might do so more effectively.[8]

The central notion of an outcome-led approach to education and
training is simple. It is that the purpose of all serious learning is to
change the learner, and that its effectiveness can only logically be
measured in terms of those changes. Learning outcome descriptions are
therefore explicit statements of achievement: what a given person can
do, know or understand as a result of a piece of formal or informal
learning – something possible now that was not possible before. I would
distinguish here between 'learning outcomes' in this sense – how an
individual is changed – from 'outputs' or 'outcomes' in a broader sense,
which usually refer to second-order factors, such as qualifications or
successful job placement, and have other implications for issues such as
institutional funding.

Learning outcomes are a form of language, designed to enable members of a community to talk to each other about a common interest in
human achievement. However, the notion of language is a complex one,
deeply intertwined with our sense of personal and social identity, and
embodying a central paradox. On one hand, it makes communication
possible. On the other, it is one of the most important tools for defining
the limits of community, by excluding those who do not speak 'our'
language, or marginalizing those who speak an unfamiliar dialect. Thus,
human societies and communities of all kinds consist of constantly
evolving linguistic groupings, first coming together around common
ways of understanding the world embodied in common vocabulary and
syntax, and then fragmenting as the community becomes too large, and
sub-groups emerge.

The languages of the professions are a classic case, where a body of
common knowledge is developed by a group, who evolve their own
ways of understanding and talking about it which gradually become
formalized. The language then becomes a defining quality of the new
professional group, with its mechanisms for inducting new members, for
testing their continuing membership and excluding those who do not
share their beliefs and concepts. The more narrowly their language is
defined, the more exclusive the membership, and, in general, the higher
their social status (and often their earnings).

The introduction of a language of outcomes into vocational education is a challenge to this exclusivity. The aim is to make the outcomes of learning in both professional and academic fields (and academic fields are themselves exclusive professions) visible to a wider group, widening the community of people able to engage in the dialogue. Not surprisingly, this is politically contentious, especially among those who 'owned' the previous language – the academic community, the professional bodies and the examining and awarding bodies, above all at the 'higher' levels, where the language is most refined, and the communities most closed. If the arguments proposed earlier, about the growth of a learning society and a knowledge-based economy, have any force, however, it is important that these barriers are broken down. We need more people to be competent in more things, and to understand those things better. However, resistance to the outcome movement at this level is more than a matter of defending traditional privilege. The attempt to make the language more accessible, and widen the community, inevitably threatens its precision, and there is a real danger that critical elements may be lost. Where the balance lies between enlarging the community and retaining the genuine quality of what is described is both contentious and critical, and it is important to examine carefully what elements may be lost before shifting the centre of gravity too far.

If we leave aside the appeals to political self-interest, there are a number of recurring objections to the outcome movement, most of which concern the difficulty of finding ways of adequately describing and assessing learning outcomes, and the consequences of this. Since the task of definition and assessment will be more difficult for some kinds of outcome than others, there is an inevitable tendency for attention and value to be diverted away from the important but difficult, to the trivial but easily assessed. This criticism is most commonly voiced in relation to personal qualities, to knowledge (at the expense of skills), and to collective outcomes. Concern is also often expressed that some qualities are not assessable in a realistic timescale, and that the model tends to be static or backward looking, neglecting the developmental and creative potential of human learning – the potential to learn the unknown.

MEASURING THE PERSONAL

Personal skills are important to individuals and to the economy. They are also centrally related to individual autonomy, but they are difficult to measure, as is autonomy itself. Nevertheless, any language to describe human achievement which did not recognize them would have failed. It is difficult to conceive of an autonomous individual who was not good at things which have often been defined as 'personal transferable skills', and research has repeatedly shown that qualities such as planning, taking initiative, making decisions, problem-solving, learning independently, and communicating with others are highly prized by individuals, teachers and employers. However, because such outcomes are less easy to describe and assess than many more mechanical activities, it has often been assumed that the only cost-effective way of measuring them is by proxy – on the basis that those who have been through a particular kind of process can be assumed to have arrived at the outcome. It is believed, for example, that there are some outcomes of traditional British higher education, fundamental to our notion of what a degree is, which are produced by three years residence in a specific place. These are rarely defined and almost never assessed, and yet despite this, in some universities, only those who have been through the process can get the qualification.

Although there may be disagreement about the degree to which such achievements can be measured, it is self-evident, as Jessup has pointed out,[9] that if an achievement can be described it must be possible to assess it. The existence of the word in our vocabulary implies that a number of people could agree about whether it was, or was not, present in a given situation, and within some limits they are likely to be able to agree about how well it was achieved. If the language of outcomes cannot articulate these qualities, it has failed, and those who are designing the language need then to review how it works, not relegate such important issues to the realm of mystery from which we have been emerging. Fortunately, there is evidence that such qualities can be assessed with a reasonable degree of accuracy. Whilst they may not be susceptible to all kinds of assessment, it is clearly possible to do so with greater accuracy and reliability than is traditional in either vocational or academic education in Great Britain. It is ironic that the formal qualification system pays little attention to the issues which figure largest in job references, and many of those who deny that qualities such as time management, creativity or leadership can be properly assessed, are happy to use such terms in recommending their students and trainees to others. Work on these areas has been going on for some years, and recent examples include the work of the National Council for Vocational Qualifications (NCVQ) on Core Skills, by the former Employment Department on Personal Competences, earlier UDACE work on Student Potential[10] and the competences of entrants to higher education[11]. However, the issue remains unresolved of how they can be best integrated into structures of formal qualification.

COLLECTIVE ACHIEVEMENT

Collective outcomes present a different problem, of particular concern to those working in adult and community education. There are a wide range of educational or development processes whose principal outcomes, central to community development models of learning, are collective rather than individual. However, despite the fact that the principal strategy for defining occupational standards in outcome terms in Britain is functional analysis, which begins with collective purposes rather than individual activity, the end result is a very individualistic one.

Collective outcomes are very varied. At the community development end of adult education, groups come together to learn how to challenge a road scheme, produce a local history or address a social problem, but collective outcomes are also evident where a quality circle learns to improve the quality of a product, or a professional group meet to refine their own practice. In all cases there can be individual achievements, but it would be perverse to suggest that they are always the most significant.

Collective outcomes present us with two problems. Most importantly, individual autonomy is often substantially enhanced by the experience of being a member of a successful team, even if the individual's measurable outcomes are very limited. Group processes, well managed, can be very powerful sources of support and motivation to individual self-confidence which is central to individual autonomy. The second problem is that the development of a language of outcomes to define individual achievement more clearly, which is important if outcomes are being used as a basis for qualifications or employment, may end up diverting attention from important collective ones. If the achievement of individual outcomes are overvalued by comparison with collective one, important educational activity in some areas may be devalued or lost.

INTEGRATION, CHANGE AND DEVELOPMENT

The final question is how far the language of outcomes can support the continuing growth of the individual, and a changing world around. The arguments touched on earlier suggest that individuals, in approaching their own learning, seek to build new achievement into a pattern which they perceive as a whole. I am likely to reject, and not learn (at any deep level) ideas and knowledge which challenge my sense of self too radically, or which I cannot relate to who I think I am, or want to be. In so far as a language of outcomes helps me to add new dimensions to my evolving self they will support my autonomy, but if they encourage me to think of myself as a bundle of dissociated skills or knowledge they will reduce my power over myself and my world. It follows that, if outcomes are to be useful to me, I need tools for integrating them, as well as analysing them, to counteract the dangers of reductionism inherent in many approaches to outcome definition.

There is a particular problem here that effective lifelong learners are continually reflecting on previous learning and experience, reconfiguring it into new 'schemes of experience'. There will thus be outcomes which do not manifest themselves or whose significance does not become apparent, for months or years. There is a danger that such learning will be devalued if the performance of education and training services comes to be evaluated against its ability to deliver outcomes in too short a timescale. If premature judgements are made about the relevance or impact of particular learning, valuable outcomes may be devalued or lost.

CONCLUSION

There are many reasons to believe in the development of individual autonomy. They include a view about the importance of individual growth and fulfilment; a commitment to a more active and democratic society; a belief about the economic need to tap the full potential of the population. They may also include equally powerful arguments about dependence and independence. In the circumstances of the 1990s, both the state and employers may be more fearful of the potential burden of looking after us, than they are of our freedom. Autonomous individuals look after themselves: dependent ones have to be provided for. Whatever the motivation, those who do believe in individual autonomy would do well to capitalize on the expressed interest, and consider carefully how the development of an outcome led education and training system might contribute.

First, explicitness matters. There is no doubt that exposing hidden criteria and standards and developing explicit descriptions of individual achievement provides individuals with greater choice, and more opportunity to exercise their autonomy. The critical issues here are to ensure that the vocabulary and structures of the language can recognize all the qualities which are valued, and do not, by accident or design, exclude important achievements. We need to ensure that the descriptions are usable, steering the course between unmanageable elaboration and over-simplification, and ensuring that the language is not formulated or policed in ways which exclude particular individuals or groups.

However, explicitness alone is not enough to develop autonomy, which is concerned with how people see themselves, and their motivation. For this people need both choice and a means to relate themselves to the changing world around. This requires that we address rather different questions, for which we need a language which can be used by those who describe outcomes, those who demonstrate them and those who use them. The central purpose of this language must be not to ask 'Has my achievement satisfied you?' but 'Do we agree that this is right?' and 'What makes it right?'. This is the characteristic form of professional dialogue (at least in its idealized form). New recruits enter, initially dependent on dialogue with senior members to help them to understand what achievement is, but as they develop and increase their competence, they internalize those definitions, criteria and values, and the language of the profession which embodies them. Thus they come to be confident in the ability to understand them, to enter into a debate in which the whole profession reflects on, challenges and evolves its understanding of achievement, and passes those findings on to new members and each other.

The challenge is to take this professional model, which is itself an empowering and developmental one, and extend it to a much larger community and a much larger range of activity. We want to find ways of ensuring that all individuals feel ownership of their own achievement, and are contributors to the constant evolution of the notion of achievement itself, in the same way that some professions have done, on a smaller scale, in the past.

There are many ways in which this can, and is, being done. Quality circles and total quality management are examples in the world of work, the use of functional analysis in staff and organizational development are others. In the educational context, processes of recording achievement, action planning and collaborative approaches to accreditation through Open College Networks, are all examples of attempts, using an outcome based language, to create the ongoing dialogue across traditional cultural barriers.

At the core of all this debate is the notion of a community of interest, in which a wide range and diversity of qualities are valued and recognized, and a language is available in which individuals can debate and develop their own understanding of their competence and opportunities. A language of outcomes might do this, and there are encouraging signs. There are also dangers, of over-formalizing and over-dependence on written language to handle things which can only be understood through discussion. More fundamentally, we cannot avoid the crucial political question of who is to be allowed into this dialogue. If we really wish to develop all the human resources of our community, we need a language which is as inclusive as possible, and where dialogue is actively encouraged. If we construct the language of outcomes in a way which excludes many people, or which prevents change or dialogue, we may increase choice, but we will not fully empower. It would be a sad end to an important enterprise.

NOTES AND REFERENCES

1 Rajan, A. (1993) *Where the New Jobs will Be*, Centre for Research in Employment and Technology in Europe. Summarized in Employment Department's Skills and Enterprise Briefing 15/93.
2 Reference to job creation and destruction – Labour Market Quarterly.

3 Metcalfe, H. (1992) *Releasing Potential: Company Initiatives to Develop People at Work*, vols 1 and 2, Sheffield: Employment Department.
4 Unpublished study of Employee Development schemes in small firms carried out by NIACE for the Employment Department, 1994.
5 Eraut, M. *Developing the Knowledge Base in* R. Barnett (ed.) *Learning to Effect*, Buckingham: SRHE/OU Press.
6 Jones, A. and Charnley, A. (1978) *Adult Literacy: A Study of Its Impact*, Leicester: NIACE.
7 See, for example, Harvey. L *et al.* (1992) *Someone Who Can Make An Impression*. Quality in Higher Education Project, University of Central England.
8 These issues are explored in more depth in, Burke, J. (1995) *Outcomes, Learning and the Curriculum*, London: Falmer.
9 Jessup, G. (1991) *Outcomes: NVQs and the Emerging Model of Education and Training*, London: Falmer.
10 Otter, S. (1989) *Student Potential in Britain*, Leicester: UDACE/NIACE.
11 Otter, S. (1991) *Admission to Science and Engineering Degree Courses: A Handbook for Admissions Tutor*, Leicester: BP/UDACE.

Chapter 14

Professions and competencies

Paul Hager and Andrew Gonczi

INTRODUCTION

A competency-based approach to education, training and assessment has re-emerged as a key educational policy in the English speaking countries. In Australia and New Zealand, governments of quite different political persuasions have joined business groups and the trade unions to promote the competency agenda, though the ways in which it is being implemented are in some respects quite different. In Britain, similar developments are occurring, though, in England at least, without the same degree of involvement and consensus from the social partners. In the United States there have been recent initiatives in developing national competency standards for the teaching profession, and for certain craft occupations. In addition, organizations such as the American Society of Orthopaedic Surgeons are developing a competency-based approach to curriculum (Green *et al.* 1990). In Canada, similar approaches have been used in social work training in a number of provinces for some time and are being tried currently in a number of middle level occupations.

What is unique about the Australian version of the competency movement, however, is the widespread involvement of the professions. Encouraged by the Commonwealth government, most of the professions have developed competency-based standards and are currently developing competency-based assessment (CBA) strategies. Obviously, this will affect higher education teaching and assessment practices as well as those of a variety of providers of continuing professional education. In addition, it will enhance the capacity of people to move up the educational/ qualifications ladder.

Most of the academic literature that has emerged recently has been highly critical of these developments. Even those authors who have seen some potential benefits in adopting competency-based approaches have usually made the assumption that they are only appropriate for middle level occupations, i.e. those at sub-professional level. (Hodgkinson, 1992, in writing about teacher education, is an exception.)

In broad terms, the argument of this chapter is that a competency based approach to education and training potentially provides a coherent framework for bringing together a range of governmental policies concerning skills formation, industrial relations and social equity and that this approach is as applicable to the professions as to any other occupations. However, as is explained below, there are a number of ways of conceptualizing the nature of competence. If inappropriate ways are adopted, not only is this potential not going to be realized, but serious damage will be done to skill formation policies in the medium term.

It is also argued that, despite the criticism of the approach, a competency-based approach to assessment of professionals is potentially (and in some cases, actually) more valid than traditional approaches. That is, it enables us to come closer than we have in the past to assessing what we want to assess, viz the capacity of the professional to integrate knowledge, values, attitudes and skills in the real world of practice. The inferences that are an inevitable part of any assessment are far more limited in this form of assessment than in traditional assessment (see Hager *et al.* 1994).

This chapter will provide:

- a brief analysis of the various ways in which the nature of competence has been conceptualized. Whilst this chapter concentrates on the professions, it is argued that the ways of thinking about competence are relevant to all occupations;
- an overview of the current state of the Australian professions' involvement with the competency movement;
- two case studies of the application of competency standards by Australian professions.

DIFFERENT CONCEPTIONS OF THE NATURE OF COMPETENCE

The first, and probably the most widely held, conception of the nature of competence is task-based or behaviourist. In it, competence is conceived in terms of the discrete behaviours associated with the completion of atomized tasks. Its aim is transparent specification of competencies such that there can be no disagreement about what constitutes satisfactory performance. In effect the task becomes the competency, so that if, for example, a mechanic can replace a fuel pump or a teacher introduce a lesson she is said to possess the competency of fuel pump replacement or lesson introduction. This approach is unconcerned with the connections between the tasks and ignores the possibility that the coming together of tasks could lead to their transformation (the whole is not greater than the sum of the parts). Evidence for the possession of the competency in this model is based on direct observation of performance.

Those who follow this approach tend to see the curriculum of education and training programmes as being directly related to the behaviours/tasks specified in the occupation's competency standards. In Australia and England, this approach has been adopted by many of the industries who first developed competency standards, and is usually the model in people's minds when they attack the competency movement (as, for example, Ashworth and Saxton 1990; Field 1991; Magnusson and Osborne 1990; Collins 1991). Although this model has the attraction of simplicity and clarity, its weaknesses are easy to enumerate. As the authors above point out, it is positivist, reductionist, ignores underlying attributes, ignores group processes and their effect on performance, is conservative, atheoretical, ignores the complexity of performance in the real world and ignores the role of professional judgment in intelligent performance (see Preston and Walker 1993). Clearly this approach is inappropriate for conceptualizing professional work and there are very serious doubts about its relevance to work at any level.

The second conception of the nature of competence concentrates on the general attributes of the practitioner that are crucial to effective performance. Such an approach focuses on the underlying attributes, e.g. knowledge or critical thinking capacity, which provide the basis for transferable or more specific attributes. Thus the general attribute of thinking critically, it is assumed, can be applied to many or all situations. In this model, competencies are thought of as general attributes, ignoring the context in which they might be applied. This approach has been popular in the management literature (see, for example, McBer 1978; Boyatzis 1982).

There are, however, a number of problems with this approach. First, there is no certainty that generic competencies actually exist. The evidence from the novice/expert research (e.g. Chi et al. 1981; Greeno 1989; McGaw 1993) and from the critical thinking literature (e.g. Ennis 1989; Norris 1985) suggests that expertise (which can be characterized as high levels of competence) is domain specific. That is, individuals demonstrate little capacity to transfer expertise from one area of activity to another. Second, these general attributes are of limited help for those involved in the practical work of designing education and training programmes for specific professions. The logic of this model for curriculum development is that one would use the same educational activities to develop critical thinking or communication skills in a medical course as in a legal course. What would be more useful for curriculum developers would be the identification of what critical thinking and communication in the practice of medicine and law are like. Indeed, given the findings from the novice/ expert literature, it will probably be necessary to identify the different types of critical thinking and communication skills in different *branches* of medicine and law. It is likely that the communication skills of a criminal lawyer will be quite different to those of a family lawyer. Traditionally, university courses have concentrated on developing and assessing generic skills in the broad context of the profession inferring that these are the basis of successful practice in the future.

The third conception of the nature of competence seeks to marry the general attributes approach to the context in which these attributes will be employed. This approach looks at the complex combinations of attributes (knowledge, attitudes, values and skills) which are used to understand and function within the particular situation in which professionals find themselves. That is, the notion of competence is relational. It brings together disparate things – abilities of individuals (deriving from combinations of attributes) and the tasks that need to be performed in particular situations. Thus, competence is conceived of as complex structuring of attributes needed for intelligent performance in specific situations. Obviously, it incorporates the idea of professional judgment. This approach has been called the 'integrated' or holistic approach to competence (Gonczi *et al.* 1990) and it is the conception that has been adopted by the professions in Australia.

This third approach overcomes all the objections to the competency movement that have been identified in the literature. It allows us to incorporate ethics and values as elements in competent performance, the need for reflective practice, the importance of context and the fact that there may be more than one way of practising competently.

The various approaches can be illustrated by looking at the introduction of competency-based teacher education in the 1970s in the US. Through the use of occupational analysis techniques, which reflected the dominant influence of behaviourist psychology in American education, teaching was broken down into the variety of tasks that teachers were expected to perform. It was felt that if teachers could perform the literally hundreds of discrete tasks identified then they would be competent teachers. Whilst this approach satisfied the desire of its proponents for observable measurable behaviours, success in performing tasks identified did not seem to have any relationship to good teaching as most experienced professionals understood it (Houston 1974). An alternative approach is to believe that teachers need only a strong knowledge base consisting of subject and pedagogical knowledge and that this base will transfer to competent practice. The integrated approach is to conceive of competent teaching as being the capacity of the teacher to employ a complex interaction of attributes in a number of contexts. Thus a knowledge base will need to mesh with, amongst other things, ethical standards and capacity to communicate with people of various ages and capacities. Unfortunately, this means that the hope of simplicity and clarity in all matters to do with the delivery and assessment of education, the things that attracted governments to the approach in the first place, are misconceived.

CURRENT INVOLVEMENT OF AUSTRALIAN PROFESSIONS IN THE USE OF COMPETENCY STANDARDS

There are presently twenty professions undertaking the development of competency standards and assessment strategies with funding provided by the National Office of Overseas Skills Recognition (NOOSR). In addition to these registered professions there are competency projects in a variety of other professions or groups within professions.

There are many reasons which favour the professions' use of competency standards:

- It will help governments to devise means of fairly assessing and granting professional status to overseas-trained professionals. This will be important in a world for the most part committed to the internationalization of trade and services.
- It is desirable to have public statements about what the qualified members of a profession are competent to do and what the public can reasonably expect of them. This will help the professions to monitor more effectively than they do currently the quality of their members' services. For the community it will lead to an enhanced capacity to choose between professionals and to judge the quality of service received. Additionally, it serves the democratic purpose of demystifying the specialized knowledge of the professions and potentially enabling more non-professionals to engage in debate about complex political issues such as health, education, justice and social welfare.
- It will facilitate mutual recognition of professional qualifications across states and territories. This is important in Federations such as Australia and in the European Union where achieving such mutual recognition has been a problem.
- It will provide the basis for assessing competence of people re-entering a profession after a lengthy absence. It will also assist in devising appropriate refresher courses for the various categories of absentee.
- It will provide clearer goals than currently exist for providers of professional education and training. This potentially will lead to much more coherent, integrated courses of professional preparation. Currently there is not much thought given to the relationship between on and off the job education/training of professionals or to the respective roles of the universities and the professions in initial and continuing professional education.

- It will help in the development of more effective continuing professional education programmes, particularly in those professions where various levels of the competency standards have been established. (See Hager and Gonczi 1991.)
- It will assist professional associations/registration authorities in the accreditation of educational programmes.
- It will assist educational providers who wish to incorporate some competency-based assessment into their programme.
- It will provide the basis for people with competencies in similar occupational areas to move more easily into the professions by making it clearer what is expected of a beginning professional. Similarly, in those professions where various levels of the competency standards have been established, it will be much clearer what is required of those seeking specialist or advanced status.
- It provides the opportunity for professionals to reflect on the nature of their work within a broader framework than they have done previously. In fact, in Australia it has resulted in the incorporation of a far wider range of attributes into the description of competent performance in many professions than has existed previously. It amounts to a rejection of the narrow model of technocratic professionalization that has characterized the professions in North America at least (Collins, 1991).
- It will help to improve the rather weak assessment procedures which lead to professional qualification in most professions, at least in Australia.

The format of the competency standards developed by the Australian professions will be familiar to people aware of the National Vocational Qualification (NVQ) model in England. They are organized into units of competence (representing a wide work function) which are subdivided in smaller elements of competence (tasks within the wider function) with their associated performance criteria (the standard by which the competence in the task will be judged). This has been mandated as the framework in both England and Australia. All the Australian professions have agreed to use this framework. However, the differences between the competency standards produced by the Australian professions and those produced by most industry bodies in England are quite startling. Rather than developing large numbers of elements of competence with long lists of performance criteria for each element, as has been the case in the English NVQ model, the professions have typically developed about thirty to forty elements of competence. In many instances, as is outlined later in the case studies, the performance criteria are 'described' standards which are not expressed as long checklists (typical in England) but in ordinary prose which is meant to suggest the holism of the nature of competence.

In Australia, NOOSR recently surveyed the professions that have established competency standards to find out what uses are being made of them. Given the various main possible uses of competency standards outlined above, it is interesting to see the definite ways in which the Australian professions are employing their competency standards (NOOSR 1994) (Table 14.1):

Table 14.1 Ways in which Australian professions employ competency standards (%)

Use of competencies by professions	Useage (%)
Assessing competence of overseas trained professionals	73
Providing public information on professional roles/responsibilities	50
Facilitating mutual recognition within Australia	47
Assisting in accreditation of education programmes	43
Assessing eligibility for professional registration	42
Developing continuing professional education courses	38
Assessing competence of lengthy absentees from practice	37
Assisting in development of university curriculum	34
Developing competency-based assessment	31
Assessing eligibility for membership of a professional body	29
Facilitating articulation between levels within a profession	26
Assessing competence of people with no formal qualifications	21
Determining individual continuing professional education needs	17
Facilitating articulation from paraprofession to profession	16
Defending professionals against legal action	13
Assisting employers to evaluate performance	12
Assisting employers in recruitment and promotion of staff	11

These figures reflect the fact that there are not just one or two main uses of competency standards. Rather, there is great diversity between the individual professions in the ways that they are employing their competency standards. This, in turn, supports claims made for the multi-purpose nature of competency standards. This diversity points to the fact that each profession has its own unique features and needs, so that the implementation of competency standards is viewed somewhat differently in each case. Overall, the development of professional competency standards has stimulated an unprecedented amount of research, development and internal debate within the Australian professions. Interestingly, the NOOSR survey found significant positive support for the use of holistic, integrated competency standards among university staff who have been involved in their implementation. This contrasts with findings by other research that academics in general, most of whom have had no experience with these sorts of competency standards, are opposed to their use.

EXAMPLES OF THE USE OF COMPETENCY STANDARDS BY AUSTRALIAN PROFESSIONS

Nursing

In 1986 in Australia a meeting of the nurses' registration authorities expressed a concern about different standards in the various States which led to the agreement to identify nationally agreed minimal competencies for the profession. These competencies (known as the ANRAC competencies – Australian Nurses Registering Authorities Conference, and subsequently as the ANCI competencies (Australian Nurse Council Inc.) were developed after a group of experts gathered together to produce a draft set of competencies which were then validated and modified by a thorough and extended empirical study. It was felt that the competencies could be utilized for four purposes:

- to determine the eligibility for initial registration of nurses prepared in Australia;
- to determine the eligibility of nurses prepared overseas for registration;
- to provide the basis of assessing nurses who wished to re-enter the profession;
- to ensure that qualified nurses are competent to continue practice.

(Percival in Gonczi et al. 1993)

Despite their commitment to the use of the competencies for these purposes the nurses' registration authorities in Australia do not desire to be prescriptive regarding university course content and, in fact, most of them would set forth no particular requirements in relation to content of courses (Cameron 1994). They are more interested in the outcomes of the course and, where content is examined in the accreditation process, it would only be to determine whether the content chosen by the school of nursing and its sequencing was adequate for achieving the course outcomes. As long as the content and its organization provides a suitable vehicle for achievement of the course outcomes, the boards are not interested in specifying content, leaving that to the universities.

Of courses universities may themselves elect to make use of the competency standards and some have chosen to do so. The nursing competencies have the potential to impact on university courses in three main areas:

- course design;
- course content;
- student assessment.

In relation to course design, the nurses' registration boards have always been quite definite that they do not wish the competencies to drive a competency-based curriculum. The competencies were not designed to reflect the narrowly behaviourist approach typical of the earlier competencies movement. Rather, they were designed to reflect the holistic nature of nursing and to represent the practice repertoire of the newly graduated nurse. Thus, course design is influenced by the competencies to the extent that individual curriculum developers wish it to be. Provided provision is made for students to demonstrate that they have achieved the competencies by the end of the course, the boards prefer to see diversity in curriculum design and would be quite uncomfortable with uniform national curricula. There are some schools of nursing who feel that the competencies do bind them and restrict their potential for developing innovative curricula. Others, however, have been able to develop curricula based on a variety of models whilst accommodating the competencies.

Another point about the competencies is that they represent the minimum standard to be achieved by graduating nurses. Universities are quite free to include additional competencies, objectives or course materials not associated with the competencies.

A major impact on curriculum content is the provision of the clinical practice that is needed in order to demonstrate achievement of the competencies. In this regard, the very first competency reads 'demonstrates a satisfactory knowledge base for safe practice'. It is clear, therefore, that theory has to be addressed in order to give the knowledge base for those competencies which are clinically based. In this respect guidance is given for content but not explicit direction.

The area of assessment is the one where the competencies have had the most impact. If these competencies are the standard to be acquired by new registrants then students must be assessed to ensure that they have acquired them. The approach to assessment of the competencies has changed from previous assessments of clinical experience. Clinical assessments tended to be based in the past on objective-style instruments such as checklists. The philosophy statement in the competencies document (ANCI 1993, p. 2) contains the sentence 'Nursing addresses the complexity and uniqueness of the whole person in the environmental context'. Thus, nursing occurs in a dynamically interactive field and one in which objective-style instruments are unsuitable. The approach to competencies assessment which has been promoted by the Council is standards-referenced and the focus is on the use of the professional and qualitative judgment of expert nurse practitioners in determining whether the standards have been met. No-one other than these experts would have the necessary expertise for making this judgment. The standards attached to the competencies become the bench-mark against which achievement is judged.

With this new focus on assessment, it was necessary to conduct workshops throughout Australia to sensitize nurse assessors to this new direction in assessment. Personnel from many of the universities have been involved in these workshops and have subsequently conducted workshops in their own institutions.

ANCI is about to undertake a review of the competencies following their first five years of use. There is widespread interest in this review as it has become obvious that the competencies must give a relevant picture of the work practices desired of the new graduate. As well, they have to be a communication tool which allows all stakeholders including the public to know what it is that the new graduate can do. For this reason there will be wide consultation during the review. This is where nurse registration authorities, the higher education sector and the workplace can engage in purposeful collaboration.

Teaching

It has been widely accepted in a range of countries that the work of teachers is becoming more complex. One of the major reasons for this is what the OECD and others have identified as the higher levels of knowledge and skill needed to be productive in the workplace. Over recent years every English-speaking nation, as well as countries such as Germany, have developed a set of core skills or competencies which are felt to be necessary for having a successful economy in the immediate future. These core competencies include things such as the need for abstract thinking, the ability to solve problems, the capacity to work in teams, the ability to communicate effectively and so on. In Australia, all teachers whether in Schools or Colleges, and also industry trainers, are expected to be able to help young people to develop these competencies in the context of their specialist subject areas.

The teaching profession has been attempting to come to grips with how to prepare its members for the new demands being placed on them. A part of the answer has been the development of competency standards as the underpinning of teacher education courses.

The teaching profession is complex and heterogeneous, and the development of competency standards needs to take account of both the similarities and differences between various categories of teacher (e.g. beginning teacher, 'master' teacher, primary teacher, secondary teacher, teacher of adults) and the variety of different specialities within these categories. Despite this complexity there have been a number of attempts to develop both generic and specific competency standards for teachers in Australia over the last two years.

The newly formed Australian Teaching Council has overseen the development of generic teaching standards for beginning school teachers in Australia since 1993. These generic competency standards have been developed collaboratively between teachers, employers and universities and are being extensively trialled: Teachers' competence has been characterized into five major areas: teaching practice; students needs; relationships; evaluating and planning; professional responsibilities. These have been further analysed into elements of competence following the template developed in the UK, though with far less disaggregation and, as a consequence, far fewer elements. Louden (1993) has illustrated each element of competence by a short case study which shows how a teacher might interpret a complex element. For example in the element 'Understands how students develop and how they learn', obviously a very broad competency, the case study describes how a teacher might interpret a piece of writing. The objective is to develop a continuum of competence rather than a list of separate skills.

In addition to the generic standards for teachers, various specialist categories of teachers have developed their own standards. One such example is adult basic education teaching (Scheeres *et al.* 1993). This is of interest because the equivalent group of teachers in the UK also have a set of standards, *The ALBSU Standards for Basic Skills Teachers* 1992). The writers of these standards have certainly taken a holistic approach. For example, there is a total of only forty elements of competence. This means that the developers of the standards have realized that competence is something more complex than simply dividing up the occupation into its smallest measurable components. They also make the important point that competence cannot necessarily be inferred directly from performance. In these UK standards, the performance criteria in any element of competence only look at outcomes. It is recognized that the knowledge and understanding needed to achieve outcomes may not be assessable by observing outcomes only.

The ALBSU report implies there is a need for understanding and knowledge that tie together the various elements into a much richer whole. Yet interestingly there is little discussion of what the developers' overall concept of competence actually is. They have realized the deficiencies of the reductionist approach without yet reaching a coherent view themselves. This seems to be confirmed by the nature of the performance criteria which obviously need to fit into the UK framework but which, as a result, are somewhat fragmented. So, for example, the ALBSU standards divide their performance criteria for each element into anything up to seven individual points. The danger here is that performance can once again be analysed as discrete tasks.

The underlying conception of competence in the Australian Adult Basic Education teaching (ABE) project is that competence consists of an individual's possession of a combination of attributes applied in particular contexts. That is, it is relational and integrated as discussed earlier. It brings together contexts and tasks with knowledge, skills and values employed in some combination. In the end, competence consists of the capacity to make intelligent judgments in a variety of complex situations, and the way of assessing this cannot be as precise as ticking off performance criteria and elements. The ALBSU project is moving to this view but has not fully embraced it.

It is also interesting that the purposes of the two projects are also somewhat different. The ALBSU project is meant to provide a basis for accreditation for a range of professional people at entry level including teachers, volunteers and industry trainers:

> We strongly felt that basic skills accreditation for staff should . . . be relevant to a wide range of professional groups including Further Education teachers, trainers working in Training and Enterprise Council funded programmes, and industrial trainers.
>
> (ALBSU) 1992, p. 3)

There appears to be a strong move to accredit a whole range of teachers with ABE/Basic Skills competence. This will lead to increased demands for recognition of prior learning and has implications for the profession. Does it mean that an industry trainer, or welding teacher may need only a short, retraining course in ABE to become a competent ABE teacher? It is certainly good for the profession if it attracts a range of people from different professional areas, but we need to tread warily along this path. In Australia, we are feeling these pressures too.

The ALBSU standards have been used to create a new qualification, the ALBSU/City and Guilds, Certificate in Teaching Basic Skills. There is no indication of the length of the course, but it is stated that it includes general teaching skills along with 'evidence of competence in the specialist basic skills subject area'. This link between the competencies and professional qualifications is essential. It is only if the competencies are used as a quick entry into the profession – a concentration on the generic teaching skills perhaps rather than the ABE element – that major problems will arise.

The Australian ABE project is about 'the good practitioner with a number of years experience'. Further, the project's principal aim 'is to map good practice and use this as a benchmark which will guide continuing professional development and, to a lesser extent, initial teacher education course' (Scheeres et al. 1993, p. 1). A further project should look at the entry level competencies and work closely with higher education institutions which have developed courses leading to professional qualifications in the ABE area.

The ALBSU attempt to develop standards relevant and applicable to a range of contexts rests on the assumption that there are no generic skills. Most of the evidence from, for example, the expert/novice literature suggests that this is not so. There is not the opportunity to discuss the generic/specific skills argument in this review, but it is important to note that the ALBSU document has 'tried to identify what is specific to different areas of teaching and what is generic (ALBSU 1992 p. 3). Consequently, the standards themselves are applicable to all contexts and there are separate sections outlining knowledge and understanding generally; for literacy 'candidates', for numeracy 'candidates' and for ESOL 'candidates'.

This is a worthwhile aim in that it recognizes in that there are things about language, literacy and numeracy which are similar. However, it suffers from the problem that the contexts are often very different and it misses the complexity and richness that the context provides. Identifying needs, designing learning programme and providing learning opportunities are three of the five key areas or 'phrases' in the ALBSU document. Even though there will be overlap, the literacy class, the ESOL classroom and so on have different histories and are different contexts and so standards as developed in the ALBSU document do not easily apply to all.

CONCLUSION

Competency standards of the right kind have many possible applications for professions. Many of these relate to professional development, curriculum development, teaching and assessment. Competency-based approaches to assessment have been attacked by some as being invalid, unreliable and capable of dealing only with the superficial and trivial. In fact, if a holistic conception of competence underpins the assessment strategies, they are likely to be more valid than current methods of assessing professionals, and equally reliable. It is possible to design strategies without much difficulty that can assess how professionals can actually perform in a variety of typical situations. However, it will not be enough to merely observe performance in the complex world of professional work. Thus competency-based assessment strategies for the professions should always use a variety of methods including, where necessary, the indirect assessment of knowledge. What is needed is breadth of evidence from which assessors can make a sound inference that professionals will perform competently in the variety of situations in which they find themselves. This judgmental model may require more time and money than more traditional indirect methods of assessment, but the cost of ignoring these methods is likely to be even greater.

REFERENCES

ALBSU (1992) *ALBSU Standards for Basic Skills Teachers*; London: The Adult Literacy and Basic Skills Unit.

Ashworth, P. D. and Saxton J. (1990) 'On competence', *Journal of Further and Higher Education*, xiv, 3–25.

Australian Nursing Council Inc. (1993) *National Competencies for the Registered and Enrolled Nurse in Recommended Domains*. Canberra: ANCI.

Boyatzis, R. (1982) *The Competent Manager*, New York: Wiley.

Cambridge Training and Development Ltd (CTD Ltd) (1992) *The ALBSU Standards for Basic Skills Teachers*, London: ALBSU.

Cameron, S. (1994) *Entry into the Professions and the Accreditation of University Courses*, IIR Conference on Professional Education and Development, Sydney.

Chi, M. T. H., Feltovitch, P. and Glaser R. (1981) 'Categorisation and representation of physics problems by experts and novices', *Cognitive Sciences*, 5, 121–51.

Collins, M. (1991) *Adult Education as Vocation*, London: Routledge.

Ennis, R. H. (1989) 'Critical thinking and subject specificity: clarification and needed research', *Educational Researcher*, 18, 3.

Field, J. (1991) 'Competency and the pedagogy of labour', *Studies in the Education of Adults*, vol. 23, (no. 1): 41–52.

Gonczi, A., Hager, P. and Oliver, L. (1990) *Establishing Competency Standards in the Professions*, NOOSR Research Paper No 1, Canberra: Australian Government Publishing Service.

Gonczi, A., Hager, P. and Athanasou J. (1993) *A Guide to the Development of Competency-Based Assessment Strategies for the Professions*, Research Paper No. 8, Canberra: AGPS.

Green, N. E., Herndon, J. H. and Farmer J. A. (1990) A Clinical Curriculum for Orthopaedic Surgery Residency Programs (mimeo available from the authors).

Greeno, J. (1989) 'A perspective on thinking', *American Psychologist*, 44, 2.

Hager, P. and Gonczi, A. (1991) 'Competency based standards: a boon for continuing education?', *Studies in Continuing Education*, 13, 1.

Hager, P., Gonczi, A. and Athanasou, J. (1994) 'General issues about the assessment of competence', *Assessment and Evaluation in Higher Education*, 19, 1.

Heywood, L., Gonczi, A. and Hager, P. (1992). *A Guide to Development of Competency Standards for Professions*, NOOSR, Research Paper No. 7, Canberra: Australian Government Publishing Service.

Hodgkinson, P. (1992) 'Alternative models of competence in vocational education and training', *Journal of Further and Higher Education*, 16, 2.

Houston W. R. (Ed.) (1974) *Exploring Competency Based Education*, Berkeley: McCutchan.

Louden W. (1993) 'Portraying competent teaching: can competency based standards help?', *Unicorn*, 19, 3.

McBer and Company (1978) *Understanding of Competence*, Boston: McBer.

McGaw, B. (1993) *Competency Based Assessment: Measurement Issues*, National Assessment Research Forum, Sydney: NSW TAFE Commission.

Magnusson, K. and Osborne, J. (1990) 'The rise of competency based education: a deconstructionist analysis', *Journal of Educational Thought*, 24, 1.

NOOSR (1994) *The Implications of the Implementation of National Competency Standards in the Professions*. Draft Report, National Office of Overseas Skills Recognition, Canberra, September.

Norris, S. P. (1985) 'Synthesis of research on critical thinking', *Educational Leadership*, 42, 8.

Preston, B. and Walker, J. (1993) 'Competency standards in the professions and higher education: a holistic approach', in C. Collins (ed.), *Competencies: The Competencies Debate in Australian Education and Training*, Canberra: Australian College of Education.

Scheeres, H., Gonczi, A., Hager, P. and Morley-Warner, T. (1993) *The Adult Basic Education Profession and Competence: Promoting Best Practice. Final Report*. Sydney: UTS. Commissioned by the International Literacy Year Secretariat, Dept. of Employment, Education and Training, Canberra.

Chapter 15

Personal skills and transfer
Meanings, agendas and possibilities

Roger Harrison

INTRODUCTION

The idea that personal skills should be developed as an explicit curriculum aim across education and training programmes has received considerable attention over the last fifteen years. Central to the discussion is the notion that there are a set of generic skills which are fundamental to effective performance across a range of settings, and which are to some degree transferable between them. The attractions of the idea are considerable, and appeal to a range of 'stakeholders' in the provision of education and training. To educational policy makers and planners they offer an integrative feature in a post-sixteen curriculum which is becoming increasingly diverse, modular and specialized; to adult learners they offer the opportunity to acquire and gain credit for skills which are useful in, and transferable between, a range of learning programmes, work settings and life situations; to employers they offer training in those skills which are seen as necessary to the flexible and autonomous workforce of the modern economy. Personal skills can be seen as offering a common strand linking the learning experience of individuals as they progress through school, further and higher education; as they pursue different specializations and study different subject areas; as they move between education and training, and between education and the world of work.

This chapter will examine the idea of personal skills and transfer; looking at the variety of definitions available, the issues of categorization, attribution of standards of attainment, and transfer. It will position current debates about personal skills and transfer in the context of contested views on the function of education as a preparation for life and work. It will suggest that it is in the idea of transfer, and the skills required to achieve transfer, that a bridge can be made between those stakeholders who seek to promote skills relevant to work, and those who seek to promote skills relevant to learning.

PERSONAL SKILLS – THE TERMINOLOGY

One of the most confusing aspects of the debate around personal skills is the variety of terminology, often used in a way which implies interchange-ability, between terms such as core skills, common skills, personal transferable skills, common learning outcomes, cross curricula skills and meta-skills. The jostling for pre-eminence, or at least recognition, amongst these terms perhaps indicates how contested the territory is, and how important it is perceived to be.

'Core skills' are those skills which have been developed by the National Council for Vocational Qualification (NCVQ), and by the Scottish Vocational Education Council (SCOTVEC). The NCVQ list covers six skills.

- Communication.
- Application of number.
- Information technology.
- Personal skills: improving own learning.
- Personal skills: working with others.
- Problem-solving.

They have been expressed in the form of units of competence at five levels of attainment, in line with other National Vocational Qualifications (NVQs), and they form an integral part of the General National Vocational Qualifications (GNVQs). NCVQ plans to complete its work on refining the standards for each of these units during 1995, after which they will be available for unit accreditation in the same way as any other NVQ. The work of SCOTVEC on core skills, in fact, pre-dates develop-ments south of the border. They have developed their own list of five core skills, at four levels of attainment, which are similar in content to those of the NCVQ, but differ in the way they define 'levels' or 'stages' of development. During 1995, both organizations will be completing their work on refining their respective frameworks, after which it will be possible to map across, identifying points of overlap and difference. How far this will deliver the policy goal of 'harmonization' between the two sets of standards remains to be seen.

'Common skills' refers to the classification used by the awarding body BTEC, which offers broadly based, vocationally oriented courses with opportunities for progression to higher education. Since 1986, BTEC have used the framework of Common Skills as a means of integrating curriculum design across all their courses, providing an antidote to the growing diversity of subject areas being covered. There is a good deal of flexibility in the selection and assessment of skills taken from the framework by the individual centres (e.g. a further education college) delivering particular programmes and courses. Whilst the major skills areas must be covered within each programme of study, they are expected to be 'filled out' into detailed statements appropriate to the vocational context and the level of the course.

'Personal transferable skills' and 'generic skills' are used to refer to the general skills and capabilities which can be applied across a range of social and work contexts. They are skills which are being promoted by government departments and some employer organizations as a necessary component of the higher education curriculum, and are increasingly required by professional bodies. The former Employment Department has stated:

> Transferable personal skills are the generic capabilities which allow people to succeed in a wide range of different tasks and jobs. They include effective communication, negotiation skills, problem solving ability, and ability to work in teams. They are characterized by a resourceful approach to tasks and are a product of applying experience and education.
>
> (Employment Department, 1991 p. 4)

These are sometimes referred to as 'social skills' and contrasted with 'cognitive' and 'intellectual' skills. However, these distinctions become increasingly difficult to sustain as we move into professional areas of practice where activities such as 'negotiation' or 'problem-solving' require the use of both social and cognitive skills of a high order (Eraut, 1985).

'Common learning outcomes' are the eight categories of skill proposed by the Confederation of British Industry (CBI), the representative body for predominantly large employers in the UK, in their 1989 report, *Towards a Skills Revolution*. As well as numeracy, problem-solving and personal skills they included more value-laden characteristics such as 'positive attitudes to change', and 'values and integrity'. The CBI (1989) proposed that these common learning outcomes should be 'applied to all stages of education and training of 14–19 year olds' as a means of 'updating' and 'expanding' skill levels.

'Cross-curricula skills' are those which are seen as applicable across a variety of cognitive domains, for instance science, maths, history, or sociology. They are sometimes described in terms of ability to interpret a diagram, use a computer or an indexing system. The National Curriculum Council (NCC) produced a list of six broad categories of cross-curricula skills: communication, numeracy, study, problem-solving, personal and social, information technology (NCC, 1990). The resemblance between these and the core skills which were subsequently elaborated by the NCVQ is striking. However, in the context of higher education there already existed a rather different notion of general cognitive or intellectual skills, which could be developed through the vehicle of disciplinary studies, but were described as 'not so much interdisciplinary but a-disciplinary' (Squires *et al.*, 1975, quoted in Bridges 1993 p. 45). These are the skills that the National Advisory Board and the University Grants Committee (NAB/UGC) had in mind when they issued a joint statement identifying a key purpose of higher education as providing students with 'transferable intellectual and personal skills', including:

> the ability to analyse complex issues, to identify the core of a problem and the means of solving it, to synthesize and interpret disparate elements, to clarify values, to make effective use of numerical and other information, to work cooperatively and constructively with others, and, above all, to communicate clearly both orally and in writing.
>
> (NAB/UGC, 1984 p. 1)

Whilst some of the skills named in this list, such as communication and problem-solving, overlap with those drawn up with vocational purposes in mind, the NAB/UGC statement also refers to the traditional liberal aims of higher education to develop the person as an individual, operating within a moral and social framework.

'Metacognition' has been associated with learning to learn and described in terms of the awareness and control of our own thinking processes (Nisbet and Shucksmith, 1984). 'Meta-competence' has been described in terms of 'competences which work on other competences . . .' (Fleming, 1991 p. 10), which allow individuals to adopt a critical, adaptable perspective on their own competence, and to make appropriate decisions on when and how to apply them. Eraut has used the term 'meta-process' to describe:

> . . . the evaluation of what one is doing and thinking, the continuing re-definition of priorities, and the critical adjustment of cognitive frameworks and assumptions.
>
> (Eraut, 1992 p. 112)

These skills can be seen as generic to any learning activity, since they have to do with the management of one's own learning and thinking. As such they offer a possible connection between the aspirations of higher education, represented in the NAB/UGC statement, and those of government and employer organizations, represented in the former Employment Department statement on Enterprise in Higher Education.

PROBLEMS OF CATEGORIZATION

This brief review of the predominant terminology does not provide the answer to the question posed by Oates:

In looking back on the 1980s and 1990s, the educational sociologists of 2020 may be amused at the plethora of developments around core skills, transferable skills, generic skills and common skills. We need to ask the same questions that they might ask: why the different terms for ostensibly the same thing?

(Oates, 1992a p. 227)

Oates answers the question by highlighting the technical and methodological problems associated with the various frameworks. He points to problems with overlapping categories, for instance 'critical skills' and 'creative skills', and to mixtures of skills with items which have more to do with attitudes and values and do not lend themselves to consistent, equitable assessment. For instance, employers might agree that 'positive attitude towards change', or 'motivation to succeed' are valuable personal qualities, but differ widely in defining the behaviour which would signify their existence. There are questions about which skills are fundamental to the widest range of tasks and contexts: for instance, communication and personal skills are clearly more generic than information technology, or modern languages. There are questions about whether generalized models of some skills are realistic, since they can be understood in quite different ways by different practitioners. For instance, a shop assistant and a psychotherapist might both be using problem-solving skills, but a detailed analysis of their behaviour might make it difficult to identify common components or a common process.

Oates argues for a development programme which will not only establish discrete and assessable categories of skills, but also clarify what we mean by 'skill transfer' (Oates, 1992a). The most comprehensive attempt to achieve the first of these goals has been through the work of the NCVQ. Begun in 1989 at the instigation of the then Secretary of State for Education, Kenneth Baker, it has continued to attract ministerial level support, and has resulted in the most rigorously researched and field-tested framework for the assessment of core skills. The skills specifications are expressed in the same way as for other NVQs, in that they have 'elements' describing the activity to be assessed, 'performance criteria' providing a means of judging successful performance, and 'range statements' describing the range of settings in which the activity should be successfully performed. Performance is defined at five levels by varying those aspects of 'communication' or 'problem-solving' which are seen to make the successful application of that skill more demanding.

Whilst the work of categorizing and ascribing levels to skills which can be taken as fundamental to a range of tasks is important, it is the second goal, that of clarifying the notion of 'skill transfer', which perhaps has the most far reaching implications for those involved in education and training. It raises questions about the relationship between learning as it occurs in the classroom, lecture theatre and laboratory, and learning as it is applied in the contexts of workplace and community; about the relationship between theory and practice, and about the processes which occur when existing skills, knowledge and understandings are adapted and manipulated to meet the demands of different situations. In other words, they are to do with our understandings of the nature and processes of 'learning'.

THE ISSUE OF TRANSFER

The expectation of transfer is central to the whole enterprise of education, since no programme of learning could ever hope to cover the knowledge and skill requirements for every future situation. Students are expected to be able to generalize from particular areas of study, and to adapt what they have learned to new situations. Jessup uses the examples of history graduates to make this point:

> Historians are valued as potential employees for a variety of reasons including the breadth of vision and perspective brought about by studying in depth our civilisation and culture, and the 'set' of enabling skills developed within the rigours of discipline, including the ability to analyse problems, sift information, weigh evidence, evaluate solutions and to communicate effectively. In essence it is believed the possession of these skills, developed to a high order, by, for example, historians, can be applied to activities other than history. This is why employers are likely to value applicants with 'A' level or degrees in history.
>
> (Jessup, 1990 p. ii)

However, studies of skill transfer have pointed up the dangers of assuming that skills learned in one setting can simply be transplanted and applied with equal success in another. The research indicates that skills such as problem-solving cannot operate in a vacuum; they are used in relation to a particular problem, and in a particular setting, and these contextual factors alter the nature of the skill required (Wolf, 1991; Blagg, 1992)). Oates has criticized the use of the term 'transferable skills', on the grounds that:

> It reproduces a very 'common sense' view of transfer, strengthened by the term itself. But this is a very static notion of skills: you learn them and then 'redeploy' them in new settings.
>
> (Oates, 1992a p. 231)

He argues that the benefits available from describing, teaching and assessing a set of core skills are not dependent on a simple form of transfer, and draws on the work of Annett and Piaget to suggest that transfer can best be understood as the adaptive modification of skills and strategies in new settings. Since even in very routine activities subtle but important differences exist between situations, modification, and therefore transfer, is occurring. This notion of transfer as an interaction between existing skills and constructs and a new task brings it very close to our understanding of 'learning' as 'lasting change in knowledge, skills and attitudes which is the result of experience rather than maturation' (Gordon P. and Lawton D., quoted in Oates 1992a p. 233). The extent to which adaptation occurs then becomes an important means of discriminating between transfer, or learning, which requires the use of simple or sophisticated cognitive processes. Perkins and Soloman (1988) have used the term 'low road' transfer to describe what occurs when there is sufficient commonality between two situations for previously learned knowledge and skills to be unthinkingly and automatically brought into play. 'High road' transfer depends on the conscious intervention of cognitive processes, such as generalizing, drawing analogies, monitoring and reflecting on performance, which enable individuals to abstract characteristics from one context and apply them appropriately in another. 'Skills of transfer' refers to a higher order of cognitive processing, involving the selection and control of skills and knowledge appropriate to the context.

Whilst the definition of a set of 'core skills', and their integration into teaching and assessment can make a useful contribution to broadening the curriculum, what is being suggested through the notion of transfer, and particularly high road transfer, is something rather more elusive. It is what Fleming has described as meta-competence; the ability to locate a particular competence within a larger framework of understanding, and to adopt '. . . a critical, adaptable perspective on, and ability to manipulate, one's own competences' (Fleming, 1991 p. 11). Using the notion of 'skills of transfer', rather than 'transferable skills' allows us to move beyond the debates about description, categorization and level definition for a particular set of skills, and focus our attention on the personal and intellectual capabilities which allow individuals to handle new and challenging situations, and to deal intelligently with change.

THE CONTEXT OF CHANGE

This summary touches on only some of the debates surrounding issues of categorization, level definition and transfer, but it is already pointing towards more fundamental questions about the principles and the purposes of education. The 'personal skills agenda' goes beyond discussions of the technical validity of one skills categorization in relation to another; it offers a challenge to established patterns of constructing teaching and learning. It forms part of a larger agenda which is seeking to shift the balance of a predominantly knowledge-based curriculum towards one which is more skills-based. The level of enthusiasm among particular stakeholders for particular models of personal skills can be a fairly reliable indicator of their position in relation to these wider debates, and provides another explanation for the diversity of terminology in use. To gain some insight into the positions being adopted, and the language being used by those who seek to influence these debates, it is necessary to look beyond research into the psychology of learning, and examine more closely the conflicting interpretations of educational purposes.

The momentum behind efforts to establish personal skills development as a key purpose of education is being driven largely by forces outside education. The pressure for curriculum change in the context of higher education has been represented by Barnett (1992) by use of the diagram in Figure 15.1. He identifies 'internal (educational)' interests as being with the development of 'discipline specific capabilities' and 'general intellectual capabilities', and 'external (vocational)' interests with the development of 'profession specific competences' and 'transferable personal skills'. The arrows indicate the direction of change in the curriculum as the dominant influence of the academic community, located in box (a), is propelled by largely external forces in the direction of boxes (c) and (d).

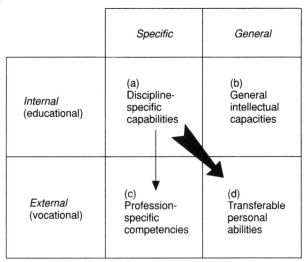

Figure 15.1 Changing structure of curriculum objectives: a schema
(*Source*: Barnett 1992, p. 2)

The voice of these external forces can be found in a range of policy documents. For instance:

Narrow discipline-based knowledge learned in the classroom, the lecture theatre or the laboratory can nowadays become out of date in a relatively short space of time. Learning how to learn rather than absorbing facts and learning how to apply a body of knowledge are increasingly being regarded as equally important as the knowledge itself . . . Education is responding to the changes in the work environment and to the needs of business and industry by looking to, and in many cases encouraging, the teaching of flexible, transferable skills, 'active' learning and more widespread use of educational technology and practical project work.   (Training Agency, 1989 p. 3)

One feature of current skill shortages is the widespread lack of generic skills such as quality assurance skills, problem solving skills, learning efficiency, flexibility and communication skills.
('Memorandum on Higher Education in the European Community'
          Commission to the European Communities, 1991 p. 4)

Graduates will require core transferable skills to enter and function effectively in the modern business. All higher education learning should develop individuals' core skills.

(CBI, 1994 p. 6)

The demand being made on educators and educational institutions is that they should pay closer attention to the perceived needs of the economy and the expressed needs of employers. These needs are articulated in terms of the ability to manage change, to routinely adapt skills and work practices in line with technological change and market demand. Core, generic or transferable skills are seen as an essential component in a curriculum which is in harmony with the requirements of the economy. Whilst education has never occupied a position entirely divorced from the society it serves, what is new about more recent developments is the extent to which the curriculum is being driven by the state. The language of personal transferable skills 'can be read as a metaphor, a search for a new curriculum code' (Barnett, 1992 p. 6). That new code is being propelled, at least in part, by forces external to the educational community, and is perceived by some as a threat to established values and practices which are rooted in the tradition of a liberal education. Higher education 'has become part of the knowledge apparatus of the modern society and is willy nilly answerable to and influenced by that wider field' (Barnett, 1992 p. 6).

The intervention of these external forces can be seen in a number of recent developments in education and training. The work of SCOTVEC and the NCVQ in developing national frameworks for vocational qualifications, which now exist at levels equivalent to graduate and postgraduate study, and are based on the notion of competence: the former

Employment Department's 'Enterprise in Higher Education' (EHE) initiative with its aims of institutional and curriculum reform, and the creation of stronger links between higher education, employers and the world of work: and the RSA's Education for Capability movement with its emphasis on learner responsibility and accountability as the basis for enabling students to deal more effectively with challenges presented by changes in society. What these initiatives have in common is the aim of developing personal effectiveness beyond the educational arena; of enabling individuals to act effectively on their environment, particularly in the world of work. As George Brown has expressed this in relation to the aims of EHE, the primary concern is with:

> Helping students to become more effective lifelong learners so that they are equipped for their future working lives.
>
> (Brown, 1992 p. 1)

The debate surrounding these interventions and initiatives can be polarized (and over-simplified) into two conflicting interpretations. For some, they are the timely interventions of legitimate stakeholders who are in close touch with the changing world of international markets and the global economy, who see clearly the imperatives of economic survival and are urging necessary changes on the more insulated and protected world of education and training, whose concerns are with a more static conception of the transmission of culture and skills. For others, they are the response of a capitalist-state facing a 'legitimation crisis' (Habermas, 1976) and forced into a deeper and more active involvement in the workings of the education system in order to maintain power and control.

Writing about the situation in the United States, Hart has argued that education is being used as a way of ensuring a ready supply of cheap, flexible and adaptable labour, intellectually and psychologically prepared for the insecurities of the modern work environment. She links this directly with the emphasis given to work on general skills:

> In other words, generic skills training is proposed as a means to adjust labour 'to long term uncertainty in the job market'
>
> (Hart, 1992 p. 86, quoting Shor)

Edwards (1993) has linked the demands on education to train a 'flexible' and 'multi-skilled' workforce with the requirements of a post-Fordist economy, and the interests of late twentieth century capitalism in achieving flexible specialization in order to maintain a competitive position in world markets.

Both Edwards and Hart have identified in the rhetoric of generic skills an attempt to establish a new discourse, designed to gain acceptance for a different sort of work ethic. For instance:

The rhetoric of constant change, flexibility and mobility today has replaced an older one of responsibility and commitment, and a corresponding indictment of irresponsibility and lack of commitment levelled against those who changed jobs frequently on their own account. Furthermore the call for flexibility is reserved exclusively for the workers themselves, a perfect illustration of the 'view from above'.

(Hart, 1992 p. 86)

The opportunity to develop 'multi-option flexilives' (Handy, 1984) is represented in this discourse as positive and empowering; a desirable form of existence for a more mobile and autonomous workforce. But this is contested, by those who perceive the possibilities for social and psychological dislocation, as individuals' sense of themselves, gained through association with work and community, disintegrates.

According to this analysis the current high profile given to personal skills in education and training is being driven by the concern of government and employers with what they see as necessary changes to patterns of employment. The main issue for them is the ability of workers to successfully manage change and live with uncertainty, which requires both intellectual skills and personal qualities. Education and training can contribute towards this development through adapting the curriculum so that generic, core, or transferable skills are emphasised as key outcomes. Through their involvement with educational processes individuals would then be 'learning to work'.

PERSONAL SKILLS AND LEARNING

How has the world of education responded to the new vocationalism implicit in this analysis of the personal skills agenda? Especially in higher education, with its tradition of independence and autonomy from outside interference, one might have expected universal resistance. The fact that this has not been the case can be understood, at least in part, by a convergence of interest around curriculum innovation aimed at developing independent and autonomous learners. Initiatives such as Enterprise in Higher Education, Education for Capability, and the developmental work on NCVQ Core Skills in further education, have been used by educational practitioners to promote the teaching of thinking and learning skills, both in the classroom and in the outside world. The primary aim has been the development of 'more effective lifelong learners' (Brown, 1992). The potential of the Core Skills Units in the development of learning skills was evident from an early stage in the NCVQ's development work. Reporting on the piloting of the draft Units with further education curriculum teams in Caring, Engineering, Business Administration and Hairdressing they noted that:

the teams felt that the Core Skills Units – particularly in 'Personal skills' – are beneficial in encouraging a much higher level of learner-centred approaches, and strongly enhance learner autonomy.

(Oates, 1992 b. p. 60)

In introducing NCVQ's report on this pilot work, Jessup was quite clear about its wider significance:

The real impact of the Core Skills Units will be in enhancing the learning experience of individuals. It is believed the units offer the potential to do this in both education and training programmes.

(Oates, 1992 ii p. 9)

In the field of higher education, both the EHE and the RSA initiatives sought to influence curriculum development in ways which paid more attention to the processes of adult learning:

These programmes have been among the first attempts at a national level to stimulate reforms in the curriculum and pedagogy of higher education. Each has sought to draw attention to teaching and learning processes and practices that are conducive to the development of broad-based transferable skills and qualities, and the capacity to know how to continue learning throughout life.

(Weil, 1993 p. 86)

For many practitioners, raising the profile of personal learning as a valued aspect of the higher education curriculum represented both a welcome reform, and a revisiting of established principles:

What it (EHE) has sought to do is to magnify and strengthen longstanding aspects within the academic tradition. It has, I would contend, given greater force and prestige to two themes: the importance of the experience of learning and self-development that students undergo; and, relatedly, the vision of higher education as a process of liberation and empowerment for those who experience it.

(Wright, 1992 p. 218)

Whilst it would be quite wrong to attribute the origin of interest in these themes to externally driven programmes, they have undoubtedly been a catalyst behind many recent developments which have sought to give a more learner-centred focus to teaching and assessment practices. Some have involved the use of portfolios, learning logs, profiles or records of achievement to raise student awareness of their own learning processes, enabling them to reflect critically on their own performance, and plan purposefully for future development (for instance, Fenwick *et al.*, 1992; Harrison, 1993; Bull and Otter, 1994). In so doing they build on a well established body of research on student learning which suggests that students' approaches to study crucially affects the quality of their learning outcomes, and that if 'deep' rather than 'surface' processing is to be achieved, attention must be given to both personal and academic understanding (Gibbs, 1992; Ramsden, 1992). Engaging learners in critiquing their own progress and development opens the way to a more active involvement in, and greater responsibility for, both the programme of learning and the assessment of outcomes. Innovations in self, peer, and collaborative assessment have been used to promote a more learner-centred and inclusive approach, where students are drawn into the whole business of assessment as an explicit part of their formative development (Fazey, 1993; Somervell, 1993). The participation of learners, not simply as passive recipients of other people's knowledge, but as active partners in learning, requires personal skills of a high order: it requires clarity of personal motivation, the ability to plan and manage one's own learning, and to reflect critically on one's own performance as a learner. These would appear to be the sort of personal skills, capabilities or qualities which are critical to successful participation in a 'learning society'. They are skills which enable individuals to make sense of, and give coherence to, an ever widening range of education and training programmes, occurring throughout the lifespan, with entry routes through credit transfer (CATS), assessment of prior learning (APL) and Access courses, by use of modular programmes with a variety of routes through and qualifications at the end, and incorporating work-based learning, professional practice and independent project work as integral and assessed components.

CONCLUSION

Issues surrounding personal skills – what they are, where they fit in the curriculum, how to develop and measure them – are central to many of the current debates, not just in higher education, but in education and training in general. In some respects they embody the 'traditional dichotomies in educational debate', Weil, 1992 p. 88), between education and training, liberalism and vocationalism, subject-centredness and student-centredness, intellectual and social development, theory and practice. What is intriguing, however, is the way in which some educational practitioners have been able to bridge and to blur these traditional divisions; exploiting the connection between the concern of the vocationally inspired competence movement with the 'skills of transfer', and the concerns of education with developing the skills of 'learning to learn'. Both involve a process for dealing intelligently with change, which is an expressed aim of education and a stated requirement of government and employers. Whilst the current discourse may be directed towards learning for the purpose of being a more effective, employable worker, there are signs that educational initiatives aiming to develop those personal skills which support reflective, autonomous learning, are capable of transcending these instrumental and utilitarian agendas.

REFERENCES

Barnett, R. (1992) 'What effects? What outcomes?', in R. Barnett (ed.) *Learning to Effect*, Buckingham: SRHE/Open University Press.

Blagg, N. (1992) *Development of Transferable Skills in Learners*, London, Employment Department.

Bridges, D. (1993) 'Transferable skills: a philosophical perspective', *Studies in Higher Education*, vol. 18, no. 1.

Brown, G. (1992) 'Enterprise learning: an introduction', *Competence and Assessment*, 17.

Bull, J and Otter, S. (1994) '*Recording Achievement: Potential for Higher Education*', Sheffield: CVCP.

CBI (1989) *Towards a Skills Revolution*, London: CBI.

CBI (1994) *Thinking Ahead: Ensuring the Expansion of Higher Education Into the 21st Century*, London: CBI.

Commission to the European Communities (1991) Memorandum on Higher Education in the European Community, Brussels: EC.

Edwards, R. (1993) 'Multi-skilling the flexible workforce in post-compulsory education and training', *Journal of Further and Higher Education*, 17, (1).

Employment Department (1991) *Enterprise in Higher Education: key features of enterprise in Higher Education. 1990–1*, London: Employment Department.

Eraut, M. (1985) 'Knowledge creation and knowledge use in professional contexts', *Studies in Higher Education*, 10, 2.

Eraut, M. (1992) 'Developing the knowledge base: a process perspective on professional education', in R. Barnett (ed.) *Learning to Effect*, Buckingham: SRHE/OU Press.

Fazey, D. (1993) 'Self assessment as a generic skill for enterprising students: the learning process', *Assessment and Evaluation in Higher Education*, vol. 18; no. 3.

Fenwick, A., Assiter, A. and Nixon, N. (1992) *Profiling in HE*, London: CNAA.

Fleming, D. (1991) 'The concept of meta-competence', *Competence and Assessment*, 16.

Gibbs, G. (1992) *Improving the Quality of Student Learning*, Bristol: Technical and Educational Services.

Habermas, J. (1976) *Legitimation Crisis*, London: Heinemann.

Handy, C. (1984) *The Future of Work: A Guide to A Changing Society*, London: Blackwell.

Harrison, R. (1993) 'Using portfolios for personal and career development', in A. Assiter and E. Shaw (eds) *Using Records of Achievement in Higher Education*, London: Kogan Page.

Hart, M. (1992) *Working and Educating for Life: Feminist and International Perspectives on Adult Education*, London: Routledge.

Jessup, G. (1990) *Common Learning Outcomes: Core Skills in A/AS Levels and NVQs*, London: NCVQ.

National Advisory Board and the University Grants Committee joint statement (1984): 'Higher Education: the needs of society' in *A Strategy for Higher Education into the 1990's: The University Grants Committee's Advice*, London: HMSO.

National Curriculum Council (1990) *Core Skills 16–19: A Response to the Secretary of State*, York: NCC.

Nisbet, J. and Shucksmith, J. (1984) 'The seventh sense', *Scottish Educational Review*, 16.

Oates, T. (1992a) 'Core skills and transfer: aiming high', *Educational Technology and Training International*, vol. 29, no. 3.

Oates (1992b) 'Developing and piloting the NCVQ core skills units: an outline of method and a summary of findings, *R&D Report No. 16*, London: NCVQ.

Perkins, D. and Soloman (1988) 'Teaching for transfer', *Educational Leadership*, vol. 46, no. 1.

Ramsden, P. (1992) *Learning to Teach in Higher Education*, London: Routledge.

Somervell, H. (1993) 'Issues in assessment, enterprise and Higher Education: the case for self, peer and collaborative assessment', *Assessment and Evaluation in Higher Education*, vol. 18, no. 3.

Training Agency. (1989) *Enterprise in Higher Education*, Sheffield: Training Agency.

Weil, S. (1992) 'Creating capability for change in Higher Education: the RSA initiative', in R. Barnett (ed.) *Learning to Effect*, Buckingham: SRHE/OU Press.

Wolf, A. (1991) 'Assessing core skills: wisdom or wild goose chase?', *Cambridge Journal of Education*, vol. 21, no. 2.

Wright, P. (1992) 'Learning through enterprise: the enterprise in Higher Education initiative', in R. Barnett (ed.) *Learning to Effect*, Buckingham: SRHE/OU Press.

Chapter 16

Policy continuity and progress in the reform of post-compulsory and higher education†

David Robertson

INTRODUCTION

Various developments in public policy throughout the late 1980s and the 1990s have opened up possibilities for a more far-reaching reform of post-secondary education than might otherwise be anticipated in an adverse economic climate. Prospects for greater flexibility and mobility for students within further, adult and higher education have been significantly improved by an understanding that the expansion of opportunities in higher education must be closely linked to greater participation throughout the post-compulsory sector generally.

In this chapter I want to argue that it is possible to discern a benign continuity of policy towards post-secondary and higher education, more long-standing than current interests in 'market forces', and more enduring, despite the apparent reversion to less welcome policies implied by the budgetary crises of the early 1990s. This long-term focus has been shaped by the need to address sustained national economic decline through, amongst other means, investment in lifelong learning. The British state appears finally to have realized that if genuine learning opportunity and achievement can be improved, there is a chance we may regain an element of international economic competitiveness.

For this to be possible, it is now widely accepted that cultures will have to be changed, structures modified and educational strategies developed to permit greater interaction between the various post-secondary sectors. The development of a national qualifications framework, vitalized by a system of cumulative credit transfer, is increasingly seen as central to this. Better national and personal performance is now held to flow from improving student choice, achievement and progression, enabling students to 'trade' within the diverse learning opportunities of

† This chapter has been rewritten from an earlier article 'Flexibility and mobility in Further and Higher Education', published in the *Journal of Further and Higher Education*, vol. 17(1), 1993.

post-secondary education, eroding divisions between academic and vocational learning, and facilitating greater participation and mobility within and between institutions and other sites of learning. Current national policy objectives and initiatives encourage the view that we are nearing a settlement on the future character of post-secondary and higher education which will bring us into closer proximity with our international competitors, repositioning our universities and colleges accordingly.

POLICY OBJECTIVES: CONSISTENCY OR INCONSISTENCY?

To justify my overall optimism in these matters, it is important to assess the strength of the contrary argument – that there has been no general consistency in policy. Those who maintain this position can marshall good evidence to support their case.

For example, public expenditure surveys and the budget statements since 1992 appear to define recent history in ways which lend little support to the view that the State has been persuaded of the need to increase investment in post-compulsory and higher education. Lines have been drawn for the time being under the expansion of university places to which we had become accustomed since 1987; capital and research allocations in further and higher education have been severely limited; funding for the Training and Enterprise Councils has been frozen at earlier levels; there have been no concessions on student maintenance; and some institutions have faced such significant threats to their revenue income that staff losses cannot be ruled out.

Some publicly acceptable 'mood music' has been added to an otherwise bleak outlook by announcements concerning the need to regenerate the national skills base through the promotion of technician-related diploma courses and engineering degrees, and vague hints have been made about a resumption of expansion in higher education after 1997. Only the 1992 decision to pursue a 25 per cent expansion of participation in post-secondary education amongst 16–19-year-olds, and the 1994 suggestion for an expansion of part-time provision, have given much cause for optimism. Both proposals have been celebrated as overdue recognition for the 'Cinderella services' – further education on the one hand, and part-time higher education on the other – after years during which policy on provision for 16–19-year-olds and part-time (mostly adult) students has been neglected and often poorly focused.

Moreover, the pessimists can argue that very few implementation incentives have been provided to makes these policies successful. Any expansion is likely to be purchased at the cost of a declining unit of resource, tightened student–staff ratios, a potential deterioration in the quality of the student learning experience, and an exploitation of individual financial resources rather than those of the State, leading to greater personal indebtedness. Indeed, they might add, public policy has never really shown a sustained commitment to expansion and reform. Budgetary crises at the start of each of the last three decades (1973–77; 1981–84; and 1992–present) have so easily blown off-course any perceived strategy that one would be hard-pressed to show evidence that a consistent policy existed in the first place.

Yet it is to this challenge that I wish to respond. There can be no disguising the fact that economic recessions compel Governments to constrain public spending requirements often with serious consequences for adult, further and higher education. This led to the stalled expansion of the 1970s and to the budgetary and participation reductions in many institutions during the early 1980s. It has now produced the policy shift in the 1990s from the relatively expensive expansion of higher education, currently locked into the system of mandatory awards and fee payments, to an emphasis on the relatively cheap (and non-statutory) 16–19 sector, and (self-funding) part-time students.

Nonetheless, if we are to understand the true character of the policy objectives in these matters, we need to dig beneath the surface of current policies. There may be a more subtle way of analysing these developments which yields a more benign interpretation of longer-term benefits and opportunities for post-secondary and higher education. Within the fabric of ideological and expedient objectives, and despite the constraints of persistent budgetary distress, it is possible to discern some threads of consistent policy.

POLICY DEVELOPMENT AND THE WHITE PAPERS

We need to place the apparent change in post-secondary and higher education policy in the wider context of policy developments over the past few years. First, the impact of the Higher Education White Paper (DES, 1987) is now well-known; participation is higher education has more than doubled from 11 per cent of the 18-year-old age group in 1987 to 28 per cent by 1992. This places well above target the growth strategy for higher education – 33 per cent of the 18-year-old age group in participation by the year 2000 – and it has allowed the Government to mix principle with expediency in calling for a period of consolidation, something that may be welcomed by many academics who have laboured under the effects of sustained but under-resourced expansion.

Second, the 1991 White Papers (DES, 1991c; 1991d) are understandably best remembered for their macro-policy impact upon the status of the polytechnics and the governance of the post-secondary colleges. The abolition of the higher education binary line, creating over forty 'new' universities, the incorporation of the further education colleges and the establishment of new funding councils (and new funding methodologies) have radically altered the shape and character of post-secondary and higher education. Many of these changes have their origins in the Robbins Report (1963) and in the Leverhulme Reports of the early 1980s (Wagner, 1982; SRHE, 1983), lending credibility to my argument that policy development, whilst proceeding in a halting and absent-minded manner, is nevertheless moving in a consistent direction over time.

In the longer term, as we accommodate the structural changes which featured in the 1992 *Further and Higher Education Act*, it is more likely that our energy and imagination will be absorbed by some of the micro-policy initiatives within the White Papers, a number of which can be identified:

- The encouragement of a more diverse student cohort in further and higher education, signalling continued support for Access courses, 'franchising', alternative entry arrangements, and more flexible definitions of 'ability to benefit'.
- Exhortations to protect and expand part-time learning provision, albeit without much indication of how institutions and individuals might be stimulated to respond.
- Support for flexible programmes, modular and credit-based learning arrangements, open learning provision and improved student guidance and information arrangements.
- The establishment of equal status for academic and vocational qualifications.
- The development of GNVQs as an additional route to NVQs and as a further bridge between post-secondary and higher education.
- The exploration of the Training Credits scheme for 16–19-year-olds, opening up the prospect of a more extensive application of 'vouchers' or some derivative as a means of resourcing a general post-secondary and higher education entitlement.
- The emphasis upon improved student choice, enhanced curriculum flexibility, greater institutional and professional accountability, with the indication that there will be shift from input to output performance assessment.
- The introduction of 'market forces', consumer sensitivity and a 'new managerialism' into the administration of institutions and their learning activities.

POLICY BEYOND THE WHITE PAPERS – THE COMMON THREAD?

When one has stripped away the ideological cladding from political statements and suspended any natural suspicions that all changes are a conspiracy against the perceived benefits of an earlier 'Golden Age', it is possible to identify a major policy thread running through these reform proposals. This can be defined as an attempt to produce in British post-secondary and higher education an accommodation with general international practice in terms of levels of participation, and with best practice in the quality of individual learning achievement. This has not been driven by any particular desire to achieve international harmonization or cross-border cooperation within Europe. Rather, policy developments have been motivated by the need to find strategies for reversing national economic decline. The overarching objective has been the pursuit of greater social equity consistent with high quality and efficiency. In this respect, the introduction of 'market forces' may be seen as merely the most recent organizing device with which to address this long-standing problem.

The volume of opinion that has been brought to bear on the general diagnosis of national underperformance has been enormous. Business strategists have noted our lack of economic competitiveness (Porter, 1990); academics and industrialists have identified a national skills deficit (Finegold and Soskice, 1988; CBI, 1989) and the over-specialized basis of much of our education and training (CIHE, 1990). Academic research has revealed our poor participation rates (Raffe, 1992; Smithers and Robinson, 1989; 1991).

Numerous policy reports have confirmed the need to invest extensively in post-secondary and higher education (Ball, 1990; 1991; Cassells, 1990; CBI, 1994; Royal Society, 1993; World Bank, 1994) whilst others have emphasized the need to modify the curriculum, institutional practice, professional values and inter-sectoral relationships (Finegold, 1992a; IPPR, 1990; 1992; Robertson, 1992; 1993; Royal Society, 1991). Two major national enquiries – the National Commission on Education (1993) and the Social Justice Commission (1994) – have underlined the need to invest massively in individual lifelong learning.

The range of agreement across the ideological spectrum has been impressive, unanimously suggesting not only that participation rates in British further and higher education must be brought in line with participation rates throughout the rest of the industrial world, but also emphasizing the need to develop greater personal flexibility and mobility for students in the context of a radically reformed post-secondary and higher education. Accordingly Britain has finally begun to cast off the legacy of an education system defined by the needs of an imperial past. It is the last major industrial nation to undertake the process of the 'massification' and democratization of post-secondary and higher education, although we should be aware that the transition to a culture of lifelong learning may not be trouble-free.

CREATING SOLUTIONS FROM DILEMMAS

As part of the strategy of transformation to a culture which encourages greater participation in learning opportunities, those working within institutions of further and higher education are likely to be faced with a significant dilemma: do they seek to predicate the right of increased access to further and higher education upon the availability of adequate resources, thereby running the risk of denying opportunity and learning achievement to many students? Or do they accommodate the likely surge of demand which is released by the increased availability of places, hoping to gain increased public support (and thereafter improved public resources), but running the risk that the unit of resource will be driven down together with the quality of the learning experience? The management of this trade-off has proved very difficult in higher education and it is likely to create some apprehension in further education as well.

There are at least two ways of approaching this problem. It will not have escaped the attention of Government that increased participation in post-secondary and higher education elsewhere in the world is generally achieved with lower unit costs, higher student–staff ratios, greater student mobility and a well-established expectation of a greater personal financial contribution from students than would traditionally be expected in Britain. It is important to note in this respect that during 1988 and 1989 officials from the then DES spent a considerable period exploring aspects of the post-secondary and higher education systems in the United States, producing a number of influential reports (DES, 1989, 1990, 1991a, 1991b). One may infer from this that the prevailing policy direction points clearly towards a system of post-secondary and higher education reflecting significant aspects of the American experience in the best features of British practice.

For many in British further and higher education, this 'solution' to the management of mass participation might be difficult to accept. We are frequently exercised by the adverse aspects of American education: poor secondary school standards under-compensated by mass entry to community colleges; questionable quality thresholds within the community colleges; assumed lack of coherence and over-fragmentation in the omnipresent modular programmes; lack of student contact with academic staff; over-reliance on personal financial support and a high wastage rate.

On the other hand, we forget at our peril that post-secondary and higher education in the United States enjoys an esteem in the public imagination which makes it unthinkable for politicians to challenge its claims on a major share of the public purse. Exceptionally, the recession and local demographic changes have produced a fiscal crisis in the maintenance of provision in some States (notably California) but it remains generally true that high levels of participation in community colleges and universities allow those institutions to mobilize public opinion in support of greater access to public (and private) resources on a scale substantially in excess of the majority of institutions in Britain or Europe. In other words, if post-secondary and higher education in Britain is ever to succeed in claiming a greater share of Gross Domestic Product in a future spending round, then it will have to achieve a far greater purchase upon public opinion than it currently enjoys. Public assent for the deployment of extra resources is usually achieved when the public is persuaded of the justice of the claim for the service in question; this in turn is closely related to public perceptions of the value of that service to immediate and on-going needs.

PUBLIC POLICY AND THE INDIVIDUAL LEARNER

The great strength of the American post-secondary system is that it is rooted in the traditions of individual access to lifelong learning opportunities. Possibly as an expression of earlier pioneer and settler values, post-secondary education is seen as the principal means of subsequent economic, social and personal progress. Investment in individual educational achievement is seen as essential to personal comfort. Further, post-secondary and higher education learning opportunities are seen as resources from which the individual learner may choose an appropriate learning programme. American learners appear quite relaxed about the market model which vitalizes these arrangements. Flexibility, mobility, diversity and choice in post-secondary education are the key organizing features around which popular consent is mobilized and democratic participation is maintained.

Does this approach to the culture, organization and management of post-secondary and higher education have any consequences or lessons for developments in Britain? If it is accepted that the structures and arrangements which may have proved effective for élite education are unlikely to be satisfactory instruments for the extension of learning opportunities to the democratic mass of students, then one is bound to consider positively those practices which encourage greater participation and which at the same time command wide public support.

Equally, one is bound to inspect the merits of existing arrangements by assessing their performance. It has been suggested earlier that a consensus exists on the inadequacy and failure of prevailing arrangements to protect Britain from inexorable economic decline. The self-attributed strengths of British post-secondary and higher education do not appear to be commensurate with national prosperity, technological inventiveness, exceptional national leadership or greater public ease. On the contrary, a large part of the population continues to be excluded from learning opportunities beyond compulsory schooling, denied access by a combination of low personal aspirations and an inadequate supply of suitable places. The expansion of both higher and further education provision therefore compels a re-examination of existing arrangements in order to promote a different culture of learning throughout Britain.

RESPONSES TO CHANGING CONDITIONS

This new culture of learning is likely to depart sharply from arrangements which rely exclusively upon professional academic definitions of appropriate learning needs, upon closely marshalled patterns of student choice, or upon the vested interests of institutions. Instead, it is likely that students-as-learners will be invited to exercise substantially greater control over definitions of personal learning needs, less constrained by the historic judgements of their tutors. This will involve students being able to exercise greater choice within learning programmes, moving between academic and vocational or work-based learning experiences, with resources perhaps following students within and between institutions as they exercise their choices. Most recent policy developments point in this direction. One can identify the emergence of some significant initiatives:

- The commitments in successive White Papers to the promotion of an open and accessible post-secondary and higher education system within which the student-as-consumer will be able to exercise greater choice, initiatives which are likely to be supplemented by structural changes within and between institutions, and by the development of a Student Charter of entitlements.
- The establishment of various Commissions and policy forums to examine the state of schools, post-secondary and higher education generally (for example, the National Commission on Education, the Higher Education Study Group established by the Royal Society, and the Social Justice Commission).
- The investment by the National Council for Vocational Qualifications in the development of GNVQs alongside NVQs, 'A' levels and other complementary awards, opening the way into higher education for a greater number of qualified students from post-secondary education, and placing centrally upon the agenda questions of assessment, performance outcomes and individual student expectations of the definitions and consequences of learning achievement.
- The explorations by the Further Education Funding Council on resource methodologies which suggest a shift from resource distributions based principally upon enrolments to resource allocations which more accurately reflect individual student learning programmes and subsequent achievements, prefiguring similar work by the Higher Education Funding Councils since 1994.

- The acceptance by the National Union of Students of the need to achieve significant structural reforms to academic programmes (modularization and semesterization) together with a readiness to negotiate constructively on alternative arrangements for student financing (see also the Flowers Committee on the reform of the academic year and Finegold, 1992b; Robertson, 1994 on student financing).
- Moves towards the development of a national framework of credit accumulation and transfer as a vehicle for the creation of a comprehensive and flexible system of student mobility and choice, reorientating the priorities of institutions from the preservation of inherited patterns of supply to the arrangements required to meet the demands of a diverse cohort of students (FEU, 1992; Robertson, 1992, 1993, 1994).

TOWARDS A NATIONAL CREDIT FRAMEWORK – THE ROBERTSON REPORT

The principal unifying feature of most recent policy initiatives is the growing awareness that they can be held together by the development of a comprehensive national credit framework. Credit systems provide the currency with which students can 'trade', enabling them to register learning achievement from diverse sites of learning and negotiate the accumulation of that achievement towards recognized qualifications. The importance of credit systems for supporting student flexibility and mobility has been recognized for many years but, with the possible exception of the system operating within the Open University, credit-based learning has remained a relatively marginal activity in most institutions. The development of credit accumulation and transfer schemes has received considerable attention within higher education, promoted by the work of the former CNAA CATS Registry and subsequent prompts from Government, but with a few notable institutional exceptions, credit schemes have tended to remain peripheral to institutional definitions of student needs.

We may regard this a feature of 'first generation' developments in which credit-based learning has been treated largely as a device for managing the demands of a restricted group of 'idiosyncratic' (usually adult) learners who wished to access academic programmes outside mainstream provision. Accordingly, the acronym 'CATS' has often been the term used to describe relatively small Combined Studies programmes, associate student schemes, accredited experiential learning arrangements or worked-based and in-company accreditation programmes. Although institutions will have learned considerably from such developments, most students have generally been expected to proceed through the conventionally structured, unmodified choice-restricted academic programmes of higher education. In the further education colleges, these limitations have been reinforced by the specific requirements of external awarding bodies.

There are now signs that a 'second generation' treatment of credit-based learning is developing, in which practitioners eschew the acronym 'CATS' as too redolent of previously marginalized activities. This new approach seeks to solve the problems of managing *increased* participation whilst encouraging the pursuit of *wider* participation by developing credit-based learning arrangements for *all* students. The creation of a national credit framework within a 'credit culture' is seen as the principal instrument by which students generally may be supplied with the means to exercise choices about their learning needs, thereby eroding boundaries between sectors, institutions, sites of learning e.g. college-based or work-based) and even subject disciplines. Credit systems become basic elements in the organization of individual learning opportunities, central to institutional life, shaping the character of the student learning experience and capable of absorbing conventional academic and NCVQ-derived approaches to the accumulation of achievement. Some institutions have begun to move in this direction, albeit with mixed results. Indeed, in *Choosing to Change*, I talk of a 'third generation' of developments in these matters, in which *academic* credit systems can be linked to *financial* resource management systems to provide a fully integrated network of student-driven programmes in higher and further education (Robertson, 1994).

The development of generalized credit systems has been made more likely by the ending of the higher education binary line; the expansion of post-secondary education now forces attention to be paid to the new boundary. If prospects for improved credit transfer between institutions within higher education remains clouded by regulations and traditions, prospects for vertical transfer from post-secondary education into higher education have been markedly improved by recent policy developments. The increased permeability of the membrane separating post-secondary from higher education is likely to be a prominent feature of developments over the next few years as the surge of participation in further education adds additional impetus to the rising volume of demand for higher education. Vertical credit accumulation and transfer will be greatly facilitated by a common cross-sector credit framework (see FEU, 1992; Robertson, 1994).

Currently a number of different credit frameworks exists. As Table 16.1 shows, arrangements have developed in different parts of the sector at different times and with different characteristics.

The earliest framework has been that developed by the various Open College Federations since 1981, principally involving further and adult education. Like other later frameworks, its characteristics have taken some time to emerge, but by 1989 its main features had been agreed by

Table 16.1 Existing credit frameworks: a comparison and evaluation

	CNAA framework	NOCN framework	NCVQ framework	FEU framework
Sector focus	Higher: academic (+ off-campus vocational)	Further and adult: academic and vocational	Further (+ Higher): vocational	Further and Adult (+Higher): academic and vocational
Architectural features	Three levels (1–3) at undergraduate level (+ emerging Level 0); Masters (M) level	Four levels (1–4) from adult basic education to 'A' level and HE Access	Five levels (1–5), with the first three relevant to further education	Eight levels (E, 1–6, M) covering FE and HE, although still under discussion
Specification of credit	Unit defined as 1/360 of degree; minimum credit = 4 = 30 hours of learning; otherwise, 120 credits/year = 360 for a degree (480 Scotland) and 120 (M) for taught Masters	Unit = 30 hours of learning = 1 credit; applicable to various qualifications; no restrictions on credit volume by level (cf CNAA scheme)	Credit = unit of assessment defined by competence statements. Units accumulated to form qualified competence (NVQ). Time-based definitions rejected	Unit = 30 hours of learning = 1 credit; applicable to all awards, including vocational and higher education qualifications if represented by outcome statements
Quality assurance arrangements	Through monitoring via CNAA, and now HEQC, but principally through individual institutions. Intrinsic QA cannot be derived from use of credit	Through peer review within OCFs; peer review within NOCN; and monitoring by SCAVA. QA can be derived intrinsically from credit system	National standards set by ILBs, and assured by assessment centres under licence from NCVQ. QA intrinsic to credit system	Not yet resolved; likely to be through individual institutions, existing arrangements BUT QA is intrinsic to the credit system
Compatibility with existing frameworks	No, its numerical system is different from others, bench-marked against a degree and problems of adoption in further education. BUT yes, since other numerical systems are compatible (NB not NCVQ)	No, time-based definition of credit is not accepted by NCVQ, although reconciliation discussions are taking place; BUT yes, very similar to FEU framework and numerical system works with CNAA (1:4)	No, formally incompatible with all numerical or time-based system of credit; establishes different approach to credit by linking it to outcome statements and units of competence	Yes, seeks to incorporate features of other systems, including numerical and time-based unit of credit derived from outcome statements; definition of credit challenged by NCVQ, but works with CNAA (1:4)

Table 16.1 Continued

	CNAA framework	NOCN framework	NCVQ framework	FEU framework
Strengths	Pragmatic; institutional degree programmes accommodated by numerical flexibility; most widely adopted HE scheme currently	Tried and tested since 1981 over full range of programmes in FE, AE and in some HEIs; biggest working credit system outside HE	Extensively adopted by vocational programmes; quality assurance by link of credit with outcome statements	Builds on best features of existing schemes; units credits, modules and outcomes; potentially adoptable by FE/HE
Limitations	Degree-centric; limited adoption of outcomes-led quality assurance; doubtfully applicable to non-HE programmes; benefit if developed educational rationale; otherwise, mechanistic	Limited exposure in HE; scheme does not generate of itself either qualifications or transfer; would benefit from incorporation within FEU proposals	Internally focused definition of credit; not easily adopted by HE (nor by any academic programmes). Would benefit from alliance with time-based credit systems	Still at design and consultation stage; may suffer in HE from having 'FE' origins. Would benefit from extensive 'pilot' developments in both FE and HE
Unresolved problems	Relationship with non-HE developments (e.g.level 0/ Access) and NCVQ; credits for Masters (120/180?). Credit for 'off-campus' and sandwich courses or other placements	Alignment of four levels with those of NVQ1–3, status of ABE work; how to achieve effective articulation between levels and with HE	How to articulate credit for vocational programmes with academic credit systems; character of GNVQ qualifications (especially at higher levels)	Negotiating operation in subscribing colleges; increasing exposure in HE; defining technical instruments, particularly levels and QA arrangements

Source: Robertson, D. (1994) Table 29, p. 142.

local open colleges and many thousands of adult learners were formally in receipt of credit through the National Open College Network (NOCN). Then, from 1986, the CNAA began to sponsor the development of a general framework for higher education, initially within the polytechnics of the period but also amongst some of the established universities. Finally, the NCVQ set out to create a national *vocational* qualifications framework from 1986–87 onwards.

By the time we reach the early 1990s, discussions over the usefulness of a national credit framework had become so extensive that it was clear to policy-makers that some attempt should be made to draw developments together. The proposals which emerged from the Further Education Unit in 1992 were the first to attempt to synthesize the ongoing work of other bodies, by combining developments in higher and further education. These efforts at a synthesis formed the basis of the recommendations which I outlined in *Choosing to Change*, and will be the platform upon which further developments may be built.

To illustrate how a national credit framework could operate, it may be helpful to consider the proposals taken from the Robertson Report itself (see Table 16.2)

An *architecture*, or structure of levels, forms the 'central spine' which runs through the qualifications framework. In this arrangement, the framework would build upon existing practice in higher and further education, together with that from the NCVQ, to produce a common 'climbing-frame' for progression. Arrangements include the specification of the *technical instruments* of the framework – a definition of 'credit' and the unit of credit; the use of modules and learning outcome statements; and prescriptions about the award of credit for demonstrated achievement.

The framework is designed as an 'open system' in that institutions, awarding bodies, professional bodies and others would *voluntarily* subscribe to it. Compulsion would never be possible or desirable since the framework would only have value if students, educational providers and employers *consent* to make it work. In this respect at least, the strength of the credit framework lies in its 'weakness' to the extent that institutions and other interested parties can begin to work with the framework from their current starting positions, *articulating* their arrangements, and moving over time through a process of *convergence* to a common national credit system.

The erosion of distinctions between education and training, between college-based and work-based learning and between academic and vocational learning, and the blurring of divisions between higher, further and adult education, are likely to require an organizing framework within which students can negotiate appropriate constellations of achievement leading towards awards. A 'political' and a professional rapprochement between the objectives of higher education, post-secondary education, the NCVQ, professional bodies and employers will need to be a major policy outcome of these arrangements.

It must be pointed out, however, that this rapprochement may take some time to be achieved. It is not at all easy to arrange the natural progression of students between largely academic and largely vocational programmes. Moreover, there are substantial forces of resistance, both within Government and within the universities, which are not yet persuaded of the merits of closer association between different sectors. Put at its most direct, some universities do not wish to see their longstanding commitment to a certain style of (élite) higher education compromised by what they perceive to be the predations of a system of democratic participation. They may be able to appeal to the natural conservatism of many professional bodies and some employers in their defence, although attitudes are changing amongst these former 'allies' (see for example, CBI, 1994). And Government for its part does not wish currently to move towards a formal cross-sectoral convergence between higher and further education in case this should prejudice the political sanctity of 'A' levels.

Then, we must anticipate that policymaking in post-secondary and higher education in the UK rarely proceeds smoothly or in an easily predicted direction. We may read consistency of progress into events over time (as I am seeking to do here) but, 'close to the action', policy implementation oftens seems much more haphazard. Crossing the implementation gap between largely agreed policy objectives and their practical realization usually requires considerable perseverance, political skill and some luck.

SOME POTENTIAL, SOME CHALLENGES

Notwithstanding the difficulties, I am confident that the development of a comprehensive national credit framework offers the prospect of fundamental changes and potential improvements throughout post-secondary and higher education. These include:

- significant changes to the structure of academic programmes (via modularization), to the organization of the academic year (via semesterization), to assessment strategies and learning delivery, to the administrative arrangements for managing complex choice-based programmes (via improved information systems) and to student financial regulations (via educational 'vouchers', 'learning accounts', and credit-led institutional funding);
- substantially improved student guidance and information systems, including a thorough reform of existing information sources to place

Table 16.2 Credit frameworks: towards a synthesis

CNAA framework		FEU framework	NCVQ framework	
CATS Level M: work equivalent to the standard required for the fulfilment of the general educational aims of a Master's programme, including an element of advanced independent work	M	HE Level M: no comment specifically but assumes consistency between HE and NCVQ	GNVQ Level 5: the specification has not yet been determined. One proposal suggests it would be equivalent to a course-based Master's programme	NVQ Level 5: competence in the application of fundamental principles and complex techniques, involving substantial personal autonomy, responsibility for the work of others, and the allocation of resources
CATS Level 3: work equivalent to the standard required for the fulfilment of the general educational aims of the 3rd Year of a full-time Degree course	6	HE Level 3: no comment specifically but assumes consistency, as above		
CATS Level 2: work equivalent to the standard required for the fulfilment of the general educational aims of the 2nd Year of a full-time Degree course	5	HE Level 2: no comment specifically but assumes consistency, as above	GNVQ Level 4: there have been initial consultations on the shape of a GNVQ 4. One current proposal is that the award should be equivalent to the first two years of a full-time degree programme, as with HND or DipHE	NVQ Level 4: competence in a range of complex technical or professional activities in a variety of contexts, involving substantial autonomy and responsibility, where the allocation of resources may be needed
CATS Level 1: work equivalent to the standard required for the fulfilment of the general educational aims of the 1st Year of a full-time Degree course	4	HE Level 1: no comment specifically but assumes consistency, as above		
NOCN framework Level 4 enables students to develop the capacity for sustained study using critical and evaluative skills and understanding. Study may prepare for entry to higher education or to other professional training	3	FE Level 3: embracing 'A' levels, GNVQ and NVQ3, Access and HE 'level 0' courses, OND and academic and vocational elements of equivalent standard	GNVQ Level 3: the Advanced GNVQ or the vocational 'A' level, A GNVQ 3 is awarded for twelve units (2 'A' level equivalent) + three core skills units	NVQ Level 3: competence is a range of complex non-routine work activities, with some autonomy, and control and guidance of others

Table 16.2 Continued

CNAA framework	FEU framework		NCVQ framework
Level 3 enables participants to acquire or develop basic concepts and principles of enquiry. It enables them to achieve functional competence in skill areas such as languages, maths, creative and interpretative arts, and community-based applications	2	FE Level 2: embracing GCSE, GNVQ2 and NVQ2, pre-Access courses, and programmes of other awarding bodies of equivalent standard	GNVQ Level 2: the Intermediate GNVQ is awarded for six units + three core skills units (equivalent to 4 GCSEs at grade C and above)	NVQ Level 2: competence in varied work activities which may be complex and non-routine, with some personal autonomy and collaboration with others in groups
Level 2 builds on existing skills or introduces a range of new foundation skills and subjects – craft and artistic skills, learning-to-learn skills, languages and maths, and group skills	1	FE Level 1: embracing initial general further and adult education, GNVQ1 and NVQ1, and equivalents	GNVQ Level 1: the Foundation GNVQ is designed for those not yet equipped to begin a GNVQ2 course	NVQ Level 1: competence in a range of varied work activities, most of which may be routine or predictable
Level 1 is the foundation level for skills necessary in everyday life – reading, writing, speaking, numeracy, and practical and coping skills	'Entry' Level	Embracing most Adult Basic Education, some special needs courses, and those programmes accredited by OCNs at Level 1	Sources: CNAA CAT Scheme Regulations, 1991; NCVQ Guide to National Vocational Qualifications, 1991; GNVQ Information Notes 1993; GNVQ at Higher Levels, 1994; Further Education Unit: A Basis for Credit?, 1992; Beyond a Basis for Credit?, 1993; UDACE: Open College Networks – current developments and practice, 1989; Manchester Open College Federation, 1984.	

National Curriculum Key Stages

Source: Robertson, D. (1994), Table 34, p. 152.

emphasis, less upon recruitment and marketing aspects of student-focused material, and more upon genuine programme-centred information and performance indicators;

- the development of credit-led student-centred resource methodologies whereby students are represented in resource terms, not by the length of their course (i.e. ftes), but by the specificity of their individual learning programme (i.e. credit-based student funding);
- improved international exchange as British post-secondary and higher education moves closer to arrangements obtaining elsewhere in the world;
- much closer engagement between individual learning programmes and personal careers in employment, where labour market prospects increasingly inform the decisions of individual learners throughout their lives;
- the creation of a genuinely democratic system of higher and further education based upon the principles of *equity, excellence, expansion* and *employment*.

Modifications to the shape and character of post-secondary and higher education outlined above have been defined as essential if we are to have any chance of deploying extensive investment in the sector to avert further national economic decline. Macro-policy considerations in this respect are likely to override the consequences of the changes for academic values, institutional culture and inherited visions of the preferred student learning experience. We have grown habituated to a benign model of post-secondary education, relatively congenial for those academic staff with access to scholarly resources, uncluttered by the demands of mass participation, relatively successful for those students who manage to enter, but hopelessly inefficient for most and palpably ineffective in meeting modern economic needs.

It is the relative congeniality and success of past arrangements that persuade many academic staff in particular that there is no premium on change, especially when there appear to be few rewards or incentives to make the change. More profoundly perhaps, there is the suspicion that proposed changes will negatively affect, not just material conditions, but the intellectual and cultural integrity of professional life itself. The power of the adherence to subject and disciplinary culture, particularly within higher education, has been well-documented (Becher, 1989) and reinforced by the recognition that the organizational arrangements of institutional life also impede radical change (Becher and Kogan, 1992).

Similarly, there is concern that mass participation and curriculum fragmentation will lead to a loss of intellectual coherence and a commoditization of learning where students will wander through an alien marketplace, isolated from their natural community of peers and tutors (Barnett,

1993; 1994). This potential loss of 'intimacy' in post-secondary and higher education has also been pointed up by some other commentators (Scott and Watson, 1992) and represents a major obstacle in winning the argument for fundamental reform.

ENDNOTE

Clearly, these reservations about the consequences of particular change strategies have to be taken seriously. The right of access to lifelong learning may be indivisible; the chances of obtaining adequate resources to meet the needs of democratic participation may currently be poor; and the case for arresting national economic decline may be overwhelming. All these factors may be true, but they do not necessarily provide a sufficiently convincing case for why we need to change the better features of the British system for some unfamiliar alternatives.

Perhaps the solution lies in learning itself. Perhaps we should learn from those features of international mass participation systems which seem to work well and be popular with academic staff and students (i.e. credit-based learning, choice-based curriculum, student mobility, student information) and ally them with some of the better features of the British way (i.e. high achievement rates, good pastoral support, good quality assurance arrangements). If we are able to match a culture of high aspiration and participation with a culture of high quality and achievement, then it is possible to win popular support for sustained investment in post-secondary and higher education whilst contributing to a reversal of national economic decline. It would be a unique international achievement.

REFERENCES

Ball, C. (1990) *More Means Different: Widening Access to Higher Education*, London: RSA.

Ball, C. (1991) *Learning Pays: the Role of Post-Compulsory Education and Training*, London: RSA.

Barnett, R. (1993) 'Knowledge, higher education and society: a postmodern problem', *Oxford Review of Education*. **19**(1).

Barnett, R. (1994) *The Limits of Competence*, London: SRHE/OU Press.

Becher, T. (1989) *Academic Tribes and Territories: Intellectual Enquiry and the Cultures of Disciplines*, Milton Keynes: OU Press.

Becher, T. and Kogan, M. (1992) *Process and Structure in Higher Education*, London: Routledge.

Cassells, J. (1990) *Britain's Real Skill Shortage*, London: Policy Studies Institute.

Confederation of British Industry (1989) *Towards a Skills Revolution*, London: CBI.

Confederation of British Industry (1994) *Thinking Ahead: Ensuring the Expansion of Higher Education*, London: CBI.

Council for Industry and Higher Education (1990) *Towards a Partnership*, London: CIHE.

DES (1987) *Higher Education: Meeting the Challenge*, Cmnd 114, London: HMSO.

DES (1989) *Aspects of Higher Education in the United States of America*, London: HMSO.

DES (1990) *Vocational and Continuing Education*, (USA series), London: HMSO.

DES (1991a) *Quality and its Assurance in Higher Education*, (USA series), London: HMSO.

DES (1991b) *Indicators in Educational Monitoring*, (USA series), London: HMSO.

DES (1991c) *Education and Training for the 21st Century*, Vol. I & II, Cmnd 1536, London: HMSO.

DES (1991d) *Higher Education: A New Framework*, Cmnd 1541, London: HMSO.

Finegold D. and Soskice, D. (1988) 'The failure of training in Britain: analysis and prescription', *Oxford Review of Economic Policy*, **2**, (2).

Finegold, D. (1992a) 'Breaking out of the Low-Skill Equilibrium', *Briefing Paper No. 5*, National Commission on Education.

Finegold, D. (1992b) 'Student finance: equity and expansion' in IPPR (1992) *Higher Education: Expansion and Reform*, London: IPPR.

Further Education Unit (1992) *A Basis for Credit?*, London: FEU.

Institute for Public Policy Research (1990) *A British Baccalaureat*, London: IPPR.

Institute for Public Policy Research (1992) *Higher Education: Expansion and Reform*, London: IPPR.

National Commission on Education (1993) *Learning to Succeed*, London: Heinemann.

Porter, M. (1990) *The Competitive Advantage of Nations*, London: Macmillan.

Raffe, D. (1992) 'Participation of 16–18 year olds in education and training', *Briefing Paper No. 3*, National Commission on Education.

Robbins, L. (1963) *Report of the Committee on Higher Education*, Cmnd 2154, London: HMSO.

Robertson, D. (1992) 'Courses, qualifications and the empowerment of learners', in IPPR (1992) *Higher Education: Expansion and Reform*, London: IPPR.

Robertson, D. (1993) 'Flexibility and mobility in further and higher education: policy continuity and progress', *Journal of Further and Higher Education*, **17**, (1).

Robertson, D. (1994) *Choosing to Change: Extending Access, Choice and Mobility in Higher Education*, London: Higher Education Quality Council.

Royal Society (1991) *Beyond GCSE*, London: Royal Society

Royal Society (1993) *Higher Education Futures*, London: Royal Society.

Scott, P. and Watson, D. (1992) Roles and Responsibilities conference paper: *Managing the University Curriculum in the Year 2000*, London, October.

Smithers, A. and Robinson, P. (1989) *Increasing Participation in Higher Education*, London: BP Educational Services.

Smithers, A. and Robinson, P. (1991) *Beyond Compulsory Schooling*, Council for Industry and Higher Education report, London: CIHE.

Social Justice Commission (1994) *Social Justice: Strategies for National Renewal*, London: Vintage.

SRHE (1983) *Excellence in Diversity*, Guildford: SRHE.

Wagner, L. (Ed.), (1982) *Agenda for Institutional Change in Higher Education*, Guildford: SRHE.

World Bank, (1994) *Higher Education: The Lessons of Experience*, Washington DC: World Bank.

Index

academic programmes, reforms 155, 284, 289
academic writing, voice 68–9
accreditation 251, 253
achievement 241–2, 244
action research 54–5
Adam, B. 211, 216
adult education 94–5; competency-based 115; critical analysis of literature 62–77; critical theory 57, 58, 123; effects of 184–5, 238; fees 158, 160–1, 277–8; funding 153, 190–1, 277–8, 279; liberal 162; political factors 72–7, 160, 175, 176; power 101–2, 107, 112, 136, 138; research 119–25; *see also* andragogy; participation in adult education; part-time education
adult education, comparisons: Australia 246–7, 250–8; Canada 246; European Union 163; Finland 164–5, 185–94; Germany 164; Netherlands 163; New Zealand 246; North America 120–2; Norway 184; Sweden 169–70, 171–3, 175–9; UK 153–4, 155–6, 166–8, 201–2; US 58, 184–5, 246, 281–2
Adult Education Research Conference, Saskatoon (1992) 69
adult education texts 60–2, 69–71
adult learners 94–8; backgrounds 61–2; classroom participation 75; coping strategies 104; experiences 36–7, 65–6, 88; formal/informal education 157–8; gender factors 103, 105; intentions 36–40,

54; learning readiness 91–2; policies 282–3; reflection 33–4, 40–51; self-assessment 273; self-esteem 67–8; Swedish 170–1; and texts 74–5; *see also* participation in adult education; students; women students
Adult Literacy Basic Skills Unit 256–8
Advisory Council for Adult and Continuing Education 158–9, 196, 200, 209
Alexander Report (1975) 159
Allman, P. 100
andragogy 3, 83; contextual factors 106–7; ego-involvement 96; experience 89–90; learning orientation 92–4; learning readiness 91–2; and pedagogy 99–100, 109; self-concept 84–9
Apple, M. W. 60
Argyris, C. 51
Aristotle 105
Aronowitz, S. 60, 64–5, 68–9, 70
assessment of prior learning 162, 257, 273
Australia: Adult Basic Education 257–8; competency-based education 246; literacy 256–7; nursing 253–5; professions 246–7, 250–8; teaching 255–8
authority: institutionalized 138–9; intellectual 139; textual 60, 68–9; tutor 103; women's experience 135–6
autonomy 105, 237–8; competence 238; economics 234–5;

education 232; as fundamental value 233; individual 243; self-concept 85; self-directed learning 112, 115; social change 232

Barnett, R. 268, 269, 292–3
Becher, J. 292
Bettelheim, B. 49
Birdwhistell, R. L. 21
Blagg, N. 266
Boud, D. 105
Bourdieu, P. 185
Boyd, E. M. 47
brain-patterns 47
Bridges, D. 264
Brockett, R. G. 213, 230
Brookfield, S. D. 69, 78, 105–6, 112, 116
Brown, G. 270, 271
Bryant, I. 65, 67, 77
BTEC 262
Burgess, R. G. 221
Buzan, T. 47

Canada, competency-based education 246
CATS Registry 284–5
change: contextual factors 267–71; cultural 83; demographic 180, 203; individual/collective 137; through learning 51; social 83, 135, 136, 137, 232; universities 284, 289
Charnley, A. 238
Choosing to Change (Robertson) 284–9
Christian-Smith, L. K. 60
Christianity, radical 130–1
class, social 123, 203, 204
classroom practice 149 (n13)
CNAA framework 286–7, 288, 290–1
collective memory work 144
collectivism 73, 74, 142
college identity 217
college time, experiencing 219–22
Collins, M. 57, 72, 72, 73, 77
Collins, R. 76
Combahee River Collective Statement 145
commons, the 113, 120
communicative action 72–3, 124, 241, 248–9; self-directed learning 115, 116–17, 118

competency: assessment 254–5; autonomy 238; context 249; nursing 253–5; re-evaluation 54; relational 249; task-based/behaviourist 247–50; teaching 255–8
competency-based education 115, 246
competitiveness 203, 280
Competitiveness: Helping Business to Win (1994 White Paper) 203
Comte, Auguste 13
concept maps 47
Confederation of British Industry 236, 263, 269, 280
conscientization 38, 133, 140
consciousness-raising 135–7
conversation 73, 221
core skills 241, 255, 262, 267, 271
Core Skills Unit (NCVQ) 271–2
correspondence courses 209
Council for Industry and Higher Education 280
Courtney, S. 183, 184
credit frameworks 6, 273, 284–9
credit-based learning 284–5
critical analysis, educational literature 60–2; communicative questions 68–71; cultural skewing 63; descriptive/prescriptive 63–4; ethical issues 67–8; experiential questions 64–8; methodological questions 62–4; political questions 72–7; psychologistic 74; self-directed learning 116; voice 68–9
critical intent, reflection 39
critical practice 57–8, 70–1
critical reflection 40, 58, 59–60, 105
critical theory 57, 58, 61, 123
critical thinking 106, 248–9
Cross, K. P. 209
Culley, M. 139
cultural capital 185, 194
cultural consumption 184–5
Cunningham, P. 76
curriculum 93, 268–70

Davies, I. K. 47
Davies, K. 214, 223, 231
De Castell, S. 60
debriefing 43, 53
democracy, education 72, 184, 234

Department of Education and
Science 196, 278–9, 281
developmental tasks 91
Dewey, John 28, 34, 35, 39
difference 128, 137–8, 144–6
Draves, W. 110
drop-outs 174, 214–15, 225–9
Dunlop, F. 54

economics, and autonomy 234–5
Educating Rita (Russell) 166–7
education: autonomy 232;
democratization 280, 282, 292;
dichotomies 152; equality of
access 173–5, 178–80, 182;
funding 153, 190–1, 279;
innovation 76–7; knowledge
transmitting 82–3, 100; market
forces 279; mass media 160;
negative experiences 85;
priorities 153–4; research in/
on 124–5; state intervention 269–
70; Tolstoy 27–8; and
training 152–3, 233, 288–9; *see also*
adult education; part-time
education
education, types: community 159;
competency-based 115, 246;
elitist 162, 233, 289; liberal 157;
liberatory 62, 76–7, 101, 116, 129,
152–3, 154; personnel 173;
recurrent 170
Education Act (1944) 158, 159
Education for Capability (RSA) 270,
271
*Education and Training for the 21st
Century* (1991 White Paper) 201,
203, 208
educational critics, feminist 128–9
Edwards, R. 270
emotions 54; and experience 147;
feminism 141; and rationality 43;
social construction 150 (n36)
employee development 164, 237
employers, training 190–1, 235
Employment Department 263, 270,
271, 273
empowerment 38, 154, 232
engineering 14
English and Welsh Education Act
(1918) 159
Enlightenment 12
Enterprise in Higher Education

initiative, Employment
Department 270, 271, 273
Entwistle, N. 39
equity, educational 235–7, 280
Eraut, M. 238, 264
erotic power 142–3
ethical issues 17–18, 67–8
ethnic minority groups 197, 204–5,
207, 208
European Union, adult education 163
Evans, S. 149 (n14)
evening classes 159
experience 49–50, 103;
andragogy 89–90;
appropriation 49–50;
association 46–7; and emotion 147;
gender differences 103;
honoured 65–6; integration 47–8;
knowledge and truth 140–4;
outcomes and action 50–1; re-
evaluated 41–2, 45–6, 53–4; in
reflection 41–4; validation 48–9;
women's 135–6, 143, 144–5, 149
(n15)
experiential learning 32, 49, 51, 90
experiments 27, 93–4, 120
expertise, professional 8–9, 18, 248

facilitators 53–4, 106, 118–19, 122;
and teachers 101, 109, 157
Fales, A. W. 47
family time, and college
schedule 216–17
Fazey, D. 273
feedback, learning 104
feelings 41, 44–5, 140–3; *see also*
emotion
feminist pedagogy 129, 134–46, 148–9
(n13)
feminist theory 128, 132
Finegold, D. 280, 284
Finland: adult education 164–5, 185–
94; gender factors in
education 186–7; municipal
institutes 186; workplace
training 186
Fisher, B. 136, 139, 140, 141, 147
Fleming, D. 264, 267
flexibility 271
flexilives 271
Flexner Report 11
Flowers Committee 284
folk high schools 170, 173

Ford (UK) 164, 237
Foucault, Michel 114, 136, 142
frame experiments 27
Frankfurt school, critical social
    theory 57, 61, 123
freedom, and contingency 117–18,
    119
Freire, Paulo: conscientization 38,
    133, 140; cultural factors 37;
    liberatory 62, 101, 116, 129;
    pedagogy 130–4; *Pedagogy of the
    Oppressed* 129, 130–4, 137;
    politics 76, 101, 124, 142;
    reflection 78; talking books 71
Fukayama, F. 72
funding, education 153, 159, 190–1,
    277–8, 279
further education colleges 278–9
Further Education Funding
    Council 202, 207, 283
Further Education Unit 284, 285,
    286–7, 288, 290–1
Further and Higher Education Act
    (1992) 202, 279
Fuss, D. 143

gender factors, adult learning 103,
    105
General National Vocational
    Qualifications 262, 279, 283
generic skills 261, 263, 270–1
Germany, adult education 164
Gibbs, G. 273
Gilbert, R. 69
Giroux, H. A. 60, 64–5, 68–9, 70, 147
Glazer, N. 8–9, 18
Gonczi, A. 249, 253
Goode, W. 10
government, UK: curriculum 269–70;
    educational priorities 153–4, 159–
    60; funding for education 153, 159,
    190–1, 277–8, 279
Graham, R. J. 69
Gramsci, A. 61, 129
Green, M. 101
Green, N. E. 246
Greenwood, E. 10
Griffin, C. 101, 102
group discussion 221
Grundtvig, N. F. S. 157, 164
Gunnarson, E. 214

Habermas, Jürgen: communicative

action 72, 124; critical intent 39;
    legitimation crisis 270; life-
    world 113; modes of knowing
    116–17; reflection 52, 61
Hager, P. 247
Hammond, M. 76
Handy, C. 271
Hanson, A. P. 103
Hart, M. 270, 271
Hassard, J. 212, 219
Haug, F. 143–4, 147
Havighurst, R. J. 91
Heidegger, Martin 118–19
hermeneutics 61, 122–3
Heron, J. 44–5, 53
Hiemstra, R. 213, 230
higher education 278, 285; *see also*
    universities
Higher Education (1987 White
    Paper) 278
Hochschild, A. R. 150 (n36)
Hodgkinson, P. 246
Hodgskin, Thomas 119, 126 (n22)
homophobia 145
Horton, Myles 58, 62, 70–1
Houle, C. 110
Houston, W. R. 249
Hughes, E. 14
Hughes, M. 225
humanization 131, 132

identity 144–5, 217
Illich, Ivan 113, 120, 124
immigrants, language instruction 172
in-service training 173
individualism 103, 235
individuals: autonomy 243; collective
    achievements 242; core skills 272;
    policy impact 282–3
industrial relations 237
industrialism 12
Inhelder, B. 22–5
Inner London Education
    Authority 196
innovation, education 76–7
insights 43–4, 45
institutions: authority 138–9;
    educational aims/assumptions 101;
    Finland 186; self-directed
    learning 114, 115
intellectuals, authority 139
intention, learning 38–40, 54
Isoaho, H. 186–7

Jarvis, P. 69
Jessup, G. 241, 266, 272
Johnstone, J. 184
Jones, A. 238

Karmiloff-Smith, A. 22–5
Kelly, G. 37–8
Kelly, T. 155
Kennedy, 225
Kivinen, O. 185, 194
know-how 21
knowing-in-action 19–21, 25
knowing-in-practice 26
knowledge: applied 269; expert 61;
   hierarchy 14; modes 116–17;
   personal/process/propositional
   238; and practice 15–16, 17, 18;
   problem solving 122;
   professional 9–10, 249;
   scientific 15; and truth 140–4
knowledge workers 235
knowledge-based economy 234–5
Knowles, M. 100, 101–2, 103, 110,
   111
Kogan, M. 292
Kolb, D. 105, 106
komvux 173, 177

labour market, skills 236
language: accessibility 70–1;
   outcomes 239–40, 244;
   professional 239; specialized 70;
   training for immigrants 172
learners: *see* adult learners
learning 94–8, 293; academic/work-
   based 283–4; affective aspects 35–
   6, 44; change 51;
   commodified 292–3;
   empowerment 38;
   environment 97–8; evaluated 88;
   experiences 36–7, 65–6, 88;
   feedback 104; holistic approach 49;
   intention 38–40, 54; internal
   process 95–6; location 206–7;
   power 101–2, 107, 112, 136, 138,
   142–3; purposes 273–4;
   reflection 32–6, 51–4; and
   status 219; *see also* adult learners
learning, types: autonomous 111–12;
   credit-based 284–5; deep/
   surface 39, 273; deliberate 32,
   196; experiential 32, 49, 51, 90;
   informal 197, 204–6; lifelong

learning 6, 156–7, 179–82, 242–3,
   276, 280; personal 272; prior 257,
   273; self-directed 60, 85, 100, 103,
   105, 109–19, 237; subject/problem
   centred 93; transformative 64, 67;
   vocational 207–8, 271–3
Learning and 'Leisure' (Sargant) 197
Learning for a Purpose (Sargant)
   197
learning contract 114
learning culture 283–4
learning journals 64, 66
learning outcomes, language 239–40,
   244
learning society 179, 273
learning-by-doing 28
legitimacy 61, 120, 270
Lehtonen, H. 185
leisure 3, 161, 197–200, 207–8
lesbians 144–5
Leverhulme Report 279
life-cycle, women's 227–8
life-history 65–6
life-worlds 112–14, 120
Linderman, E. 58, 72, 111
listening role 53
literacy 256–8
Lorde, A. 141–3
Louden, W. 256
Lowe, J. 164

Manpower Services Commission
   156
Mansbridge, A. 157, 162
Marcuse, H. 123
market forces, education 279
Martin, B. 146
Maslow, J. E. 21
mass media, education 160
Massachusetts Institute of
   Technology 28–9
McGivney, V. 209
medical education 11–12, 14
meditation 45, 53
men: as adult learners 186–7;
   patriarchy 129, 139; self-
   direction 105; study subjects 204;
   time 223
metacognition 264
meta-competence 264, 267
meta-process 264
methodological questions, critical
   analysis 62–4

Mezirow, J. 38, 40, 61–2, 72, 78, 102, 104–5
Miller, J. P. 49
Mills, C. Wright 58, 76
modernism, rational analysis 59
Mohanty, C. 146
Moore, W. 9
Morgan, D. H. J. 214
motivation 95–6, 209, 237–8

National Advisory Board 264
National Commission on Education 280, 283
National Council for Vocational Qualifications 241, 262, 265, 269, 271; credit framework 286–7, 290–1
National Curriculum Council 263
National Institute for Adult Continuing Education 196–7, 209
National Office of Overseas Skills Recognition 250, 253
National Union of Students 284
National Vocational Qualifications 251, 279, 283
natural sciences 119–20, 121
Netherlands, adult education 163
New Zealand 246
Newbattle Abbey College, Dalkeith 153
Nisbet, J. 264
NOCN framework 286–7, 288
non-participants 208–9
non-vocational provision 161
Nordhaug, O. 184
North America, educational research 120–2
Novak, J. D. 47
novice/expert research 248–9
nursing 253–5

Oates, T. 264–5, 266, 272
occupational groupings, participation in adult education 190
occupational training 153
OECD 176–7, 179
Open College Federations 244, 285, 288
Open University 155, 157
oppression 128, 129–30, 132, 145
Osborn, A. F. 47
outcomes, language of 50–1, 239–40, 263

part-time education 105–6, 212–13; research study 215–16; support for students 229–31; women 213–25
participation in adult education 184–5, 200–1; age groups 187–9; demographic changes 203; Finland 183, 185–7; higher education 278; increased 281–2; labour force 194; occupational groupings 190; previous education 191–3; public policy 282–3; regional differences 201–3; socio-economic status 189–90, 193; Sweden 173–5
participatory research 121–2, 126–7 (n24)
patriarchy 129, 139
pedagogy 61, 82–3, 99–100, 109
Pedagogy of the Oppressed (Freire) 129, 130–4, 137
performance: assessment 265, 282; competency 248; intuitive 21–2, 25; skills 261
Perkins, D. 267
personal construct theory 37–8
personal skills 240–1, 261, 262–4, 267–73
personnel education 173
perspective transformation 38, 76, 104–6
Peters, J. 69
phenomenology 122–3
Podechi, R. 102
policy: adult education 276–8; equity 280; and individual learner 282–3; market forces 279, 280; and outcomes 239–40
politicization 136
polytechnic colleges 278–9
Pöntinen, S. 190, 194
Porter, M. E. 280
Portuges, C. 139
positivism 12, 14, 19, 248
postmodernism 59, 128, 138, 143, 144, 146
power, learning 101–2, 107, 112, 136, 138, 142–3
practice 25–6; adult education texts 71; critical 57–8, 70–1; and knowledge 15–16, 17, 18; and research 11, 125; and theory 57–8; *see also* professional practice

practitioners 15–16, 19–20, 248
Preston, B. 248
prior learning 257, 273
problem setting 16
problem solving 15–16, 122, 266
professional practice: conflicts 17;
    dialogue 243–4; ethics 17–18, 19;
    expertise 8–9, 18, 248;
    judgment 248; problem solving
    15–16; reflection 19, 55
professions: categorized 8–9; and
    competency-based education 246–
    7, 250–8; knowledge 9–10, 249;
    language 239; research/practice 11;
    rigour/relevance dilemma 17, 18;
    specialization 26; uncertainty 16–
    17
Provonost, G. 212, 214, 216, 222, 231
public libraries 167
public provision, education 160

qualifications 241, 250, 276–7;
    GNVQs 262, 279, 283; NVQs 251,
    279, 283
quality circles 244

racism 145
radical Christianity 130–1
Raffe, D. 280
Rainer, T. 45, 47, 53
Rajan, A. 235
Ramsden, P. 39, 273
rational analysis 59; see also critical
    analysis
rationality 8–12, 43, 113, 140–3; see
    also Technical Rationality
re-evaluation, experience 41–2, 45–6,
    53–4
reading, self-guided 222
Reagon, B. 147
reality testing 48
Reason, P. 54
recession, and education 163–4
reductionism 111, 242, 248
Reed, D. 38
reflection: components 42; critical 40,
    58, 59–61, 105; in learning 32–6,
    38–40, 105–6; process 51–4;
    promoting 40–51
reflection-in-action 21–2, 26–7, 29–30
reflection-in-practice 25
refresher courses 250
reification 73–4, 117, 120

research 11, 15, 125
Ressner, U. 214
Riesman, D. 184
Rigg, M. 200
Rinne, R. 183, 185
Rivera, R. 184
Robbins Report 279
Robertson, D. 284–9
Robertson Report (HEQC) 284–9
Robinson, P. 280
Rockhill, K. 72
Rogers, C. R. 49, 53, 101
Rowan, J. 54
Royal Society of Arts 270, 283
Rubenson, K. 165
Russell, M. 136
Russell, Willie 166–7
Russell Report (1973) 158
Ryle, G. 20

Sarachild, K. 135–6, 143
Sargant, N. 197, 204–5
Scheeres, H. 256, 257
Schein, E. 9, 11, 18
Schniedewind, N. 149 (n13)
Schön, D. A. 55
school certification, inadequate 162
schools, custodial function 197
Schultz, A. 21
scientific enquiry 13–14
scientific knowledge 15
Scotland: Alexander Report 159;
    Newbattle Abbey College 153;
    participation in adult
    education 201–2; SCOTVEC 262,
    269
Scott, P. 293
Scottish Office Education
    Department 153
Scottish Vocational Education
    Council 262, 269
self, unstable 147
self-concept 84–9, 228, 237–8
self-development 187
self-directed learning 60, 85, 100, 103,
    105, 109–19, 237
Self-Directed Learning Readiness
    Scale 114
self-improvement 166–7
Sellman, J. V. 165
sexism 129, 145
Shor, I. 76, 78
Shrewsbury, C. 148–9 (n13)

Shucksmith, J. 264
Simon, H. 18
skill transfer 265–7
skills 11, 264–6; basic 256;
    cognitive 263; core 241, 255, 262,
    267, 271; critical/creative 265;
    generic 261, 263, 270–1;
    flexibility 271; labour market 236;
    lack of 280; and outcome 263;
    personal 240–1, 261, 262–4, 267–
    73; social 263; transferable 266–7
Smithers, A. 280
Smyth, W. J. 78
social change 83, 135, 136, 137, 232
social class 123, 203, 204
Social Justice Commission 280, 283
social science 61
socialization 105
Solomon 267
Somervell, H. 273
Soskice, D. 280
specialization 26, 280
specialized knowledge 250
sport 199
state: *see* government
student guidance 289–90
students: academic texts 61; college
    identity 217–18; as consumers 283;
    expert knowledge 61;
    financing 284, 289; learning
    272–3; mature 103; NUS 284; *see
    also* women students
subjects: choice 198, 203–5; for future
    study 207–8; informal
    learning 204–5
surprise, reflection-in-action 22
Sweden: adult education 169–79;
    adult learners 170–1; all-round
    education 163, 165–6; demographic
    changes 180; economy 177–8, 179;
    education cut-backs 174, 176;
    employment training board 181–2;
    komvux 173, 177; labour market
    policy 173; School Act (1991) 172,
    177; unemployment 174, 179–80

Tart, C. T. 49
tasks, in learning 91, 111, 247–50
teacher 52–4; andragogy 83, 86, 88;
    communicative action 118–19; as
    facilitator 101, 109, 157; role 133,
    137, 138–40; specialization 256
teacher education 28–9, 249

teaching: competencies 255–8; and
    facilitation 65; learner-centred 272;
    learning conditions 97–8
Technical Rationality: limits 15–19;
    origins 12–14; professionals 8–12
Technological Programme 12–14
texts: see critical analysis
textual authority 60, 68–9
theory-in-action 23–5
Thorndike, E. L. 94
Thorne, B. 11–12
Tight, M. 162
time: collective 214, 216–17; at
    college 219–22; and
    education 213–14, 216–17;
    family 216–17; invisible 222; lack
    of 225–6; male view 223; in
    study 222; use of 212–13
time diaries 222–5
time management skills 230
Tolstoy, L. N. 27–8
total quality management 244
Tough, A. 32, 101, 110–11, 158, 196,
    200
Toukonen, M. L. 164–5
trade unions 164, 175, 180–1, 284
training: and education 152–3, 233,
    288–9; employers 190–1, 235; full/
    part-time workers 201; in-
    service 173; work-related
    153–4; in workplace 186, 197–8
Training Agency 269
Training Credits 279
Training and Enterprise
    Councils 207, 277
transformation: learning 64, 67;
    perspective 38, 76, 104–6;
    social 136
truth 140–4, 146
Tuomisto, J. 185
tutors 106; *see also* facilitators;
    teachers

UK: adult education 153–4, 155–6,
    166–8, 201–2; class, social 167;
    funding 153, 159, 190–1, 277–8,
    279; governmental educational
    priorities 153–4, 159–60; individual
    autonomy 236; literacy 256–7;
    political dichotomies 152
uncertainty, professions 16–17
unemployed 161, 174
UNESCO 'Learning to Be' 156

UNISON, Open College 164
universities: continuing education
    departments 165; extra-mural
    departments 153, 154, 155; new
    creations 278; place allocations
    277; resistance to change 289;
    structural reforms 284, 289
University Grants Committee 264
University of the Third Age 167
US: adult education 58, 184–5, 246,
    281–2; competency-based
    education 246; critical adult
    education 58; education's
    function 270; feminist
    pedagogy 129; research 15; teacher
    education 249
Usher, R. S. 61, 65, 67, 77

values 49, 113, 233–4
Veblen, T. 14
Venn diagrams 47
vocational learning 207–8, 271–3
voice 68–9

Wales, adult education 202
Walker, J. 248
Watson, D. 293

Weedon, C. 144, 147
Weil, S. 272, 273
Westwood, S. 122
White, R. T. 47
Whitehead, A. N. 82–3
Wolf, A. 266
women students 213; adult
    education 200–1; Black
    women 143, 144–5; domestic
    roles 213; drop-outs 225–9;
    experiences 135–6, 143, 144–5, 149
    (n15); fragmented lifestyles 213,
    225, 230; life-cycle 227–8; part-time
    education 213–25; study
    subjects 204, 208
women's studies 134, 137, 138
Woodley, A. 200, 215, 225–6
work-related courses 153–4
Workers Educational
    Association 153, 154–5
workforce, equity 235–7
workplace training 186, 197–8
Wright, P. 272

Yeandle, S. 214
Yonge, G. 102